WildCity

A Guide to Nature in Urban Ontario, from Termites to Coyotes

DOUG BENNET & TIM TINER

ILLUSTRATIONS BY MARTA LYNNE SCYTHES

M&S

National Library of Canada Cataloguing in Publication

Bennet, Doug
  Wild city : a guide to nature in urban Ontario, from termites to coyotes / Doug Bennet and Tim Tiner ; illustrations by Marta Lynne Scythes.

Includes bibliographical references and index.
ISBN 0-7710-8569-9

  1. Urban animals – Ontario.   2. Urban plants – Ontario.   3. Urban ecology (Biology) – Ontario.   4. Natural history – Ontario.   I. Tiner, Tim   II. Scythes, Marta   III. Title.

QH106.2.05B454 2004   577.5'6'09713   C2004-902245-8

We acknowledge the financial support of the Government of Canada through the Book Publishing Industry Development Program and that of the Government of Ontario through the Ontario Media Development Corporation's Ontario Book Initiative. We further acknowledge the support of the Canada Council for the Arts and the Ontario Arts Council for our publishing program.

Typeset in Goudy by M&S, Toronto
Printed and bound in Canada

This book is printed on acid-free paper that is 100% ancient forest friendly (100% post-consumer recycled).

McClelland & Stewart Ltd.
The Canadian Publishers
481 University Avenue
Toronto, Ontario
M5G 2E9
www.mcclelland.com

1 2 3 4 5   08 07 06 05 04

CONTENTS

Fish

Mammals

Reptiles & Amphibians

PLANT KINGDOM

Plants

Trees

THE HEAVENS

Day Sky

Night Sky

Acknowledgements

We would like to sincerely thank the following people for their advice and help in writing this book:

Richard Aaron, Bob Anderson, George Argus, Norma Barnett, George Barron, Peter Beckett, Michael Berrill, Ron Brooks, Chris Brousseau, Bev Carter, Nancy Clark, Paul Cooper, Doug Currie, Chris Darling, Charles Dondale, J.E. Eckenwalder, David Francey, David L. Gibo, Darryl Gwynne, Andy Hamilton, Chris Hayden, Bob Johnson, Ellie Kirzner, Jackie Kaiser, Jaime Kirzner-Roberts, Henry Kock, Donald Kramer, Innocenzo Lippa, Steve Marshall, Lubomir Masner, Ross MacCulloch, Chris McDonell, Ken McGregor, Tim Myles, Norm North, Rick Rosatte, Bill Rose, Jocelyne St-Onge, Heather Sangster, Frederick Schueler, Alex Schultz, Nik Sheehan, David Sherry, Stephen Smith, Susan Smith, Richard Ubbens, Dennis Voigt, Alan Watson, Jan Whitford.

We would also like to acknowledge the following organizations, to which many of the above individuals are attached: Agriculture and Agri-Food Canada's Cereal & Seed Research Centre, Canadian Museum of Nature, Canadian Wildlife Service, City of Toronto Urban Forestry, Eastern Ontario Biodiversity Museum, Laurentian University, McGill University, Mount Hollyoke College, Ontario Maple Syrup Producers Association, Ontario Ministry of Natural Resources, Royal Ontario Museum, Trent University, Toronto Zoo, University of Guelph and the UofG Arboretum, University of Toronto, University of Western Ontario, Urban Forest Associates Inc.

INTRODUCTION

Wild city is generally used as a paradoxical phrase, often to describe the seeming juxtaposition of animals associated with the wilderness turning up or living in built-up areas. The scope of this book, however, is much broader, and we use *wild* in the sense of all those aspects of nature that, though near at hand, are not domesticated and directly controlled by us. We also cover the most common street and yard trees that, though intentionally planted and tended, play a central role in urban ecosystems.

Cities are commonly thought of as being outside of nature, and certainly there is no landscape more altered and intensely dominated by humans. Nature, however, has adapted to and evolved with urban settlement for perhaps 10,000 years. Pigeons, dandelions, house mice, starlings, houseflies and an assemblage of other familiar species, together with domestic garden plants, grasses and trees, form a cosmopolitan urban ecosystem. Individual cities are a combination of that basic framework on top of the natural habitat on which they are placed. Certain native species, such as squirrels, crows, blue jays and raccoons, have learned to prosper in the new, human-structured environment. Many others persist in the less-disturbed, protected or neglected spaces within cities. Their number and diversity may not rival that found in the near-pristine wilderness or even in the rural countryside, but for the more than 80 percent of us in Ontario who live in urban environs, it's the nature most immediate to us in our everyday lives.

Many people ask, upon hearing about a book on urban nature, whether it will tell them how to get *rid* of their garden- and bird-feeder-raiding squirrels, garbage-dining raccoons or eaves-nesting sparrows and starlings. Such information is featured seasonally in almost every daily newspaper and is available in great detail in public information handouts from all three levels of government and on innumerable Internet Web sites. This book, rather, is intended as a handy guide to some of the most common wild urban plants and animals that, like them or not, will always be with us and may, on occasion, find their way into places where they're not wanted. We've tried to answer some of the most oft-asked questions about their natural lives and look into their place in folklore, culture and history.

With the vast majority of Ontario's urban population living in areas south and east of the Canadian Shield, *Wild City* concentrates on the plants and animals found primarily in those regions. Many introduced and common native species habituated to urban life also occur in the north, as well as in cites across Canada. Northern cities, though, also have more immediate and frequent experiences with animals such as moose, bears, porcupines and many birds commonly associated with remote wilderness.

For ease of use, we have followed the same format in *Wild City* as in our previous two books, *Up North* and *Up North Again*, which covered the mixed-forest hinterland region of central Ontario. There are three main sections: "Animal Kingdom," "Plant Kingdom" and "The Heavens." Subsections within the chapters are arranged alphabetically; thus, "Birds" comes before "Creepy-Crawlies." Finally, within each subsection, individual entries are arranged alphabetically by common name. Vital statistics and tidbits of information are featured in a sidebar with each entry, and included in the entries on featured subjects is information on many other species. Their names appear in **bold** wherever mentioned in some length. At various points throughout the book, we've also included a dozen special entries on selected urban nature subjects and habitats. Finally, there's an index for quick reference at the back. We hope the book will help illuminate the commonplace and everyday experiences of nature in the city.

Tim Tiner
Doug Bennet

ANIMAL
KINGDOM

Birds

THE VARIED URBAN landscape ranges widely in the richness of the avian life it hosts. Everywhere, even in the most built-up spaces, there are pigeons, starlings and house sparrows, age-old devotees of human settlement that seemed to arrive as part of the package with the urban mode of life brought from the Old World. Highly adaptable native crows and gulls have also taken to cities in a big way and can be found almost anywhere, while Canada geese and mallards have multiplied in city parks and waterfronts.

Along tree-lined streets and in shrubby residential yards and gardens, blue jays, robins, cardinals and mourning doves abound, often joined by sweet-voiced house finches, recent transplants from the western United States. High above, twittering chimney swifts remain almost constantly aloft as they scoop flying insects from the sky, and are replaced after dark by seldom-seen but often-heard nighthawks. Chickadees, goldfinches and cedar waxwings often visit suburban yards, especially those well provisioned with bird feeders in the winter. Neighbourhoods with about 40 percent crown cover of trees overhead and lots of shrubs providing shelter and berries can support a great diversity of birds.

Valleys, ravines, large parks, cemeteries and woods are also rich birding grounds within cities. Red-winged blackbirds and song sparrows call out from cattails and shrubby meadows, while red-tailed hawks cruise overhead for field mice and other small prey. And in canyons of high-rise towers in some cities, peregrine falcons have even returned in recent years to pick off pigeons and other urban offerings.

1

BARN SWALLOW
Mud-dabbing Master Builder

B ARN SWALLOWS HAVE attached their homes and fortunes to those of humans since the coming of the longhouse to southern Ontario. Originally, the swirling, fork-tailed flyers nested only on scattered waterside cliffs or caves. But sheltered vertical surfaces, beams and ledges on human habitations proved ideal places to stick their mud-cup nests, above the reach of most predators. Today, 99 percent of barn swallow nests are on human structures, sometimes even festooning boats and boxcars. In cities, the red-throated, cinnamon-bellied birds turn up hunting for flying insects around bridges and in parks and suburbs with rivers, ponds or lakesides and plenty of open space.

Masters of masonry, pairs of barn swallows spend one or two weeks building their nests, each bird scooping up hundreds of dabs of mud in its beak, forming pellets and sticking them together with grass against a ledge or wall. The thick-walled mud-cups may last as long as five years, needing only to be refurbished when the builders return to their northern domiciles after flying to South America and back. In choice locales, condo communities of 10 or more swallow nests spring up, with neighbours as close as a few metres (six to 10 feet). The gregarious little birds have an adulterous streak, though, and males jealously guard the small spaces around their quarters.

Maximum number of daily sorties flown to feed nestlings: More than 1,000

Flying speed: 18–61 km/h (11–38 mph)

Length: 15–20 cm (6–8 in)

Wingspan: 30–34 cm (12–13.5 in)

Weight: 14–24 g (0.5–0.8 oz)

Markings: Dark blue-black back; red on throat and between the eyes; pale rusty-beige undersides; male's tail 20% longer

Alias: House swallow, common swallow, l'hirondelle des granges, Hirundo rustica

Calls: Soft, liquid chittering song; also chirping call notes

Food: Mosquitoes, midges, horse flies, beetles, flying ants, caddis flies, mayflies, moths, small amounts of berries and seeds

Whereabouts: Parks, large suburban yards and other open areas around rivers, ponds, lakeshores and marshes

Home range: Usually within 200 m (220 yd) of nest

Nest: Thick-walled half-cup of mud pellets and grass, 10–18 cm (4–7 in) wide, 2.5–4.5 cm (1–1.8 in) high, lined with feathers; built on a sheltered platform, bridge girder or against a wall beneath eaves

Average clutch: 4–5 pumpkin-seed-sized eggs, white with reddish-brown spots

Incubation period: 13–17 days

Fledging age: 18–23 days

Age at first breeding: 1 year

Average annual survival: 20–30% in first year; 30–60% for adults

Lifespan: Most less than 4 years; maximum 15 years

Predators: Kestrels, sharp-shinned hawks, Cooper's hawks; nests raided by cats, squirrels, raccoons, weasels, grackles

Average first arrival in southern Ontario: Early Apr.

Average last departure from southern Ontario: Early Oct.

Nesting range: Throughout most of Ontario, but sparse in north; also in all other provinces and territories except Nunavut

Winter whereabouts: Panama and the Caribbean to Argentina

Number of swallow species nesting in Ontario: 6

Number of swallow species worldwide: 89–100

Also see: Chimney Swift

An average of 30 percent of Ontario barn swallows start a second family after their first brood learns to fly around late June. In a really good year, a few over-achievers may even go for a third. One of the young from the first batch sometimes remains with its parents to help feed and warm its younger siblings.

When not tending their young, the tiny-beaked birds are almost constantly in swirling flight chasing down their dinners. They usually pick off mosquitoes and midges six to eight metres (20 to 27 feet) above the ground or water, but sometimes sweep down after pestering swarms around people's heads. Long, narrow wings and sleek bodies allow them to stay aloft on far fewer calories than most other birds. Even to drink or bathe, they prefer to swoop their breaks or bodies through the water rather than wade into it. Early American ornithologist Alexander Wilson estimated that barn swallows log almost 1,000 air kilometres (620 miles) a day, and that one reaching the ripe old age of 10 years will have flown more than 3.2 million kilometres (2 million miles) in its lifetime. While perhaps an overestimate, it stands as a testament to the bird's aerial nature. Among Ontario's birds, only chimney swifts spend more time in the air.

Little wonder such tireless flyers migrate as far as southern Argentina between late August and October, in effect becoming birds of endless summer. Some fly 565 kilometres (351 miles) non-stop across the Caribbean Sea. Their fleet wings, in fact, have taken them all over the world. Barn swallows are also native to Eurasia, Africa and Australia, and occasionally reach Hawaii and Greenland. In the folklore of many cultures, the skybound bird brings fire to humans from supernatural realms, its back covered with soot, its breast singed red and its tail feathers burned into a V. From ancient Rome to China, it was deemed good fortune to have barn swallows nest on a house and very bad karma to disturb them.

BLUE JAY
Resourceful Feeder Favourite

WHETHER SCREAMING through old, leafy downtown neighbourhoods or bellying up at suburban feeders, the blue jay has done extremely well for itself in the city. One of the most common and colourful birds in urban Ontario, it was a natural to represent Toronto alongside baseball's Cardinals and Orioles. Well-treed communities, especially those with plenty of mature oaks, sometimes host more than 100 pairs of nesting jays in one square kilometre (0.4 square mile), far more than in the forest or countryside. The success of the blue-jacketed birds, however, has been tempered in recent years by the West Nile virus, which has seriously diminished their numbers in some areas.

Like crows – probably the hardest-hit West Nile victims – jays are members of the celebrated Corvidae family, and as such are considered among the brainiest of birds. Brash, bold and alert, they are highly adaptable forest opportunists that have learned plenty of street smarts in the city, dining on berries and caterpillars from ornamental shrubs, combing moist turf grass for grubs and worms and ambushing large wasps emerging from the cracks between aluminum siding.

In winter, blue jays don't merely rely on bird feeders to get through hard times. Like squirrels, the resourceful birds retrieve seeds, nuts and acorns from buried caches and the nooks and crannies of tree trunks where they've hidden them earlier in autumn and summer. One jay can stash or bury up to 5,000 acorns and nuts in a single season. Many commonly fly 1.5 kilometres (0.9 miles), sometimes even up to five kilometres (three miles), to a fruitful stand of trees. Cramming their throats and beaks with up to five acorns or 15 beechnuts, they then return home to hide the loot. Forgotten nuts and seeds often

Flying speed: Average 33 km/h (20 mph) in town, 37–42 km/h (23–26 mph) in migration

Length: 25–30 cm (10–12 in)

Wingspan: 41–42 cm (16.1–16.5 in)

Weight: 70–100 g (2.5–3.5 oz)

Markings: Blue back, white undersides, black necklace, blue crest

Alias: Blue coat, common jay, jay bird, northern jay, nest robber, corn-thief, *le geai bleu*, *Cyanocitta cristata*

Origin of name: Old German *gahi*, meaning "quick"

Name for a group: A party of jays

Calls: Wide variety, including short, loud, harsh screams, a "queedle" sound like a squeaky clothesline, and whistles

Whereabouts: Shady neighbourhoods, parks, forest edges

Food: Acorns, beechnuts and other nuts about two-thirds of diet in Oct.–Mar.; also seeds, berries, caterpillars, beetles, grasshoppers and other insects, their eggs and cocoons, spiders, snails, millipedes, frogs, mice, minnows, roadkill, small birds, their eggs and nestlings

Favourite feeder foods: Sunflower seeds, peanuts, suet

Nest: Bulky bowl of sticks, grasses, bark and mud, lined with moss, feathers and rootlets, about 18 cm (7 in) wide, wedged between a forked branch, usually 2–15 m (6–50 ft) above ground in an evergreen

Average clutch: 4–6 cherry-tomato-sized light-green, blue or buff eggs, with brown specks

Incubation period: 17–18 days

Fledging age: 17–21 days

Age of first-time breeders: 2 years

Annual adult survival: About 50%

Lifespan: 6 years common; up to 18 years in wild, 26 years in captivity

Predators: Hawks, owls, falcons, dogs, cats; nests raided by crows, raccoons and squirrels

Nesting range: Southern Ontario to southern edge of boreal forest; also in all other provinces

Winter whereabouts: Most remain in Ontario; probably less than 20% fly to the central and southern United States

Number of jay species nesting in Ontario: 2

Number of jay species worldwide: 42

Also see: Crow, Mosquitoes, Red Oak

germinate, making the birds important agents of long-distance nut dispersal in forests. Experts studying buried pollen records believe blue jays may have played a big part in the rapid advance of oaks into southern Ontario after the glaciers retreated 11,000 years ago.

In spring, jays add the occasional batch of scrambled birds' eggs or nestlings to the menu. Though nest robbing accounts for less than 1 percent of their fare, it's enough to make them notorious among other feathered species. Small birds sometimes gang up and mob a jay to force it away, berating and diving at it in the air. For their part, blue jays frequently mob crows, hawks, owls and foxes, which can threaten them or their nests.

As early as mid-February, jays turn their aggression on each other, with small groups of males trying to out shout, intimidate and trounce each other as they pursue unattached she-jays. After the roughest, toughest customer finally wins and settles down with his new mate, the raucous brigand actually whispers softly whistled love songs to her. A pair usually remains together for life. By late April or May, unlike most other songbirds, a hitched male jay clams right up and becomes inconspicuous as he helps his spouse build a well-hidden nest, usually within the dense, inner branches of an evergreen. He also fetches food and feeds his partner like a nestling, strengthening their bond and providing her with the energy and protein needed for producing eggs.

Blue-jay young, like many other birds, hatch featherless, blind and unable to generate enough heat to warm their blood to normal survival temperatures. For their first two or three days, they are closely brooded and not fed, instead living off the yoke absorbed from their eggs. After those first critical days, their circulatory systems rev up, their blood warms and they acquire downy insulation. Their bright-red, opened mouths trigger an automatic feeding response in their parents, who nourish them with a rich soup of regurgitated caterpillars and other juicy insects. By June, jays are again calling loudly to each other over rooftops from street to street as four-week-old fledglings accompany their foraging parents.

CANADA GOOSE
Wanderlust Muted by the City

A V FORMATION of Canada geese passing overhead, traditionally a sign of seasonal change, in the city is more likely to signify hungry birds heading out for a bite to eat. Beating the snarled commuter traffic below, urban geese move easily between waterside parks and choice grazing spots on fairways and highway embankments, cruising low over rooftops with an audible droning whirr from their powerful wing strokes.

The Canada goose is one of the most celebrated wildlife comeback stories of recent decades, though many cities are no longer celebrating. A prized game bird, it was virtually extirpated as a nesting species from southern Ontario by the 1920s, save for some remnant flocks on Lake St. Clair. Strict hunting regulations and conservation measures later allowed North America's Canada goose population to rise from about 250,000 around 1935 to probably more than five million – before the fall hunt opens – in recent years. Most are geese that nest in the Hudson Bay Lowlands and other northern areas and winter in the United States.

Urban geese are a breed apart, or rather a subspecies, known as giant Canadas. They nest locally and can weigh up to 10 times as much as some northern-nesting varieties, such as the mallard-sized cackling Canada geese. The bigger birds were almost extinct in the 1950s,

Flying speed: 65–85 km/h (39–51 mph)
Wingbeats per second: 2
Migrating altitude: Average 300–1,000 m (1,000–3,280 ft), up to 3,350 m (11,000 ft)
Length: 56–114 cm (1.8–3.7 ft)
Average height: 63–102 cm (2–3.3 ft)
Wingspan: 1.1–2 m (3.7–6.7 ft)
Weight: Females average 3.4–6.4 kg (7.5–14 lb); males 3.7–7.5 kg (8–16.5 lb); up to 10 kg (22 lb)
Weight of Arctic-nesting cackling Canada goose: 1.4–1.8 kg (3–4 lb)
Markings: Black neck and head, white chin strap, light-brown back, off-white breast and tail
Alias: Giant Canada goose, honker, wild goose, Canada, white-cheeked goose, grey goose, *la bernache canadienne, Branta canadensis maxima*
Goose name origin: From proto-Indo-European word *ghans,*

7

probably an imitation of the honking call

Name of a group: Gaggle

Call: Honk; female higher-pitched than males

Whereabouts: Grassy areas of parks, sports fields, golf courses, lakes, rivers, ponds, reservoirs, marshes

Food: Grass, sedges, grain, seeds, berries, willow buds, aquatic vegetation, insects

Nest: Sticks, reeds and down lining a ground depression, 75–90 cm (2.5–3 ft) wide, near water

Average clutch: 4–6 dull white eggs, about the size of average potatoes

Incubation period: 28–30 days

Fledging age: 9–11 weeks

Age of first-time breeders: 2–3 years for most; less than 10% at 1 year

Portion of goslings that survive to fledge: 60–80%

Lifespan: Up to 23 years in wild, 33 years in captivity

Predators: Coyotes, foxes, eagles; nests raided by gulls, crows, raccoons; goslings taken by hawks, owls, snapping turtles

Flightless moulting period: About 40 days, in Jun. and Jul.

Spring break: Many flocks of adolescents leave southern Ontario in Jun. and fly to the lowlands of James and Hudson Bays, where emerging vegetation is still new and succulent and they find abundant lakes on which to moult; adolescents and unsuccessful breeders from inland areas of southern Ontario and the northern United States also

except for small numbers nesting mainly in Manitoba. Ontario's Ministry of Natural Resources began a captive nesting program for giants and started releasing the offspring in the province's cities in 1968, hoping to both increase their numbers and provide big trophy birds for hunters during migration. With plenty of Kentucky bluegrass to feast upon and few predators in the cities, the great urban geese flourished. Many don't even bother to migrate. They've grown to a southern Ontario late-summer population of probably half a million.

The thronging gaggles, however, can have a considerable impact on their surroundings. They chomp vast swaths of turf grass to the roots and foul sports fields, suburban lawns and swimming areas with up to 150 droppings per well-fed goose a day. With secluded waterside nesting real estate at a premium, geese forced to set up in less-favourable spots (such as suburban corporate office grounds, flat-topped garage roofs or even high-rise apartment balconies) sometimes lunge at humans who come too close. (Geese are powerful birds capable of a nasty bite and it's probably not a good idea to let preschoolers chase after them in the park.)

Attempts to control swelling goose populations in cities across North America have ranged from trying to spook them away with scarecrows, dead-goose decoys and inflatable alligators, to employing border collies fitted with life jackets, remote-controlled model boats and cars (in one case draped in fox skins), noisemakers, firecrackers and lasers. Some U.S. jurisdictions have opted for capital punishment, with New Jersey gassing up to 10,000 geese a year.

Ontario has instituted special hunting seasons in early September and mid-winter to help keep down resident populations of giant Canadas in rural areas. But city birds are another story. A proposed cull of 2,000 problematic waterfront geese in Mississauga in the late 1990s was called off after fervent protests from animal rights activists and the general public. Instead, Mississauga, Toronto, Oakville and Whitby have deported thousands of the big birds – rounded up while moulting in early summer and unable to fly – to conservation areas near Lake Erie and, in the past, to remote marshes in New

Brunswick and northwestern Ontario. Parks departments also try to keep populations down by spraying eggs with mineral or vegetable oil, which prevents them from hatching, and by planting areas frequented by geese with obstructing bushes, shrubs and less-tasty grasses. Bread-tossing goose feeders are discouraged or threatened with fines.

Though biologists say bread isn't particularly good for waterfowl, winter feeding is one of the reasons tens of thousands of geese usually find enough to eat in urban parks and waterfronts to stay put for the winter. They also make country picnic forays to glean waste corn from farm fields close to cities. Others migrate to the United States in the fall, cold fronts sometimes pushing them south 300 kilometres (180 miles) or more in a single flight. Migrating flocks are made up of several family groups that merge in the air. They fly in a shifting V formation because it cuts wind resistance and the suction created by the powerful downstrokes of one bird helps carry the goose following it, like a bicycle behind a truck. Adults take turns at the forward point, according to some experts, because they're the strongest and they know the route.

Both returning migrants and overwintering geese begin nesting in March, when parents, who mate for life, send their yearlings off to join flocks of other one- and two-year-olds. A gander closely guards his mate while she remains almost constantly on the nest for a month, losing considerable weight, before the eggs hatch around early May. Afterwards, while she rebuilds her strength grazing with her new downy yellow goslings, her mate continues to stand sentinel, keeping other geese away from the family's feeding space. The largest families claim the best grazing sites, with their ganders given the highest deference by other geese. Extended families, usually consisting of the adult breeding offspring of an older dominant pair and their broods, also sometimes pool their goslings together, forming "crèches" of 20 or more youngsters that are looked after communally.

fly to the shores of the Great Lakes to moult

Famous geese: Mother Goose, Goosey Gander, goose that laid the golden egg

Cost of automated park goose-dropping sweeper: $15,000

Nesting range: Most of southern Ontario, with scattered populations as far north as Cochrane and west to Thunder Bay; northern subspecies in James and Hudson Bay Lowlands; also in all other provinces and territories

Spring migration peak: Mid-Apr. to early May

Fall migration peak: Late Sept. to mid-Oct.

Winter whereabouts: Most southern Ontario birds fly to bordering Great Lakes states or Chesapeake Bay area of the U.S. Atlantic seaboard; some stay as far north as Collingwood and Ottawa or go as far south as Georgia and Arkansas

Winter population in southern Ontario: 50,000–60,000

Number shot each fall in Ontario: Almost 150,000, including about 110,000 giant Canadas

Population breeding in Ontario's Hudson Bay Lowlands: More than 600,000

Oldest waterfowl fossils: 80 million years old

Number of goose species nesting in Ontario: 3

Number of goose species worldwide: 14–90, depending on species definition

Also see: Mallard, Lawn & Garden

CARDINAL
Scarlet Bird from Dixie

NESTING CARDINALS ARE among the most alluring of backyard blessings. And cardinals like nothing better than a bushy, well-treed yard to call their own. The red-robed birds make themselves comfortable even in older neighbourhoods in the hearts of cities, remaining through the winter to adorn bare branches and snow-covered evergreens.

Their vibrant, tropical good looks once made cardinals popular cage birds, trapped and shipped off to Europe by the thousands until native songbird imprisonment was outlawed in Canada and the United States in the early 20th century. "Northern" cardinals, in fact, are most closely related to birds living in or near the tropics and originally seldom ventured north of Kentucky. But the patchwork of forest, farm and town that developed in the U.S. midwest in the 19th century proved much to their liking, and they gradually spread northward with each new generation of dispersing young birds. The scarlet-crested pioneers were first spotted homesteading in Ontario in 1901, at Point Pelee, and within the following two decades were hitting the city, nesting in London and Toronto.

Cardinals went along for the ride in the postwar boom years of the 1940s and 1950s, with the widespread rise of suburban bird feeders giving them a big boost in winter. They prospered in numbers and moved to

Peterborough in 1951, Kingston in 1964 and Ottawa 10 years later. Today, they abound throughout the heavily settled portions of the province below the Canadian Shield and settle more sparingly in communities as far north as Sudbury.

Dense evergreen boughs, thick understory shrubbery, even the inner thorny tangles of old, unruly rose bushes, are all favourite places for cardinals to conceal their tiny nests of slender stems and grass in spring. If there's plenty of food around, mates will remain together near their nesting site year-round. Males reassert their land claims with loud bursts of song starting around mid-February, though they occasionally sing in the earlier off-months as well. Cardinals also stand out for being among the few songbirds whose more plainly clad females answer their whistling wooers with similar melodious airs. In close quarters, mates raise their crests, crane their necks and sway back and forth as they sing softly to each other. Later on, nest-bound hens whistle in their foraging spouses whenever more grub is needed.

Though cardinal nests are well hidden, many are found by neighbourhood cats, squirrels and other predators. More than two-thirds of all nesting attempts usually fail. The cardinal rule, however, is never to give up. If they lose one clutch, they renest five or six days later. They also nest again if they successfully raise a brood by early summer, with dads tending the fledglings while mothers settle on the next set of eggs. Indeed, so strong is the parental drive to nurture, apparently chickless male cardinals have been seen feeding the nestlings of other species. One was even observed feeding a surrogate school of goldfish at a pond where they had previously learned to beg for handouts from humans.

Young cardinals, recognized by their dark bills, continue to sponge off their parents for several weeks after they learn to fly. Eventually, they leave and go off in search of their own space. Following river valleys and other natural corridors, they may wander throughout the winter looking for an unoccupied territory, sometimes – with the help of feeders stocked with cracked corn and sunflower seeds – pushing their species' frontier still farther north in the process.

beetle grubs, caterpillars, grasshoppers, crickets, cicadas, dragonflies and other insects, spiders, centipedes, snails; also buds and sap in early spring

Favourite feeder foods: Cracked wheat, sunflower seeds, safflower seeds, corn

Territory: 0.2–2.6 ha (0.5–6.4 acres)

Nest: Neat bowl, about 9 cm (3.5 in) wide, of grass, plant stems, shredded bark, pliable twigs, rootlets, leaves, paper or cellophane; usually 1–3 m (3.3–10 ft) above ground

Average clutch: 2–3 brown-speckled or blotched greenish-white or greyish eggs, about the size of grapes

Incubation period: Usually 9–10 days

Fledging age: 9–10 days

Age at first breeding: 1 year old

Average annual survival: 54–66% for adults

Lifespan: Up to 15 years in wild, 22 years in captivity

Predators: Cats, dogs, raccoons, foxes, skunks, opossums; nests raided by squirrels, chipmunks, blue jays, crows

Nesting range: Southern Ontario north to about Sudbury; also in Quebec, New Brunswick and Nova Scotia

Closest Ontario relatives: Rose-breasted grosbeak, indigo bunting, dickcissel

Number of cardinal-grosbeak family species worldwide: 42

Also see: Mourning Dove, House Finch, Grey Squirrel

CEDAR WAXWING
Amiable Berry Lover

Average flock: 30–60 birds

Flying speed: 34–50 km/h (21–31 mph)

Length: 15.5–20 cm (6–8 in)

Wingspan: 28–31 cm (11–12 in)

Weight: 27–38 g (1–1.3 oz)

Markings: Brown breast, back and head crest; black mask; yellow bar at tip of black tail; waxy red tips on secondary feathers of black wings

Alias: Cedarbird, cherry bird, southern waxwing, Carolina waxwing, cankerbird, *le jaseur des cedres, Bombycilla cedrorum*

Call: High, dry, reedy "zeee," frequently repeated

Whereabouts: Around fruit- and berry-bearing trees in large parks, suburban yards, rail and hydro corridors, ravines, shorelines and wetlands

Food: Raspberries, strawberries, serviceberries and mulberries in early summer; later dogwood berries, cherries, caterpillars, dragonflies, ants, mayflies and other insects; from fall to early spring, crabapples, mountain ash berries, wild grapes, hawthorn and Russian olive fruits, red cedar berries, rosehips, sumac and alder seeds; also sap in late winter; flowers in spring

Community density: 5–44 nests/ha (2.5 acres)

Nest: Bulky cup, 10–13 cm (4–5 in) wide, of grasses, twigs, rootlets, bark and lichens;

ORMING ROVING BANDS of black-masked fruitopians, cedar waxwings flock to suburban backyards, large parks and riversides crowded by trees and bushes brimming with berries. The sleek, genial, pointy-crested nomads are the most fruit-focused birds in eastern North America and travel widely from one ripening crop to another. They're sometimes seen perched in a row politely passing berries up and down the line to each other. In May, when there's not much fruit around and sweet blossoms provide almost half the birds' sustenance, courting couples also daintily pass flower petals back and forth, accompanied by a little dance.

Waxwings choose their mates by sizing up each other's wings for the sealing-wax-like red dabs for which they're named. The dabs are much more prominent on birds that are two years of age and older, marking them as experienced, dependable food providers. For most other songbirds, real-estate appraisal is key in mate selection, with females settling with partners holding territories with the most bountiful supplies of caterpillars and other insect meals. Fruit-eating cedar waxwings, however, don't establish individual breeding territories because there are seldom enough varieties of berries in any one spot to last the duration of the nesting period. Instead, they nest in loose clusters of up to a few dozen pairs in a small grove of hawthorns or cedars, from which flocks of males commute as far as a kilometre (0.6 miles) to forage. After gorging himself, one of these providers may fill his throat and beak with up to 30 chokecherries to bring back home to the missus, who almost never leaves the nest while incubating her eggs.

Cedar waxwings don't settle down to nest until June, when egg-laying females can fatten up on ripe red raspberries, strawberries and other early fruits. When the hatchlings emerge, they're initially plied with a high-protein insect mash that allows them to grow very quickly. At this time of year, waxwing parents are often seen hunting from tree perches, snatching insects from the air like flycatchers. Within a few days, however, the nestlings are weaned onto regular waxwing fruit fare.

Some successful parents, less than a third, nest again after their first brood takes wing around early August. As the breeding season ends, flocks resume their nomadic ways. Some groups begin flying south in mid- to late September, amalgamating into larger loose flocks as they go. Others choose to stay behind, taking shelter with overwintering robins in scrubby thickets in creeks and ravines, especially in areas with scraggly red cedar trees, which bare powdery dark-blue, berrylike fruits that are a winter waxwing mainstay. Sometimes they have an unplanned winter bash, when fermented fruits, such as clusters of black pokeweed berries, actually make them drunk, causing them to sway and even topple from their perches. Sloshed waxwings can be oblivious to the point of allowing themselves to be picked up, a dangerous prospect when winter predators lurk nearby.

usually wedged in a forked branch 1–4 m (3.3–13.3 ft) up in a hawthorn, cedar, apple or pine tree
Average clutch: 3–5 olive-sized blue, grey or greenish eggs with black spots
Incubation period: 11–14 days
Fledging age: 14–18 days
Portion of eggs that hatch: 54–75%
Portion of eggs that produce fledglings: 39–57%
Average annual survival: About 45% for adults
Lifespan: Very few live more than 3 years; up to 7 years in wild, 14 years in captivity
Predators: Red-tailed, sharp-shinned and Cooper's hawks, merlins, grackles; nests raided by squirrels, raccoons, blue jays and house wrens
Average first arrival of migrants in southern Ontario: Late Apr.
Average last departure of migrants in southern Ontario: Late Oct.
Nesting range: All Ontario to the treeline; also in all other provinces
Winter whereabouts: From about Sudbury, Sault Ste. Marie and Ottawa south to Central America
Also see: Goldfinch, Robin, White Cedar

BIRD GARDENS
Growing Native Plants Provides an Ideal Haven for a Variety of Nesters and Migrants

Ripening times of common seeds and fruits eaten by birds:

Spring: Silver maple, white elm, Pennsylvania sedge

Early summer: Wild raspberry (illustrated), blackberry, wild strawberry, fly honeysuckle, Solomon's seal, wild sarsaparilla

Midsummer: Serviceberry, red-berried elder, flowering raspberry, currants, gooseberries, trilliums

Late summer: Wild cherries, dogwoods, Canada elderberry, hairy honeysuckle, wild raisin, nannyberry, wild rose, bunchberry, violets

Autumn: Oaks, ashes, beech, white cedar, sugar maple, maple-leaved viburnum, hobblebush, climbing bittersweet, sunflowers, jack-in-the-pulpit

Autumn (fruits persisting into winter): American mountain ash, hawthorns, Virginia creeper, riverbank grape, red cedar, staghorn sumac, juniper, highbush cranberry, hackberry, winterberry, partridgeberry

Autumn (seeds persisting into winter): White birch, Manitoba maple, white pine, white spruce, hemlock, speckled alder, goldenrod, asters

Common non-native trees with fruits eaten by birds:

Crabapples, Russian olive, autumn olive, European mountain ash, white mulberry

Common non-native lawn and garden weeds with seeds

BIRD FEEDING, for many, is an extension of gardening, communing with nature in the backyard. Growing native plants takes that marriage of popular pastimes a big step further. Restoring original components and natural diversity to the urban landscape, even in neighbourhoods near the core of Ontario's biggest cities, vastly increases property values in the estimation of a great many birds. After thousands of years of co-evolution, native trees, shrubs and perennials best serve avian interests and require far less care and watering than the alien commercial cultivars that predominate in most gardens. Bird-friendly, pesticide-free yards also benefit from feathered attendants that are only too happy to keep plant-nibbling insects in check.

The wider a yard's vegetative variety, offering food, cover and nest sites, the more diverse its inhabitants. But even select flower plantings can make a big difference. Beyond the many reddish tubular blossoms sought by hummingbirds, celebrated spring forest beauties such as trilliums, violets and Solomon's seal develop summer seeds sampled by a number of different songbirds. So too are purple coneflowers, black-eyed Susans, coreopsis and other showy species that both flower and seed throughout the summer.

Other colourful, sun-loving natives (such as goldenrod, asters and, above all, sunflowers) bear autumn seeds that, if left standing, bring in all manner of hungry passing migrants and overwintering juncos, tree sparrows and northern finches. Some common garden flowers, including cosmos, marigolds, zinnia and phlox, yield bountiful quantities of seeds that attract many birds as well through the summer and into winter if left in place.

Even when there's plenty of food around, though, most birds need at least some shelter nearby in which to perch before they feel secure enough to tuck in to a good meal. In yards too small for a lot of trees and shrubs, vines can turn fences and walls into lush sanctuaries and even roosting and nesting sites for cardinals, house finches, wrens and others. Virginia creeper – with leaves that turn reddish purple in autumn – and riverbank grape also proffer clusters of hearty wild grapes that continue to feed many birds after the snow comes.

Virginia creeper, wild raspberry (illustrated) and blackberry often turn up in yards after being planted by birds themselves from seeds in their droppings. Indeed, the hand of nature is the best guide for creating gardens to attract wildlife. Trees and shrubs are more appealing to birds when they're clumped, rather than regimented in rows. The denser the tangles of branches, the more inviting they are to nesters and ground foragers.

Large yards with tall maples and oaks sometimes host high-canopy nesting orioles and warbling vireos, as well as treetop-foraging red-eyed vireos. Feasts of acorns draw blue jays, flickers, nuthatches, crows and many other eager diners to oak trees in early autumn. Ripe chokecherries and wild black cherries in late summer have the same effect on dozens of different songbirds.

Long-lasting mountain ash berries, both native and European, are staples of overwintering robins and cedar waxwings, and sometimes remain long enough to reward early-arriving migrants in spring. Hawthorns similarly offer bounties of fruit though the winter as well as a dense shroud of heavily spiked branches to protect nightly boarders and nesters from cats, raccoons and other tree-climbing predators. Evergreens afford the warmest, coziest winter digs of all and premium pre-leafout cover for early nesters, including crows, blue jays, mourning doves and house finches.

eaten by birds: Lamb's quarters, chickweed, prostrate knotweed, common plantain, lady's-thumb, climbing nightshade, dandelion, sheep sorrel, crabgrass, pigweed

Garden nibblers eaten by birds: Beetle grubs and adults; cutworms, cankerworms and other moth caterpillars; fly maggots and adults; wireworms, slugs, snails, crickets, ants, sowbugs

Native plant sources: Many garden centres and nurseries are beginning to offer an assortment of native species; seed can be collected from wild plants, though no more than 10% should be taken from one source; local naturalist clubs sometimes organize "rescues" of native plants from construction sites and road clearances; otherwise, in most cases, native plants should never be transplanted from the wild

Bird baths: Greatly increase a yard's draw, with most birds appreciating a good bath and a cool, refreshing drink; a bird bath should be shallowly sloped, at least 1 m (3.3 ft) above the ground and well away from shrubs and other cover in which cats and other predators can hide; should be cleaned out at least once a week

Also see: Hummingbird, Transient Migrants, Winter Wayfarers, Red Oak, Lawn & Garden

CHICKADEE
Big Vocabulary & Expanding Mind

AFTER THE FAIR-WEATHER birds have all fled south, black-capped chickadees come to the fore as they tamely troop to suburban winter feeders. The cheerful bundles of energy edge out blue jays as the most frequently reported visitors at feeding stations across the province. Belying their cheerful, diminutive demeanour, the densely feathered sprites defy the season's odds through a combination of focused teamwork, intelligence and grit.

Through October and November, each chickadee collects and hides hundreds or even thousands of seeds, berries, cocoons, egg sacks and bug bodies every day. They disperse the immense larder inside knotholes, under strips of bark and within tufts of pine needles and in dead curled leaves. Studies suggests that chickadees not only remember where they've hidden things, but which caches contain select entrees and break into them first during winter. Neuroscientists have also found that to handle all this data, black-caps actually expand their memory banks around October, growing new neurons in the hippocampus, the part of the brain that deals with spatial recollection. Humans brains are incapable of such a feat.

Quick access to winter grub is essential for chickadees. While roosting, they often burn all of their body fat shivering their muscles to produce heat and must replenish it every day, meaning they need far more food than in the summer. To keep from running out of fuel on particularly cold nights, they shiver less and enter a state of regulated hypothermia, allowing their body temperature to drop by 10–12 °C (18–22 °F).

Small flocks of black-caps fiercely defend winter territories containing their scattered secret stockpiles from neighbouring chickadee bands. Comrades keep in contact, announce food discoveries, warn of danger and otherwise relate with one another using at least 15 different types of vocalizations. Their namesake buzzing "chick-a-dee-dee" call is uttered in innumerable different combinations, key shifts and repetitions that some researchers liken to human sentence structure, carrying a wide variety of distinct messages. Their repertoire also includes tweets, twitters, gargles and hisses.

Chickadees begin distilling their most hopeful of calls on sunny midwinter days, when males start laying claim to breeding territories by whistling their high, lingering mating song. The simple two- or three-note verse can be heard into early summer, but its debut bears the promise of spring. Flocks break up in March and the birds disperse over a wider area. The top one or two males reserve choice territories within the flock's winter-foraging area, often pairing up with their previous year's spouse. Younger or meeker chickadees are pushed out to the boonies until the breeding season ends toward late summer. On average, only one couple per flock survives from one breeding season to the next, most often the dominant pair with the best feeding and sheltering locales. In the absence of an unoccupied woodpecker hole, a black-cap couple pecks one out themselves in a week or two. Lower-ranking females sometimes fly to the manor of a dominant male for an illicit liaison, then return to their nests on the wrong side of the tracks to have their cuckolded husbands help raise their blue-blooded brood.

Average breeding territory: 1–7 ha (2.5–17 acres)

Nest: Cavities in rotted tree trunks, limbs or stumps, especially birch, most often 1–4 m (3–13 ft) above ground; entrance about 2.5 cm (1 in) wide; lined with moss, fur, grass, pine needles and feathers

Average clutch: 6–8 reddish-brown-spotted, dull white eggs, the size of pistachio shells

Incubation period: 11–13 days

Fledging age: About 16 days

Dispersal: Young join unrelated flocks when 6 weeks old

Age of first-time breeders: 1 year for most

Average annual adult survival: 60%

Lifespan: Adults average 2.5 years; up to 12 years

Predators: Kestrels, sharp-shinned hawks, owls, northern shrikes, cats; nests raided by squirrels, raccoons, chipmunks, weasels

Often seen with: Nuthatches, juncos, downy and hairy woodpeckers in winter flocks; also kinglets, brown creepers, warblers and vireos in autumn

Nesting range: All Ontario, except for northwest; also in all other provinces and territories, except Nunavut

Winter whereabouts: Most stay put; flocks of young birds sometimes migrate to northern United States in mid-Sept. to Nov., especially in years of food shortage; return Apr.–May

Number of chickadee and titmouse species nesting in Ontario: 3

Number of chickadee and titmouse species worldwide: 65

CHIMNEY SWIFT
Tireless in Flight

H IGH OVERHEAD on warm summer days, small squadrons of chimney swifts streak and sweep through the air like tiny fighter jets, their long chittering bursts taking the place of screaming engines. Swifts are dark, stub-tailed little birds with stiff, flickering wings more than twice as long as their bodies. Almost never landing where someone can see them up close, they spend virtually all their waking hours in the air chasing down flying insects, generally cruising at much loftier heights than swallows, whom they resemble. The indefatigable aeronauts also drink, bath, feed their young and reportedly sometimes mate on the wing. Studies have confirmed that the European common swift often even flies in its sleep, ascending to heights of 1,000 to 2,000 metres (3,280 to 6,561 feet) to spend the night gliding and slowly flapping into the wind as it nods off.

Swifts have no use for terra firma. Their tiny legs barely have the strength to push off the ground. But while their feet weren't made for walking, their stout claws are like grappling hooks, enabling them to hang on to or catch an edge of virtually any vertical surface. Chimney swifts originally roosted by clinging to the inner walls of large, hollow dead or dying trees, but switched to the wide flues of old-fashioned brick chimneys as old-growth forests fell to the axe. As long as chimneys are not in use – usually the case during the warm months – the already-sooty-hued birds have a safe and secure dorm and nesting chamber.

Though many modern chimneys are capped, wired, lined with sheet metal or too narrow for roosting occupants, swifts remain among the most urban of birds.

Foraging altitude: 20–150 m (66–492 ft)

Flying speed: Average 30–60 km/h (18.5–37 mph)

Width of chimney flue used for nests: At least 25 cm (10 in)

Time swifts return to roosts: About 20 minutes after sunset

Body temperature: Normally 41.5–43°C (107–109°F); in torpor 11–16°C (52–61°F), when bugs scarce on cold days

Wingspan: 30.5–33 cm (12–13 in)

Length: 12–14 cm (5–5.5 in)

Weight: 17–30 g (0.6–1 oz)

Markings: Mostly dark grey-brown, lighter grey on cheeks, throat and upper breast; blackish wings and tail

Alias: Chimney bird, chimney swallow, chimney sweep, le martinet ramoneur, Chaetura pelagica

Calls: Loud, rapid-fire chittering

They still occupy large chimneys in the best neighbour-hoods as well as old factory smoke stacks, air shafts, church steeples, garages and derelict buildings. Loving their own company, they sometimes hang from the cracks and mortar of choice locations in overlapping rows of roosting birds. Large flocks can be seen swirling over and funnelling into such large traditional roosts when they return at dusk.

After flying in from Peru, chimney swifts appear over Ontario cityscapes in May performing noisy, acrobatic courtship flights. Once paired, they spend up to three or four weeks carefully making their nests, though they may start laying eggs three or four days after construction begins. Nest builders collect thin twigs by snapping them off trees and bushes with their Vise-Grip claws as they fly by and paste them together with their trademark thick, gluelike saliva onto the insides of chimneys or walls. Swift saliva glands, in fact, swell to 12 times their normal size during the nesting season. Some southeast Asian swiftlet species make their nests entirely of their own quick-drying morsels of mucus. The six-centimetre-wide (2.4-inch-wide), white translucent structures are col-lected from colonial caves by the thousands and used as the base for the Chinese delicacy known as bird's-nest soup – in effect, bird's-spit soup.

Chimney swifts usually keep to one nest per site, though the natal flue may be shared with a number of non-breeders. In many cases, one or more of these roomies may become mother's helpers, assisting the breeding pair in building their nest and incubating, brooding and feeding the nestlings. After the young fledge, swifts begin joining in larger flocks, flying in zigzag zoning patterns for their prey. As insect numbers drop in late summer, they begin heading south again, often joining with migrant nighthawks in sky dining along the way.

Whereabouts: Sky throughout city; open brick chimneys, roofs, garages

Food: Mosquitoes, flies, wasps, bees, caddis flies, mayflies, crane flies, beetles, flying ants and other flying insects

Foraging distance from nest: Commonly less than 0.5 km (0.3 mi), up to 6 km (3.7 mi)

Nest: Shallow half-cup of twigs, 5–7.5 cm (2–3 in) wide, stuck on inside wall of a chimney, air shaft, church steeple, aban-doned building or beneath a garage roof joist

Average clutch: 4–5 white, jelly-bean-sized eggs

Incubation period: 19–21 days

Fledging age: 28–30 days

Age at first breeding: 1 year

Annual adult survival: 63–81%

Lifespan: Adults average 4–5 years; up to 15 years

Predators: Kestrels, sharp-shinned hawks, peregrine falcons

Nesting range: Southern Ontario north to about Cochrane and Wawa, and between Thunder Bay and Kenora; also in Saskatchewan, Manitoba, Quebec and Maritimes

Average first arrival in southern Ontario: Late Apr. to early May

Average last departure from southern Ontario: Late Sept.

Winter whereabouts: Coastal and Amazonian regions of Peru and adjacent Brazil

Closest Ontario relative: Ruby-throated hummingbird

Number of swift species world-wide: 96

Also see: Nighthawk, Barn Swallow

CROW
The Smartest Bird in Town

Flying speed: 40–53 km/h
(24–32 mph)
Portion of nesting crow parents assisted by 1 or more off-spring from a previous year: 37–94% of year-round residents
Portion of bird species worldwide in which nest helpers are common: About 3%
Length: 43–53 cm (17–21 in)
Wingspan: 84–100 cm (2.7–3.3 ft)
Weight: 420–640 g (1–1.4 lb)
Weight of a raven: 0.9–1.5 kg (2–3.3 lb)
Markings: Completely black
Alias: American crow, common crow, eastern crow, corn thief, *la corneille américaine, Corvus brachyrhynchos*
Name origin: Imitation of call
Name for a group: A murder of crows

RISING EARLY from wooded roosts and patrolling neighbourhoods in small foraging parties, urban crows always seem to have something on the go as they call back and forth over wide spaces. They're normally among the city's top-five avian inhabitants, and undoubtedly the smartest. Having taken to the spread of agriculture in a big way, the sable-winged omnivores also learned to thrive in Ontario's cities, scavenging roadsides, feasting at garbage dumps and fast-food parking lots and sampling the delights of lawns and gardens.

In recent years, though, crows have been devastated by the West Nile virus. Within two years of the mosquito-borne disease reaching Ontario in 2001, crow numbers in Toronto, Mississauga, Oakville and Burlington dropped by more than 90 percent. Dead crows were used as harbingers to track the spread of the virus across the province. Blue jays and chickadees were also hit hard. If, however, West Nile follows the usual course of most new epidemics, its impact should decrease over time, allowing bird populations to recover.

Crow populations in many other Ontario communities seem to have remained relatively healthy. Some would argue too healthy. Smaller cities and towns in southwestern Ontario in particular often have to cope with immense flocks of cawing, defecating black-feathered squatters moving in from farther north for the winter, starting around November. The birds roost en masse in town trees by night and fan out each day over hundreds of square kilometres of surrounding countryside, gleaning leftovers in harvested cornfields. Recent winters of low snowfall have made for good eating. Chatham hosted a winter flock of some 160,000 until bird control professionals, packing projectile "bangers" and whistles, shooed most of them away late in the year 2000. The problem, however, may simply reform somewhere else, with the pros having since also been called in to harass flocks of 120,000 crows in Essex, near Windsor, and almost 40,000 in Woodstock. Roosts in the American midwest can reach up to four million birds.

Extreme prejudice is also used to deal with crows, among the few non-game birds not legally protected in Ontario. But their sharp wits have enabled the black brainiacs to persevere. Crows are said to commonly recognize shotguns and fly away long before irate farmers can squeeze off a shot. Studies have shown that crows are smart enough to learn how to solve puzzles and count to at least four or five. Some naturalists suggest they already know how to count.

Crows also have strong communication skills, with between 20 and 300 types of calls according to various authorities, including specific greetings, warnings, alerts and directions for each other. They can yell, gurgle and even mimic human laughter and words. Tall tales abound of crows being taught to talk. In Greek mythology, a crow named Corvus was the messenger of the god Apollo. Originally a white bird, Corvus angered his master by being tardy and bringing bad news. In consequence, Apollo turned him black and banished him to the night sky, where he can still be seen early on spring evenings, forming the four-star, diamond-shaped constellation Corvus, low in the southwest below the zodiacal constellation Virgo.

One call – a long, constant cawing – is said to be summons for the flock to gather. There are many

Calls: Loud caw, many variations

Whereabouts: Throughout city and suburbs

Food: Human food scraps, roadkill, fruit, nuts, berries, seeds, corn, grain, grasshoppers, beetle grubs and other insects, worms, snakes, starlings, sparrows, robins and other small birds, nestlings and eggs, frogs, squirrels, mice, fish

Waste corn content of annual diet: More than one-third for most crows

Territory: 0.8–28 ha (19–69 acres) in city; up to 10 times as large in countryside

Nest: Jumble of sticks and bark, usually about 40–50 cm (16–20 in) wide, 10–38 cm (4–15 in) high; lined with grass, moss, roots and fur; often hidden in the inner branches of an evergreen, 5–18 m (16–60 ft) above ground

Average clutch: 4–6 dark-brown-spotted, bluish-green or olive eggs, about as big as golf balls

Incubation period: 16–19 days

Fledging age: 28–35 days

Age at first breeding: 2–6 years

Average annual survival: 43–63% in first year; 70–95% for adults

Lifespan: Most adults 2–6 years; maximum 14 years in wild, more than 20 years in captivity

Predators: Great horned owls, red-tailed hawks, goshawks, foxes; raccoons, cats, Cooper's hawks raid nests

Average nestling feeding rate: About once every 35 minutes

Body temperature: 39.5–41°C (103–106°F)

Famous crows: Heckyll & Jeckyll, Corvus

Species that reuse old crow nests: Hawks, great horned owls, long-eared owls, merlins, squirrels; raccoons use them to sleep in

Nesting range: All Ontario; also in all other provinces and the Northwest Territories

Size of migrating flocks: Usually 30–200 birds, sometimes up to 1,000

Winter whereabouts: From about Pembroke, around the Great Lakes and Kenora south to Arkansas, Tennessee and North Carolina

Age of the oldest corvid (crow family) fossils: 25 million years old

Closest Ontario relative: Northern raven

Number of crow and raven species worldwide: 47

Also see: Blue Jay, Mosquitoes

accounts of crows holding councils, sometimes raucously conversing back and forth for hours. The big birds are also known for teamwork and for sticking up for one another, often coming to the calls of injured or distressed confederates. They co-operate closely, keeping one or two sentries posted while a flock forages, and joining together to mob potential predators such as hawks or owls. A group of crows kicking up a ruckus during the day often betrays the presence of a roosting owl.

Starting around mid-February, flocks of overwintering urban crows are bolstered by large numbers of returning migrants. But the corvid communities gradually break up as couples pair off. Wooing males fly in courtship displays, diving and driving off competitors. Mates bow repeatedly to each other and utter soft, melodious sweet nothings, quite unlike the harsh caws of everyday crow parlance. They usually spend a week or two in March or early April building large, well-concealed nests within the upper branches of evergreens. Their nestlings become boisterous around May, and by the time they make their first clumsy flights they are already black and adult-sized, though with bluish eyes and higher voices. They're not the much-smaller black birds often seen close on the heels of crows, erroneously taken by some to be babies following their mothers. The little followers are red-winged blackbirds, angrily mobbing crows, which make regular snacking raids on other species' nests.

Flocks begin reforming again in late June, parents bringing their fledglings with them to learn the ways of society. Sometimes, youngsters stick around and help their parents raise one or more batches of siblings in following years. Most, however, become youthful rovers after gaining independence, wandering widely until finding a mate for life and settling down.

FLICKER
Woodpecker with a Terrestrial Bent

THE MOST ABUNDANT and strikingly attired woodpecker in many Ontario cities is often not recognized as a member of its tree-boring family. Flashing golden yellow beneath its wings and tail as it dips through the air, the common flicker sports a boldly spotted white belly, smart black neckerchief and red-triangle neck nape ensemble. But unlike other local woodpeckers, the blue-jay-sized bird spends much of its time on sandy ground probing ant holes. Capturing its quarry with a barbed, sticky tongue that darts the length of a human pinkie beyond its bill, the avian anteater has been known to fill its stomach with up to 5,000 of the tangy-tasting colonial insects.

Similar foraging habits of the European green woodpecker earned it a place in Greek and other Indo-European mythologies as the father of the inventor of the plough. Woodpeckers in general were closely associated in Europe and Asia with agriculture, rain and thunder gods. In many languages, they were called "rainbirds," both because they produced thundering sounds when knocking on wood and because they frequented oaks, which were considered sacred trees in many cultures.

Flicker tongue length: Extends 7.5 cm (3 in) beyond beak

Drum roll: Loud, even, 25 beats per second, lasting up to 1.5 seconds

Flying speed: 13–42 km/h (8–25 mph)

Average number of wingbeats between dipping "bounds": 1–5

Body length: 30–35 cm (12–14 in)

Wingspan: 47–52 cm (18.5–21.5 in)

Weight: 110–160 g (3.9–5.6 oz)

Markings: Dark-brown bands across tan back and wings; tan neck and face with a grey cap and a red, arrowhead-shaped patch on the back of the neck; wide black bib at top of the breast; black spots covering a white belly and sides; white rump; blackish-brown pointed tail is yellow on the underside, as are the wings; male has a black "moustache" across cheek

Alias: More than 130 known aliases, including common flicker, northern flicker, yellow-shafted flicker, golden-winged woodpecker, antbird, yellowhammer, wood pigeon, wick-up, clape, gaffer, harry-wicket, heigh-ho, *le pic doré, le pic flamboyant, Colaptes auratus*

Name origins: Imitation of "flick-a" call; may also have roots in Old English, *flicerian,* meaning "to flutter" or "fluttering of birds"; *Colaptes* comes from the Greek word for "hammer," *kolapter, auratus* means "gilded" in Latin

Name for a group of woodpeckers: A descent

Calls: Song a rapid "wick, wick, wick, wick" or "yuck, yuck, yuck, yuck," sounding like a car trying to start, continuing up to 6 seconds; also a "wicka" call, a creaky "clear" call note and several other vocalizations

Buzzing babies: A unique buzzing noise made by flicker nestlings when anything comes near them is suspected by some biologists to trick predators into believing the nest cavity is occupied by angry bees

Whereabouts: Sandy ground in parks, lawns, open and patchy woods, waterfronts

Food: Ants and ant eggs and larvae make up about half of fare; beetles, grasshoppers, crickets, wasps, wood lice, caterpillars, grubs, worms and flying insects; acorns, nuts, berries and seeds provide about a quarter of its diet

Territory: About 300 m (330 yd) wide

Average width of flicker nest entrance hole: 6–7 cm (2.4–2.8 in)

Width of downy woodpecker hole: 3–4 cm (1.2–1.6 in)

Width of pileated woodpecker hole: 10–12.5 cm (4–5 in)

Nest: Round cavity, 11.5–25 cm (4.5–10 in) wide, 25–100 cm (10–39 in) deep; usually facing south or southeast; bottom lined with fresh wood

When they alight on tree trunks, flickers assume the classic woodpecker posture: head up, feet grasping the bark, stiff tail feathers braced against the tree. During mating season, both sexes also drum like the rest of their kin, marking territories or attracting mates by hammering their beaks against any sufficiently resonant surface, from dead trees to TV antennas, metal road signs and aluminum siding. Strong head bones and neck muscles act as shock absorbers. In addition, territorial birds proclaim their presence with a loud, ratcheting cry reminiscent of a car engine turning over without starting. The call's junglelike quality inspired the nickname "Tarzan bird."

Aside from a few resourceful individuals frequenting generous bird feeders, most flickers migrate south on autumn nights, mainly to the Gulf Coast states, and begin returning in March or April. Males usually arrive a few days ahead of their mates. The guys are the real workers in any flicker marriage. Two females will even face off against each other to win a devoted husband, flaring their wings and tails, bobbing their heads and circling haughtily upturned beaks in an attempt to intimidate. Contentious males deal with each other in a similar manner. Strangely enough, this pugnacious behaviour becomes seduction between two birds of the opposite sex. And the only way the lovebirds can actually tell each other's gender is by the male's black moustache. A clever biologist proved this by painting a moustache on a mated female. Her hubby quickly rejected the cross-dressed flicker but took her back when the black mark was removed.

After pairing, males choose a nest site in a soft, rotted tree, or sometimes a Hydro or telephone pole. One pair of determined flickers forced the last-minute cancellation of a space shuttle flight in 1995 after drilling more than 100 exploratory holes in the foam insulation cover of the multibillion-dollar craft's fuel tank. When a good site is found, both mates usually spend one or two weeks excavating with their long, curved beaks, though sometimes they simply renovate an old hole or occupy a backyard nest box erected for them. Occasionally all their efforts come to naught when they're evicted by aggressive, cavity-nesting starlings, squirrels or kestrels. Though flickers can still carve out another nest hole and lay a second batch of eggs if a suitable tree is available, the delay decreases their chances of nesting success. Competition from starlings, an alien interloper, is thought to be at least partly responsible for a 50 percent decline in North American flicker populations during the last third of the 20th century.

Males are the chief incubators and brooders, sitting on the nest through the night and doing most of the feeding by day. Nestlings are fed heaping helpings of regurgitated ants about twice an hour. After they fledge, the raucous young continue to demand preprocessed meals with loud, high-pitched calls. Later, they join with their parents to make the ravaging of ant cities a family affair.

Another common member of the flicker's brethren in urban areas is the **downy woodpecker**, a black-and-white, sparrow-sized bird that taps erratically along branches and tree trunks in search of insects, spiders and their eggs. Unlike flickers, most downies don't migrate, though some tag along with mixed flocks of transient kinglets, nuthatches, brown creepers, chickadees and white-throated sparrows as they forage through the woods. The little woodpeckers also often show up at winter bird feeders, where they relish suet balls and sunflower seeds.

Almost identical to downies, but less common in cities, are **hairy woodpeckers**. Hairies are larger, though, about the size of robins, and have proportionally bigger beaks, which are about as long as the width of their heads. Still larger is the much rarer crow-sized **pileated woodpecker**, which flaunts a lofty, conical red head crest and usually inhabits the deepest woods. **Yellow-bellied sapsuckers**, whose males have matching red foreheads and beards, are also relatively uncommon forest woodpeckers in urban environs, but are often seen passing through during spring and fall migration.

chips; usually 2–5 m high (7–16.5 ft) in dead trees, often poplars; also in utility poles, posts and embankments

Average clutch: 5–8 peach-pit-sized, glossy white eggs

Incubation period: 11–14 days

Fledgling age: 24–28 days

Age at first breeding: 1 year

Lifespan: Up to 12 years in wild

Predators: Sharp-shinned and Cooper's hawks; nests raided by crows, blue jays, raccoons, cats, squirrels, chipmunks and weasels

Number of Ontario bird species that usually nest in tree cavities: 36

Number of Ontario mammal species that den in tree cavities: At least 7

Nesting range: Throughout Ontario; also in all other provinces and territories

Average first arrival in southern Ontario: Mid-Mar.

Average last departure from southern Ontario: Mid-Nov.

Winter whereabouts: Most Ontario flickers go to the southeastern United States, a few linger as far north as Pembroke and Parry Sound

Number of woodpecker species nesting in Ontario: 9

Number of woodpecker species worldwide: About 200

Also see: Starling, Ants, Red Oak

GOLDFINCH
Wild Canary of the Garden

Calls: Song a long, musical, canarylike series of high, squeaky chips, twitters and trills; also a flight call of 3 quick, repeated "per-chicory" notes, and a springy call that drops and rises, sounding like a cork twisting in a wine bottle

Flying speed: 30–62 km/h (19–39 mph)

Length: 11–13 cm (4.5–5 in)

Weight: 11–13 g in summer (0.4–0.5 oz), 13.5–20 g in winter (0.5–0.7 oz)

Wingspan: 21–23 cm (8–9 in)

Markings: Males yellow with black wings, tail and cap and a white rump; females olive-green back, dull yellow breast, black wings and tail and white wing bars; in autumn both sexes turn more olive-brown, with buff breasts; juveniles light brown above and dull grey-yellow below

Alias: American goldfinch, wild canary, yellow bird, thistle bird, common goldfinch, *le chardonneret jaune, Carduelis tristis*

Name for a group: A charm of goldfinches

Whereabouts: Backyards, parks, forest borders, meadows, shrubby bottomlands, open woods

Food: Seeds of thistles, dandelions, goldenrods, asters, grasses, teasel, mullein, chicory, evening primrose, burdock, birch, alder, elm, willow, cedar, and spruce; also fruit tree and elm flower buds, birch and alder catkins and tender bark from

O F THE FEW yellow birds that make the city their home, goldfinches are by far the most populous. Bouncing through the air in deeply dipping flights, they frequent suburban yards to sample seeds of cosmos, zinnias, coreopsis and other common garden flowers. Elsewhere throughout the city, nimble-toed sprites occupy ravine meadows, hillside thickets and tree-lined riverbanks. Donning drab but warm olive-brown coats in winter, they throng to bird feeders, delighting in thistle seeds, peanuts and small black sunflower seeds.

Many people call the black-winged, bright-yellow birds wild canaries. Goldfinches are indeed closely related to the long-domesticated cage birds originally from the Canary Islands, off North Africa. The European goldfinch was also tamed for the cage long ago and widely admired for its beauty; it's often depicted in medieval manuscript illuminations with the child Jesus and was also widely associated with Easter.

Certainly, a goldfinch can sing like a canary. The loquacious male, with his pushed-forward black beret, is given to long bouts of twittering and sputtering whistles from early spring to late summer. Nesting, however, doesn't begin until late June or July, when the first meadow-plant seeds ripen. Fresh seeds are more palatable for nestlings than old, dry leftovers. Parents make them further digestible by munching them first, often mixing in a caterpillar or some aphids, and then serving up the fortified gruel. Thistle seeds are especially favoured and their downy fibres line the nest. So closely are goldfinches associated with thistle, their scientific name, *Carduelis*, derives from the Latin name of the prickly plant.

Ever gregarious, goldfinches nest as close as three or four metres (10 to 13 feet) from each other in small groups. After the young fledge, families forage together for a while. Then, gradually, the drably coloured youngsters drift away and form large, wandering flocks of adolescents. Adults hunker down in their own groups in the shelter of streamside thickets and cedar woods until late September or early October while they moult, becoming less buoyant and agile during the transition, like other moulting songbirds.

As the first snow falls in November or December, many adults head south in large flocks, the females tending to fly a little farther than the males and returning about two weeks later in spring. Mobs of juvenile birds, on the other hand, don't seem to know enough to retreat. Goldfinch young stick it out in the land of their hatching for their first winter, subsisting on seeds from the dead standing stalks of goldenrod, mullein, evening primrose and aster, or from birch and conifer cones while sheltering in woods. Thanks to bird feeders, and perhaps a warming climate, more and more adults have also been braving winters in southern Ontario in recent decades. Their numbers are bolstered by migrant goldfinches from northern hinterlands. Winter flocks of more than 200 are common, often mixing with chickadees, tree sparrows and northern finches such as redpolls and pine siskins. The birds will fly up to seven kilometres (four miles) from roosts to well-stocked feeders and are particularly ravenous during stormy weather.

twig shoots in spring; small amounts of insects and berries

Favourite feeder foods: Thistle and sunflower seeds, peanuts

Nest: Tidy, tightly woven, rounded cone, 6–10 cm (2.4–4 in) wide, 4.5–11 cm (1.8–4.3 in) high, with thick walls of grass and bark strips; lined with thistle and milkweed down, bound with spiderwebs; usually wedged between upright forked branches in bushes, hawthorns, serviceberries or maple saplings

Average clutch: 4–6 kidney-bean-sized, pale-blue eggs, often with light spotting

Incubation period: 10–14 days

Fledging age: 11–17 days

Lifespan: Up to 11 years in wild, 13 years in captivity

Predators: Cats, squirrels, kestrels, sharp-shinned hawks, shrikes; nests raided by blue jays, garter snakes, weasels

Classical homage: Antonio Vivaldi's Flute Concerto No. 3 in D, opus 10 *Il Cardellino* (The Goldfinch)

Nesting range: Southern Ontario to the southern edge of the Hudson Bay Lowlands; also in all other provinces

Average first arrival of migrants in southern Ontario: Late Mar. to early Apr.

Average last departure of migrants from southern Ontario: Early Dec.

Winter whereabouts: From about New Liskeard and Lake Nipigon to the Gulf of Mexico

Also see: Cedar Waxwing, Winter Wayfarers, Goldenrod, Thistles

GRACKLE
The Golden-eyed Blackbird

Largest colonies: 200 nests
Flying speed: 32–63 km/h
(20–39 mph)
Length: 28–34 cm (11–13.5 in)
Wingspan: 43–47 cm
(17–18.5 in)
Weight: Females 85–100 g
(3–3.5 oz), males 110–125 g
(3.9–4.4 oz)
Markings: Males completely black,
with iridescence sometimes
shining purple, blue, green and
bronze in the sun, especially
around the head; females are
duller; juveniles dark brown till
their first autumn
Alias: Common grackle, blackbird,
bronze grackle, keel-tailed
grackle, purple jackdaw, *le quis-
cale bronzé*, *Quiscalus quiscula*
Calls: High, squeaky screech like a
rusty hinge; a sharp, harsh
"chack," harsh "waa," nasal
"brrt," clucks and whistles
Food: 70–75% vegetarian, including seeds throughout year,
berries, nuts and acorns in late
summer and fall, grain in fall
and winter; in breeding season
mainly worms, caterpillars,
beetles, grubs, grasshoppers,
ants and other insects, spiders,
snails; also frogs, salamanders,
crayfish, minnows, mice, small
birds, eggs and nestlings
Whereabouts: Lawns, parks, riversides, wet meadows, swamps,
open woods, forest edges
Nest: 16–22 cm (6–9 in) wide,
of sticks, mud, weeds and
grass; usually 1–4 m
(3.3–13.2 ft) up in ever-

S OME PEOPLE CONFUSINGLY mislabel starlings
as grackles. True grackles are larger, blacker,
glossy-coated birds with longer tails and piercing
golden eyes. While starlings, introduced from Europe,
are usually closely tied to built-up areas, the native
grackle is a flexible, omnivorous jack of all trades.
Characteristically foraging in small groups, grackles are
most abundant along wooded riversides, swamps and
other wet places. But they also turn up on lawns on rainy
days, either picking their own worms or stealing them
from robins and other birds. Nor are they above pilfer-
ing from picnics and garbage baskets in parks. They'll
also pick off the odd house sparrow and other feathered
half-pints.

Grackles richly profited from human settlement and
roads that have carved up woodlands and created more
of the forest-edge habitat they love. Shrinking woodlots
also expose more forest birds to grackle nest raids.
Though eggs and nestlings generally make up less than
1 percent of their diet, grackles and blue jays are blamed
for contributing to the decline of songbirds that has
come with forest clearing.

After a winter of southern hospitality, male grackles
return from around Kentucky or Tennessee in large
mixed flocks with red-winged blackbirds, cowbirds and
migrant starlings in March and early April. They can be

told from other blackbirds by their long, rudder-shaped tails and level flight (red-wings usually flap and dip). The slightly smaller females, in flatter, dark-brown attire, show up about a week later. Soon, they're followed about by multiple suitors uttering weak, screechy mating calls, while drooping their wings, puffing their feathers and raising their lengthy beaks straight in the air.

Unlike their fiercely territorial red-winged relations, the golden-eyed blackbirds usually settle into loose colonies of 10 or so nests, spaced as close as five metres (16.5 feet) from each other. Large, dense evergreens are their favourite quarters, often located in parks or along quiet suburban streets. Starting earlier than most birds, female grackles spend about five days in April building nests of sticks, mud and plant stems. All the while, their mates closely guard them and wait to mate when the nest is complete. The honeymoon ends when, after laying an egg a day for the better part of a week, mothers begin incubating their clutches. While some males stick around to help raise their offspring, about half respond by hitting the road.

After the brown-eyed progeny fledge, by mid-July, grackles again join with ever-growing mixed flocks of other blackbirds – which can soon reach into the thousands – foraging and roosting together. Older adults usually occupy the best and safest perches in trees at the centre of a large roost, pretty much ensuring those snatched by predators will be the rookies on the periphery. Still, the inexperienced young learn where to find the best grub by sticking with the flock. By the time mixed blackbird migrants congregate at traditional winter sites in the southern United States, they can number up to five million in a single roost.

greens; sometimes in marshes, tree cavities or beneath bridges
Average clutch: 4–5 peach-pit-sized, light blue-green or brown eggs with dark-brown, black or purple squiggles
Incubation period: 11–15 days
Fledging age: 13–17 days
Portion of eggs that produce fledglings: 33–65%
Average annual adult survival: About 50%
Lifespan: Up to 22 years
Predators: Red-tailed hawks, Cooper's hawks, great horned owls; nests raided by cats, raccoons, squirrels, chipmunks
Nesting range: Southern Ontario to the southern portion of the Hudson Bay Lowlands; also in all other provinces and the Northwest Territories
Average first arrival in southern Ontario: Early Mar.
Average last departure from southern Ontario: Mid-Nov.
Winter whereabouts: From about Toronto and Grand Bend south to Texas and Florida, with most southern Ontario birds flying about 1,000 km (620 mi) to the U.S. mid-south
Estimated North American common grackle winter population: About 110 million
Estimated winter population of all North American blackbirds: 400 million
Number of grackle species nesting in Ontario: 1
Number of grackle species worldwide: 7 (all in the Americas)
Also see: Starling, Red-winged Blackbird

HOUSE FINCH
Melodious Western Newcomer

Calls: Long, very melodious but jumbled warbling song of rapid, bubbling notes; also sharp cheeps

Average number of different songs sung by each male: 2–6

Number of songs sung per minute: Up to 15

Length: 13–15 cm (5–6 in)

Wingspan: 21.5–25 cm (8.5–10 in)

Weight: 18–27 g (0.6–1 oz)

Markings: Males have a red eyebrow stripe and other splashes of red on head, breast and rump; brown back, wings and tail; dark strips on whitish belly and sides; females have brown backs and heads and darkly streaked light undersides

Alias: Hollywood finch, red-headed linnet, papaya bird, Mexican house finch, *le roselin familier*, *Carpodacus mexicanus*

Name origins: Finch comes from Old English *fringil*, meaning "colourful"; *Carpodacus* is Latin for "fruit-biting"

Whereabouts: Yards, street trees, parks, riversides

Food: Mostly seeds of dandelion, thistle, grasses, knotweed, wild mustards and other plants; tree buds, maple sap in early spring; some berries, cherries; occasionally plant lice and other insects

Favourite feeder foods: Almost any seeds, corn, nuts

Nest: Neat, shallow cup, 8–17 cm (3–6.7 in) wide, of grass, twigs, leaves, rootlets, hair,

SEEN FROM AFAR, a house finch can easily be mistaken for the similarly named common house sparrow. That is, until the finch opens its mouth and sings. Unlike the monotonous squeaky chirps squeezed out by house sparrows, the song of the red-splashed male finch is a cascading, melodious jumble of notes that pour forth for many seconds at a time from street trees and backyard bushes. While the house finch is the new bird in town, its colourful attire and sweet California sound have won it a considerable fan base in its ongoing contest for urban food and space with the longer established but even more alien sparrow.

Native to the arid U.S. southwest, house finches were shipped east by the thousands during the 1930s and sold as caged singing "Hollywood finches" by pet stores. When authorities cracked down on this illegal trade in 1940, New York City's Macy's department store, so the story goes, released its contraband charges on Long Island to avoid prosecution. The liberated birds propagated a small feral population that lingered in the area until the late 1950s. Then, apparently having perfected a lifestyle closely tied to human habitation, they suddenly began to increase exponentially and expanded from one town and city to the next.

The first house finch pioneers reached Ontario in

1970 and were confirmed nesting eight years later, at Niagara-on-the-Lake. Demonstrating how far dispersing young birds can travel after leaving their parents, the finches spread throughout southern Ontario during the 1980s, while the entire population in eastern North America was doubling every three years. In many places, the rise of the finch was accompanied by the fall of the sparrow. After dominating residential neighbourhoods in most of the continent for close to a century, house sparrows finally ran into a feisty bird their size that they couldn't bully out of small nest holes or away from their place at winter feeders.

In the mid-1990s, however, the house finch boom went bust. An epidemic of "finch eye," a variant of a blinding disease known previously only in poultry, caused eastern North America's population of several hundred million house finches to drop by an estimated 60 percent between 1994 and 2001. The outbreak's virulence was probably caused by the narrow genetic diversity among the eastern birds, which descended from just a small number of freed finches. Though the epidemic peaked, the disease continues to strike between 5 and 10 percent of the population.

In good times house finches are gregarious throughout the year. They forage and roost in loose flocks and nest together in blue spruce trees, cedar hedgerows and ivy-covered walls. While some migrate south in mid-autumn, many remain through the year and begin sweet warbling solicitations on sunny days as early as January. Singers with the brightest, most extensive patches of red are the top choice of husband-hunting, sandy-brown females. The feminine finches sometimes sing their own simplified songs, usually to entice courtship feeding or mating services from their spouses. All of the nest building and egg tending is done by mothers, starting in late March, while males continue to sing, guard and feed their nest-bound mates. Among the most strident of vegetarians, house finches bring their nestlings up almost exclusively on seeds, unlike most other finches, who add substantial supplements of insect protein to the kids' menu. If all goes well, the west-coast transplants usually raise two broods though the nesting season.

string, and other fibres; usually 1.5–10 m (5–33 ft) above ground, deep inside a spruce or cedar, bush, rose trellis or ivy; often in a crevice or hole in a tree trunk, in or on garages, a ledge or vent on a house or in a birdhouse; sometimes in hanging plants, street lights or old nests of other birds

Space between nests in colonies: As little as 1 m (3.3 ft) in good sites

Average clutch: 4–5 dark-speckled, blue-tinged white or bluish-green eggs, about the size of almonds

Incubation period: 12–17 days

Fledging age: 11–19 days

Age at first breeding: 1 year for most; 2 years for up to 40% of males

Average annual adult survival: 50–60%

Lifespan: Up to 11 years in wild

Predators: Cats, sharp-shinned hawks, Cooper's hawks; nests raided by crows, blue jays, grackles, squirrels, chipmunks

Portion of nests bearing cowbird eggs: Up to 42%

Body temperature: 41–42°C (106–108°F)

Nesting range: Southern Ontario to North Bay, Sudbury and Sault Ste. Marie; also in all other provinces except Prince Edward Island and Newfoundland

Number of true finch species nesting in Ontario: 9

Number of true finch species worldwide: About 140

Also see: House Sparrow, Goldfinch, Winter Wayfarers

TRANSIENT MIGRANTS
Great River of Birds

S PRING AND AUTUMN migration offer urban eyes a chance to behold, if only in passing, the incredible, colourful diversity of birds that nest beyond the city. They are part of a vast river of wings that twice annually flows over every town, village and metropolis in its path from the tip of South America to Canada's high Arctic.

The first waves come early in southern Ontario. Warm spells in February bring flocks of starling-sized horned larks as well as migrant crows and ring-billed gulls north to rejoin their overwintering brethren in many communities. The black, white and yellow-faced larks commonly pick their way along urban waterfronts and weedy roadsides before fanning out into the countryside or flying on to the tundra beyond the Arctic Circle.

The waterfront is an ideal place to greet many of the earliest migrants, as well as the last to come in autumn. Waterfowl flock to waters off Hamilton, Kingston, Toronto and other harbours and sheltered spots along the Great Lakes and St. Lawrence and Ottawa Rivers while they wait for the ice to break up farther inland. In March, new faces start showing up among the rafts of long-tailed ducks, buffleheads, common goldeneyes, greater scaup and other ducks that spend the winter at these staging areas. Green-winged teal and lesser scaup are among the first to arrive, as well as smaller numbers of pintails, ring-necked ducks, redheads, hooded mergansers and canvasbacks. Smatterings of wigeons and northern shovelers follow around the end of the month, while loons, grebes, blue-winged teal and red-breasted mergansers splash down in April.

At the same time, the land-bird migration builds considerably through April, spilling across the Niagara

Fastest migrant: Canvasback duck, up to 110 km/h (68 mph)

World's longest distance migrant: Arctic tern, flies up to 17,700 km (11,000 mi) from Canadian Arctic to Antarctica, via coast of western Europe and Africa

Non-stop distance flown by Hudsonian godwits: Up to 12,870 km (8,000 mi)

Non-stop flight by semipalmated sandpipers from the Bay of Fundy to South America: 96 hours

Time it takes tropical songbirds to reach Ontario: 4–5 weeks

Time taken by songbirds to return to tropics from Ontario: 6–8 weeks

Highest recorded altitude of a migrating bird: 8,840 m (29,000 ft), whooper swans over Ireland

and St. Lawrence Rivers and strategic lake crossings, such as Point Pelee, southeast of Windsor, and Long Point, south of Hamilton. In addition to robins and other early birds that nest in the city, many more transient travellers come through, starting with hyperactive flocks of golden-crowned kinglets. They're often accompanied by small numbers of tree-trunk-spiralling brown creepers, while visiting winter wrens and phoebes tend to keep to themselves. Though almost any bird can turn up in backyards and street trees during migration, most like to put down in urban woodlots, ravines, lakefronts, riversides, wetlands, parks and other green corridors. Much of the action is along brushy forest edges. Cemeteries, with a good mix of open space and a great variety of trees and shrubs, also lure a corresponding wide variety of migrants.

Contingents of ruby-crowned kinglets (illustrated) join the parade in mid-April, accompanied by the drum beats of yellow-bellied sapsuckers. The lingering whistles of white-throated sparrows also rise above other early-spring stylings, making them the most prominent of a number of sparrow species that begin filing through. Yellow-rumped warblers begin arriving around the same time, heading up the pageantry of nearly three dozen different multihued warblers, rose-breasted grosbeaks, scarlet tanagers, orioles, indigo buntings, thrushes, flycatchers and vireos that follow over the next two months. Shorebirds bound for the far north also usually build to a peak toward the end of May as they drop down on southern Ontario's abundant lakesides to refuel. Hamilton's Cootes Paradise, Oshawa's Second Marsh, Whitby Marsh and many other areas of mud flats and sandbars in the urban shadow are ideal shorebird rest stops.

Though most early migrants come from the central and southern United States, later arrivals usually hail from the tropics, some from the other side of the equator. Most songbirds migrate at night, when there's less turbulence and the air cools feverishly working muscles. In ideal conditions, on clear nights, advancing waves of up to two million migrating songbirds have been detected by radar. Between flights they usually

Average songbird migration altitude: 150–300 m (492–984 ft)

Average hawk migration altitude: Most at 300–800 m (1,000–2,600 ft), up to 2,500 m (8,200 ft)

Shorebird migration altitude: More than 3,000 m (9,840 ft) for some species

Distance a broad-winged hawk is able to glide without flapping: Almost 6 km (4 mi)

Average songbird migrating speed: About 50 km/h (31 mph)

Average shorebird migrating speed: About 70 km/h (43.5 mph)

Estimated number of birds that migrate south from Canada and the northern United States: 5 billion

Portion of Ontario's bird population that leaves the province: More than 75%

Number of North American shorebirds nesting in the Arctic: More than 20 million

Raptor fall migration peaks: Broad-winged hawks, mid- to late Sept.; Cooper's hawks, late Sept. to early Oct.; turkey vultures, early to mid-Oct.

Highest single-day broad-winged hawk count over Holiday Beach, south of Windsor: 95,500, on Sept. 15, 1984

Average number of turkey vultures passing over Holiday Beach each fall: More than 10,000

Average number of all fall migrant birds counted at Holiday Beach: 600,000–750,000

spend a few days resting and catching insects to replenish their fat reserves.

Prolonged heavy cloud or rain may ground night migrants for longer than they'd like, since they navigate by the stars. In studies conducted inside planetariums in spring, white-throated sparrows, indigo buntings and other species flutter and orient themselves toward the North Star in night-sky projections. Other studies reveal most learn the skill rather than genetically inherit it. Birds also follow landscape features and some may navigate using the Earth's magnetic field, the pressure shifts of weather fronts or low-frequency background sounds, such as ocean waves or winds thousands of kilometres away.

Unfortunately, night migrants are disoriented by the light of tall buildings, especially when forced low upon encountering rain or fog. Failing to see glass exteriors and windows, or flying toward reflections of trees in them, hundreds of birds can slam into one office tower in a single night, becoming the largely unknown victims of lethal light pollution. Amazingly, about half of them usually survive the impact and fall to the ground, but are then weakened and imperilled by continued disorientation, scavenging gulls and crows and the desperate need to find food and shelter.

Volunteers with Toronto's Fatal Light Awareness Program rescue about 3,000 stunned or exhausted birds a year, representing 131 different species, from beneath the city's financial district towers in the wee hours of the morning during migration. Good Samaritans also work the downtown streets of Ottawa and other Ontario cities. Birds that recover are released in city parks or outlying areas. Activists have also succeeded in getting many buildings to turn off, reduce and alter their lighting, or simply pull their drapes and blinds, during migration.

Though spring migration peaks around mid-May, the last stragglers pushing north in June can encounter the vanguard of the return southbound birds of autumn. Some species – especially far-northern-nesting shorebirds such as least and solitary sandpipers, short-billed dowitchers and lesser yellowlegs – begin coming back through southern Ontario around late June and early July. The first warblers are not far behind, and by late August the departure of many tropical migrants is in full flight. But even for these birds, the fall migration is much more spread out and leisurely than the race to be first in the nesting grounds in spring.

The autumn passage is also generally not as spectacular as spring, with the bright breeding colours of many songbirds having faded and the males no longer in singing voice. But in a number of choice locations along the north shores of Lakes Ontario and Erie, fall is the best season for seeing lots of hawks, vultures, falcons and even eagles. Most birds of prey minimize the energy expended in flapping their wings when travelling long distances by circling upwards for hundreds of metres (or yards) on columns of warm, rising air, called thermals, and then gliding off until they pick up the next warm updraft. Thermals, however, do not occur over large bodies of water, so when southbound hawks reach the big lakes, they bunch up in large numbers as they follow the shorelines until they reach a point where they can continue south over land.

Toronto's High Park hawk watch ranks with Beijing and Istanbul as one of the world's three best spots for seeing migrating raptors in an urban setting. Organized, eagle-eyed watchers have tallied more than 23,000 hawks, from 16 different species, passing over the site in a single autumn, including almost 11,000 broad-winged hawks in a three-day stretch in mid-September. Other urban hawk-watching sites include Whitby's Cranberry Marsh, while Lake Erie's premier watches, Hawk Cliff and Holiday Beach, lie within 20 kilometres (12 miles) respectively of London and Windsor. Grimsby also hosts a busy hawk watch in the spring, when northbound raptors follow the Niagara Escarpment along the south shore of Lake Ontario.

ovenbirds, common yellow-throats, brown creepers, hermit thrushes

Window collision deterrents: Special film covering, called Scotchcal, allows clear view from inside but makes glass opaque on outside; sticking on raptor silhouettes; promo CDs hung in front of windows twirl and glimmer in the breeze, tending to keep birds away

Portion of Canada's bird species showing significant population decline: Almost 20%

Portion of Canada's bird species showing significant population increase: About 10%

Portion of Canada's birds on World Conservation Union's list of species at risk: Almost 10%

Number of northern bird species seen in southern Ontario only during migration: About 60

Number of southern Ontario nesting species in which all of population migrates: About 110

Number of southern Ontario nesting species that are mainly or partially migratory: About 55

Number of non-migratory bird species in southern Ontario: 19

Also see: Winter Wayfarers

HOUSE SPARROW
Winging Along with Civilization

Flying speed: 29–55 km/h
(18–34 mph)

**Average number of wingbeats
per second:** 13

**Number of clutches laid per year
if most lost to predators:** Up
to 8

Length: 14–16 cm (5.5–6.3 in)

Wingspan: 24–25 cm
(9.5–10 in)

Weight: 27–31 g (0.9–1.1 oz)

Alias: English sparrow, domestic
sparrow, European house
sparrow, tramp, hoodlum, *le
moineau domestique, Passer
domesticus*

Calls: A slow, monotonous repeti-
tion of shrill, unmusical cheeps
sung year-round by both sexes,
though less often by females;
also chips, peeps, chattering
and chuckles

Markings: Males have mottled
brown back and sides, grey head
with chestnut-brown band

NOISY, TUNELESS CHANTS of "cheep, cheep, cheep, cheep" were first laid down on the soundtrack of urban civilization perhaps 10,000 years ago, when house sparrows began tucking into spilled grain and livestock feed in the Middle East. Recognizing a good thing, the little ground foragers dropped their traditional migratory routes and hitched their wagons to the course of human history. They moved in to the dwellings of their unwitting food providers and learned to keep always just a hop beyond their grasp, becoming one of human kind's oldest and closest independent associates throughout Eurasia and North Africa.

Taking hold wherever large-scale European settlement has occurred, house sparrows were first brought to North America in the 1850s, appropriately at the continent's greatest immigrant portal, New York City. Others were released in a number of additional cities, including Ottawa in 1870 and Strathroy, near London, Ontario, in 1874. They quickly spread to farms and communities everywhere. The avian immigrants' sponsors reasoned that in addition to bringing a familiar touch of home to the new land, the birds might curb leaf-eating caterpillars on urban shade trees as well as agricultural insect pests. Unfortunately, house sparrows are actually only sparing insect eaters, but quite accomplished farm pillagers themselves.

Worse still, house sparrows shut many native birds that are big insect eaters out of their former homes. Stunning bluebirds and red-headed woodpeckers were once common cavity-nesters in residential neighbourhoods in southern Ontario. They suffered serious declines after house sparrows appeared on the scene and have remained largely absent from urban areas. Purple martins and other hole-nesting species were also knocked for a loop. Non-migratory house sparrows, as well as alien starlings, set up shop in nest cavities in and around houses well before native birds return from the south. Even when tree swallows and other natives manage to secure a spot, house sparrows often ruthlessly turf them out and destroy their eggs or kill their nestlings.

After their numbers peaked in the 1920s, house sparrows themselves began to decline somewhat in cities and towns. As cars replaced horses, the sparrows lost a major urban food source in the undigested grass seeds and grain in equine road apples. Severe winters in the following decades and competition with house finches after the 1970s also reduced their numbers.

Still, the plucky mites probably remain, together with starlings, the most commonplace of birds in Ontario's cities. Being small and a little less noisy, house sparrows are not as widely disliked as the other Eurasian immigrant. Many people, in fact, are happy to feed them. Because of their tameness and ubiquity, house sparrows offer front-row viewing of behaviour and aspects of their life cycle that they share with many more retiring birds. They're not shy about taking a shower in a public fountain, or a dust bath – which helps absorb excess feather oil and may ward off lice – in a downtown flower bed or suburban garden. Throughout much of the year, small groups of droop-winged, puff-chested hopping suitors can be seen circling a single female, often tangling and rolling on the ground with each other, in an effort to win her affections. Males with the biggest black bibs are preferred. Once paired, sparrows also hardly keep their frequent matings a private affair.

running back from eye, white cheeks, black throat and bib; grey undersides; females and juveniles have brown back and sides, grey undersides, a grey-brown eyestripe; both sexes have a white stripe on each wing

Whereabouts: Around buildings throughout city and suburbs

Food: Mostly seeds of ragweed, knotweed, crabgrass, foxtail and other grasses and plants or from bird feeders; also discarded bits of human foods; invertebrates such as beetle grubs, grasshoppers, crickets, caterpillars and spiders make up to 10% of diet in spring and summer; also small amounts of fruit and nectar

Nest: In a hole or narrow sheltered space, with entrance at least 5 cm (2 in) wide, under eaves, behind a drainpipe or in other nook on a house or building; also often in a birdhouse or cavity in a tree, utility pole or fencepost; most often 3–6 m (10–20 ft) above ground; nest space filled with grass, stems, leaves, feathers, paper, string, hair, cloth and other bits of litter; sometimes a dome of grass and stems with a side entrance built in dense tree branches or an ivy-covered wall; fresh mint and mustard plants added to nests in midsummer to help ward off parasitic insects

Average house sparrow occupancy of martin house apartments: 20%

Average clutch: 4–5 olive-sized, darkly marked white, light-green or bluish eggs

Incubation period: 10–14 days

Fledging age: 14–17 days

Nestlings resulting from adulterous matings: About 8%

Average time between fledglings leaving nest and first egg of next clutch being laid: 6–9 days

Portion of eggs that hatch: About 62%

Portion of nestlings that survive to fledge: About 65%

Average annual survival: About 20% in first year; 50–60% for adults

Lifespan: Up to 13 years in wild, 23 years in captivity

Predators: Cats, dogs, grackles, kestrels, sharp-shinned hawks, peregrine falcons, shrikes; nests also raided by raccoons

Portion of young that disperse from their natal areas: 50–75%

Estimated North American population: 150 million

Nesting range: Southern Ontario to Moosonee and Red Lake, in northwestern Ontario; also in all other provinces and the Northwest Territories

Closest Ontario relative: Water pipit, nesting on tundra of Hudson Bay coast (native sparrows belong to a separate family)

Other alien birds introduced in Ontario: Starlings, pigeons, mute swans, ring-necked pheasants, grey partridge

Also see: Starling, House Finch, Alien Invaders

House sparrows actually begin looking for nest sites in autumn and guard them throughout the winter. If there's nesting material in the cavities from the previous year, they clean it out and start afresh with new grass, leaves and litter. Males take the lead in assembling the nests and help incubate the eggs and brood the hatchlings during the day. Parents stoke their tiny charges mostly with high-protein insect meals 15 to 19 times an hour for their first few days before gradually weaning them on to regurgitated seeds.

By laying their first batch of eggs in April and nesting into August, house sparrows can raise up to three broods a year, ensuring their prominent place among the city's feathered masses. While mothers rebuild their strength to lay their next sets of eggs, fathers continue feeding the fledglings for seven to 10 days after they leave the nest.

Young sparrows gradually form small foraging flocks that grow with each new wave of siblings taking wing. They commonly roost in large neighbourhood evergreens and the ivy-covered sides of houses, joining in ringing, if monotonous, chirping singalongs at dusk and dawn and flying to weedy fields and parks to forage during the day. Through the winter, the hardy scroungers persist on the continual rain of tiny seeds from tall, standing stalks of grass and weeds, as well as on the birdfeeder fixings they kick to the ground and the discarded or proffered crumbs and scraps tossed their way by human hands.

HUMMINGBIRD
Sacred Aztec Hyperflapper

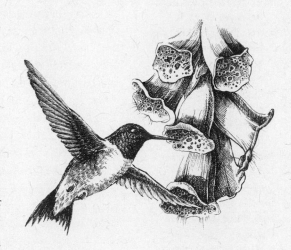

SEEMING TO BUZZ from out of the blue, ruby-throated hummingbirds can turn up almost anywhere during migration, even in small, inner-city gardens. Most pass through, but suburban locales with large, profusely flowering yards and woods nearby entice some hummers to settle in where the living is easy. The fastidious little birds sometimes make themselves at home to the point of showering in sprinklers and hose-nozzle spray and have even been known to hum along with water-can-bearing gardeners.

In addition to hovering at sugar-water feeders furnished for them, hummingbirds arriving in May lap up nectar from lilacs and apple blossoms. If nothing else is available, they may apply their long, brushy tongues to fuzzy yellow willow catkins. In the woods, they often turn to the sweet sap oozing from rows of holes drilled into tree trunks by yellow-bellied sapsuckers, which come north a few weeks ahead of their tiny associates.

Toward summer, more of the tubular flowers favoured by ruby-throats come into bloom. They're especially attracted to red flowers, which often have no scent but big nectar payloads. Nectar provides sugar that can be burned immediately as energy, keeping the whirring-winged little birds in perpetual hyperflap, allowing them to veer sideways on a dime, or fly straight up, down, backwards and even upside down. Insects lapped up with the nectar or caught separately provide protein for building body tissue. To keep their high-octane engines running, hummers refill their bellies about every seven to 12 minutes. They may consume and burn food equal to half their weight every day. To sustain their metabolic rate, an 80-kilogram (176-pound) man would have to pack away 45 kilograms (100 pounds) of Smarties a day

Average number of wingbeats per second: 40–80; up to 200 in courtship dives

Flying speed: Up to 43 km/h (27 mph) in level flight, up to 97 km/h (60 mph) in a dive

Heartbeats per minute: 500–600 at rest, 50–180 in torpor, up to 1,260 in flight

Respiratory rate: 250 breaths a minute at rest

Weight: 3–4 g (0.125 oz)

Weight of a loonie: 7 g

Length: 7–9 cm (2.8–3.5 in)

Wingspan: 10–13 cm (4–5.2 in)

Markings: Iridescent green back, grey-white belly; males have an iridescent bright-red throat and a forked tail

Average number of feathers: 940

Alias: Ruby-throated hummingbird, *le colibri à gorge rubis*, *Archilochus colubris*

Call: High-pitched, twittering squeaks

Whereabouts: Gardens, parks, forest edges, watersides

Food: Nectar, sap, mosquitoes, spiders, flies, bees, aphids, caterpillars, insect eggs

Number of licks per second: 11–13

Nest: Neat, deep, thick-walled cup of moss, lichens, grass, bud scales and plant down, bound with spiders' silk; about 4–5 cm (1.5–2 in) wide; usually 3–6 m (10–20 ft) high in a small tree or shrub

Average clutch: 2 pea-sized, oblong white eggs

Incubation period: 12–14 days

Fledging age: 18–22 days

Lifespan: Up to 9 years in wild, 12 years in captivity

Predators: Kestrels, sharp-shinned hawks and large fish sometimes catch adults; nests raided by crows, chipmunks, weasels, snakes and yellow jackets

Number of hummingbirds killed annually in tropics for fashion accessories in late 1800s: About 5 million

Nesting range: Southern Ontario to Lake Abitibi, the north shore of Lake Superior and Red Lake; also in Quebec, prairie and Maritime provinces

Average first arrival in southern Ontario: Early May

Average last departure from southern Ontario: Early Oct.

Winter whereabouts: Southern Florida and coastal Texas to Costa Rica

Number of hummingbird species worldwide: About 322

and drink five cases of beer to keep his skin from catching fire.

Hummingbirds are especially active just before dusk and after dawn, storing up or replenishing vital fuel. On cool nights, they save fuel by slowing down their heart and breathing rates by 90 percent, dropping their body temperature to half the daytime average. In the cold highlands of their wintering grounds in Mexico and points south, hummingbirds go into a prolonged torpor. Their ability to revive from this deathlike state made them sacred to the Aztecs, who considered hummingbirds to be the spirits of dead warriors. Inca women roused the tiny hummers from their deep sleep by warming them between their breasts. In British Columbia, hummingbirds were depicted on totem poles as messengers of the dead.

Miraculous enough is the tiny ruby-throat's long journey to Ontario from the tropics, including an 800-kilometre (500-mile) non-stop flight across the Gulf of Mexico. Males arrive first, claim their turf and defend it against each other, calling out in high squeaks. The females stake out their own ground. These territorial half-pints aggressively fend off much larger brutes, from chickadees to turkey vultures, using their darting speed to advantage.

Hummingbirds engage in only the briefest of romantic liaisons, involving an elaborate swinging-pendulum male courtship flight followed by four or five seconds of sex. Then the female goes off to nest and raise a family alone while the red-cravated libertine looks for new partners. A pair of honeybee-sized, blind, naked chicks usually hatches around early summer and is fed nectar and insects from their mother's crop. When they fledge, they're good flyers right off the mark, their wings buzzing away like windup toys. They become independent in another four to seven days. By then, some hummingbirds are already setting off for their tropical retreats. Most leave by late August, though a few may stick around until the first light frosts of early autumn pulverize the succulent stems of late-blooming jewel-weed flowers.

KILLDEER
A Ringing Endorsement of Spring

THOUGH NOT AS well known as the robin or red-winged blackbird, the killdeer is one of the feathered harbingers of early spring. The cryptically coloured, comically bobbing member of the plover family shows up from the south just as soon as the melting snow exposes bare patches of open ground that have thawed enough to be probed for sleeping beetle grubs and rousing worms. While difficult to see as it goes about its business, the boisterous bird proclaims its arrival by calling out its own name in a shrill, repetitive "kill-dee, kill-dee, kill-dee."

Many other shorebirds migrate through southern Ontario later in the season, but none take to the city so readily as their early-bird relative. Ground-nesting killdeers take up residence in open fields, golf courses, highway corridors and even on large, flat-topped roofs or gravel parking lots. They sometimes fly to sprinklers for the bounty of creepy-crawlies they bring to the surface. The pointy-winged opportunists also stay up late and gather at the bright night lights of baseball diamonds and large parking lots to feed, meet and greet.

Killdeers are able to make it in the city because as open-ground nesters they must, like magicians, be masters of invisibility and slight of wing. Their dull-brown back and sides blend perfectly with the scrubby, muddy and stony terrain they frequent, with their most

Flying speed: 40–88 km/h (25–55 mph)

Length: 20–28 cm (8–11 in)

Wingspan: 48–53 cm (19–21 in)

Weight: 84–92 g (3–3.5 oz)

Markings: Brown back, wings and head; white belly, neck and between and around eyes; bold black collar and breast band separated by a white band; in flight, a long white stripe on top of wings and gold-orange rump

Alias: Field plover, chattering plover, killdee, *le pluvier kildir*, *Charadrius vociferus*

Call: A loud, piercing, repeated "kill-deee, kill-deee" or "dee-kidee" rising up, then down; also a rising "dee-ee" and low trills

Whereabouts: Shorelines, gravel river bars, sports fields, golf courses, expansive lawns, short-grass meadows, construction sites, airports, road shoulders, Hydro corridors

Food: Beetle grubs and adults, grasshoppers, dragonflies, ants, caterpillars and other insects; spiders, worms, snails, crayfish and a few seeds

Territory: 300–400 m^2 (375–500 sq yd)

Nest: A shallow, scraped-out ground depression, sometimes lined with smooth stones or a little grass

Average clutch: 4 walnut-sized, light-grey or buff, darkly blotched and squiggled eggs

Incubation period: 24–28 days

Fledging age: 22–31 days

Portion of pairs that raise 2 broods: About 10%

Age at first breeding: 1 year

Lifespan: Up to 11 years

Predators: Foxes, red-tailed hawks, merlins, great horned owls; chicks eaten by kestrels, coyotes, dogs; eggs taken by raccoons, opossums, weasels, crows, gulls

Nesting range: Throughout most of Ontario; also in all other provinces and territories except Nunavut

Average first arrival in southern Ontario: Late Feb. to mid-Mar.

Average departure from southern Ontario: Mid-Nov. to early Dec.

Winter whereabouts: Most in southern United States; small numbers stay in southern Ontario in mild winters

Number of plover species nesting in Ontario: 3

Number of plover species worldwide: 63

Also see: Nighthawk

prominent feature, two black breast bands, helping to break up their outlines. Meanwhile, their sound and fury appears to be aimed at distracting other animals, including humans, from stumbling across their imperceptible clutches and young ones. By nesting in wide, open spaces, killdeers have unobstructed sight lines for long distances. Once an intruder is detected, the skilful plover steals away from its nest or chicks before calling out and drawing attention away from them.

If a predator continues toward a nest, a killdeer will fly over to the threat and perform its famous broken-wing display. The bird flops on the ground, spreads its tail and drags a quivering wing as if broken, twittering in feigned pain. Hobbling along, the bird keeps just out of reach until it has lured the assailant a safe distance away. Then it explodes into the air and escapes on swift, bent wings designed for speed.

Still, for all their craft, killdeers lose 50 to 80 percent of their vulnerably located nests to predators or other disturbances. To make up for it, females can lay up to eight replacement clutches in a breeding season. It's killdeer males, however, who are the most dedicated parents. Though both mates take turns incubating the eggs during the day, the male usually handles the entire night shift. Some mothers will lay a second clutch once their first brood has fledged, usually in June, but don't always stick around to raise the young fully, leaving the task instead to the diligent fathers.

Like many birds that hatch downy and ready to roll, killdeer chicks can peep and listen to the calls of their parents through their shells a couple of days before hatching. The white-bellied, brown-backed chicks leave their nests and trot after their parents as soon as their down is dried, a few hours after hatching. Before long, they're probing the ground for insects. They freeze instantly if their fathers or mothers launch into their distraction strategies. If all else fails, the chicks scatter on their parents' command, sometimes even plunking into the water and swimming submerged to evade a cruising raptor. Those hatching on flat rooftops are hardy enough to survive sun-heated surfaces as hot as 59°C (138°F) and falls of as much as 15 metres (49 feet).

KINGFISHER
Bank-burrowing River Rattler

A WALK ALONG sandy-banked riversides and lakeshores, pleasant in itself, can sometimes be rewarded with the sight of one of the most exotic-looking birds in the city. With a huge beak, high-topped head crest and tiny feet, the cartoonlike, blue-mantled belted kingfisher announces its presence with a distinctive rattling call that rises above the din of traffic and other urban noises as it patrols its stretch of waterside. The pigeon-sized bird may hover briefly before dropping six to 12 metres (20 to 40 feet) straight down, its wings fixed like a little fighter jet, to catch a fish as deep as 60 centimetres (2 feet) below the surface. Its oversized headgear is designed to take the impact of hitting the water beak-first.

Kingfishers also hunt from favourite perches in trees or on wires above clear, shallow water. Captured fish are brought back to a tree perch, banged about, flipped in the air and swallowed headfirst. The tail end of a really big catch may stick out of a kingfisher's mouth while the bird's digestive juices go to work on the rest of the fish. A pile of regurgitated bones and scales on the ground below usually marks a regular kingfisher hunting perch.

In Greek mythology, the gods turned the sea-tossed queen Alcyone and her husband into kingfishers and

Call: Loud, harsh rattle, like the sound of changing bicycle gears; also screams and squeaks

Flying speed: Up to 60 km/h (36 mph)

Length: 28–37 cm (11–15 in)

Wingspan: 56–58 cm (22–23 in)

Weight: 125–175 g (4.5–6.2 oz)

Markings: Grey-blue bushy crest, breast band and back; white undersides; red stomach band on females

Alias: Belted kingfisher, lazy bird, alcyon, *le martin-pêcheur*, *Ceryle alcyon*

Whereabouts: Lakeshores, streams and marshes with clear water and high banks

Food: Minnows, sculpins, sticklebacks, perch, young brook trout and other small fish, usually less than 10 cm (4 in) long; also frogs, tadpoles, crayfish, salamanders, dragonfly nymphs, grasshoppers and mice

Average breeding territory: 800–1,200 m (880–1,320 yd) of shoreline

Average non-breeding territory: 300–500 m (330–550 yd) of shoreline

Nest: Burrow, 0.9–1.8 m (3–6 ft) long and about 25 cm (10 in) wide, in a sand, clay or gravel bank

Average clutch: 6–7 glossy white eggs, about the size of large chestnuts

Incubation period: 22–24 days

Fledging age: 27–29 days

Age at first breeding: 1 year

Predators: Red-tailed hawks, Cooper's hawks, great horned owls, foxes, cats; nests raided by skunks, raccoons, mink and snakes

Average first arrival of migrants in southern Ontario: Early to mid-Mar.

Average last departure of migrants from southern Ontario: Mid- to late Nov.

Nesting range: All Ontario; also in all other provinces and territories except Nunavut

Winter whereabouts: Rare in southern Ontario to about Arnprior, Lindsay, Guelph and Grand Bend; south to Panama and West Indies

First appearance of kingfishers: 40–50 million years ago

Number of kingfisher species nesting in Ontario: 1

Number of kingfisher species worldwide: 87

Also see: Minnows

afterwards stilled the winds for two weeks around the winter solstice each year – a time still known as the halcyon days – so that they could build a floating nest of fish bones. Kingfishers don't really nest in the water, but their scientific name, *alcyon*, pays tribute to the story.

Belted kingfishers nest, amazingly enough, in burrows dug into lakeshore, riverside, and rail and road embankments near water. The availability of shoreline territory and nest sites limits their numbers. To secure good sites and keep away rivals, males usually arrive in March or April, about a mouth before their mates. Female kingfishers – who with rusty red belly bands are among the few avian matrons more colourful than their spouses – join in the constant shoreline patrols after they arrive. Both mates take turns pickaxing a nest burrow with their great long beaks and kicking out the sand, a task that may take three weeks to complete.

After laying their eggs in May or early June, females do most of the incubating. The young hatch featherless and about a week later sprout tiny pinfeathers in sheaths, making them look more like porcupines than birds. After two more weeks, full feathers explode from the sheaths all at once. Parents teach their fledglings to hunt by dropping fish into the water for them when they're hungry. Families break up when the young are about six or seven weeks old. Many kingfishers remain well into autumn and a few sometimes stay for the winter, as long as the fishing is good and the water doesn't ice over.

MALLARD
Citified Duck of Ages

LIKE HUMANS, pigeons, house mice and cock-roaches, mallard ducks possess a penchant for adaptability that has made them part of the standard set of urban fauna much of the world over. Recognized by anyone who's visited a park pond or the local waterfront, they're the most common and wide-spread ducks in North America. They also nest across most of Eurasia, winter in North Africa and have been introduced to Australia. Mallards have been paddling around human settlements since ancient times and, indeed, are the ancestors of white farm ducks, domesticated more than two thousand years ago. They still often mix and breed with their distant hayseed cousins.

In North America, mallards were originally mainly prairie birds. They gradually spread east after forest barriers fell and started nesting in Ontario in the 1930s. Some 1.7 million mallards were also released from game farms in northeastern North America in the mid-20th century. As the web-footed westerners became more common, they began interbreeding with and displacing Ontario's native black ducks. When the two meet, with their courtship rituals virtually the same, brightly coloured mallard drakes seem to win out over the less-glamorous black duck males in competition for mates.

Mallards, blackies and other marsh ducks are "dabblers," gleaning most of their food from the surface of the water or foraging for it on shallow, weedy bottoms,

Top flying speed: More than 100 km/h (62 mph)

Length: 50–70 cm (20–28 in)

Wingspan: 79–102 cm (31–40 in)

Weight: 1–1.3 kg (2.2–2.9 lb)

Markings: Males green head, yellow bill, white neck ring, chestnut-brown chest, grey back and sides, blue wing patch, black back end, white tail; females mottled brown, with blue wing patch, off-white tail, smudgy orange-and-brown bill

Alias: *Le canard colvert, Anas platyrhynchos*

Name origin of *duck*: From Old English *ducan*, meaning to dive or to dip

Name for a group: A paddling of ducks

Calls: Females quack loudly; males utter softer, rasping "raeb" calls and, during courtship, short flutelike whistles and grunts

Whereabouts: Calm rivers, lakes and bays; ponds, waterside parks, marshes, swamps, sewage lagoons, ditches, fields

Food: Seeds of grass, sedges and aquatic plants; pondweed, aquatic roots, grain, berries, acorns, aquatic insect larvae, snails, earthworms, tadpoles, mussels, crayfish, occasionally frogs and toads

Nest: Saucer of grass, leaves, reeds or cattails, 26–29 cm (10–11.4 in) wide, lined with down; near water, hidden in grass, bushes or debris

Average clutch: 7–10 greenish- or grey-brown eggs, about size of large chicken eggs

Incubation period: 23–30 days

Fledging age: 52–70 days

Ducklings that survive to fledge: 22–68%

Lifespan: Adults average 1.8 years; up to 29 years in wild

Predators: Foxes, raccoons, coyotes, red-tailed hawks, falcons; eggs also eaten by skunks, crows and snakes; ducklings killed by herring gulls, night herons, cats, dogs, snapping turtles and pike

Nesting range: All Ontario; also in all other provinces and territories except Newfoundland

Average peak of spring mallard migration in southern Ontario: Mid-Mar. to mid-Apr.

Average peak of fall mallard migration in southern Ontario: Early to late Oct.

Winter whereabouts: From about Ottawa and Orillia south to Florida and Arkansas

Number of duck species nesting in Ontario: 26

Number of duck family species worldwide: 148

heads submerged, tails raised to the sky. Beyond this apparent mooning, there's actually much more to dabbling than meets the eye. Mallard bills are highly sensitive and efficient food processors, tipped with 28 nerve endings per square millimetre (human fingers have only 20 per square millimetre). Thin, closely spaced ridges inside their bills filter food from the water. Urban ducks also nibble plenty of grass, especially in the early morning and late afternoon, sometimes a fair distance from the shore, and are more than happy to accept bread and other human offerings.

Mallard hens are especially ravenous at egg-laying time around May. To produce up to a dozen large eggs, they usually eat twice as much as their closely guarding mates, hoovering all the protein-rich invertebrates they can find. But once they have a full clutch and begin incubating, females feed only briefly, once or twice a day, and spend the rest of the time on top of the eggs. They lose an average of 25 percent of their weight by the time their eggs hatch several weeks later. Meanwhile, the handsome green-headed drakes, finding their incubating mates no longer interested in their affections, fly off to moult with the guys in the cover of large marshes. Members of these secluded boys-club flocks seem to put on female attire in changing into their drab "eclipse" plumage, becoming flightless for about a month while their new feathers come in.

Single mothers left behind lead their downy brown-and-yellow day-old broods out into the water in June. Shortly after the youngsters fledge in late summer, they're left on their own while mothers seek cover while they moult. Ducks of all ages and both sexes gradually flock together by September. Many migrate south in the weeks to follow, but thousands of other southern Ontario mallards usually stick around through winter, as long as there's some open water and food to be had. Males, having regained their breeding plumage in late summer, may court potential mates at any time through autumn and winter. Experienced ducks on the make show no particular preference for mates of the previous year. Most are paired by January.

MOURNING DOVE
Lifting Off on Whistling Wings

WHILE FERAL PIGEONS rule the roost among street-foraging birds downtown, mourning doves have moved into the quieter neighbourhoods of the city and suburbs in growing numbers in recent decades. The demure, slender-necked doves habitually lounge on utility wires and tree branches, being far more adept at gripping slender perches than their portly, pigeon-toed cousins. They're far shyer birds, though, and often take flight when even remotely approached, spreading their luxuriant, white-trimmed, spear-shaped tails and producing a characteristic springy whistling noise with the sound of their rushing wings.

The wary doves are named for their soft, mournful, lingering cooing, mistaken by some as the hooting of an owl. Rather than notes of despair, the coos are the woos of bachelors and may be heard copiously between early April and July. Occasionally, females answer back with their own faint coos. Mourning dove mates are notably affectionate birds, interacting with much nuzzling and intimate small talk. Males bring nesting material to their partners, take over incubation duties during most of the day and take their turns feeding and brooding the little ones after they hatch. Like other dove species, mourners initially feed their nestlings a rich, creamy liquid, known as "pigeon milk," produced by glands inside the crop, a food-storage chamber at the bottom of

Calls: Song starts with 1 or 2 short, soft coos, followed by 3 longer, lingering ones; also a short, quiet yodel and a quick "ork"

Flying speed: Usually under 56 km/h (35 mph), up to 90 km/h (56 mph)

Length: Females 22.5–31 cm (9–12 in), males 26.5–34 cm (10.5–13.5 in)

Wingspan: 43–48 cm (17–19 in)

Weight: Females 100–140 g (3.5–5 oz); males 110–170 g (4–6 oz)

Markings: Beige on top, with black spots on wings; lighter face and undersides; black cheek spot; tail trimmed in white; males have bluish hue on top of the head and back of neck, and red-tinted throat and breast (fainter on females)

Alias: Carolina turtle dove, wild dove, wild pigeon, *la tourterelle triste, Zenaida macroura*

Name origin of *dove*: From Old English, *dufan*, meaning "dive"

Whereabouts: Parks, backyards, street trees and wires, roadsides, open woods, forest edges, fields

Food: Mostly seeds of grasses and field plants such as ragweed, lamb's quarters, smartweed, wild sorrel, purslane; waste grain and occasionally acorns, beechnuts, snails and insects

Favourite feeder foods: Cracked corn, millet, sunflower seeds and milo, all preferably spilled onto ground

Average daily seed serving: 10–35 g (0.35–1.2 oz)

Nest: Loose, flimsy dish of twigs and grass, often 3–8 m (10–26 ft) up in an evergreen tree, or in a shrub

Average clutch: 2 peach-pit-sized white eggs

Incubation period: 13–15 days

Fledging age: 12–15 days

First year survival: 40–60%

Lifespan: Up to 31 years in wild

Predators: Sharp-shinned hawks, Cooper's hawks, falcons, cats, dogs, raccoons; nests raided by blue jays and squirrels

Nesting range: Southern Ontario north to about Wawa and Timmins; also between Thunder Bay and Kenora and in all other provinces except Newfoundland

Winter whereabouts: Most Ontario birds go to the U.S. Gulf States and Georgia; some remain as far north as Sault Ste. Marie, Sudbury and North Bay

Also see: Pigeon, Peregrine Falcon, Red Oak

the esophagus. Fathers continue to tend the young for a couple of weeks after they fledge, while mothers usually lay a new pair of eggs between one and six days after the first batch leaves the nest.

While parents attempt to raise up to three broods through spring and summer, their newly independent offspring gather in small foraging flocks and begin heading south as early as mid-August. All mourning doves once largely vacated the province by late October, but the growing popularity of bird feeders since the early 1950s has helped convince many to remain through the winter. Small flocks forage in city parks and other open spaces, as long as the snow doesn't get too deep.

As birds of the forest edge and field, mourning doves in general prospered with the clearing or shrinkage of woodlands that came with agricultural settlement. Their North American population is estimated at about 400 million, despite the fact that they are the most heavily-hunted game birds on the continent, with shot-guns blasting 23 million annually in the United States. In Ontario, they're left in peace.

The extinct passenger pigeon – which looked very much like a larger version of a mourning dove, with a pink neck and red eyes – once flourished in even greater numbers. It may well have boasted the biggest bird population the Earth has ever known, with some migrant flocks estimated at more than 2 billion. One such flock took three days to pass over Niagara-on-the-Lake in 1866. Huge passenger pigeon nesting colonies, however, fell easy prey to hunters. One was just outside Toronto, at Mimico, which means "pigeon gathering place" in the Mississauga language. Nor could the multitudes cope with the loss of a great portion of the hardwood forests upon which they depended for beechnuts, acorns and chestnuts. The large flocks disappeared in Ontario after the late 1870s, and the last wild passenger pigeon was seen in 1902. The species became extinct with the death of a female named Martha at the Cincinnati Zoo in 1914.

NIGHTHAWK
Mystery Voice in the Dark

Foraging altitude: Usually up to 175 m (574 ft), occasionally up to 250 m (820 ft)

Average flying speed: 32–56 km/h (20–35 mph)

Average number of attempts to catch prey per minute: 18

Wingspan: 53–61 cm (21–24 in)

Length: 22–24 cm (8.5–9.5 in)

Weight: 65–98 g (2.3–3.5 oz)

Markings: Mottled grey, brown, black and white, with prominent white bars under wings; males also have a white chin and a bar across underside of tail

Alias: Common nighthawk, mosquito hawk, moth hunter, will-o'-the-wisp, bullbat, pisk, l'engoulevent d'Amérique, Chordeiles minor

Scientific name meaning: Genus name comes from the Greek words choros, "a circular dance" and deile, "evening"; the Latin minor means "smaller"

Call: short, loud, nasal, buzzy sound, usually written as "peent"; sounds something like the whispered word "beard"

Whereabouts: High above city streets in twilight, often around street lights and sports field night lights; flat-topped gravel roofs by day

Food: Mosquitoes, flying ants, beetles, grasshoppers, moths and other flying insects

Meal servings: Up to 500 mosquitoes, or 2,200 flying ants

Average distance from nest to foraging grounds: 2.5–3 km (1.5–2 mi)

J UST ABOUT EVERYONE has heard a nighthawk, even if they don't realize it. Disembodied but familiar, the fleet-winged spectre's thin, sharp, nasal cry is the most common bird call heard on summer nights in most southern Ontario cities. A trained eye can sometimes find the robin-sized evening flyer high in the sky at dusk, sleek and fluttering on long, pointy wings. After night falls, it may be glimpsed swooping closer to the ground in pursuit of moths and other insects attracted to street lights and ballpark flood lamps. If the bird comes low enough, a bold white bar bisecting the underside of each sharply crooked wing clearly identifies it.

Nighthawks take over from day-flying chimney swifts at an airborne feast many dozens of metres above city streets. Wide mouths agape, they swirl, dip and dart though a virtual soup of flying insects, wind-borne mites and newly hatched spiders and caterpillars "ballooning" on strands of silk. The presence of these countless billions of minute, high-altitude travellers – dubbed "aerial plankton" – was unknown until discovered by airplanes, sometimes as much as 4.5 kilometres (2.7 miles) above the ground.

Ontario's aerial plankton is rich enough to entice nighthawks all the way from South America to raise their families. Flat gravel rooftops in cities offer five-star accommodation, protected from many predators. In the

Nest: Eggs usually laid within 0.5 m (1.6 ft) of a parapet bordering a large, flat gravel roof

Average clutch: 2 darkly mottled whitish or olive eggs, about size of peach pits

Incubation period: 18–20 days

Fledging age: 17–18 days

Lifespan: 4–5 years common; up to 9 years

Predators: Cats, dogs, owls, kestrels, peregrine falcons; nests raided by crows, gulls, raccoons, skunks

Best sense: Sight; eyes weigh more than the brain; night vision enhanced by light-reflective lining in back of eyes

Body temperature: 34–40°C (93–104°F)

Average urban density: 1 breeding pair per 19 ha (47 acres)

Nesting range: Throughout Ontario; also in all other provinces and territories except Nunavut and island of Newfoundland

Average first arrival in southern Ontario: Mid-May

Average last departure from southern Ontario: Early Oct.

One-way migration distance: 4,000–11,000 km (2,500–6,800 mi)

Winter whereabouts: South America to northern Argentina

Number of nightjar (nighthawk family) species nesting in Ontario: 3

Number of nightjar species worldwide: 67–84

Also see: Chimney Swift, Moths, Spiders

wild, the cryptically coloured birds lay their eggs on open rocky ground, blending in so well with their grey-and-brown surroundings they're virtually impossible to see. Males claim choice digs and entice potential brides by performing deep dives and suddenly pulling out, causing air to pop through their wing feathers with a soft, whirring mini-boom, sounding a little like a fleeting drone of a bullfrog. The aerodynamic overtures are often heard in May and June, but less frequently after females finish laying their eggs. Spartan to the extreme, they don't actually build nests and instead often move the eggs around, sometimes into shade or out of pooling water.

Fuzzy nighthawk chicks hatch in July. They're raised on regurgitated bugs provided by both parents until they've had a few days of flight school. Then they join their elders in the air to bag bugs by the hundreds and even thousands. Most nighthawks depart for their evening dinners about a half-hour before sunset and return to their roosts 90 minutes to two hours later. They rouse again for breakfast about an hour before the sun rises and eat until it appears on the horizon. Then they retire again to sleep away the day. Flocks of sometimes hundreds also gorge above in broad daylight while migrating along lakeshores and river valleys in late August and early September.

In recent decades, urban nighthawk numbers have declined, possibly because the birds spurn the craze for aluminum or rubberized rooftops. They appreciatively take up residence, however, on gravel pads specially laid out for them. The insectivores are also frequent innocent victims in areas sprayed for mosquitoes.

PEREGRINE FALCON
Speed Demon of Concrete Canyons

A PIGEON SWIRLS nonchalantly over a busy downtown street. Suddenly, a dark, angular figure slices through the air from above. Talons strike, feathers fly. A lifeless form drops to the ground and is swiftly retrieved by the author of its demise, reputed to be the fastest bird on Earth.

The meteoric peregrine falcon is a cliff-dwelling flock predator by trade. It once lived well off the vast nesting colonies of passenger pigeons that blanketed wide areas of Ontario. Now the famous raptor haunts office-tower canyons and dines on the imported squab that replaced the vanished multitudes of native pigeons, nearly a century extinct. Though one of the rarest birds in the city, the crow-sized falcon enjoys a celebrity far exceeding its scant numbers. Peregrines are one of the most cosmopolitan birds in the world, flying over every inhabited continent. They were coveted by kings and nobles for more than 4,000 years for the exclusive sport of falconry, which originated in China. Even today, together with red-tailed hawks and merlins, they're employed to keep airports, marinas and golf courses clear of geese, gulls and pigeons, whose inbred terror of the raptors keeps them clear of an area for hours after catching sight of one.

It is as a victim of modern progress, however, that the ancient icon of speed and grace is most famous. In 1963, a year after Rachel Carson's watershed book *Silent Spring* alerted the public to the dangers of DDT and other pesticides, Ontario's original population of peregrine falcons nested for the last time. As top predators of insect- and seed-eating birds, peregrines received the most concentrated levels of DDT and other chemicals that, because they take so long to break down, steadily accumulate in body tissues as they are passed up through the food chain. Massive reproductive failure resulted. In particular, falcon

Top diving speed: At least 282 km/h (175 mph)

Level flying speed: Average 40–55 km/h (25–34 mph), up to 112 km/h (70 mph)

Altitude at start of predatory dives: Usually 215–320 m (705–1,500 ft); up to 1,080 m (3,543 ft) and more than 1.5 km (0.9 mi) from target

Distance a peregrine can spot a sparrow from its hunting perches: 2 km (1.2 mi)

Cities that have had nesting peregrines in recent years: Toronto, Ottawa, Hamilton, London, Mississauga, Niagara Falls, St. Catharines

Length: Males 36–49 cm (1.2–1.6 ft); females 45–58 cm (1.5–1.9 ft)

Wingspan: Males 81.5–92.5 cm (2.7–3 ft); females 95–104.5 cm (3.1–3.4 ft)

Weight: Males 530–810 g (1.2–1.8 lb); females 760–1,200 g (1.7–2.6 lb)

Markings: Dark blue-grey to black back and head, black "side-burns," white neck and breast, barred and spotted white undersides, with rust tinge to belly

Alias: Duck hawk, American falcon, ledge hawk, rock hawk, bullet hawk, *le faucon pèlerin*, *Falco peregrinus*

Name origins: *Falcon* comes from the Latin *falx*, meaning "sickle," in reference to the shape of beak and talons; *peregrine* means "traveller," deriving from the Latin *per ager*, "through country"

Original falconry terms: "Callow" referred to a falcon nestling; a "codger" was an older falconer who used a cage or portable perch to carry his bird

Calls: Rapid, rasping "kek kek kek kek"; a long, rising two-syllable wail; a creaking, squeaky-hinge call

Whereabouts: Amid tall buildings and along waterfronts

Food: Mostly pigeons and mourning doves; also ducks, shore-birds, starlings, house sparrows, robins, blue jays and many other birds; occasionally bats, mice, squirrels, rats, grasshoppers, crickets, dragonflies

Pigeon servings per falcon: 1 every 2–3 days

Hunting attempt success rate: Average 20–40%

Home range: About 15–50 km^2 (6–19 sq mi); forage up to 18 km (11 mi) from nest

---

egg shells became so thin, they broke during incubation. Peregrines disappeared from all of eastern North America south of the boreal forest. Populations of bald eagles, ospreys, cormorants and herring gulls were also pushed to the brink before U.S. and Canadian laws severely restricted DDT use in the early 1970s.

Following the lead of a number of provinces and states, Ontario's Ministry of Natural Resources, with the Canadian Wildlife Service, began releasing young pere-grines from captive breeding facilities in Alberta into Algonquin Park in hopes of re-establishing them. Most of the birds were from the Rockies and members of the same subspecies that had occupied the east, though some were from Arctic and other races. After having little luck in the wilderness, partly due to fledgling-nabbing great horned owls, the program started turning the birds loose from tall buildings in Toronto, Ottawa, Hamilton, Thunder Bay, Sudbury and other Ontario cities. In 1983, the province's first peregrine nestlings in 20 years hatched on a church steeple in Arnprior.

After more than 600 fledgling releases over 25 years, more than 40 peregrine pairs now nest across Ontario, including at least 10 in urban areas. The province is even considering downgrading the bird's status as an endangered species. Using an assortment of high-tech devices and 24-hour video surveillance in several Ontario cities, the Canadian Peregrine Foundation monitors high-rise nests from nearby command centres run by teams of up to 50 volunteers, whose aid and quick rescues of fallen fledglings have tripled the young birds' survival rate to 75 percent. Real-time video footage of the nests is broadcast on the group's Web site, which gets about 17 million hits a year from all over the world.

The foundation also monitors Ontario falcons fitted with mini-lighter-sized transmitters that are tracked by satellite. One transmitter-collared young bird released in Richmond Hill in the summer of 2001 created an international incident after it turned up a few months later at a public monument in the Dominican Republic, killing and eating local doves. A Dominican permit to kill the falcon was set aside after a flood of diplomatic and scientific pleas convinced local authorities to spare the endangered, expensively monitored predator.

Young peregrines in general suffer high mortality when they migrate. Those from Ontario mostly fly to the southern U.S. Atlantic seaboard and the Caribbean, while the Arctic-nesting peregrine subspecies head to Central and South America, usually passing over the province in late September and early October. Flying with steady, rapid beats of their point-tipped wings rather than soaring and gliding like most migrant hawks, they average a couple of hundred kilometres (124 miles) a day. They often pick off migrating shore-birds and sometimes kestrels, merlins – both smaller falcons – or sharp-shinned hawks along the way.

Most urban-nesting pairs, though, remain together in the city for the winter, finding plenty of winter-plump pigeons, mourning doves and starlings that do the same. They usually perform soaring, acrobatic courtship flights and pick out nesting ledges in the winter, then lay their eggs in late March or early April. A male peregrine helps out with the incubation, but mostly provides captured prey, lovingly plucked and beheaded, for his consider-ably larger mate while she's on the nest. She in turn tears up the offerings for the downy white nestlings once they hatch. After the young fledge in early summer, they continue being fed by their parents for up to 10 weeks as they learn to hunt for themselves. Once fully independ-ent, they drift off on their own or migrate south.

While catching sight of a peregrine remains a rare treat, the unsung but beautiful **kestrel** is much more common in urban environs. Often seen perched on wires, poles, TV antennas and dead trees along highways and open areas, the blue-jay-sized falcon has a barred, reddish-brown back, spotted white undersides and elab-orate blue-grey, black and tan markings on its head. Males also sport blue-grey wings. Usually first noticed by their screechy call, kestrels characteristically hover in one place in midair before swooping down to catch mice, small birds or grasshoppers. They nest in tree cav-ities, most often old flicker holes, but sometimes take up residence in the crevices of old buildings and nest boxes built specially for them in parks and urban nature areas.

Nest: Scraped-out depression, 17–22 cm (7–9 in) wide, in debris on ledges, from 15 m (50 ft) to more than 61 m (200 ft) above ground

Highest known falcon nest in Ontario: 40 floors up on Toronto's Sheraton Centre hotel

Average clutch: 3–4 white to creamy pink eggs, sometimes with brown or reddish markings; size of medium chicken eggs

Incubation period: 33–35 days

Fledging age: 38–45 days

Age at first breeding: Usually 2 years

Lifespan: Adults average 5–10 years; up to 20 years in wild, 25 years in captivity

Predators: Great horned owls, eagles, gyrfalcons

Nesting range: Scattered in south-ern and eastern Ontario to about Temagami and eastern Lake Superior; also around northwestern Lake Superior and in all other provinces and territo-ries except Newfoundland and Prince Edward Island

Peak of spring migration: Late Apr. to mid-May

Peak of fall migration: Late Sept. to mid-Oct.

Winter whereabouts: From breed-ing range to U.S. Atlantic seaboard and the West Indies

Estimated Ontario population at end of breeding season: 200–250

Estimated North American popu-lation: 40,000–50,000

Also see: Pigeon, Mourning Dove

WINTER WAYFARERS
Hardy Visitors from the North

JUST AS WINTER drives many of the city's winged inhabitants to warmer climes, it also brings in some hardy northerners for whom southern Ontario is a balmy refuge. Of these cold-season visitors, dark-eyed juncos are the most familiar in many backyards. Always appearing in small, ground-foraging groups, the slate-grey, white-bellied, pale-beaked sparrows fly in on early-autumn cold fronts from remote spruce-birch forest clearings. They form winter flocks of 10 to 30 birds that visit the same daily circuit of feeders, gardens and wooded, weedy roadsides until April, flashing their signature white-flanked tails whenever they take wing.

Like juncos, small flocks of tree sparrows also forage for the seeds that rain down from tall, dead stalks of grass and wildflowers throughout winter. Sporting a black spot in the centre of a plain grey breast, the streaky-brown, rusty-capped birds are off-season vacationers from the stunted birch and willow northern treeline. Though many pass through in late October and November and again in early spring, some put down in southern Ontario for as long as their seed sources remain above the snow in brushy fields and valley bottoms or there are generous backyard feeders to visit.

Snow buntings have the same criteria for sticking around. The white-breasted Arctic voyagers nest farther north than any other land bird, to the upper reaches of Ellesmere Island and Greenland, before coming south to spend the winter in open, snowy fields. Large, skittish snow bunting flocks gravitate to rural areas, but occasionally turn up along deserted urban beaches or around airports, swirling up en masse on wings displaying large white patches. True to their name, they burrow into the snow on cold nights for a warm, insulated sleep.

Number of waterfowl that winter around Canadian shores of Lake Ontario: Up to 282,000

Number of waterfowl species wintering on Lake Ontario: Up to 36

Maximum time underwater for long-tailed ducks: 1.5 min

Closest cities to a winter concentration of bald eagles in Ontario: Kingston and Brockville, with 20–40 bald eagles usually spotted along the St. Lawrence River between the two communities

Other winter eagle concentration spots: Bruce Nuclear Power Station, north of Kincardine on Lake Huron; Nanticoke Thermal Power Station, east of Simcoe on Lake Erie; Peterborough Crown Game Reserve, northeast of Peterborough

Migrant waves of golden-crowned kinglets, horned larks, brown creepers, and red-breasted nuthatches also all leave small contingents behind to winter in southern Ontario, their numbers varying with the weather. The presence of northern finches, on the other hand, depends on erratically fluctuating evergreen cone crops throughout Ontario. Flocks of the rambling seed-eating finches pile into the south during winters when cones are scarce over large areas of the north. They often come in February, but may arrive as early as mid-October.

Evening grosbeaks (illustrated), the most popular of northern finches, throng to suburban bird feeders during these irruptions. The stocky, cardinal-sized birds also feast on Manitoba maple seeds in southern cities. The greyish females have a stronger tendency to come south and usually outnumber the more colourful, yellow-visored males. Smaller wandering pine siskins and purple finches sometimes join them at feeders. Both the heavily brown-streaked siskins and female purple finches resemble sparrows, while the male purple finch, in the words of birding great Roger Tory Peterson, looks like "a sparrow dipped in raspberry juice."

Another visiting northern finch, the common redpoll is a sparrowlike bird with a bright red cap and a reputation for surviving colder temperatures than any other songbird. In addition to digging in at feeders, the tiny scrub and tundra nesters happily pick away at the cones in ornamental birch trees and cedar hedges. Much more rarely, tame flocks of red crossbills and white-winged crossbills visit pine or spruce groves on urban outskirts. They use their specialized, crossed-over upper and lower beak tips to pry open cone scales to get at the seeds inside. Crossbills are so footloose, they may nest wherever and whenever they find extremely bountiful cone crops, occasionally even in the dead of winter.

Cyclical drops in the number of mice, lemmings and hares, as well as particularly deep snows that make hunting difficult, can also send northern birds of prey south. Snowy owl irruptions occur roughly every four or so years, with the big, seemingly tame birds often turning up like white ghosts in broad daylight on or near the ground around waterfronts, airports and other open

East-west migrants: Flocks of sometimes more than 1,000 nomadic Bohemian waxwings from western Canada sometimes irrupt into central Ontario cities such as North Bay and Ottawa during winters of bumper mountain ash berry crops

Average daily number of mice or voles eaten by snowy owls: 7–12

Pressure exerted by bills of evening grosbeaks to crack open nuts, pits and seed shells: Up to 11 kg (25 lb)

Throat storage: Large chambers in esophagus of redpolls and crossbills allow them to bring a large number of seeds back to their roosts and gradually swallow them, ensuring they have enough energy to get through extremely cold nights

Favourite feeder food for juncos and other sparrows: Millet

Favourite feeder food for pine siskins and redpolls: Thistle seed

Average annual quantity of bird seed provided at a feeder: 27 kg (59 lb)

Portion of North American households that feed birds: One-third

Local forest nesters often at winter bird feeders: White-breasted nuthatches, downy woodpeckers, chickadees

Official season for winter bird sighting lists: Dec. 1–Feb. 28

Christmas Bird Count: First held on Dec. 25, 1900, by conservationists at 25 locations in the United States and Canada as an alternative to traditional

Christmas "side hunt" competition by teams to see who could shoot the most birds; 55,000 volunteers now take part annually in 1,000 local counts, each tallying the species and total number of birds seen within a 24-km- (15-mi-) diameter area over a one-day period, across the United States, Canada and parts of Latin America

Number of local Christmas Bird Counts held in Ontario: 94

Number of species tallied on Christmas counts in recent years: Niagara Falls 93–100, Toronto 79–89, Ottawa 72–82, Sudbury 33–43

Number of northern nesting species wintering regularly in southern Ontario: About 12

Number of bird species with frequent winter irruptions into southern Ontario: About 20

Number of bird species with at least a portion of population wintering in southern Ontario: About 100

Also see: Transient Migrants, Mallard, Canada Goose, Manitoba Maple

areas. Large rough-legged hawks usually come at the same time as snowies. Both birds normally dine upon the same kinds of rodents in the high Arctic.

Smaller numbers of great grey and northern hawk owls, flying in from northern boreal forests, also hunt during the day, paying little attention to humans, whom they seldom see on their nesting grounds. Other birds of prey that nest in parts of the south, such as goshawks and great horned owls, can also become more common in winter when food shortages farther north send refugees into urban areas. Up to 75 normally rare long-eared owls, which are more regularly migratory, have been counted in a single southern winter woodlot.

Though most of southern Ontario is a little north of the traditional winter ranges of Cooper's and sharp-shinned hawks, both are increasingly staking out neighbourhood bird feeders through the cold months to snatch unsuspecting chickadees and house sparrows. Robin-sized northern shrikes also sometimes show up at suburban feeders to attack songbirds during winters when lemmings are scarce in the far north's stunted forests.

Cities on large lakes and rivers that remain unfrozen are further graced with tens of thousands of overwintering northern-nesting diving ducks, which forage for snails, mussels, crayfish, aquatic insect larvae and small fish.

The deepest of the divers, going down to 60 metres (197 feet), are long-tailed ducks (formerly known as old-squaw), which breed in the high Arctic, their males standing out with striking black-and-white markings and spikelike tails. Large flocks of dark-headed greater scaup, also tundra nesters, usually dive closer to shore, along with buffleheads – diminutive boreal-forest ducks with puffy white bouffants – and common goldeneyes, which nest across the Canadian Shield. Smaller numbers of other divers, such as mergansers and redheads, are also often present in winter, while in the shallows, dark-feathered gadwalls, black ducks and other marsh species dabble amid resident mallards, geese and the occasional feral mute swan.

PIGEON

Consummate Bird About Town

FERAL PIGEONS ARE hallmarks of urban civilization the world over. Their numbers seem to rise in tandem with human density. Long habituated to people, they thrive in vertical streetscapes that replicate their ancestral cliffside homes but have relatively few predators. They find the city's streets virtually paved with pigeon feed, especially at the foot of curbs where all manner of tiny delectables accumulate. Pigeons fan out over parking lots, snap up the seeds of common plantain, knotweed and other bountiful lawn and sidewalk plants, and stake out doughnut shops, convenience stores, hot-dog stands and small parkettes for spillage and handouts. The success of city pigeons stands as a testament to fast food, snacks and human generosity.

Defying to be pigeon-holed, however, the quintessential urban bird is a master of many guises. Simply a pigeon to most, the head-bobbing connoisseur of ornate architecture is actually only one member of a family of more than 250 pigeon and dove species, most living in or near the tropics. The sidewalk-strutting city pigeon's other name, rock dove, points to its origins as a cliff nester of rocky Mediterranean lands. The wild birds were domesticated and being raised for food in Egypt and Syria by 4000 B.C. But they were also esteemed for their beauty and gentle nature and became an early symbol of love, as reflected in the biblical ode, the Song of Solomon:

> O my dove, in the clefts of the rock,
>   in the covert of the cliff,
> let me see your face,
>   let me hear your voice,
> for your voice is sweet,
>   and your face is comely.

Top flying speed: 97 km/h (60 mph); up to 151 km/h (94 mph) with a tail wind
Wingbeats per second: 5–8
Pigeon hearing range: As low as 0.1 Hz
Human hearing range: As low as 30 Hz
Lowest bass tuba note: About 50 Hz
Length: 29–36 cm (11.4–14.2 in)
Weight: 300–400 g (10.6–14.1 oz)
Wingspan: 62–70 cm (24.4–27.6 in)
Markings: Either mostly blue-grey and darker around head and tail, or more uniformly dark throughout; iridescent green and purple sheen on neck; whitish rump; black wing bars and band at edge of tail; whitish-grey underwing; orange eyes; red

feet; recent descendants of domesticated birds can have varying degrees of reddish, white and other colours
Calls: Soft, low, gurgled coos
Alias: Rock dove, rock pigeon, domestic pigeon, street pigeon, feral pigeon, *le pigeon biset, Columba livia*
Name origins: *Pigeon* comes from the Latin *pipio*, a young bird that "pips"; *Columba*, "dove" in Latin; *livia* is the Latin word for "blue-grey"
Whereabouts: Streetsides, sidewalks, buildings, parking lots, alleys, parks and yards, especially downtown
Food: Weed seeds, nuts, berries, insects, grain, birdseed, bread and other human-food scraps; sand, grit and tiny pebbles also swallowed to aid grinding of seeds and nuts against hard ridges of gizzard
Nest: Wide, shallow, loose disk of sticks, roots, leaves and stems, usually built on a ledge, under eaves, or bridges
Average clutch: 2 white, golf-ball-sized eggs
Incubation period: 16–19 days
Fledging age: 25–32 days in summer; up to 45 days in cold months
Fat content of pigeon milk: 7–15%
Fat content of human milk: 4%
Portion of eggs that produce fledglings: 20–45%
Age of independence: About a week after fledging
Age of first-time breeders: Males 5½–12 months; females 7–12 months

A pure white dove – lighter-coloured breeds were common in the bleached, dry lands of the Middle East – was associated with the Babylonian deity Ishtar, the Canaanite Ashtart and Greek Aphrodite, all goddesses of love and fertility. Kamadeva, the Hindu god of romantic love, also rode on a dove. Over time, the white bird came to represent the soul and was adopted by early Christians to signify the Holy Spirit. Today, it's the most widely recognized symbol of peace everywhere.

White doves of peace may seem antithetical to the messy, common street urchins reviled by many, but all urban pigeons are feral descendants of domesticated birds. Pigeon breeding spread throughout the ancient world and became as much a passionate hobby as a means of sustenance. By Greek and Roman times some varieties were developed as carrier pigeons, making use of the rock dove's extraordinary tendency to return to its home over unfamiliar ground after being released up to 1,600 kilometres (1,000 miles) or more away. News of Caesar's conquests in Gaul and Napoleon's defeat at Waterloo first reached distant capitals on the wings of a dove. In the Middle Ages, both the Arab and Mongol empires set up carrier-pigeon mail services that spanned their vast lands. During the First World War, the French army awarded a pigeon named Cher Ami the Croix de Guerre for delivering a message through the thick of combat that saved an entire battalion.

No one knows for sure which of the bird's acute senses are responsible for such feats. Homing pigeons are believed to use smell for at least short-distance orientation in returning to their lofts. They also have much keener eyesight than humans and can make out sounds eight octaves below middle C, meaning they could theoretically hear a volcano erupting on the other side of the planet. Studies show, as well, that all pigeons can somehow detect the Earth's magnetic field and orient, and possibly navigate, by it.

The rock dove's homing abilities were also used to develop long-distance pigeon racing – the national sport of Belgium – starting in the early 1800s. Despite seeming to be plump, unhurried and always loafing about, pigeons possess powerful flight muscles, accounting for

31 percent of their total weight, compared with 20 percent for weak-flying birds. They're actually among the swiftest of birds, having evolved to avoid other cliff-dwelling predators such as falcons. Pigeons can fly at a steady speed of 70 kilometres (43.5 miles) per hour or even faster with a favourable tail wind. As soon as they are released, usually early in the morning anywhere from 200 to 800 kilometres (124 to 497 miles) from their coops, racers immediately orient themselves and then wing their way home before the end of the day. Top prizes in some races sometimes reach up to $40,000, while the offspring of big-money champs can sell for more than $100,000.

In all, more than 300 breeds of domesticated rock doves come in all shapes and colours. But when they escape, or are released, light-coloured birds tend to be singled out by hawks, falcons and other predators, keeping their genes scarce in feral populations. In fact, sooty-feathered pigeons abound in gritty downtowns much more than in the suburbs and countryside, where the classic blue-grey-hued birds, known as "blue-bars," predominate.

Canada's first feral birds may have flown the coop shortly after being brought to the country's oldest permanent settlement, Port Royal (Annapolis Royal) in Nova Scotia, in 1606, just three years after the colony's founding. The birds flocked along with the national dream in towns and cities as they spread across the country, even as native passenger pigeons perished.

Thriving feral pigeon populations, however, make for perilous lingering beneath ornate edifices. Acidic pigeon droppings can corrode paint, stone and brick. Large dried accumulations can also cause allergies and bare fungal spores that, in rare instances, have caused illnesses in humans. The federal government has employed full-time shooers to keep pigeons off statues and ledges on Parliament Hill. Many European and American cities have tried curbing oversized populations with feed spiked with sterilizing chemicals or outright poison.

But the urban rock dove is not without its defenders. An attempt in London, England, to outlaw the tradition

Average annual survival: About 57% in first year; about 65% for adults

Lifespan: Average of 2.4 years for adults; up to 31 years in captivity

Predators: Red-tailed hawks, peregrine falcons, kestrels, great horned owls, raccoons, cats, opossums, traffic; nests raided by crows, blue jays, grackles, squirrels, chipmunks and store owners whose signs have been occupied by nests

Record mission by a U.S. Army signal corps carrier pigeon: 3,700 km (2,300 mi)

Most recent war service: Pigeons rode with U.S. Marines in invasion of Iraq in 2003 to serve as an early-warning system for chemical weapons

Famous pigeons and doves: Dove of Peace, Noah's dove, Cher Ami

Number of pigeon racers in Canada: About 3,000

Stool pigeon: Captive passenger pigeons tethered to small perches, called stools, were used by hunters to lure others with their calls to within shooting range, in effect betraying them

Clay pigeon: Passenger pigeons were once so numerous, thousands were caught for gun-club target practice in trapshooting. With their extinction, the bird targets were replaced by projected clay disks

Pigeon pie: The renowned Québécois tortiere was originally made with passenger pigeons, *tourte* being a French word for *pigeon*

Art appreciation: A Japanese study found pigeons could distinguish a painting by Pablo Picasso from another by Claude Monet

Nesting range: Southern Ontario to about Kapuskasing and Kenora; also in all other provinces

First appearance of doves on Earth: More than 20 million years ago

Number of dove species nesting in Ontario: 2

Number of dove species worldwide: 255

Also see: Mourning Dove, Peregrine Falcon, Red-tailed Hawk

of feeding Trafalgar Square's 35,000 pigeons led to two years of protests and civil disobedience by animal rights groups until a compromise was struck in 2003 aimed at gradually weaning the birds off of handouts to avoid mass starvation.

As one of the most ubiquitous and easily watched of city creatures, pigeons have plenty of admirers in Ontario as well. Being very gregarious, they can often be seen interacting, though they don't form distinct, structured flocks. Their congregations are fluid and form where the eating's good. But they do mate for life. Though a bowing, cooing, swollen-necked male may appear to be trailing a shy debutante through a crowd of other pigeons, the two could well be an old couple. The birds may court and nest from mid-February through autumn, raising three broods or more, food and weather permitting.

Both mates scrape together their loose nest of twigs and debris on a ledge or windowsill. The cock takes over from his partner to sit tight on their two-egg clutch through most of the day, so that it's almost always covered. When the nestlings hatch, both parents feed them "pigeon milk," a thick, nutritious, curdlike substance made from fluid-filled glandular linings inside the crop, a food-storage chamber located at the bottom of the esophagus of many birds. Crop milk, though, is unique to the dove family and has a higher protein and fat content than human or cow milk, while lacking sugar and other carbohydrates. After a few days, parents supplement the crop milk with spewings of regular food. As much as two weeks before the squabs even leave the nest, they're often joined by two more potential siblings as their mother drops her next clutch, continuously procuring fresh recruits for the burgeoning ranks of urban rock doves.

RED-TAILED HAWK
Soaring Over the City

Ability to distinguish details at a distance: 2½ times as good as humans

Number of visual cells in a hawk's retina: Up to 1 million per mm²

Number of visual cells in a human's retina: Up to 200,000 per mm²

Flying speed: 32–70 km/h (20–43.5 mph)

Wingbeats per second: 2.6

Average hunting altitude: 10–50 m (33–164 ft)

Average migrating altitude: About 840 m (2,756 ft)

Height at which hawk disappears from view: 1,100 m (3,609 ft)

Portion of time spent gliding while in migration: 79%

Wingspan: 1.2–1.5 m (4–5 ft)

Turkey vulture wingspan: 1.7–2 m (5.8–6.6 ft)

Bald eagle wingspan: 1.8–2.3 m (6–7.5 ft)

Length: Males 45–56 cm (18–22 in); females 50–65 cm (20–26 in)

Weight: Males 0.7–1.3 kg (1.5–2.9 lb); females 0.9–1.5 kg (2–3.3 lb)

Markings: Mottled dark brown on top, with a rusty red tail; undersides white with dark streaky belly band and specks or splotches on wings; immature birds' tails dark brown or grey with fine dark bars on both sides

Alias: Chicken hawk, eastern red-tailed hawk, red hawk, *la buse à queue rousse, Buteo jamaicensis*

THE HIGH, FIERCE, piercing raptor screech, "keeeeeer," dubbed into countless movie and TV jungle or desert scenes to enhance the wild setting, is actually the voice of one of urban Ontario's most magnificent birds. Soaring high above parks and ravines on broad, expansive wings, North America's most widespread hawk flashes the top of its namesake rust-red tail in the sun as it banks in wide arcs. In the city, the red-tailed hawk, which averages slightly larger than a crow, is a skilled pigeon snatcher, even cruising over busy downtown streets and civic squares frequented by their cooing quarry. Most of the time, though, it hunts for voles and mice from perches on trees, fence posts or Hydro towers overlooking fields and lining highways.

Like most species that prosper in cities, red-tailed hawks are opportunists, cashing in on whatever prey is plentiful and easy to catch. In spring, when songbirds are nesting and most vulnerable, about 10 percent of the hawks' diet is feathered. In late summer, they'll land in meadows and hunt thronging grasshoppers on foot. They prefer a mix of fields for hunting and small, open forests for taking cover, roosting and nesting. Their presence in urban and suburban woodlots is sometimes betrayed by a cacophony of angry crows swooping down trying to drive the big predators away.

Origin of word *hawk*: From Old English *haf*, meaning "seize"

Calls: High-pitched, piercing screech, 1–3 seconds long, rising and then descending; also loud chirps and a harsh, rising, repeated "klow-eek"

Whereabouts: Open areas mixed with woods; ravines; along highways and rail lines

Food: Voles, mice, rabbits, rats, pigeons, snakes, ducks and small birds; sometimes chipmunks, squirrels, shrews, amphibians, grasshoppers, earthworms and fresh roadkill

Average daily food requirement: 3–4 meadow mice or 1 chipmunk in summer; almost twice as much in winter

Average number of bone, fur and feather pellets regurgitated a day: 1

Territory: 1.3–5 km² (0.5–1.9 sq mi)

Nest: Bulky, 0.7–1 m (2.3–3.3 ft) wide, 10–13 cm (4–5 in) deep, made of sticks; lined with shredded cedar or wild grapevine bark, moss, green sprigs of pine, cedar, hemlock and plants; usually 5–21 m (16–70 ft) high in main fork of a deciduous or pine tree with good view, close to forest edge; occasionally on utility poles or cliffs

Portion of great horned owl clutches laid in old red-tailed hawk nests: About 75%

Average clutch: 2–3 brown-spotted white eggs, sometimes bluish-white or unmarked; about the size of large chicken eggs

Incubation period: 28–35 days

Red-tails were once fairly rare in the vast forests that covered most of Ontario, being less agile than the slightly smaller red-shouldered hawk in flying through densely branched canopies. Even in the early 1900s, red-shoulders outnumbered their bigger relatives four to one in southern Ontario. Gradually, the thinning of woodlots, cutting the largest, mature trees, tipped the balance decidedly in the red-tail's favour, especially after the 1950s. Studies show that once a forest's crown cover drops below 70 percent, the larger, more aggressive hawk tends to exclude red-shoulders from their former domain. Since many red-tails overwinter in southern Ontario, while others are among the earliest migrants to return, starting in February, they can occupy the other species' old nests and territories before red-shoulders begin arriving in mid-March. The smaller hawks are now rare and their population officially considered vulnerable in the province.

Migrant red-tailed hawks themselves sometimes have their old nests expropriated by great horned owls, which stay put through winter and begin nesting in February or March. Though not as abundant as the hawks in urban areas, great horns prefer largely the same habitat, usually hunting unseen by night instead of day. Red-tails that lose their nests to owls may spend a week or so building a new one nearby, snapping off sticks from dead branches and piling them up in the crotch of a tree. But they stand only about a one-in-three chance of success because the big owls will prey on their young if they get the opportunity.

Red-tails usually space their nests an average of about 1.5 kilometres (0.9 miles) apart from each other. Non-migratory pairs remain together and defend their nesting territory year-round from their own kind. They roost in evergreens and eat more in winter than during the warm months because they have to burn more calories to stay warm. They also conserve energy while roosting on winter nights by lowering their normal 41°C (106°F) body temperature by an average of 3.2°C (6°F).

Wintering hawks begin their courtship flights on sunny days in February or March, with pairs soaring in circles, dipping and diving together. Migrants do the same soon after returning, with most arriving by early April. Females usually lay each of their eggs in intervals of two days or more and do most of the nest-minding, while their mates fetch food for them and later their young. Mothers do the actual feeding of the downy white chicks, which hatch in late spring. Parents continually replenish the nest with the foliage of cedar, hemlock, pine and other green plants that are known to contain natural bug-repellent substances.

The young fledge around mid-July, but are still fed by their parents for a couple more months while they learn to hunt. Some may stay close to their natal territory into winter, while others drift, usually more than 100 kilometres (62 miles), in search of new horizons, sometimes gathering with other young hawks. Many migrate ahead of adults, starting in September or October, and generally travel farther, sometimes all the way to the Gulf of Mexico and Central America.

Fledging age: 6–7 weeks

Average number of daily feedings at nest: 10–15

Age at first breeding: 2 or 3 years

Average number of young that survive to fledge per nest: 0.9–1.4

Average annual survival: About 46% in first year; about 80% for adults

Lifespan: Less than 20% of adults live more than 10 years; up to 23 years in wild, 29 years in captivity

Predators: Raccoons, crows, blue jays and great horned owls raid nests

Average heartbeats per minute: 202 during day, 134 at night

Nesting range: Most of Ontario to the treeline, though rare in northwest; also in all other provinces and territories except Newfoundland and Nunavut

Average peak of spring migration: Mid-Mar. to early Apr,

Average peak of fall migration: Late Oct. to early Nov.

Record one-day count of migrating red-tails over Toronto's High Park hawk watch: 1,680

Winter whereabouts: From about Pembroke, Haliburton and Midland south to Mexico

Estimated North American population: 350,000–1 million

First appearance of raptors: About 50 million years ago

Number of day-hunting birds of prey nesting in Ontario: 14

Number of day-hunting birds of prey worldwide: About 292

Also see: Transient Migrants, Crow, White Cedar

RED-WINGED BLACKBIRD
Bellicose Master of the Marsh

He'll be there beside the river,
When Winter finally breaks its bones,
He'll be king among the rushes,
He'll be master of his home.
– David Francey, "Red-Winged
Blackbird"

THE FLICKERING of red wing patches in flight, like technicolour strobe lights, often brightens urban riversides, marshes and ponds well before the first robins of spring show up on residential lawns. Male red-winged blackbirds arrive in flocks mixed with grackles and cowbirds, often when marshes are still frozen. They snap up weed seeds in fields and tear into fluffy cattail seedheads for the tiny, overwintering caterpillars of the cattail worm moth nestled within. Though males forage and roost together for several weeks, they gradually begin staking out turf, singing boldly from prominent perches, chasing and tussling in a never-ending game of border encroachment.

A dominant male red-winged blackbird in his prime is an iron-fisted patriarch commanding the best and biggest stretch of marsh, a small harem and the fear and respect of his community. He is a warrior troubadour who, many bird experts believe, has learned more songs than his rivals, warding them off with his virtuosity. While he sings, he flashes bright-scarlet epaulets, badges of age and experience that similarly convince others not to challenge him.

The less-dominant red-wings are probably the ones most often encountered by people in the city. Pushed out of prime marsh real estate, they try their luck in scrubby meadows, thickets, patches of cattails and rushes in roadside ditches and sometimes backyards. A pair of blackbirds once even nested inside a Toronto subway station.

Length: 17–25 cm (7–10 in)
Wingspan: 30–36 cm (1–1.2 ft)
Weight: Females 37–47 g
(1.3–1.7 oz); males 62–70 g
(2.2–2.5 oz)
Markings: Males black with scarlet-and-yellow wing epaulets; females streaked brown and beige, with yellowish-orange tints around head; juveniles similar to females
Alias: Red-wing, marsh blackbird, red-winged starling, red-winged oriole, *le carouge à épaulettes, Agelaius pheoniceus*
Calls: Song a gurgling "conk-a-ree," rolling at the end; also loud clicks, clacks, high whistles, chirps and chatters
Whereabouts: Marshes, swamps, meadows, scrubby fields, roadside ditches
Food: Mostly seeds, small fruits and grain from late summer to early spring; caterpillars,

Females, who arrive two to four weeks after the males, do not marry for love. They look for the richest, safest patch of marsh for raising a family, and mate with whatever lug happens to occupy it, usually in May. Males will breed with and defend as many females as are interested in settling in their domain. Each female maintains her own nesting zone within her mate's territory, driving away potential new concubines. Two or three wives are common for a well-situated male. Some may have four or more. With these red-patched sultans monopolizing virtually all available females, there are many luckless bachelors, mostly one- and two-year-olds, forced to be non-territory-holding floaters.

Female red-wings are certainly not stand-by-your-man types. Although they may return to the same territory to mate every year, they show no qualms about having flings with interloping scoundrels when the lord of the manor is away feeding. Studies suggest between one-quarter and a half of hatchlings are fathered through extramarital affairs, usually involving next-door neighbours.

Resembling big, brown-streaked sparrows, female blackbirds are effectively camouflaged in their nests. If predators are close by, the bright males try to distract or drive them away, exploding from the cattails with a loud burst and splash of colour. Red-wings also commonly band together to mob owls, crows, hawks and foxes. Despite their vigilance, predators often make suppers of the contents of about half of all blackbird nests.

Later in the summer, though they continue to roost in marshes, large red-wing flocks feed on seeds and berries in dry fields, females and young flying separately from males. Blackbirds commuting between roosting and foraging areas can often be seen scooting over the city. Many also patrol road shoulders for dead grasshoppers, dragonflies and other insect roadkill. Flocks gradually gravitate to traditional migration staging areas, such as Holland Marsh and Long Point, where many thousands may roost together between late August and September. Some winter roosts in the United States swell to several million.

dragonflies and other invertebrates during breeding season

Nest: Deep, woven basket, about 9 cm (3.5 in) wide, of strips of cattail leaves, sedges and grass, built on cattails, reeds, small trees or shrubs

Average clutch: 3–5 black-and-purple speckled or streaked light blue-green eggs, about the size of grapes

Incubation period: 10–12 days

Fledging age: 10–13 days

Age at first mating: Females 1 year; males 2–3 years

Nestlings that survive to fledge: 30–60%

Average annual adult mortality: 40–60%

Lifespan: Average 2–2.5 years, up to 15 years in wild

Predators: Sharp-shinned hawks, owls, herring gulls, foxes; nests raided by raccoons, skunks, crows, blue jays, grackles, marsh wrens, water snakes

Nesting range: Most of Ontario, except for far northwest; also in all other provinces and territories except Nunavut

Average first arrival of migrants in southern Ontario: Early to mid-Mar.

Average last departure of migrants from southern Ontario: Late Nov. to mid-Dec.

Winter whereabouts: From about Toronto to northern Florida, with most in U.S. deep south

Number of blackbird species nesting in Ontario: 11

Number of blackbird species worldwide: About 100

Also see: Grackle, Wetlands

RING-BILLED GULL
Happiest in High-Density Haunts

LOUD, AGGRESSIVE, THRONGING and revelling in garbage, ring-billed gulls embody for some the more unsavoury aspects of urban life. Looked at another way, they're a native species that has survived a concerted assault by western society and emerged as a consummate city slicker. It was the great building boom of downtown Toronto in the 1960s and 1970s, in fact, that directly gave rise to one of the biggest ring-billed colonies in the world.

As colonial birds, ring-billed gulls were particularly vulnerable to egg-collectors and the late-19th-century craze for feather-adorned women's hats. Their waterside nesting sites were also often developed or otherwise irreparably disturbed. By the early 1900s, the ring-bill's raucous calls had all but faded from the Great Lakes, save for a few isolated islands in Lake Huron.

Ring-bills were finally legally protected, along with most other non-game birds, by the Canada–U.S. Migratory Birds Treaty of 1916. Their population stabilized after 1940. Then something funny happened. Freed from human persecution, the gulls gradually lost their wariness of people and began frequenting cities, dining at garbage dumps and raiding picnic grounds. The explosive spread of alien alewives and rainbow smelt in the Great Lakes also provided a plentiful new food source. Ring-billed gull numbers increased correspondingly, more than twenty-fold in the two decades after 1960.

Because their ideal water-edge colonies are eventually spoiled by fluctuating lake levels and successional vegetation, ring-bills have evolved as a shifting population, able very quickly to take advantage of rapidly changing conditions. As they recovered, the gulls began living on breakwaters, dikes, sewage lagoons and other artificial nest sites. In 1973, 21 pairs first nested on Toronto's Leslie Street Spit, a five-kilometre (three-mile) finger of landfill jutting into Lake Ontario created, mainly after 1965, from the excavations for the city's huge office towers and countless suburban plots. Two years later, there were 10,000 nests, and by the mid-1980s, almost 75,000 nests were contained within a 41-hectare (101-acre) site. The population has since decreased as dogwoods, willows and cottonwoods, as well as predators, encroach on the gullery.

Breakwaters and berms built out into Lake Erie at Port Colborne and in Hamilton Harbour, in the shadow of the city's flame- and smoke-spewing steel mills, have similarly been colonized by thousands of ring-billed gulls, as well as large numbers of cormorants, common terns and black-crowned night herons. As the sun rises in these densely packed nurseries, ring-bills fan out like early-morning commuters far and wide over cityscapes and beyond. Gulls are scavengers par excellence and will eat almost anything. Though most migrate south in mid- to late autumn, thousands find food through the winter by flying out to city dumps. In April and May, particularly after rainfalls, they venture beyond the urban fringe to fill up on earthworms and grubs in newly ploughed fields, often following directly behind farm tractors as they turn up the soil. They relentlessly patrol waterfronts for small fish year-round, but especially in early summer, when annual mass die-offs of alewives serve up beachside feasts. Open fields, where they snap up grasshoppers, caterpillars, beetles and even meadow voles, are also a major focus throughout the summer.

As well, pillaging gulls can make themselves less than welcome around city parks, amusement grounds, fast-food outlets and outdoor cafés, sometimes even presenting hazards on airport runways. Toronto's most

young are mottled sooty brown, gradually gaining adult colours over three years

Call: Wide variety of loud wails, squeals, clucks and mewing

Alias: Seagull, lake gull, common gull, common American gull, shit hawk, *le goéland à bec cerclé*, *Larus delawarensis*

Name origin: *Gullan*, Cornish for "wailer"

Whereabouts: Throughout city and suburbs, especially along waterfronts, at dumps, parks and fast-food restaurant parking lots

Food: Alewives, smelt and other small fish, worms, grubs, grasshoppers, caterpillars, other insects, bird eggs and nestlings, ducklings, songbirds, mice, voles, grain, fruit, seeds, berries, vegetable shoots, carrion and garbage scraps

Distance of foraging flights during nesting season: Average 5–17 km (3–10.5 mi), up to 30 km (18.6 mi)

Nests per 10 m² (1.2 sq yd) in large colonies: 5–25

Nest: In a ground depression, about 5 cm (2 in) deep, 25–63 cm (10–25 in) wide, often lined with grass, sticks, leaves and feathers; usually in an inaccessible, flat, sparsely vegetated waterside location

Average clutch: 2–3 brown-spotted and blotched brownish-white or olive eggs, about the size of large chicken eggs

Incubation period: 23–31 days

Fledging age: 34–41 days

Age at first breeding: 3 years

Average survival: Eggs usually more than 80%; chicks

60–65%; gulls in their first 2 years 40–50%

Lifespan: Very few live more than 7 years; up to 21 years in wild, 31 years in captivity

Predators: Foxes, coyotes, dogs, hawks, falcons, great horned owls kill adults; eggs or chicks also eaten by raccoons, skunks, mink, weasels, rats, snakes, crows and herring gulls

Famous gulls: Jonathan Livingston Seagull; Gertrude and Heathcliffe; the slain gull of Chekhov's *The Seagull*, symbol of the destructive force of human whims

First aircraft crash caused by a bird: 1910, in Long Beach, California, from a collision with a gull

Nesting range: Around Great Lakes, St. Lawrence and Ottawa Rivers, large lakes such as Simcoe, Nipissing, Temagami, Lake of the Woods, and James Bay; also in all other provinces, except Nova Scotia, and in the Northwest Territories

Average first arrival of migrants in spring: Late Feb.

Average last departure of migrants in fall: Dec.

Winter whereabouts: Some along shorelines of Lake Ontario, Erie and Huron to about Grand Bend; most go to Florida

Portion of bird species that are colonial nesters: About 12%

Number of gull species nesting in Ontario: 6

Number of gull species worldwide: 45

Also see: Smelt

famous deceased ring-bill was part of a large flock that regularly attended Blue Jays baseball games at Exhibition Stadium until it was killed on the field during a warmup in 1983 by a ball thrown by New York Yankees outfielder Dave Winfield. Observed by thousands, the fatal toss and resulting furore earned the star a night in jail on a cruelty-to-animals charge.

Like baseball players, most wintering ring-bills enjoy the warm sun of Florida before returning to southern Ontario, starting around late February and early March. Experienced gulls have a strong tendency to come back to the same nest site within the colony, though their memories or loyalties are not as strong for their past amours. Many end up mating with the previous year's neighbour instead. Females often feed on spawning rainbow smelt in nearby river mouths at night to build up food reserves for egg production. Both parents build the nest and take turns incubating the eggs, laid around late April and early May, so that they're virtually always tended. The chicks hatch covered in grey down, with their eyes open, and can walk well when two days' old. They're provided with a spread of regurgitated fish, worms and insects by their parents twice a day. Soon after they learn to fly, around midsummer, the colony starts breaking up, with the birds congregating at roosting sites closer to food sources.

Southern Ontario's other common wailer, the **herring gull**, looks much like the ring-bill, but is about 20 percent larger, lacks the black ring around its beak and has pink instead of greenish-yellow legs. It nests in much smaller colonies than ring-bills, generally with less than 100 nests, but is usually the gull seen farther inland, often well away from the larger lakes and rivers. Urban herring gull numbers actually increase in winter as birds from northern wilderness areas fly in to fish in the open waters of the Great Lakes and Niagara River between September and April.

Some 100,000 or more gulls, representing up to 14 species, gather at the Niagara gorge in winter, to scavenge fish killed or injured by the Falls or in Hydro turbines. They come from as far as the Arctic, the prairies and even Europe.

ROBIN
Perennial Springtime Favourite

ONCE A SHY, retiring thrush of the wilderness, the robin transformed itself by taking up residence in human society, gaining success and fame. Urban robins are celebrated songsters, fabled harbingers of spring, front-lawn fixtures and frequent household tenants. Prime suburban areas can support up to several hundred nesting bobbers per square kilometre (0.4 square miles). Mowed lawns and ornamental trees, hedges and shrubs are custom-made foraging grounds for the erectly postured birds, whose natural habitat is the forest edge and clearings. European settlement even introduced multitudes of juicy earthworms to Ontario, served up on or just below the close-cropped surface of turf grass during rainfalls and frequent waterings.

Robins are most admired when they first show up in early spring. No matter how commonplace they later become, the first sleek red-breast hopping amid the dark, squat forms of starlings after a long, cold winter is always one of the best-loved bird sightings of the year. In much of southern Ontario, though, the first robins may be those emerging from seclusion rather than returning from the south. While most of the birds leave the province in autumn, some retire to dense brushy ravines, thick cedar swamps, abandoned orchards and other sheltered places. Their numbers vary with the severity of the season and abundance of durable hawthorn

Average number of nest-material-collecting trips made by female a day: About 180

Flying speed: 27–51 km/h (17–32 mph)

Length: 23–28 cm (9–11 in)

Wingspan: 37.5–42 cm (14.7–16.3 in)

Weight: 70–95 g (2.5–3.35 oz)

Markings: Males have brick-red breast, dark sooty-grey back; females have duller orange-red breast, grey-brown back; spotted breast on juveniles

Alias: American robin, Canada robin, common robin, redbreast, northern robin, *le merle d'Amérique, Turdus migratorius*

Name origin: A nickname for *Robert*, originally applied to the English robin in the form "Robin redbreast"; *Robert* comes from an Old German name meaning "bright fame"

Name for a group: A nest of robins

Calls: Loud, long bursts of repeated rising and falling

whistled musical phrases, each with several syllables, often varying, but commonly described as "cheer up, cheerily, cherry"; also a stuttered, laughing call, chirps, squeaks and tweets

Whereabouts: Lawns, shrubby gardens, street trees, parks, forest edges and open woods

Food: In spring and summer, mostly earthworms, beetle grubs and adults, caterpillars, ants, grasshoppers and other insects, spiders, snails; through summer, increasing amounts of raspberries, serviceberries, wild cherries, dogwood berries and other fruits; in fall and winter, 90% mountain ash, buckthorn, poison ivy, juniper and red cedar berries, rosehips, sumac seeds, fruits of hawthorns, honeysuckles and other trees and shrubs

Favourite feeder foods: Bread, raisins, bits of apple

Average breeding territory: 0.1–0.25 ha (0.25–0.6 acres)

Area of a football field: 0.8 ha (2 acres)

Nest: Deep, tidy cup, 8–20 cm (3–8 in) wide, of mud, grass and twigs, usually 2–6 m (6.6–19.7 ft) above ground in understory trees and shrubs, with branches above for concealment and shelter; also on ledges and platforms beneath porch roofs, eaves and decks

Average clutch: 3–4 light blue-green eggs, about the size of peach pits

Incubation period: 12–14 days

Fledging age: 9–16 days

apples, mountain ash, juniper, buckthorn and other berries. In bumper berry years, many thousands may winter in southern Ontario, many of them migrants from farther north. But if the snow cover in their sanctuaries persists above about five centimetres (two inches), they often flee farther south, only to return as the snow pack diminishes. When late-winter warm spells start thawing the ground, the overwintering birds re-emerge on city lawns to scare up stirring earthworms and insect larvae.

Migrant robins similarly follow the leading edge of thawing ground northward from Dixie in early spring, usually coinciding with mean daily temperatures of about 3°C (37°F). Males normally return and set up shop a few days or a week ahead of their more dully coloured better halves. Experienced nesters usually reoccupy their old stomping grounds. Before long, they begin waxing eloquent. To human ears, their melodic carolling is a simple joyful ode to spring, one of the most widely recognized of all birdsongs. An Ojibway legend explains that robins sing to cheer people because they descended from a boy who became a bird to escape the suffering of a too-difficult vision quest – an initiation rite involving fasting and dreams – set by his father.

Male songsters are most prolific early in the breeding season, leading off with revelry well before daybreak. The hours around dawn are generally the busiest for breeding birds, the time when they most vigorously define their territories through song and confrontation. Male robins are highly territorial, chasing each other as they carve out their turf. Their songs, by serving as proprietary proclamations and warnings, help to minimize dangerous and exhausting combat. Early morning is also often when mates first pair up. A second peak of activity comes before sunset.

Beyond their serenades, the dusky-backed thrushes often treat humans to intimate views of their family lives permitted by few other songbirds. Female robins seek out nest sites with overhead shelter to ensure their mud-cup nests don't dissolve in the rain. Ledges and recesses above windowsills and doorways or beneath eaves are often ideal. Beams under raised decks, balconies and grape trellises are also prime digs. Expecting mothers spend three to 10 days adding layers of mud and grass to their emerging nests. Sitting inside, they mould them into shape by pushing with their wings and stamping their feet for up to 10 seconds before turning a few degrees and repeating the process, occasionally until they have completed several full rotations.

After laying three or four eggs, usually one a day, robin hens do virtually all of the incubating and brooding, while their partners feed them and their little ones. The chicks usually hatch in April, helpless and blind like most songbird nestlings. But stoked six or seven times an hour with high-protein earthworms and insects, they grow so quickly they're 10 times their birth weight after 10 days and make their first flights within another week. Father robins take the fledglings under their wings, tutoring them in the ways of finding their fare. Tireless mothers, meanwhile, lay another batch of eggs, often after building a new nest, free of parasites that may have built up in the old one. In really good years, they raise up to three broods.

Throughout the nesting period males continue to diligently guard their territories from each other. Yet when it comes time to knock off each day, the boys leave their wives behind and bunk down together in thickly branched trees. The roosts swell when fathers start admitting their fledgling charges to the formerly all-male evening clubs. After the last broods fledge, they too arrive, along with their mothers. Gradually building by the score, or even hundreds, flocks become highly noticeable by September, prior to and during migration.

Age at first breeding: 1 year

Lifespan: Rarely more than 4 years; up to 14 years in wild, 17 years in captivity

Predators: Cats, kestrels, crows, great horned owls, sharp-shinned and Cooper's hawks; nests raided by blue jays, grackles, house wrens, squirrels, raccoons, chipmunks and garter snakes

Number of feathers: About 2,900

Accolades: Last companion of Queen Elizabeth on the Canadian $2 bill; state bird of Wisconsin, Michigan and Connecticut

Early casualties: Die-offs of robins poisoned by contaminated earthworms on the grounds of Michigan State University being sprayed for Dutch elm disease in the mid-1950s first alerted scientists to the dangers of DDT

Nesting range: All Ontario and Canada below the treeline

Average first arrival of migrants in southern Ontario: Early to mid-Mar.

Average last departure of migrants from southern Ontario: Late Nov. to early Dec.

Winter whereabouts: From about Ottawa and North Bay south to Mexico; most Ontario migrants go to Gulf of Mexico states

Highest number of robins tallied in Toronto's annual Christmas Bird Count: 1,467

Number of thrush species nesting in Ontario: 7

Number of thrush species worldwide: About 175

Also see: Cedar Waxwing, Earthworms, Poison Ivy

SONG SPARROW
The Spot-chested Virtuoso

I N LATE WINTER, peals of exuberant song sparrow melodies signal the turning of the season. The most urban of native sparrows, they are luckily also among the most eloquent. Staking out nest sites in shrubby backyards and bushy fields and riversides, song sparrows, in Latin *Melospiza melodia*, belt out complex tunes for hours on end. Each male singer draws from a repertoire of eight to 10 songs – sometimes as many as 20 – to create kaleidoscopic stylings. Even female song sparrows sing short, soft tunes early in the year. The most vocally versatile males command the greatest attention from the opposite sex and respect from rivals. They must also be good listeners, learning to recognize dozens of different songs performed by next-door neighbours in order to distinguish them from strangers.

Though most song sparrows arrive on early fronts of fine weather from the south, some may be gritty holdouts that hunker down in the city for the cold months, sidling up to chickadees and cardinals at winter feeders. They begin nesting as early as mid-April in southern Ontario, allowing time to raise up to three consecutive broods by the end of summer. Males continue to sing and guard their nesting territories throughout the period, their refrains rising to the fore as the calls of other songbirds trail off in midsummer.

Females usually spend four to 10 days in April or early May building their first nests on the ground, hidden amid shrubs or the previous year's long, dry plant stems. Later, after the leaves open and their spouses take charge of the newly fledged first broods, they turn to the cover higher up in bushes to locate their second nests. A mother bird may begin laying a new clutch as soon as six days after her last batch of young takes wing. Despite the equal amount of care given to later broods, sparrows born in the first clutch have better chances for survival because they have more time to gain experience in their first summer.

Youngsters become independent when about four weeks old. Males spend the next couple of months learning the craft of their species, listening intently to the songs of surrounding adults. Adding their own improvisations, they begin singing original ditties by autumn. By the time they begin their first breeding season the following spring, they have an expansive songbook they follow for the rest of their lives. Most return each spring to the hometowns where they hatched. Since they learned to sing in that milieu, generations of birds perpetuate each area's distinctive musical styles. Song sparrow enthusiasts estimate the birds may have up to 900 local "dialects" across the continent.

grasses, smartweed, ragweed, knotweed, clover and many other field plants; 40–45% insects during breeding season, especially caterpillars May-Jun. and grasshoppers and crickets in Aug.; also berries and other fruits in summer and fall

Average territory: 0.2–0.6 ha (0.5–1.5 acres)

Nest: Neat cup, 11–20 cm (4–8 in) wide, 5–10 cm (2–4 in) high, of grass, stems, bark strips, leaves and rootlets

Average clutch: 3–5 olive-sized, light-green or pale-blue eggs covered in brown spots

Incubation period: 10–14 days

Fledging age: 16–17 days

Age at first breeding: 1 year; 2 years for some males

Annual survival: About 20% in first year; 40–60% for adults

Lifespan: Adults average of 2.5 years; very few live more than 4 years; up to 11 years in wild

Predators: Cats, foxes, sharp-shinned hawks; nests raided by crows, blue jays, garter snakes, squirrels, mink, opossums, rats

Nesting range: Throughout Canada to the treeline

Average first arrival of migrants in southern Ontario: Early to mid-Mar.

Average last migrant departure of migrants from southern Ontario: Mid- to late Nov.

Winter whereabouts: From about Ottawa and Midland to Mexico

Number of native sparrow species nesting in Ontario: 19

Number of New World sparrow species in the Americas: 156

Also see: Yellow Warbler

STARLING
Often Outnumbering Humans

Calls: Great variety of harsh chirps, loud whistles, shrill squeals, low gurgles, clicks, twitters, creaks, burbles and rattles

Number of bird species whose calls are known to be mimicked by starlings: 56

Number of different segments of each male's song: 20–70

Flying speed: 60–80 km/h (37–50 mph)

Length: 20–23 cm (8–9 in)

Wingspan: 37–41 cm (14.5–16 in)

Weight: 70–95 g (2.5–3.35 oz)

Markings: Glossy black with brown spots and trim and iridescent blue-green sheen; bright-yellow beak; strongly specked, with grey beak, in autumn and early winter; juveniles dusky grey-brown

Alias: European starling, common starling, l'étourneau sansonnet, Sturnus vulgaris

FROM BEIJING to Rome, Thunder Bay to Amsterdam, starlings throng in the cities of the world in numbers that often exceed their human populations. Gathering in favourite trees in huge, murmuring masses, their gurgling, whistling, clacking cacophony can drown out even the sound of traffic on busy streets. Flocks often suddenly explode into the air, hundreds or even thousands of the squat, stubby-tailed birds swirling, ascending or diving as one, eventually settling on another group of trees or buildings.

Starlings, in effect, talked their way into North America. Members of the same family as the more renowned talking myna bird from India, starlings too have impressive vocal abilities and commonly mimic the calls of other birds as well as cats, dogs, flutes, chimes and machine sounds. They were originally grassland birds and became commonplace around the farms and cities of the ancient world, where they were taught by the Romans to speak Latin words and phrases, with proper gender and tenses. In Shakespeare's *Henry IV*, after the king forbids the name of his rival, Edmund Mortimer, to be uttered, the defamed earl's ally, Henry Percy, malevolently jests:

> I'll have a starling shall be taught to speak
> Nothing but 'Mortimer,' and give it him
> To keep his anger still in motion.

This brief mention on stage bought the starling a ticket to America. In 1890, a wealthy drug manufacturer, Eugene Schieffelin, released about 60 imported starlings in New York's Central Park in his project to establish all of the birds mentioned in the plays of Shakespeare in the United States. It was a classic example of romantic human ignorance resulting in ecological disaster.

While Schieffelin's attempts to introduce nightingales, skylarks, song thrushes and chaffinches all failed, his starlings began their invasion of North America in earnest, symbolically building a nest within weeks of their Central Park release under the eaves in the tower of the nearby American Museum of Natural History. Prospering, multiplying and spreading forth, they crossed onto the Niagara Peninsula in 1914 and nested for the first known time in Ontario in 1922, at Burlington. Ten years later, they were already the most common bird in many southern areas of the province.

Starlings had a devastating impact on native birds. Cavity nesters, already hard hit with competition from alien house sparrows for natal spaces, met an even more formidable adversary in the glossy-black, dagger-billed bruisers. Starlings will evict flickers, larger than themselves, from their newly chiselled chambers and eat purple martin eggs, nestlings and parents before claiming their apartments in multistoreyed bird boxes. Bluebirds, tree swallows, red-headed woodpeckers, great-crested flycatchers and many others can lose their homes if their doorways are more than five centimetres (two inches) wide, allowing a starling to squeeze through.

In addition to nesting in tree cavities and bird boxes, starlings set up in almost any well-sheltered space with a good perch nearby from which to defend it. Recesses on the sides of houses, holes in soffits, vents, old mailboxes, even the interior of traffic lights are sometimes used. After securing a site during the winter, a male perches outside of it and advertises for a roommate. Glimmering in the sun in his iridescent breeding best, hunching low, ruffling his neck feathers and fluttering his wing tips, he pours forth a continuous stream of whistles and clicks, squeals and twitters and all manner of acoustics. By vibrating either side of his syrinx – the vocal organ at the bottom of a bird's windpipe – independently from the other, the balladeer can make two different sounds at the same time. It may not be the prettiest of bird-songs, but it's certainly one of the most complex. The most versatile vocalists are the most successful in love.

Name origin: *Starling*, meaning "little star," may refer to the four-pointed star shape of the bird in flight or to starry speckles on its winter plumage

Name for a group: A murmuration of starlings

Whereabouts: Throughout city and suburbs, fields, forest edges

Territory: 50 cm (20 in) around nest hole defended; parents usually forage within 180–450 m (197–492 yd) of nest

Food: 40–60% insects, especially beetle grubs and adults, grasshoppers, crickets, caterpillars, and wood lice; also earthworms, millipedes, slugs, snails, spiders, weed seeds, berries and other fruits, corn, grain, buds, human food scraps, carrion

Average daily helping: 7–23 g of invertebrates or 20–40 g of plant food

Nest: Grass, twigs, leaves, bark and scraps of garbage in a cavity with a 6–7-cm-wide (2.4–2.8-in-wide) entrance in a tree, post or side of a house, usually 3–8 m (10–26 ft) above ground

Parasitic mites per nest: Up to 8,000 in nests lined with pest-repelling green plants, and up to 780,000 in nests without

Average clutch: 4–6 brown-marked, light-blue or pale-green eggs, about size of peach pits

Incubation period: 11–13 days

Fledging age: 21–23 days

Age at first breeding: 2 years for most; 1 year for some females

Average annual survival: 35–45% in first year; 33–75% for adults

Lifespan: Up to 21 years in wild

Predators: Cats, dogs, rats, weasels, sharp-shinned hawks, owls, peregrine falcons; nests raided by squirrels

Urban population density: Often 100–1,000 nests per km² (0.4 sq mi)

Notable starling roosts: Burlington Skyway Bridge, Windsor's Ambassador Bridge, Toronto's Bloor Street Viaduct and Gardiner Expressway

Estimated North American population: More than 200 million

Literature in which starlings play important parts: *A Sentimental Journey through France and Italy* by Laurence Sterne; *Headhunter* by Timothy Findley; *Pilgrim at Tinker Creek* by Annie Dillard

Greatest starling accident: About 6 in a flock of 20,000 were sucked into a jet engine in 1960 near Boston causing it to crash, killing 62 people

Nesting range: Throughout Ontario; also in all other provinces and territories

Winter whereabouts: Most remain in nesting range; some migrate to central United States

Starling family members native to Ontario: Mockingbird, grey catbird and brown thrasher

Number of starling family species worldwide: 114

Also see: House Sparrow, Flicker, Red-winged Blackbird

Legend has it that Mozart's pet starling influenced him in composing the aria "Trostlos schluchzet Philomele," or a least learned to whistle the tune. Some experts also believe that the great composer's bizarre divertimento for sextet (K. 522), nicknamed the Musical Joke, was really a replication of a starling's intertwining of off-key whistled snatches of song, noting that Mozart wrote the piece eight days after he held a funeral, with memorial hymns and poetry, for his dark-feathered muse in 1784.

A beseeching starling bachelor also often holds a long stalk of grass in his beak to let females know he already has a furnished pad. When the little lady moves in, around late March, she usually tosses out most of the material he's sloppily assembled and remodels the space into a proper feather- and down-lined nest. She also continuously replenishes the cavity with green sprigs of yarrow, fleabane, wild carrot or similarly strong scented plants whose chemical compounds ward off nest parasites such as fly maggots, mites, ticks, fleas and bird lice.

With the eggs laid in April or May, fathers help with the incubation for about a third of the daylight hours. Mothers sit tight on the nests the rest of the time. On average, parents feed the nestlings insects, especially lawn grubs and caterpillars, about once every three minutes. A week or so after the young fledge, around June, many couples build a new nest and start a second family.

As the breeding season ends in late summer, starlings gather in big, noisy flocks, feasting on grasshoppers and crickets in fields and roosting in large trees, under bridges or around buildings. In early autumn, their beaks fade to grey and they moult into white-speckled winter coats. Most remain in southern Ontario for the winter, switching to evergreen tree roosts, warming themselves on chimney tops and adeptly prying open spaces in cold or frozen turf beneath the snow to find dormant grubs and other sleeping insects. Some join large massings of red-winged blackbirds, grackles and cowbirds to migrate south. They usually start returning in February. About the same time, starling beaks turn yellow and the white tips of their feathers wear off, putting them in shimmering breeding form once again.

YELLOW WARBLER
Stunning Streamside Songster

THE VAIN VERSE of urban Ontario's most abundant warbler seems to boast "sweet, sweet, sweet. I'm so sweet!" The author of the rapid, ringing, oft-repeated song is a striking lemon-yellow bird with rich, rusty breast streaks. Appropriately christened the yellow warbler, the euphonious songster haunts shrubby streamsides that run through suburbs and into the hearts of many cities. Nearby backyards with lots of shrubs and trees also attract yellow warblers and sometimes even cradle their nests.

There are more brightly coloured summer wood warblers than any other group of birds in the vast forests that cover most of Ontario. But not many of the insectivorous, mostly tropical migrants regularly nest in built-up areas. Of the feisty few, the yellow warbler is far less reticent to show its colours than most of its reclusive, skulking kin. The best time to see one is in early May, when males perch on prominent, still mostly bare branches to boldly croon for perspective mates, who usually arrive nine or 10 days after them. Later, when their spouses begin nesting in June, fully leaved trees make the singers harder to see, they call out less frequently and use a shorter, less emphatic version of their song to mark their territorial borders.

Nesting females are especially inconspicuous. They weave their tiny, tidy nursery cups well concealed, low in the shrubbery, and seldom leave once they start to incubate their eggs. Later, parents feed the young every few minutes, stuffing them with their own weight in caterpillars and other insects every day. The high-protein diet turns hatchlings into fledglings in less than two weeks.

Frequently, however, one member of the brood turns out to be an almost grotesquely oversized, loud-mouthed

Maximum daily number of songs sung by a male: 3,240

Portion of young sired by extra-marital matings: One-third in one Ontario study

Length: 12–13 cm (4.7–5.1 in)

Weight: 9–11 g (0.3–0.4 oz)

Wingspan: 20 cm (8 in)

Alias: Yellowbird, golden warbler, wild canary, *la paruline jaune, Dendroica petechia*

Markings: Males rusty-streaked lemon-yellow undersides, yellow head; greenish-yellow to olive back, wings and tail; females and juveniles usually without or only faint breast streaks and often greener on back

Calls: Loud, variable song, usually with 5 or 6 syllables, often inflected up near end; also musical "chip" calls

Whereabouts: Usually in trees, often willows, along edges of streams, ponds, scrubby fields, wetlands and backyards

Food: Caterpillars, beetles, midges, grasshoppers, aphids, plant lice, wasps, other insects and spiders; occasionally berries

Nest: Tight, neat cup, 4.5–9 cm (1.8–3.5 in) wide, 4.5–11 cm (1.8–4.3 in) deep, of grass, stems and shredded bark; lined with seed down, feathers and fur; usually in an upright fork of willow, hawthorn, cedar, dogwood or raspberry canes, 0.9–1.5 m (3–5 ft) above ground

Average clutch: 4–5 raspberry-sized, cream-coloured or light-green eggs with brown, grey or olive spots or splotches

Incubation period: 11–12 days

Fledging age: 8–10 days

Age at first breeding: 1 year old

Average annual survival for most adult warblers: Less than 50%

Lifespan: Few live more than 2 years; up to 8 years

Predators: Cats, weasels; nests raided by raccoons, foxes, skunks, squirrels, crows, blue jays, garter snakes

Nesting range: All Ontario and Canada below treeline

Average first arrival in southern Ontario: Late Apr.

Average last departure from southern Ontario: Late Sept.

Winter whereabouts: Mexico and West Indies to Bolivia

Number of warbler species nesting in Ontario: 34

Number of warbler species worldwide: 115

thug that bares little resemblance to its siblings. The lout, in fact, is a freeloading imposter. Yellow warblers, together with song sparrows, are the most common victims of the brown-headed cowbird, a rogue that lays its eggs in other species' nests and then disappears. The alien nestling usually hatches first, grows faster and aggressively elbows its foster siblings out of the way at feeding time, sometimes pushing them out of the nest.

Cowbirds developed their devious parasitic nest strategy because they were once high-plains drifters, following roving buffalo herds to devour the bugs and seeds kicked up by their hooves. They didn't have time to stay put to raise a family. When the bison were slaughtered to near extinction by Buffalo Bill and his ilk, the cowbird simply switched its focus to cattle and spread east with the opening of forests to farmland. Sooty-grey female cowbirds – only the males have brown heads – take little more than a minute to slip into a temporarily vacant nest, toss out one of its eggs and lay one of their own in its place. But if a female yellow warbler catches one in the act, or even near the nest, she clues in to the dirty deed. Though a cowbird egg is too big for her to lift out, if she hasn't already laid most of her own eggs, she builds a new floor over all of the eggs, so they will never be incubated, and starts a new clutch on top. Yellow warbler nests have been found with up to five false floors covering abandoned eggs.

When all the nesting drama is finally over, yellow warblers don't stick around for long. They're one of the first songbirds to initiate fall migration, most leaving for the tropics in August as the caterpillars and other insects they glean from leaves and branches diminish in numbers. Having the greatest range of any warbler, they're joined by other yellows from as far north as Labrador and Alaska in vast unseen fronts of migrants passing high overhead in the late-summer night sky.

Creepy-Crawlies

AS THE MOST successful group of animals to roam and fly around the Earth, insects can hardly be expected to consider cities off limits. They are everywhere, in gardens, on trees, beneath the water, under asphalt, inside houses and in the air, comprising the vast majority of all things that fly. With close to one million insect species known worldwide, and perhaps tens of millions more to be identified, their ranks include specialists operating in almost every imaginable microhabitat, from birds' nests to home libraries.

Many insects – such as butterflies, ladybugs and dragonflies – are much admired for their beauty when they visit backyards and are spotted in parks and fields. Others, including cockroaches, clothes moths, carpenter ants and termites, are among the most unwelcome home intruders. Yet, for all the negative attention pest species receive, we have far more insect friends than generally realized, including legions of pollinating bees and flies, as well as predatory wasps, beetles and bugs that keep pest insects in line. Other insects are key agents of decomposition and major links in the food chain. The vast majority play vital ecological roles that we are only beginning to understand.

Spiders too are extremely important predators of insects, though underappreciated in human company. Together with earthworms, they are among the most widely recognized non-insect creepy-crawlies in the city. Others include centipedes, mites, sowbugs and many more tiny animals that go about their daily lives in untold multitudes throughout the city.

ANTS
Strength in Numbers

F OR ANTS, CITYSCAPES are just another part of the vast and varied assortment of landforms over which they claim domain. One of the most recently evolved and successful insect families, they're by far the most abundant six-legged things on Earth, estimated to equal collectively the weight of all humanity. From grasslands to tropical jungles and northern forests, they make up about 10 percent of the total animal biomass. Ants hunt down more insects, spiders and other creepy-crawlies than any other predators. They collect more than 90 percent of all insect corpses and turn up more soil than earthworms, making immense volumes of nutrients available for terrestrial ecosystems.

Many ants also forage for leaves, seeds and nectar, cultivate subterranean fungi, "milk" and tend other insects like livestock and enslave or con other kinds of ants to work for them. They form essentially female societies, most only producing a small number of males, equipped with wings, together with winged potential queens, once a year. Most drones are picked off by predators after leaving the nest in nuptial swarms. The rest die soon after mating. Fertilized females shed their wings, crawl beneath stones or other debris and lay eggs to start a new colony of mostly sterile female workers. Chemical communication is the key to their success, with varying pheromones from scent glands identifying fellow nest-mates, marking colonial boundaries, signalling alarm and eliciting mouth-to-mouth feeding. Workers lay down scent trails on foraging trips that mark the way back home and lead others to food.

Among the most common troopers marching along urban sidewalks, patios and backyards, especially at night, are dark, sesame-seed-sized **pavement ants**. Possibly introduced in colonial times from Europe in cargo-ship ballast sand, they forage up to nine metres (30 feet) from nest entrances between concrete slabs or at the edges of asphalt and cracks in walls. Workers scavenge for other insects, collect seeds, tap sap from roots and stems, drink sweet honeydew excreted by aphids and sometimes dine on spattered grease, spilled sugar and other foods inside houses.

Another ant of similar size and habits is responsible for many of the familiar sand-crater nest mounds that multiply through the summer on lawns, roadsides and golf courses. Known as the **turf-grass ant**, it's also sometimes called the Labour Day ant because it often swarms by the thousands to mate on humid afternoons after a good rain in late August or early September.

Slightly smaller, reddish **pharaoh ants** are even more persistent indoor pests, eating all manner of human foods, as well as silk, rayon, rubber and sponge. Originally stowaways from Africa or tropical Asia, they commonly nest in small cavities inside furniture, boxes, between floors, or behind baseboards. The closely related **little black ant** also often shows up in houses. But far more vexing are staple-sized black **carpenter ants** (illustrated), building to colonies of 3,000 or more. The tree-dwellers are drawn to damp, easy-to-chew wood, often around leaky plumbing, windowsills, door frames and plugged eavestroughs. Rather than eating wood, they expel small piles of sawdust and shavings as they bore honeycombed nest galleries, from which they forage for other insects, nectar, honeydew and household food scraps. Fixing the leaks and puffing boric acid powder into cracks and crevices is about the least-toxic means of control.

chambers for eggs, larvae, pupae, food stores, refuse, aphid pens and growing fungi

Eggs: Usually white, round, microscopic to pinhead-sized, stuck together in clumps; most species hatch in 3–4 weeks

Larvae: Whitish, glistening, legless; most complete growth in 3–4 weeks

Pupae: Transform into adults in white, parchmentlike cocoons over 3–6 weeks

Lifespan: Pharaoh ant workers live only a few weeks as adults, while workers of many other common species can live 1–3 years; most queens can live more than 5 years

Predators: Many birds, amphibians, mammals and insects

Bites and stings: Bites cause burning irritation because ants spray wounds with formic acid from their abdomens; a fraction of Ontario species, such as pavement ants, also have stingers but are not aggressive

Slave societies: Several Ontario ants, with red heads and midsections, raid the nests of close relatives and carry off their larvae and pupae, which are raised to work obediently for and feed their new masters

Winter whereabouts: Most species dormant inside nests

Range: Throughout Canada to a little beyond the treeline

Number of Ontario ant species: 93

Number of ant species worldwide: About 10,000 named; probably 10,000 more unnamed

Also see: White Trillium, Termites

BEES, WASPS & HORNETS
Societies of Heavily Armed Females

G ENERALLY CONSIDERED ARMED and dangerous, even when they keep to themselves, bees, wasps and hornets are traditionally the most feared of the city's diminutive inhabitants. Their stingers, perhaps the ultimate symbol of feminine power, are modified ovipositors, or egg-laying tubes, used by most insects to deposit eggs with accuracy. Stingers instead inject venom while sawing through the skin with tiny barbs. Honeybee stingers are so barbed, they often break off while being pulled out, leading to the death of the bee. Bumblebees, wasps and hornets, on the other hand, can live to sting again. Hornets are reputed to be particularly painful, though yellow jackets are more aggressive and more likely to administer multiple stings. With only the females bearing such awesome weapons, there's little wonder that social bees and wasps form solidly matriarchal societies.

Wasps comprise a very large group, or order, of insects, within which bees are really only one relatively small, unique family. Unlike most of the others (including hornets and yellow jackets), bees are strictly vegetarians, living on flowers. Over millions of years, bees evolved in tandem with flowering plants, forming one of the most vital links in nature. Flowers produce nectar solely for the purpose of attracting bees and like-minded creatures. Their sweet fragrances and bright colours are designed to advertise their wares to insects, which pick up and spread pollen as they buzz from one flower to the next. Plants help ensure their own survival by taking turns, blooming in succession, one species after another through the year, which allows bees and others to stay fed and get around to them all.

Among the first hardy pollinators to appear in early spring are husky, densely furred bumblebee queens (illustrated). Their insulation allows them to be active in temperatures too cool for most other species, though they often avoid the midday heat. After hibernating alone all winter beneath the ground or within a crevice in a building foundation, a bumblebee queen searches out silver maple flowers, willow catkins and other early blossoms for protein-rich pollen needed to produce eggs. Having mated and obtained a year's supply of sperm the previous fall, she builds a small wax-chambered nest in the ground, often in an abandoned mouse hole or under a tree stump, and lays eight to 10 eggs.

Some 20 to 30 days later, the larvae have hatched, grown, pupated and become working adults. These infertile female bumblebee workers take over the tasks of collecting nectar and pollen, enlarging the nest and serving as nannies for another generation of young. The queen concentrates on laying more eggs.

Toward the end of summer, when the colony has grown to 100 to 400 bumblebees, the queen lays a batch of unfertilized eggs that hatch into male drones. Other late eggs, which are given large chambers, extra food and special care, become new queens. The sole job of the drones is to leave the nest, establish territories and mate with young queens that come their way. They die soon afterwards. The workers in the colony, along with the old queen, also perish with the killing frosts of fall. Only young, fertilized queens, after loading up on nectar from goldenrods, asters and other late-blooming flowers, survive by crawling beneath the ground for the winter, the future of a whole new colony resting with them.

The other major colonial nesting bee in Ontario is the honeybee. Its colonies of up to 80,000, usually in tree cavities and crevices, are like permanent cities, persisting through the winter, sometimes lasting for years or even

Average amount of honey in a bumblebee nest: About a teaspoon

Number of calories burned by a flying bumblebee per minute: 0.5

Average lifespan of a bumblebee worker: About 4 weeks

Lifespan of honeybee queen: Usually 2–3 years, up to 5 years

Average lifespan of a honeybee worker (from hatching as a larva): 6–8 weeks

Average honeybee length: 1–1.6 cm (0.4–0.6 in)

Honeybee markings: Striped black or brown and yellow abdomen, mostly black head and thorax

Temperature at which honeybees become active: 15°C (59°F)

Suicidal liaisons: With thousands of male honeybees for every queen, very few get a chance to mate, and those that do die instantly for their success, their reproductive organs exploding upon contact

Foraging trips required to make 1 g (0.03 oz) of honey: About 60

Number of honeybee lifetimes required to produce a teaspoon of honey: 12

Maximum lifetime distance a honeybee worker travels: 800 km (500 mi)

Amount of honey needed by an average honeybee colony to get through the winter: 25 kg (55 lb)

Annual honey production of a commercial beehive: More than 50 kg (110 lb)

decades. Honeybees survive the cold months on large stores of honey, made from nectar. Huddling together for warmth, they conserve their energy and live longer than quickly burned-out summer honeybee workers.

Until sugar became widely available in the past few centuries, honey was Europe's main sweetener. Indo-European peoples learned the art of domestic beekeeping, or apiculture, more than 4,000 years ago, and brought the first honeybee colonies with them to North America in the early 1600s. Native peoples called honeybees the white man's flies. The bees spread quickly into the wild, since queens frequently lead swarms from crowded nests to start new colonies in late spring or early summer, leaving pupal heirs behind to assume their old thrones. Since 1984, however, much of North America's wild honeybee population has been devastated by parasitic mites from Europe.

Some wasps are also colonial. Bald-faced hornets and yellow jackets, both members of the same family of wasps, have life cycles very similar to bumblebees. Hornets – which specialize in killing flies – and aerial yellow jackets build the familiar large, grey, oblong aerodromes that become noticeable among bare tree branches in autumn and winter. They are the original paper producers, chewing wood fibre into sheets of saliva-soaked pulp that dries into the fine, grey paper walls of their nests. Starting out small, the nest expands in progressive layers as the colony grows through the summer. Paper wasps use the same material, but their umbrella-shaped nests consist of an unwalled, single-layer comb of paper cells suspended by a central stalk from a tree branch or beneath a house ledge.

Other kinds of yellow jackets usually construct their spherical nests in cavities dug underground, or inside cracks in the walls and eaves of houses. Several of these species are primarily scavengers of dead insects and carrion, which provide protein for their larval siblings. For themselves, adult yellow jackets sup on nectar, ripening fruits, aphid honeydew and any other sweet food sources. These are the wasps that raid picnics, backyard barbecues and open garbage pails in late summer, when their numbers are peaking. German

---

Honeybee colony population: 40,000–80,000 in summer; 5,000–20,000 in winter

Average yellow jacket colony population: 2,000–4,000 by end of summer

Yellow jacket length: 1.2–1.8 cm (0.5–0.7 in)

Yellow jacket markings: Smooth, bright yellow-and-black bodies

Wasp food: Insects, spiders, insect eggs, nectar, plant tissues and juices, honeydew

Bald-faced hornet length: 1.2–2 cm (0.5–0.8 in)

Bald-faced hornet markings: Black body with white markings on abdomen and head

Bald-faced hornet colony population: 100–600 by late summer

Only true hornet species in Ontario: European hornet, 3 cm (1.2 in) long

Paper wasp length: 1.5–2 cm (0.6–0.8 in)

Paper wasp markings: Black, brown or amber body with two large reddish spots on sides of abdomen, very thin waist and long legs

Paper wasp colony population: 30–50

Length of wasp and yellow jacket stingers: About 4 mm (0.16 in)

Mud dauber length: 3–3.5 cm (1.2–1.4 in)

Sweat bees: Small metallic green bees, some species attracted to human sweat, may sting if touched but not as painful as major stingers

Carpenter bees: Resemble bumblebees but chew holes

yellow jackets, an introduced species that took hold in Ontario around 1975, are particularly aggressive and have become the most common yellow jacket species in urban areas, being long adapted to city life in Europe.

Entomologists – bug experts – liken each selfless member of an insect colony to a single cell of an organism. The vast majority of bees and wasps, however, are solo flyers, hunting or foraging alone and very rarely ever stinging humans.

Most wasps are parasitoids, using non-stinging ovipositors to inject their eggs into or on live insects, many of which are harmful to garden plants and trees. Spider wasps and sand wasps, on the other hand, dig holes in the ground for their eggs and stock them with flies, spiders or caterpillars they have paralyzed with their stings. When the larvae hatch, their food is laid out in front of them, fresh, alive and immobile. Mud dauber wasps work the same way, building numerous mud chambers, often stuck on the walls of houses, and leaving several spiders and one egg in each.

Many species aren't readily recognizable as wasps. A large number are extremely small. Others are coloured black and white, or completely black. Spider wasps spend most of their time running along the ground rather than flying. At the same time, hover flies, bee flies and clear-winged moths look like bees or wasps, having evolved to imitate the bright colours that warn birds and animals to stay away from many stinging insects.

0.6–1.2 cm (0.25–0.5 in) wide in wood to lay eggs provisioned with pollen

Parasitoid ichneumon wasp length: Up to 4 cm (1.6 in)

Smallest wasps: Fairyflies, which parasitise insect eggs, as small as 0.2 mm (0.01 in)

Bee and wasp predators: Spiders, bee flies, robber flies, flycatchers, skunks, mice, raccoons

Portion of world's crops pollinated by bees: About 75%

Portion of world's crops pollinated by wasps: About 5%

Other common pollinators: Hover flies (a.k.a. flower flies), bee flies; many members of the longhorn, soldier and checkered beetle families; moths and butterflies

Range of bees and wasps: All Ontario and rest of Canada to the Arctic Circle

Portion of Ontario bee species that are solitary: More than 90%

Number of Ontario bee species: About 200

Number of Ontario yellow jacket species: About 15

Number of bee species worldwide: About 30,000

Number of species of bees, wasps, ants and sawflies worldwide: At least 108,000

Also see: Ants, White Trillium, Red Oak, Lawn & Garden

CABBAGE WHITE BUTTERFLY
Familiar Backyard Flutterer

WHILE UNDOUBTEDLY the plain Janes of their kind, cabbage whites are usually the most abundant of urban butterflies, flitting erratically about backyards and garden flowers from mid-April until the killing frosts of autumn. Like many of the most common city dwellers, they're from the other side of the Atlantic, and are among the few butterflies to be considered pests. Perhaps sailing with provisions of cabbages on immigrant ships, the small newcomers with the black-dotted wings disembarked at Quebec City in 1860 and in little more than 25 years spread through farms and vegetable gardens all the way to the Rockies and Gulf of Mexico.

The cabbage white's close association with humans probably began with the domestication of the wild progenitor of broccoli, cabbage and cauliflower around 5000 B.C. in southern Europe. Little green cabbage white caterpillars relish all manifestations of cabbage as well as the other plants in the mustard family, blending almost imperceptibly with their leafy fare. Two to five weeks after hatching, they fasten on to stems and pupate for about 11 days. Adults are short-lived. Males fly for up to two and a half weeks. Females last only about three days. But their numbers build through the year, with those flying in October the descendants of grandparents or great-grandparents that emerged in early spring.

Adult female cabbage whites spend most of the little time they have laying eggs, each spaced out on its own on the undersides of leaves. Once mated, they spurn the advances of additional suitors by characteristically spiralling up as high as 18 metres (59 feet) until the Johnny-come-latelies lose interest.

A member of the same butterfly family, the **clouded sulphur**, looks a little like the cabbage white and is also common in suburban yards and meadows from mid-May to October. Its wings are lemon yellow on top, with black borders and two black spots, and whitish with a couple of dark-rimmed white spots on the bottom. Some females, especially in spring and autumn, are white on the upper surface of their wings as well. They lay their eggs on white clover, alfalfa and other legumes.

As relatively unadorned as whites and mustards may be, their flitting, bouncing, light-as-air flight still holds the whimsical butterfly essence that has captivated human imagination from the dawn of time. In a famous Taoist parable, the protagonist Chuang Tzu awakens after dreaming he was a butterfly and becomes perplexed at the thought that he doesn't know whether he was really sleeping or if he himself is the figment of the butterfly's dream. Because butterflies transform and emerge from a deathlike pupal state, they were associated with immortality and the spirits of the deceased in cultures around the world. The ancient Greeks used the same word, *psyche*, for both the soul and butterflies. The Aztec mother goddess of love, art and beauty, Xochiquetzal, was depicted in the form of a swallowtail butterfly who gave comfort to warriors killed in battle.

An Ojibway story tells of how butterflies were created after the first humans – a pair of twins – were born. The children would not learn to walk, so the Great Spirit told their benefactor, Nanabush, to collect colourful stones in the western mountains and throw them in the air. The stones became butterflies, followed Nanabush back to the twins and, by staying just beyond their grasp, enticed them to sit up, walk and run for the first time.

long, with thin, sharp edges

Caterpillar mortality: Many battered and drowned by rain when very young and tiny; a virus commonly kills two-thirds of older larvae

Pupa mortality: About one-third commonly killed by parasitic insects

Predators: Birds, ambush bugs, parasitic flies and wasps

Best senses: Sight and smell; chemoreceptors on antennae and leg tips direct butterflies to their preferred nectar sources and pheromone emissions of the opposite sex; butterflies cannot hear

Winter whereabouts: As a chrysalis attached to plant stems

Range: All Ontario; also in all other provinces and southern Nunavut

Vegetables developed from wild cabbage plant: Head cabbage, cauliflower, broccoli, Brussels sprouts, kale

Only other Ontario butterfly caterpillar considered a pest: European skipper, eats timothy grass in hayfields

Also see: Monarch Butterfly, Moths, Butterfly Gardens

CICADA
The Sound of the Heat

The crickets creak, and through the noonday glow,
That crazy fiddler of the hot mid-year,
The dry cicada plies his wiry bow
In long-spun cadence, thin and dusty sere.
– Archibald Lampman, "Among the Timothy"

THE LOUDEST INSECTS on Earth, cicadas are set off like whistling kettles on the hottest days of summer. Their long, raucous treetop buzz, rising with the temperature, is an exultation of lust terminating years of silent, solitary subterranean existence. Flat-headed and as thick as a thumb, a male cicada is an enormous insect, but most of his cone-shaped abdomen is hollow and resonates, like an empty pop can being clicked, when a pair of tightly flexed membranes beneath the wings pop in and out hundreds of times per second. The resulting sound, roughly likened to the high-pitched whine of a mini-circular saw cutting into a board, beckons females from far and wide to the noise-maker's perch.

The object of fascination through the ages, the cicada's song delighted Socrates and stumped Galileo. It turns up as a recurring theme in ancient Greek culture from Homer's *Iliad* on down. Around 700 B.C., the pastoral poet Hesiod wrote that the constant, ubiquitous, shrill serenade of the sun-scorched Mediterranean summer marked the time to knock off work, find a shady tree and drink wine.

At the same time, the emergence of cicada nymphs from the ground to burst from their juvenile shells into winged adults also made them symbols of resurrection, rebirth and immortality for the Greeks and Romans. To China's Taoists, the transformation represented the departure of the soul from the body at death.

Cicada nymphs start out as ant-sized creatures, hatching in wooden natal chambers created by the long, sharp ovipositor at the end of their mother's abdomen, which she uses like a tiny keyhole saw to cut slits into low twigs on trees and shrubs, especially pines. Plunging to the ground, the hatchlings dig below the surface in search of tender, juicy tree rootlets, which they siphon for sap with their pointy snouts. The most widespread and commonly heard species in Ontario cities, the appropriately named dogday cicada remains underground, usually within a metre (3.3 feet) of the surface, sucking and growing for seven or more years.

Around early July, burly, fully grown dogday nymphs begin resurfacing from pinky-sized holes at night and crawling up trees. Fastening themselves to secure spots, often on the trunk, they take about an hour to break free from their old nymphal husk, emerging moist and immaculate from a split in the back. It takes a few more hours for their new black-and-green armour to harden and for their wings to inflate. Males usually space themselves well apart and belt out their harsh, swelling entreaties on afternoons when the thermometer hits 25°C (77°F) or higher. Some often continue well into September.

While dogday cicadas call every summer, a population of periodic cicadas in the Grand Bend area appears only once every 17 years, most recently in 2004. In the eastern United States, where these smaller, red-eyed cicadas are much more common, mass emergences of millions in late spring produce clamouring, deafening choruses until early July, when the throngs die off.

Markings: Black with touches of green and tan; green-tinted clear wings

Alias: Dogday cicada, eastern dogday cicada, annual cicada, dogday harvestfly, *la cigale coniculaire*, *Tibicen canicularis*

Whereabouts: Trees in backyards, streetsides, parks, woods; nymphs live in the ground beneath the same trees

Food: Tree sap

Eggs laid per female: Probably several hundred; split into many batches, with a few laid in each slit in a series, about 2–3 cm (0.8–1.2 in) long, within dead twigs

Lifespan: At least 7 years; 1–2 months as adults

Predators: Cicada killer wasps, hornets, birds, raccoons, cats, moles

Winter whereabouts: Nymphs live at least 2.5 m (8.2 ft) deep in ground

Earliest known depictions of cicadas in art: 1700 B.C., in Chinese bronze

Dog days of summer: About Jul. 3 to Aug. 15, when the winter Dog Stars, Sirius and Procyon, are closest to the sun, which ancient Egyptians believed added to the solar orb's warmth, creating the heat of summer

Ontario's largest cicada: Scissor grinder cicada, up to 7 cm (2.8 in) long

Number of Ontario cicada species: 8

Number of cicada species worldwide: About 2,000

Also see: Grasshoppers & Crickets, Stars & Constellations

COCKROACH
Skittering Across the Ages

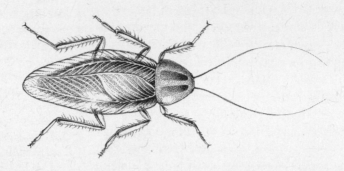

F OR MORE THAN 340 million years, cockroaches have endured by eating almost anything and skittering with lightning speed into the narrowest cracks and crevices whenever trouble looms. Long before the dinosaurs, the swampy fern-tree jungles of the Carboniferous era were virtually ruled by primordial cockroaches, which may have outnumbered all other winged insects. Though time and two cataclysmic die-offs have since profoundly altered the look of almost every living thing on Earth, history's most successful scavengers remain little changed from their oldest fossil records.

Cockroaches are so resilient, they're favoured modern lab-research subjects. The sacrifice for science seems a small price considering the huge boon humans have been for the spiny-legged, flat-bodied opportunists. Moving in with their benefactors and operating mainly at night, cockroaches are the most accomplished of pilferers. When cast in light, they scurry for cover on limbs reputed to be the fastest in the insect world. Their sticky feet carry them effortlessly up sinks, windows, walls and refrigerators, while their oily, waxy armour helps them squeeze into the tiniest, most inaccessible spaces.

Although Ontario has several native cockroach species, often called wood roaches, they live in forests under rocks, decaying bark and leaves and seldom enter houses. Home-intruding roaches, especially abundant in the province's biggest cities, are all accomplished stowaways that originated in the tropics or subtropics and rarely go outdoors. By far the most common, the German cockroach, is thought to have been transported along ancient trade routes from East Africa into southern Europe. In the centuries since, the adventurous omnivore has journeyed with cargo and food supplies to the ends of the Earth, establishing itself from the islands of the South Pacific to Canadian Forces installations at Alert, on the north coast of Ellesmere Island.

Domestic cockroaches seldom use their wings and still rely mainly on humans to shuttle them about, with cardboard boxes or cartons providing their preferred travelling accommodations. Most arrive in houses along with the groceries. They take hold where they have access to starchy foods, sweets, greasy residues and a steady supply of water from leaky taps and sweaty pipes. Under such conditions, a female German cockroach will lay up to eight batches of eggs in her seven-month lifespan. Cockroach nymphs look like small, squat, wingless versions of adults, often huddle in little herds and moult five to seven times over six or seven weeks before becoming sexually mature.

Cockroach infestations often leave a foul odour on food and packages from their droppings, saliva and moulted skins. The same excreta, carried in dust, is a leading allergen for humans in urban areas and is identified in some studies as a trigger for 40 to 50 percent of asthma sufferers. Cockroaches can also carry some 40 pathogens known to affect humans, including salmonella, *E. coli*, pneumonia, tuberculosis and typhoid, though they generally harbour far fewer germs than house flies. True to their indefatigable nature, they often develop resistances to many of the most common, and potentially hazardous, insecticides ranged against them, including diazinon and bendiocarb. Less-toxic weapons, such as boric acid and hydramethylnon bait stations, are effective, but keeping a squeaky clean kitchen and securing food in refrigerators and tightly sealed containers is probably the best way of keeping unwanted guests at bay.

cupboards and behind fridges, stoves, baseboards, door and window frames

Food: Almost any kind of human or animal food, dead or living vegetation, insects and their eggs, flakes of skin, fingernail clippings, leather, woollens, glue, wallpaper paste, books, paper, wine corks, ink, watercolour paints, plaster

Survival time without food: Up to 45 days

Eggs: 30–48 contained within a light-tan, rectangular egg case, 6–9 mm (0.25–0.33 in) long, carried partially sticking out of mother's abdomen for 4 or more weeks, until a few hours before hatching

Nymphal development period: 38–63 days

Lifespan: 3–7 months

Predators: Mice, cats, house centipedes, spiders

Intelligence: Cockroaches can memorize the routes of mazes, putting them among the smartest of invertebrates, not far behind octopi

Average frequency of breaking wind: Every 15 minutes

Range: Southern Ontario at least to Ottawa and Midland; also in Thunder Bay and in all other provinces and territories except Manitoba, New Brunswick and the Northwest Territories

Number of Ontario cockroach species: 5 introduced, 3 native

Number of cockroach species worldwide: At least 5,000 named; probably another 5,000 unnamed

DRAGONFLIES
A Mosquito's Worst Nightmare

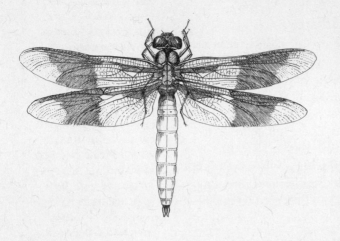

LONG ADMIRED in Japan as *katsumushi*, "the invincible insect," the dragonfly once adorned the swords and helmets of samurai warriors to ensure victory in battle. The earliest Japanese poetry tells of an irreverent horse fly that bit an early emperor and was then swiftly dispatched by a loyal dragonfly, prompting the grateful monarch to proclaim his realm as the Dragonfly Islands. Ancient Japanese entomological understanding seems considerably more advanced than notions once held in the West, where dragonflies were sometimes called horse stingers because they were often seen around skittish horses. In fact, the hovering behemoths don't sting, though they do tear into other insects, including biting marauders that drive both horses and humans to distraction.

From the moment they hatch in the water, dragonflies are fearsome predators. Their larvae, called nymphs, are stocky, crablike aquatic creatures that inhabit the muddy bottoms or weedy tangles of ponds, lake shallows, rivers and creeks. Like a living nightmare from the movie *Alien*, they have hooked, snap-action lower "lips" that spring forward in a fraction of a second to snatch other aquatic insects or even tadpoles and fish fry.

In late spring and summer, most often after sunset, fully grown nymphs crawl just above the surface on emergent plants or the water's edge and spend a couple of hours wiggling out of their juvenile skin. In the poem "The Two Voices," Alfred, Lord Tennyson, eloquently recounts the emergence of the adult dragonfly:

An inner impulse rent the veil
Of his old husk: from head to tail
Came out clear plates of sapphire mail.

He dried his wings: like gauze they grew;
Thro' crofts and pastures wet with dew
A living flash of light he flew.

Newly minted dragonflies rove widely through patches of urban meadows, ravines and woods, sometimes venturing into backyards in search of insect prey. After two or three weeks, they return to prime egg-laying waterside sites and establish mating territories. The cleaner the local ponds and watercourses, the greater the number and variety of dragonflies. For avid birders and butterfly listers, the broad-winged insects present a rich new frontier for their binocular viewing. Being most active, like butterflies, in the warm midday hours, dragonflies are especially appealing for nature admirers who like to sleep in.

The first dragonfly to appear in spring is usually the **green darner**, one of the largest, fastest and most common species in Ontario. Though most species overwinter as nymphs beneath the ice, some green darner populations migrate, flying south after cold fronts in early fall, often in large squadrons. Hundreds of thousands are known to congregate at spots along Lake Erie, such as Point Pelee. No one knows their main destinations, though they're known as far south as Central America. Like monarch butterflies, only their descendants return, starting around early May. Though the migrants mate, lay eggs and generally die off by mid-June, non-migratory green darners begin emerging soon after and fly through the summer. Then, after they dwindle away, the nymphs of the southbound population emerge to transform in September.

All of the large darner species constantly patrol their breeding territories for prey, mates and interlopers, usually cruising relatively high in the air along the edges of slow streams and ponds. In contrast, skimmer family species, among the most territorial and aggressive of dragonflies, generally dart low and erratically over the surface of the water. One male's domain may cover an entire small pond, or many may occupy a larger water body. A **common whitetail** (illustrated) – abundant throughout southern and central Ontario – may

Alias: Mosquito hawks, darning needles, horse stingers, snake charmers, *les libellules*, order Odonata; larvae called nymphs, naiads or bass bugs

Whereabouts: Various species specialize in meadows, ponds, slow or fast-flowing streams, lakeshores and wetlands

Food: Adults eat mosquitoes, black flies, deer flies, horse flies, midges, butterflies; nymphs eat other insect larvae, midges, butterflies, worms, snails, crayfish young, tadpoles, tiny fish

Average number of mosquito larvae eaten during nymph stage: 3,000

Best sense: Sight; huge eyes contain some 30,000 separate lenses, providing a 360-degree field of view and ability to see objects up to 15 m (49 ft) away; estimated 80% of brain is devoted to vision

Sunbathing: Dragonflies bask in the morning and shutter their wings to warm flight muscles enough to fly

Peak activity times: Midday, warm, sunny weather

Shady characters: A few species, such as shadow darners and fawn darners, fly in shade, on overcast days or at dusk

Eggs laid per female: About 500 to more than 3,300

Egg-development period: A few days to 9 months, depending on species; 1–4 weeks for most

Nymphs: 2–60 mm (0.08–2.4 in) long, various shades of plain to heavily patterned brown, green or yellow

Period spent as a nymph: A few months to a year for most species; nymphs in the Arctic may live up to a decade before transforming

Period spent as an adult: From a few days to about 10 weeks for most species; up to 6 months for some species

Winter whereabouts: Most species overwinter as inactive nymphs at the bottom of ponds, lakes and streams; some populations of green darners migrate south, others lay overwintering eggs

Predators: Red-winged blackbirds, swallows, kingbirds, kestrels, hawks, ducks, frogs, fish, robber flies, wasps, spiders; nymphs also eaten by giant water bugs and turtles

Earliest dragonfly depictions in art: Seal-stone engravings on Crete from 1500 B.C.

Range: Throughout Ontario; in all other provinces and territories

Damselflies: Also members of the Odonata order, differ from dragonflies in being more slender and having widely spaced eyes and a slower, more fluttering flight; dragonflies hold their wings horizontally when resting, while damselflies fold them in

Number of Ontario dragonfly and damselfly species: About 165

Number of regular migrant species in Ontario: At least 11

Number of dragonfly and damselfly species worldwide: 5,500–6,000

Also see: Mosquitoes

command anywhere from 17 to 150 square metres (20 to 180 square yards) over a shallow stream, pool or marsh. Scrambling from one of a number of oft-used perches, it engages in frequent but brief aerial dogfights with competitors, often accompanied by the loud sound of opposing wings thrashing together.

Dragonfly mating equipment is so varied and specialized, entomologists make no qualms about magnified examination of their private parts to make a positive ID on difficult species. Before mating, a male doubles over to deposit sperm from the tip of his tail into a special storage space beneath the base of his abdomen. When a receptive female arrives in his territory, they form an acrobatic circle with their two bodies, the male holding her head by the tip of his tail while the female's tail swings forward to take the sperm from his cargo hold. The act takes only a number of seconds. A female can store the sperm for a long time and go on to mate with other dragonflies. Since the last one to mate with her usually has the biggest share of offspring, a male often jealously guards his partner, remaining attached to her or flying just above, driving off competitors until she lays her eggs. Ambitious males may try guarding two mates at once.

Varying egg-laying methods are largely responsible for the naming of major groups of dragonflies. Female skimmers "skim" low over the water for four or five minutes as they drop their eggs, two dozen or more at a time, each sinking to the bottom to hatch. Darners use the sharp tip of their abdomens to slice open stems just beneath the surface of the water and deposit their eggs inside. Spiketail dragonflies swiftly dunk into the shallows to inject one egg at a time into the bottom, while in weedy waters, basket-tails drop just one big payload of eggs, which are strung together and become strewn over submerged vegetation.

EARTHWORMS
The Intestines of the Earth

ARISTOTLE PROCLAIMED earthworms the "intestines of the Earth." Darwin dubbed them "nature's ploughmen." He estimated they could turn over up to 10 tonnes of soil a year per hectare (2.5 acres), ultimately replacing the top three surface centimetres (one inch) every decade. Through digesting grains of sand along with any organic matter small enough to fit into their mouths as they move, earthworms excrete castings of soil compounds high in nitrogen, calcium, potassium and phosphorus that are delectable to plant life. Their tunnels also loosen and aerate the soil, opening up passages for rootlets and fungal strands and increasing the ground's ability to retain water.

Ontario, however, has not always been graced with earthworms and their works. In the 18,000 years since the glaciers of the last Ice Age began to recede from their maximum limits in the northern United States, plants and animals have gradually followed in their wake from the south. But earthworm populations, expanding at a maximum rate of about 10 metres (33 feet) a year, could not have wiggled their way back into Ontario in that time span from refuges beyond the reaches of Ice Age permafrost, somewhere deep in the American south. Instead, they arrived over the past 200 years or so, mostly from Europe, in soil holding imported

Population density: Up to more than 80 per m² (sq yd) in prime locations

Number collected annually in Ontario for bait and research: More than 1 billion

Longest Ontario earthworm: Nightcrawler (illustrated), 9–30 cm (3.5–12 in)

Smallest Ontario earthworms: Several species mature when less than 2 cm (0.8 in) long

Markings: Various species are brown, pink, red, purple, greenish, grey or whitish, many of them with lighter-shaded bellies

Alias: *Les vers*, oligochaetes

Name origin or *worm*: From proto-Indo-European *wrmi*, meaning "snake," possibly from the word *wer*, meaning "twist" or "turn"

Whereabouts: Rich, moist soils, compost, beneath rocks and aquatic plants in lakes and streams

Food: Decaying leaves, seeds and other vegetable and animal matter; micro-organisms

Worm sex: Each worm has both male and female organs in front of the distinct band called the clitellum, which produces a slime coating that fuses the sexual areas of two worms when they meet and exchange packets of sperm

Clutch: 1–20 eggs in a rubbery, yellow-brown case of hardened slime the size of a small pea

Egg-development period: 3–20 weeks

Age at first breeding: 3½–13 months

Lifespan: Most live less than 2 years; some live 4–10 years in captivity

Predators: Robins, starlings, killdeer, gulls, moles, shrews, mice, rats, skunks, garter snakes, red-bellied snakes, toads, salamanders, cluster fly larvae, beetle grubs, centipedes, ants

Severance survival: Back half may wiggle after cut off, but soon dies; front may survive and regenerate a new tail if it retains clitellum band and at least 10 segments back from it

Winter whereabouts: Below frost line, rolled in a ball

Range: Southern Ontario north to about Lake Abitibi; also in all other provinces

Number of Ontario earthworm species: 19

Number of earthworm species worldwide: More than 8,000

Also see: Ants, Robin, Starling, Ring-billed Gull, House Fly, Woods, Lawn & Garden

plants and used in ships for ballast. Before then, soil improvement chores were left to ants and other native subterranean creatures.

Worms remain most abundant in southern Ontario's farm land, cities and other human-altered habitats. Mounting evidence, however, suggests that they can adversely alter more natural settings, such as wooded parks and ravines. Because worms pull fallen leaves into their burrows to shred and devour, they significantly thin the forest litter layer, upon which many native plants, animals and fungi depend. Red-backed salamanders, sugar maple seedlings, trilliums, wild ginger and a dozen other common spring wildflowers generally dwindle or disappear in earthworm-invaded forests.

Avoiding the deadly, drying rays of the sun, worms generally wait until nightfall before rising to check for decaying delectables on the surface near the entrances of their burrows. The largest and best-known among their ranks is the nightcrawler, or dew worm, which dwells as deep as 1.8 metres (six feet) below ground during the day. The reddish-brown wriggler with the lighter, orangish belly is snatched by the millions on golf courses, sports fields and other prime grassy areas by nocturnal red-filtered-flashlight-wielding worm pickers who supply fishing bait dealers.

Much smaller, reddish-purple manure worms, also known as red wigglers, are also sold as bait, but are especially prized in composters. They normally dwell in the organic surface layer in urban yards and are even sold with increasingly popular vermicomposting bins that fit beneath the kitchen sink in apartments. Snuggled in a bedding of shredded paper or cardboard, red wigglers can consume about half their weight in food scraps a day, converting them into rich castings to fertilize house plants and window boxes. In an age of never-ending urban garbage crises, the intestines of the Earth are only too happy to lend their digestive prowess.

HOUSE & HOME
We Are Not Alone: Domestic Ecosystems
Include a Cast of Millions

AS MUCH AS nature may seem like an ideal that lies beyond city streets, all houses, apartments and other indoor confines contain their own ecosystems in which humans are just one of many species. And the more life we ourselves bring in and nurture – house plants, any number of pets and the odd brother-in-law – the more opportunities there are for unbeckoned lifeforms from without to join in. Squatting sparrows, starlings, raccoons and squirrels may be shut out, mice, cockroaches and ants scrupulously exterminated, but something else that has flown, crawled or been carried in will turn up sooner or later. Many more tiny, uninvited cohabitants, some beyond our perception, go undetected as we live our lives.

Silverfish   9–13 mm (0.35–0.5 in) long

Sometimes seen skittering across the bathroom or kitchen floor when a light is turned on, silverfish are carrot-shaped, silvery-grey insects with long antennae and three-pronged tails. They've been around for about 300 million years and never developed wings like the vast majority of insects. Craving warm and humid places, they squeeze through gaps where plumbing passes through walls and find comfortable lodgings beneath sinks and stoves, behind baseboards and inside closets and bookcases. A damp bathroom without an exhaust fan but plenty of reading material provides them with the best of all possible worlds, since they savour the glossy coatings of magazines, book-binding glue, dust shed by toilet-paper fibres and bits of lint from towels and clothes. The stealthful, silvery-scaled scroungers also eat flour, dry cereals and other starchy crumbs in the kitchen, though they can go without food for up to months at a time. Active year-round in heated environments, they lay several batches of seven to 12 white eggs every week, which hatch two to eight weeks later into nymphs that resemble their elders but may grow for more than two years before reaching adult size.

Bug name origin: In medieval England, *bug* meant "scarecrow," "ghost" or "goblin," from which came "bug-eyed, bogeyman, bugbear" and "bugaboo"; first applied to insects around the early 1600s when bedbugs and other terrifying little monsters from the tropics arrived on English shores with returning trading ships

Earwig **name origin:** From Old English *earwicga*, "ear insect"; *wicga* probably originates in the Germanic base word *wig*, from which also comes "wiggle"

Portion of Canadian homes harbouring fleas: About 12%

Number of flea larvae that can be raised in a teaspoon of house dust: 10,000

Earliest known reference to scholars as "bookworms": Early in 1st century A.D., by Philippus of Thessaloniki

Tropical centipede length: Up to 25 cm (10 in), with up to 362 legs

Delusory parasitosis: Association of rashes and bites with insects responsible for neither

Average number of daily droppings produced by a dust mite: 10–20

First appearance of mites: More than 400 million years ago

Number of lice species that feed on humans: 3

Number of sucking lice species worldwide: About 250

European Earwig (illustrated)   9–15 mm (0.35–0.6 in) long

Luckily, there's no truth behind the creepy folklore for which earwigs are named. They do not burrow into the ears of sleeping humans. Their fearsome-looking tail pincers are used for defence rather than boring out brains. The slender, shiny-brown omnivorous insects do like to crawl into dark, narrow cracks and crevices to take shelter during the day, usually in logs, under bark and leaf litter outdoors, where they hunt aphids, mites and other creepy-crawlies at night. They're also sometimes found inside flowers and under garden vegetable leaves, but generally eat more plant pests than plants themselves. Few people, though, find their vaguely crocodilian appearance endearing when earwigs take shelter indoors, seeking out warm, moist, dark refuges, slipping under doormats and settling into damp washcloths. The insects also probably get moved around a lot in potted plants and garden soil. They were first reported in Ontario in 1942, in a woodpile on the Bruce Peninsula. After spreading slowly across central Ontario, they started turning up in cities to the south in the early 1980s.

House Centipede   2.5–4 cm (1–1.6 in) long

Believed originally to hail from warm Mediterranean climes, the disconcertingly long-legged house centipede learned to live indoors in colder lands and reached Canada, probably from the United States, just prior to the First World War. The flat-bodied, splayed-legged creature frequents damp basements and bathroom drains. Despite its name – Latin for "100 feet" – the house centipede has only 30 legs, which it moves so rapidly, in a fuzzy blur, it seems like much more. The limbs are progressively longer from front to back, with the last pair outstretching the centipede's black-lined orangish body. At the other end, two antennae are equally far-reaching and used to feel out insect prey, including cockroaches. Though a centipede's venomous bite is likened to a wasp sting, it's very rarely applied to humans, generally only if the sprinting beast is captured and handled. Like many other household creepy-crawlies, it can go a long time between meals, making subsistence possible even where there are relatively few insects.

Millipedes have more cylindrical bodies than centipedes and much shorter legs, placed directly below them. They eat mainly decaying vegetation and fungi, have no venomous bite and often coil up when at rest. Most species have closer to 100 legs rather than the 1,000 suggested by their name. They usually don't come indoors except during very dry or rainy periods and usually die within a few days if they don't find food.

Whiteflies   1–2 mm (0.04–0.08 in) long

Hiding out on and sucking sap from the undersides of leaves, whiteflies rise up in a little cloud of pale flying specks when an infested house plant is given a shake. Stricken leaves develop white speckles, fade to pale green and yellow before eventually dropping off. Whitefly nymphs remain largely stationary suckers under waxy white secretions for three to five weeks before turning into winged, mini-mothlike adults, which may live up to another month. Like aphids – their little wingless relatives that occasionally come in from the garden to siphon house plants – they also excrete sticky honeydew that attracts black mould. Other sap-sippers that sometimes move indoors include thrips, which look like roving, dark, narrow specks, and slightly larger oval white mealy bugs and scale insects.

Boxelder Bug   10–15 mm (0.4–0.6 in) long

When the sun shines warmly on winter and early-spring days, red-trimmed black boxelder bugs often emerge from refuges in crevices in windowsills, attics and basements and fly about the house in anticipation of getting outdoors to lay their eggs. The attractive, red-eyed insects dine on Manitoba maple leaves and seeds and are also known as maple bugs. Their red nymphs hatch later in spring and gradually become more black as they grow. Swarms sometimes buzz around the outside walls of houses and buildings before they retire in autumn.

Carpet Beetles   2–5 mm (0.08–0.2 in) long

Several very tiny, oval carpet beetle species invade houses. As adults they feed on nectar and pollen and are often attracted through open windows to indoor flowers or are carried inside in bouquets from the garden. Females lay eggs in clumps of dust and lint collecting in air ducts, under baseboards and other nooks and crannies. In the wild, their wormy, bristly tailed offspring feed on fur, feathers and shed or dead insect exoskeletons in nests and burrows. In houses, they seek out hair, fur and woollens around the edges of rugs, inside closets, upholstered furniture and other hidden places. The grubs can also bore right through packaging to infest flour, cereals and other stored foods. Black carpet beetle grubs, the most common of their kind, are usually yellowish-brown and grow to about eight millimetres (a third of an inch) in five to 11 months before pupating into adults.

Cigarette Beetle   2.5–3 mm (0.1 in) long

Often inhabiting supermarkets and processing plants, a bevy of other confetti-sized beetles boldly squeeze and force their way into packaged foods to lay their eggs. Flour and other loose food particles adhere to the sticky bodies of their wiggling young, keeping them well concealed. Though they don't spread diseases, carpet beetle grubs do spoil food. Yellow-brown cigarette beetle larvae fill up on everything from cereals, rice, flax, pet food, nuts, candy and spices to dead leaves and the cigarettes and tobacco products for which they're named. They feast for three or four weeks before pupating into light-brown, oval adults that are attracted to lights. There may be up to six generations a year.

Drugstore beetles have a very similar look and lifestyle, but hold the dubious distinction of being able to down almost any pharmaceutical. The grubs of the likewise intriguingly named confused flour beetle have a taste for chocolate, dried fruit and beans.

Powder-post Beetles   1–7 mm (0.04–0.28 in) long

After hatching from eggs laid in the surface pores of unfinished hardwood, thread-thin powder-post beetle grubs may spend many months eating their way into floorboards, door and window frames, mouldings and, less often, furniture. After transforming into adults, usually in spring, they chew through to the surface and fly off to look for mates, leaving exit holes about the size of the tip of a ballpoint pen. Affected wood is riddled with tunnels filled with sawdust as fine as talcum powder. Most infestations begin in lumberyards with improperly seasoned wood.

Book Lice   1–4 mm (0.04–0.16 in) long

Though they definitely have a literary bent, book lice are not really lice at all, resembling the minute parasites only in size and their lack of wings. The pale-grey, fungus-feeding insects love nothing better than digging into an old, musty book in dark, dank basement cloisters, often damaging the bindings in the process. They also sup on mould and mildew spreading over damp papers, cupboards, windowsills, wallpaper and plaster. Small numbers are probably present in most houses, with populations jumping in humid summer weather.

Many other insect bibliovores are loosely referred to as "bookworms," including silverfish, the caterpillars of certain moths and cigarette, drugstore and wood-boring beetle grubs. These creatures are in turn chased through the pages by crab-clawed book scorpions no bigger than the periods at the end of sentences. Other tiny pseudoscorpion species, like true scorpions related to spiders, prey on insects throughout the house.

Fleas   1–4 mm (0.04–0.16 in) long

Lacking wings, but able to leap with explosive force more than 30 centimetres (one foot) straight up in the air, fleas hop aboard cats and dogs outdoors and may live for up to 18 months on the blood of their hosts. Females scatter eggs in the pets' fur, their bedding, under carpets and in tumbleweeds of dust and lint, where their white wormy larvae hatch and scavenge decaying bits of skin, parental droppings and dried blood. After one to five weeks, they spin silk cocoons in which they pupate into adults. Pupae may remain dormant for up to a year and then suddenly stir to action upon feeling the vibrations of an approaching potential host. They sometimes jump onto humans, biting around the feet and leaving itchy red bumps. Their slippery, hard, vertically flattened bodies are maddeningly hard to squash. Reproducing quickly in warm weather, populations peak in August and September.

Bedbug   4–7 mm (0.16–0.28 in) long

Sleeping tight and not letting the bedbugs bite was more than an idle jest in the 19th century, when the flat, oval, reddish-brown bugs were familiar in almost every home. Though far less prevalent today, the infamous night biters have made a bit of a come-back in recent years, attributed by some to ever-increasing numbers of people travel-ling abroad, who bring them home from hotels and motels in their suitcases. Others point to the popularity of yard sales, through which bedbugs stowed away in old furni-ture and electronics move from one house to another. Hiding by day in the folds and crevices of bed covers, mattresses, baseboards and wallpaper, the flightless bugs crawl upon their sleeping victims and commonly leave a line of several blood-crusted itchy bites and red streaks on sheets. A female lays up to 300 eggs over her lifetime. Nymphs mature in anywhere from six weeks to a year, depending on the blood supply, and may live up to 15 months without food.

Mites   0.1–30 mm (0.004–1.2 in) long

While large parasites such as bedbugs may be relatively uncommon, everybody har-bours their own personal ecosystem, featuring millions of bacteria, pollen grains and spores of mould and other fungi. More than 90 percent of us have hundreds of micro-scopic face mites – related to spiders and ticks – living harmlessly in pores and hair fol-licles around our eyebrows, eyelids, nose and ears. They feed on oily sweat gland secretions and dead skin cells.

A number of parasitic mites, some just barely visible, suck human blood and cause irritating rashes, but are uncommon in the home. Bird mites occasionally invade from nests in eaves or chimneys. Mange in dogs and cats is also caused by several types of follicle mites.

Tiny, pale, web-slinging spider mites infest house plants, gradually sapping their strength. Dust mites, on the other hand, are microscopic scavengers that throng in incredible numbers in every house, devouring minuscule flakes of skin constantly being shed by humans. An average of two million live in most beds and more than 15,000 in every square centimetre (0.15 square inches) of carpet. Their droppings are among the chief causes of indoor allergies and triggering asthma. Like most other little household critters, they thrive in humid conditions.

GRASSHOPPERS & CRICKETS
Late-Season Instrumentalists

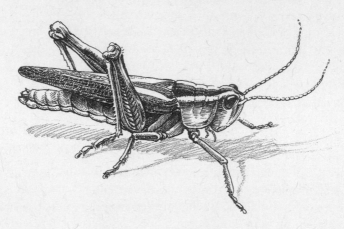

EVEN IN THE CITY, behind the din of noise and traffic, nature lays down its own backing tracks that gradually change throughout the year. As summer wears on, choirs of songbirds give way to insect instrumentalists. A discerning ear on a warm, sunny day or calm evening can often pick out a number of distinct stylings from within the symphony of grasshoppers and crickets rising from creeks and meadows. Each is strummed by a different species of wooing musical hopper whose particular song is only truly appreciated by a female of his own kind.

Grasshoppers perform during the day, cranking out rasping washboard rhythms by running their saw-toothed back legs along hardened veins in their folded forewings. After scattered early-summer warmups, their concerts hit full pitch around late July and continue until the first hard frosts of autumn. Band-winged grasshoppers, comprising a number of Ontario species, also put on aerial courtship displays, many making clicking, crackling or buzzing sounds by rubbing their wings together during short bursts of erratic flight. While most are drably attired, they unfold bright-yellow, orange or reddish hind wings when they fly, which may both attract mates and startle predators.

The big, grey-brown Carolina locust, which blends almost imperceptibly with bare patches of ground along dusty roadsides and bicycle paths, is perhaps the most commonly seen band-wing in Ontario cities. When the grasshopper, also known as the road duster, springs into air, it seems to turn into a fluttering butterfly, spreading 10-centimetre-wide (four-inch-wide), yellow-bordered black wings that can carry it for up to 21 metres (69 feet), or even farther in the wind.

Many other grasshoppers are silent. For **two-striped grasshoppers** (illustrated), common grazers of wildflower and garden plant leaves, mating is a matter of little sound but a lot of fury. When a male comes upon a member of the opposite sex, he unceremoniously hops on her back, though she's usually almost twice his size. The little guy has to hold on during her initial attempts to throw him. If he proves himself a steady rider, she acquiesces and accepts his packets of sperm, called spermatophores, released from the curled tip of his abdomen into hers. Mating lasts about 45 minutes for many species, though some may couple for up to a day and a half. Fertilized females store their sperm until late summer or early fall, when most lay multiple batches of eggs in bare patches of soil or at the base of tufts of grass. Each clutch has a frothy coating that hardens into a pod.

Female crickets, in contrast, appear quite eager to hook up with the first eligible bachelors they can find, and often come running in response to male serenades. Though members of the same group, or order, of insects as grasshoppers, crickets are often much more sedentary, and males are highly territorial. They're also more accomplished songsters. Crickets produce whistlelike musical chirping, commonly heard at night as well as during the day, by scraping a toothed ridge on the underside of one raised front wing across the hard, leading edge of the other. Among field crickets, for every territory-holding musician, there are often several silent males that lurk on the periphery of his turf in hopes of intercepting and mating with some of the incoming traffic. Female crickets are distinctive, their abdomens tipped with long, needlelike ovipositors, used to inject eggs into the ground, plant stems or twigs.

Most cricket and grasshopper eggs are laid in late summer and fall and hatch the following spring and early summer. The jumping nymphs that result look like small

Cricket markings: Ground crickets black, brown or reddish brown; tree crickets pale green

Ears: Located on sides of first abdominal segment on grasshoppers; on front legs of crickets

Number of grasshopper muscles: 900

Number of human muscles: 792

Grasshopper aliases: Short-horned grasshoppers, locusts, grigs, acridids, *les sauterelles*, Acrididae family

Cricket aliases: True crickets, grigs, *les grillons*, Gryllidae family

Name origin of *cricket*: From French *criquer*, meaning "creak"

Whereabouts: Meadows, fields, woods, thickets, backyards, parks, vacant lots, roadsides, railway embankments

Food: Grasshoppers eat grass and other plants; tree crickets eat aphids, caterpillars, other small insects and vegetation; field crickets are omnivorous, eating leaves, seeds, fruits, fungi, dead or living insects and their eggs

Eggs: Grasshoppers produce 4–25 separate pods, each holding 4 to more than 100 eggs; crickets lay several hundred individual eggs

Number of moults during nymph stage: 4–6 for grasshoppers; 8–12 for many crickets

Age at moulting to become an adult: 30–60 days for grasshoppers; 60–90 days for crickets

Lifespan: Most 3–6 months; up to about 11 months for species overwintering as adults

Predators: Robber flies, beetles, wasps, spiders, garter snakes, toads, leopard frogs, rodents, skunks, raccoons, foxes, cats, gulls, crows, killdeer and many other birds

Winter whereabouts: Most species in egg stage underground, vegetation, in stems or twigs

Cereal crop losses during grasshopper outbreaks: Often 5–10%

Densities during severe outbreaks: More than 24 per m^2 (1.2 sq yd)

Famous crickets: Jiminy, Buddy Holly's band

Grasshopper and cricket range: All Ontario; also in all other provinces and territories

Age of oldest grasshopper fossils: More than 190 million years old

Katydids: Grasshopper and cricket relatives, green or brown, with extremely long antennae, like crickets; most produce whispery ticks and buzzes; some live on meadow plants, others on trees or on ground

Number of Ontario grasshopper species: About 50

Number of true cricket species in Ontario: 15

Number of Ontario katydid species: 26

Number of grasshopper, cricket and katydid species worldwide: More than 23,000

Also see: Cicada, Toad, Leopard Frog, Ring-billed Gull, Killdeer

versions of adults, with disproportionately large heads, like a puppy or kitten, and lacking fully developed wings. Spring field cricket nymphs are among the few that hibernate. They transform into adults around early June, their slow, wavering chirps becoming one of the first insect songs of the year. They're particularly hermitlike, however, usually remaining in or near their burrows beneath rocks or debris, and are seldom abundant.

Fall field crickets, virtually identical in look and sound to their earlier performing cousins, start chirping in late July. They're the squat black crickets familiar to most. In autumn, a few sometimes try to prolong their lives by squeezing through spaces in windowsills and passageways into buildings. House crickets, on the other hand, commonly come indoors to get warm, snack on crumbs and lay their eggs. Their weak incessant chirping sometimes drives human cohabitants to distraction. Believed to have come to North America more than 200 years ago in cargo ships from tropical Asia, the yellowish-brown chirpers adapted to breed almost any time of year, as long as they have warm, cozy surroundings.

Long, continuous, high-pitched trills heard on late-summer and early-fall evenings in many city neighbourhoods, however, are usually the work of black-horned tree crickets, whose males often join in synchronized choruses. Despite their arboreal name, they usually call from tall plant stems and low shrubs, especially goldenrod and raspberry canes, in backyards, vacant lots, weedy roadsides and creeks. Pale green, smaller and more slender than familiar field crickets, they're rarely seen during the day.

The closely related snowy tree cricket is a little less common, but has a very distinctive loud, high, resonant whistled chirp that's often in the background of campfire scenes in movie westerns. Snowies are also called thermometer crickets because their even chirp rate, which like those of other singing insects rises with the temperature, lends itself to easy measurement. Adding four to the number of chirps heard in eight seconds equals the approximate temperature in Celsius. Adding 40 to the chirps made in 13 seconds yields a Fahrenheit reading.

HOUSE FLY
Most Wanting of Table Manners

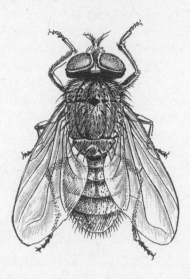

PROBABLY THE MOST constant of humankind's unwelcome guests, house flies are part of the same cosmopolitan cast of continent-hopping creatures found in cities around the world. The hairy-legged sneaks possess atrocious table manners, zooming directly from the garbage to the dinner plate, or shimmying down glasses of milk. Before digging in, they sample their fare with taste receptors on their feet. Worst of all, because a fly's spongy-tipped proboscis can only sop up liquids, the slurping vulgarian dissolves sweets, mashed potatoes and other foods by spewing on them first, the odious "vomit drop" style of dining all too well re-enacted in David Cronenberg's Technicolor remake of the B-movie classic *The Fly*.

House flies are renowned for a phenomenal reproductive rate that ensures they'll probably always take their uninvited place at the table. In hot summer weather, successive generations can be spaced only a couple weeks apart. Eggs hatch eight to 24 hours after being laid in fresh animal droppings, garbage food scraps, piles of grass clippings and any other moist, decaying organic matter. After burrowing into and feasting upon their rotting nursery piles for a week or so, creamy, blind, legless fly maggots wiggle away to dry, consume moist, decaying organic matter, including animal droppings, fruits and vegetables, grass cuttings

Eggs: White, about 1.2 mm long, shaped like rice grains, laid in batches of about 75–150; females living a full lifespan average 4–6 batches

Larva: Yellowish-white, wormlike, with a thin, pointy front end and widest at rear; reaching 8–12 mm (0.3–0.5 in) after moulting twice

Pupa: 6–8 mm (0.2–0.3 in) long, pine-cone-shaped, yellowish at first, darkening to orange, reddish brown and finally black

Development time from egg to adult: 10 days at 30°C (86°F), 21 days at 21°C (70°F), 45 days at 16°C (61°F)

Lifespan: Usually about 3–5 weeks in the summer; most survive less than a week as adults, but males may last up to 15 days and females up to 26 days

Predators: Eggs, maggots or pupae eaten by hister beetles, rove beetles, soldier beetle larvae, parasitic wasp larvae, mites, black dump fly and sweat fly maggots; adults or pupae eaten by spiders, house centipedes, dragonflies, hornets, robber flies, preying mantids, toads, mice, shrews, rats and many birds

Nighttime haunts: High on walls, ceilings, outdoor wires, trees and shrubs

Winter whereabouts: Hibernates as an adult in spaces inside

shady spots to pupate. Six or seven days later, they emerge as winged adults raring to breed, with each female afterwards laying multiple piles of eggs every three or four days.

Given their foul, malodorous breeding grounds, it's not surprising that house flies are among the filthiest things on the wing. The average urban fly harbours between one and two million bacteria, especially on the sticky pads of its taste-testing feet, which permit the scaling of walls and ceilings. More than 100 pathogens can be transmitted from house flies to humans or animals, including dysentery, *E. coli*, salmonella, diphtheria, tuberculosis, scarlet fever, cholera, typhoid, anthrax, polio, smallpox and tapeworms. Thanks to modern medicine and health practices, most such diseases are now rare in North America. But cities once had far greater numbers of flies around to spread them when horse stables and manure piles were commonplace and sewage systems and regular garbage pickup, not to mention stoop-and-scoop bylaws, were wanting.

Few house flies, which probably originate in the warm regions of the Old World, survive winter hibernation in Ontario's cities. The descendants of those that do generally don't become abundant until July and August, when they usually comprise more than 90 percent of all types of flies showing up indoors. In the late spring and early summer, however, the small **lesser house fly** also sometimes appears inside, characteristically flying in sharp-angled turns around ceiling-light fixtures in rooms, porches and garages. Unlike common house flies, they often hover and seldom seem to land. They breed in bird droppings and many of the same sites as their larger cousins, but hot weather and parasites cause their numbers to fall in midsummer.

Another member of the house fly's large family, and one of the few that bites and sucks blood, the **stable fly** also sometimes ventures indoors on very humid days, leading to the old belief that impending rain turned house flies vampiric. A long, bayonetlike proboscis that can penetrate through socks and thin clothing sets the stable fly apart from its similar-sized, sponge-mouthed relation. As its name suggests, the flying viper's main victims are cows and horses, but it also shows up in the open areas of city parks and beaches, usually biting humans around the ankles and dogs on their ears.

The big, sluggish flies that bask on the sides of houses in late summer and turn up indoors buzzing around windows on sunny late-winter and early-spring days, on the other hand, are **cluster flies**, which hibernate inside walls and attics. Non-natives, like most other house-frequenting flies, they're especially abundant after rainy summers because they start life as earthworm-infesting maggots, slowly devouring their hosts alive until ready to pupate. In outlying suburbs close to pasture lands, window congregations also include overwintering **face flies**, the merciless pests that relentlessly swarm around the eyes, noses and mouths of cattle and horses, feeding on their mucus, tears and saliva.

Much more common in cities are the **green bottle** and **blue bottle flies** often seen around garbage or dead animals. They're members of the blow fly family, as are cluster flies. The infamous maggots of a succession of blow fly species, as well as those of flesh flies and coffin flies, specialize in dining on different stages of animal decomposition. Patrolling widely and employing antennae that can pick up the first scents of death – subtle gases imperceptible to human noses – females usually arrive to lay eggs within minutes of their subject's demise.

A galaxy of other flies, forming more than 100 different families, display a vast diversity of lifestyles. Many, such as bristly-bodied **tachinid flies**, **robber flies** and **long-legged flies**, are considered highly beneficial garden predators, parasites or parasitoids of plant-eating insects. The large **bee fly** and **hover fly** families, most of whose members look like bees or wasps, feed on nectar and are the world's second biggest group of pollinators. Unlike most other insects, all true flies – including fruit flies, horse flies, black flies, mosquitoes, midges and gnats – have just two wings instead of four. While cities seem to have their share of dipterans (from the Greek words *di pteron*, "two wings"), a recent survey of a single wedge of shore and forest stretching a short distance back from one lake in Algonquin Park found some 600 different species of them.

---

walls, in attics or under loose bark, or as a maggot or pupa in rotting vegetation

Range: All Ontario; also in all other provinces

Portion of the world's crops pollinated by fly species: About 19%

Number of biblical plagues that involved flies: At least 2, possibly 4

Small fruit flies: Also called pumace flies, 2–4 mm (0.08–0.16 in) long, often appear in houses around over-ripe fruit, on which they lay eggs; larvae eat yeast on fruit; leading insect subjects for studies on genetics for past century because they produce a new generation every 10–20 days and they have huge, easy-to-read salivary gland chromosomes

Love bugs: Also known as March flies, they form large, low-flying breeding swarms over fields, parks and suburban gardens in spring and early summer, with some pairs mating for up to 56 hours straight

Parasitoids: Parasitic insects that kill their hosts

Oldest fly fossils: 225 million years old, of a crane fly

Number of fly species worldwide: About 120,000

Also see: Mosquitoes, Cockroach, House & Home, Lawn & Garden; Bees, Wasps & Hornets

LADYBUGS
Honoured in Many Tongues

REGARDED AS A GODSEND since ancient times
for their services in eating aphids and other soft-
bodied, crop-damaging insects, ladybugs have
been named after saints and deities in dozens of languages. In medieval England, they were associated with
the mercy of the Virgin Mary and known as the beetles
of "Our Lady." Today they're still generally greeted with
delight upon landing on a human hand.

Yet, the familiar **nine-spotted ladybug** that most
adults grew up with in Ontario may not even exist here
any more. It's believed to have been replaced by the alien
seven-spotted ladybug and the multicoloured **Asian lady
beetle** (illustrated), which have become the most
common species in much of the province. Both were
intentionally introduced in the United States in recent
decades to rid farm fields and orchards of pests, with the
European seven-spots spreading to Ontario by 1981 and
the north Asian ladybugs arriving in 1994. Whether
through direct competition for prey or because of greater
resistance to pathogens, no one knows for sure, the immigrants are also suspected of threatening, if not completely
displacing, at least two other native ladybug species.

Asian lady beetles became very well known after the
hot, dry summer of 2001 produced a plague of little
soybean-eating green aphids, also recent invaders from
China, that briefly blew into downtown Toronto,

closing swimming pools and sending Blue Jays fans at SkyDome running for cover. The Asian ladies – which can be orange, yellow or black, with zero to 19 spots – followed the aphids wherever they went and multiplied in tandem. On the Niagara Peninsula, so many ladybugs turned up in vineyards close to soybean fields that they left their mark on the vintage of 2001. Though little creatures are strained out in the wine-making process, ladybugs, like many other brightly coloured beetles, are bathed inside their shells by a rank, bitter orange or yellow fluid that's extremely displeasing to larger predators. If seized, some can "bleed" the liquid from their leg joints to secure a quick release. The bug juice is so potent, more than a few bottles of Ontario chardonnay and Riesling were imbued with a subtle peanutty bouquet.

Fluid-squirting Asian lady beetles also invaded many homes around late October 2001, entering through cracks and door jambs to hibernate between walls and in groups of hundreds and sometimes thousands. Most ladybug species, however, huddle together in dormitories beneath fallen leaves or under bark for the winter, some emerging soon after the snow melts in spring. The pinkish-red native **spotted lady beetle**, which is much more streamlined than most of its cousins, is particularly common around early May, when it pigs out on pollen from the first big bloom of dandelions before aphids become plentiful.

Employing their stubby pair of antennae to pick up the pheromones of others of their kind, ladybugs meet, mate and gradually lay batches of yellow or orange eggs on the undersides of leaves. A few days later, spiny, segmented, six-legged grubs hatch and go hunting for aphids. Their dark bodies become coloured with red, yellow or orange spots or bands as they grow and moult four times over two to four weeks, before pupating for another three to 12 days and turning into adults. Like other beetles, they acquire fliptop lids, with a pair of modified wings forming hard, protective covers over most of their bodies. The shields raise forward to allow a second, functional set of transparent wings beneath to spread when the ladies take flight.

Lifespan: 1–12 months for most species; up to 3 years for multi-coloured Asian lady beetles

Predators: Parasitoid wasps and flies; occasionally birds

Playing opossum: When threatened, ladybugs often freeze and play dead because predators such as birds commonly avoid eating insects that don't move and may be a little "off"

Temperature at which ladybugs become active: About 13°C (55°F)

Winter whereabouts: Beneath fallen leaves and inside bark crevices, usually at the south-facing base of big trees; also in the corners of unheated porches, garages; sometimes inside houses

Range: All Ontario; also in all other provinces and territories

Age of oldest known beetle fossils: About 250 million years old

Number of Ontario ladybug species: 83

Number of ladybug species worldwide: More than 5,200

Number of beetle species worldwide: 300,000–370,000

Number of known insect species worldwide: More than 1 million

Probable number of insect species worldwide: 3–10 million

Portion of known animal species that are beetles: About 25%

Also see: Lawn & Garden, Alien Invaders

MONARCH BUTTERFLY
Destiny Bound by Mexican Siesta

I N LATE SPRING, and more noticeably toward the end of summer, monarch butterflies sail through backyards, parking lots, parks and cafés in cities across Ontario in one of nature's most celebrated migrations. Tanked up on nectar, converted to fat to fuel their long journeys to and from Mexico, monarchs collect in large numbers in cities along the shores of the Great Lakes as they search for the shortest crossings over the water. An estimated 120,000 monarchs passed in 90 minutes along the Burlington Skyway bridge into Hamilton on one late August day in 1997. They rest en masse in trees at night and on days when the wind is against them, with thousands sometimes gathering around points, such as Toronto's Leslie Street Spit, or even in well-sheltered suburban yards along migration thoroughfares.

Monarchs employ the same strategy as migrating hawks, spiralling upwards on warm columns of rising air, called thermals, climbing up to 1,500 metres (5,000 feet), then gliding in the wind until they hook on to another thermal. By early November, often hundreds of millions of the orange wind-riders from all over eastern North America converge on about a dozen volcanic mountains in central Mexico's Sierra Madres. Yet none has ever made the trip before.

The monarch masses settle into a handful of colonies 3,000 metres (10,000 feet) above sea level, in stands of fir trees, each covering one to three hectares (2.5 to seven acres). Turning the sky and scenery orange, they crowd onto tree limbs and go into intermittent semi-dormancy for several months, the cool mountain air, hovering around the freezing point, enabling them to conserve energy. Mexicans living near wintering sites traditionally said that monarchs were the souls of children,

Estimated number of monarchs that passed through Point Pelee, on Lake Erie, in 90 minutes on September 17, 1996: 350,000

Average distance covered by one generation migrating north: 1,700 km (1,000 mi)

Distance covered by one generation migrating south: Up to 4,800 km (3,000 mi)

Duration of trip from Ontario to Mexico: 6–8 weeks

Average daily migration distance: 71 km (44 mi)

Flying speed: Up to 18 km/h (11 mph) in still air and 50 km/h (31 mph) with strong tailwinds

Wingbeats per second: 5–12

Minimum temperature needed to fly: 13°C (55°F)

Wingspan: 9–10.5 cm (3.5–4 in)

their arrival coming around the time of All Souls' Day, on November 2, an important festival in Latin America known as the Day of the Dead.

The whereabouts of the butterflies' Mexican rendezvous was long a mystery to the rest of the world. It was finally pinpointed in 1975, the culmination of a lifetime of work by the University of Toronto's Fred and Norah Urquhart, who invented tiny, effective butterfly wing tags and organized an international monitoring effort. They were later awarded the Order of Canada. The discovery may have come just in time, with logging having reduced the butterflies' wintering grounds to about 10 percent of what they once were.

The Mexican government has designated the mountain refuge area as the Monarch Butterfly Biosphere Reserve, but illegal cutting continues to encroach, reducing the insular effect of large tracts of forest, leaving sheltering butterflies more vulnerable to the elements. Severe rain or snow storms in some recent years have claimed up to 75 percent of wintering populations. Luckily, so far, monarch numbers seem to have bounced back quickly after such calamities. Still, the International Union for the Conservation of Nature describes the monarch migration as an "endangered phenomenon."

The generation of northern-bred monarchs that spends the winter in Mexico is very long-lived by butterfly standards. The key to their longevity is remaining chaste until longer late-winter days and rising temperatures stir them from their siesta. Then their delayed hormones kick in and the butterfly fiesta begins. For males, it's the last hurrah. Females, however, once mated take off around late March in a race to be the first to lay eggs on milkweeds emerging from the ground in the northward advance of spring. Most burn out after laying eggs in Texas and the other Gulf states, though a tough, tattered few may reach Ontario in late May. The bigger waves that arrive in June and early July are a second generation, hatched from eggs in northern Mexico and the southern United States.

In Ontario, monarch butterflies have the strange predicament of being officially listed as a species at risk,

Weight: 300–750 mg (0.01–0.03 oz)

Fat content: About 25 mg (0.0009 oz) in summer; 150 mg (0.005 oz) before migration; 225 mg (0.0075 oz) going into hibernation in Mexico

Markings: Black-veined, bright-orange wings with white-spotted black borders; black body also marked with white; males have a black spot on hind wings and thinner black veins than females

Alias: Milkweed butterfly, King Billy, *le papillon monarque, Danaus plexippus*

Whereabouts: Fields, meadows, forest edge, backyards, parks, shorelines

Food: Caterpillars eat milkweed leaves; adults sip nectar of milkweeds, goldenrods, asters, Joe-pye weed and many other flowers

Mating: Couples meet in afternoon and spend night together; both sexes may mate several times with different partners

Average number of eggs per female: 100–300 pinhead-sized green eggs attached singly beneath milkweed leaves

Egg development period: Usually about 4 days; up to 12 days

Caterpillar: Up to 5 cm (2 in) long; yellowish green after hatching, turning to bands of bright yellow, black and white

Time from hatching to emergence as an adult: 3–4 weeks

Adult survival in spring and early summer: 2–6 weeks

Survival of adults emerging in late summer: 7–8 months

Predators: Birds, mice, shrews, wasps, spiders

North American population: 250–650 million

Population cycle: Peaks about 7–11 years

Total area occupied by colonies in Mexico each winter: 3–21 ha (7.5–52 acres)

Accolades: Official emblem of the North American Free Trade Agreement; state insect of Vermont, Illinois, Texas, West Virginia, Idaho and Alabama

Range: Southern Ontario to James Bay; also in all other provinces

Lookalikes: Viceroy butterflies smaller, with a black band running across the veins of the hind wings

Also see: Red-tailed Hawk, Moths, Cabbage White Butterfly, Butterfly Gardens; Meadows, Vacant Lots & Roadsides

while its only caterpillar food, milkweed, is designated as a noxious weed that property owners are legally bound to uproot. Growing in meadows and fields, most milkweed species produce toxins in their milky sap that usually protect them from cows and many other browsers. Monarchs find milkweeds a safe haven for their caterpillars, which have evolved a tolerance for the poisonous tissues themselves. In fact, milkweed toxins stored in the insect's body make both the caterpillars and adults unpalatable to most vertebrate predators. After heaving once from a monarch meal, birds steer clear of the butterfly's bright colours. The unpleasant reputation allows monarchs to flutter lazily about with relative impunity. The smaller **viceroy butterfly**, which looks so much like a monarch, also sometimes packs toxins, depending on which of a number of possible host plants it fed upon as a caterpillar.

Starting off less than two millimetres (one-tenth of an inch) long, monarch caterpillars eat constantly for nine to 14 days, go through five skin sheddings and grow to 2,700 times their hatching weight. In human terms, it would be like a three-kilogram (6.6-pound) infant putting on eight tonnes. The caterpillar then suspends itself from a silk pad stuck to a branch or leaf and transforms into a beautiful turquoise pupa. The pupal covering gradually becomes transparent and, after about 10 to 15 days, a butterfly emerges. It spends about an hour inflating its wings with fluid, then flies away. Two or three generations of monarchs hatch through the summer in Ontario, the last returning again to Mexico.

BUTTERFLY GARDENS
Sweet City Sanctuaries Can Lure a Colourful Parade of Winged Beauties and Provide a Home for Future Generations

Fallen flower I see
Returning to its branch –
Ah! A butterfly.
– Arakida Moritake, founder of haiku

B Y HAPPY CIRCUMSTANCE, butterflies are attracted to beautiful flowers. A true butterfly haven, however, offers more than a sweet slurp of nectar for the odd resplendent drifter happening by. The much-admired sprites feast mainly in their youth, as leaf-munching caterpillars. Backyard oases full of the favourite foods of their formative days entice fluttering adults to stick around to mate and lay eggs, turning gardens into butterfly nurseries. While the little ones chow down upon hatching, they're seldom numerous enough to seriously defoliate their host plants.

Most butterflies don't need a large area to survive and successfully reproduce. With the right host plants and amenities, even a few backyards in one neighbourhood can provide enough habitat locally to sustain a number of different species. Such efforts can go a ways to boosting populations depressed by habitat destruction and the past use of DDT and other chemicals. Even today, pesticides sprayed to control mosquitoes and other insects also take down many innocent butterflies.

With a wide-enough selection of the right plants, shrubs and trees, a yard and garden can bloom from spring to autumn amid an ever-changing kaleidoscope of brightly coloured wings. The forest sleepers are the year's scouts, sometimes fluttering like a dream through sun-drenched backyards on the first warm days of early spring. Of the half-dozen or so southern Ontario species

Butterfly capital of Ontario: Windsor and environs, which host many rare southern species that seldom reach much farther north into the province

Ontario's biggest butterfly: Giant swallowtail, with a wingspan of 10–15 cm (4–6 in)

Butterfly lifespan (as a flying adult): Less than 2 weeks for most species; 2 days for spring azures; 7–10 months for winter hibernators

Butterfly amenities: Flat rocks placed in sunny, but sheltered, spots for basking; a bucket or basin of damp earth for lapping up moisture

Important native nectar plants for butterflies: Butterfly weed and other milkweeds, goldenrods, asters, wild bergamot, bee balm, Joe-pye weed, sunflowers, black-eyed Susan, purple cone-flower, dogbane, wild geranium, blackberry, coreopsis, honey-suckles, phlox, fleabane, blazing stars, wild mint, honey-suckles

Native butterfly caterpillar host plants: Violets, nettles, wild columbine, dogbane, asters, sun-flowers, pearly everlasting, pussytoes, meadowsweet, turtle-head, vervain, tick trefoil, rock cress, native grasses, sedges

Native butterfly caterpillar host shrubs: Viburnums, currants, New Jersey tea

Native butterfly caterpillar host trees: Willows, aspens, birches, black cherry, chokecherry, oaks, hawthorn, dogwoods, staghorn sumac, hackberry, alder, hickory, wild plum

Non-native caterpillar host plants: Clover, Queen Anne's lace, St. John's wort, lamb's quarters, sheep sorrel, burdock, vetch, alfalfa, plantain, curled dock, timothy grass

Common non-native nectar sources: Bull thistle, Canada thistle, ox-eye daisy, spotted knapweed, dame's rocket, bird's-foot trefoil, wild mustards, yarrow, blueweed, orange hawkweed, speedwell

Common garden flower nectar sources: Lilacs, butterfly bush, marigolds, zinnias, cosmos, hol-lyhocks, day lily, lavender

Other foods eaten by some but-terflies: Juices from rotting fruit and fungi, sap, carrion, animal droppings

Carnivorous caterpillars: Harvester butterfly caterpillars

that regularly overwinter as adults in narrow tree cavi-ties and hollow logs, the unmistakable mourning cloak, with chocolatey wings trimmed in yellow, is the most common. Like the others, it thirsts for the juices of rotting fruit and sap dripping from tree wounds, making yards with sugar maples or hawthorns centres of attrac-tion. Willows, birch, aspens and elm trees are also big draws, serving as natal sites for the crawling offspring of most of the early-spring flyers. Many of the same trees also host the caterpillars for some of the most striking butterflies of early summer, including tiger swallowtails, white admirals and monarch-mimicking viceroys.

Around late April and May, red admirals begin sailing into Ontario from the southern United States, though some may successfully overwinter here during mild years as well. Among the most familiar of butter-flies, bearing dark wings with a broad, circular reddish-orange band and white spotted tips, they too prefer tree sap and fruit juices. Though they lay their eggs on sting-ing nettle, which grows in damp woods and along rivers and roadside ditches, red admirals also often wing through residential neighbourhoods.

As nefarious as stinging nettle may be, devoting an out-of-the-way section of a yard or garden for plants commonly regarded as weeds can reel in considerable beauties. Violet-trimmed question marks also lay eggs on nettles, while black-and-orange painted ladies often lay theirs on thistles and burdock. The caterpillars of American coppers eat sheep sorrel. Common sootywing larvae nibble lamb's quarters.

Violets are among spring's early-blooming butterfly plants. After the caterpillars of great spangled fritillaries and other closely related species emerge from hiberna-tion in the leaf litter, they crawl onto violet leaves and snack away until undergoing metamorphosis into large, black-spotted orange-and-brown butterflies later in the spring and summer. Meanwhile, the buds and white flowers of wild cherries, dogwoods and various vibur-nums are devoured in late May and June by the cater-pillars of the little, ethereally blue-winged spring azure. After spending the winter in a chrysalis, the azure briefly takes flight, any time between April and early June.

Clouded sulphurs, eastern-tailed blues and silvery blue butterflies also overwinter as pupae and flock to clover, vetches and other legume-family plants to deposit their eggs. As red clover begin blooming in May, they also attract large, long-tongued butterflies, such as newly transformed black swallowtails, with rich pools of nectar. Smaller butterflies lap from the shorter florets of white clover flowerheads.

Butterfly pageantry is richest between June and August, fuelled by a wide array of sun-loving, summer-long-blooming flowers, including milkweeds, wild bergamot, black-eyed Susan, purple coneflower and coreopsis. Such native species are much stronger butterfly magnets than most common garden cultivars, which have been bred for large, showy flowers but usually lack the quantities of nectar and alluring scents needed to reproduce in the wild.

Clumps of tall native grasses are also centres of attraction throughout the summer, especially for a large family of small-winged, mostly brownish butterflies known as skippers. Though they sip nectar from a variety of sources, most skippers lay their eggs on specific kinds of grasses and, unlike most butterflies, usually pupate within cocoons of leaves woven together with silk.

From summer into autumn, Joe-pye weed, sunflowers, goldenrods and asters are the big nectar sources for most butterflies. Many late bloomers, such as jewelweed (illustrated), die with the first frosts, making butterfly survival more difficult. But purple New England asters often linger into late October, sustaining the last grizzled orange sulphurs and cabbage whites, as well as a few monarchs that seem to have missed the boat to Mexico. Mourning cloaks and sculpted-winged hop merchants also sometimes flit through backyards in farewell flights on fine Indian summer days before finally retiring for their long winter rests.

eat woolly aphids on beech and alder trees

Common urban butterflies: Cabbage whites, clouded sulphurs, mourning cloaks, red admirals, spring azures, eastern-tailed blues, pearl crescents, silver-spotted skippers, Peck's skippers, tawny-edged skippers

Ontario butterflies that hibernate as adults: Mourning cloaks, question marks, hop merchants, Compton tortoiseshells, Milbert's tortoiseshells, grey commas, green commas, satyr commas; occasionally red admirals and black swallowtails

Number of migratory and semi-migratory Ontario butterflies: At least 23

Butterfly range: Throughout Ontario and Canada to the high Arctic

World's most widespread butterfly: Painted lady, found in North America, Eurasia, Africa and Australia

Minimum butterfly body temperature needed to fly: 27°C (81°F)

Butterflies that have been extirpated in Ontario: Karner blue (last seen in 1991), frosted elfin (last seen in 1988), southern hairstreak, Persius duskwing, regal fritillary

Number of resident or regular migrant butterfly species in Ontario: About 140

Number of butterfly species worldwide: About 17,500

Also see: Monarch Butterfly, Cabbage White Butterfly, Moths, Bird Gardens

MOSQUITOES
Straw-nosed Marauders

I N A COUNTRY of viciously biting bugs, southern Ontario cities get off comparatively lightly. Still, mosquito-friendly weather some years can turn backyard barbecues and evening strolls into slapstick miseries. Steady April showers, then warm, sunny spells, sustain multitudes of wriggling aquatic larvae in innumerable temporary early-spring ponds, puddles and ditches. Collectively known as snowmelt mosquitoes, numbering many species, great hordes of the early-season hatchers take wing in May and June, but have only one generation a year, laying eggs in ground depressions that fill up again the following spring. Many other straw-nosed blood bandits, however, go through multiple generations and continue to pester through the summer.

Two closely related summer marauders became infamous in recent years as the chief West Nile virus villains in Ontario. The nearly identical northern house mosquito and the white-dotted mosquito are adept city dwellers, overwintering as adults in storm sewers and sometimes taking up in damp basements. Four generations of them emerge from May to August, breeding in street-grate catch basins, eavestroughs, swimming pool covers, discarded tires, even containers as small as empty bottles and tin cans. They're primarily nocturnal pests of roosting birds, from whom they pick up and then widely spread the West Nile virus. The two only rarely bite humans, when feathered fare isn't handy, but eight other Ontario mosquitoes with more varied tastes are known occasionally to pick up the virus from birds.

Only about 20 percent of people infected with the West Nile virus become sick, developing flulike symptoms, while a much smaller fraction become seriously ill. The disease struck at least 319 people in Ontario in 2002 and killed 18, prompting many municipalities to treat catchment basins with larvicides. The Toronto and

Distance humans can be detected by mosquitoes: Up to 30 m (100 ft)

Wingbeats per second: 300–600

Length: Most species 3–9 mm (0.1–0.4 in)

Largest Ontario species: Gallinipper (*Psorophora ciliata*), about 2.5 cm (1 in) long

Monster "mosquitoes": Crane flies, up to 5.5 cm (2.2 in) long, with very long legs; attracted to lights but do not bite

Alias: Skeeters, *les moustiques*, Culicidae family

Name origin: Spanish *mosca*, meaning "little fly"

Most troublesome Ontario biter: *Aedes vexans*, also called floodwater mosquito, common at dusk, Jun.–Aug.

Other common urban species: Cattail mosquito, northern house mosquito, white-dotted mosquito, eastern tree-hole mosquito

Breeding grounds: About half of Ontario species in temporary

Oakville areas were particularly hard hit. Some health authorities estimate that without knowing it, some 100,000 Canadians may have been infected, thereby acquiring immunity to the virus. The following year, only about a quarter as many West Nile cases occurred in the province, following the trend in New York State, where the virus first appeared in North America in 1999.

Despite its legions of biting bugs, Ontario is seldom visited by the scourges of insect-borne diseases that plague warmer parts of the world. The house mosquito also figured in an outbreak of St. Louis encephalitis, centred around Windsor, in the mid-1970s. Sporadic malaria epidemics occurred in the province up until about 1900, including one that halted construction of the Rideau Canal in the late 1820s, slaying hundreds of Irish labourers. A few hundred people still return to the province from abroad every year with malarial infections, most of which are treated and cured. The spotted-wing common malaria mosquito, which occurs in urban areas, and perhaps a couple of its close relatives are capable of carrying the disease in Ontario, but there has been only one known case in recent decades of transmission from an infected foreign traveller to another person in the province. Luckily, the AIDS virus is too fragile to survive in the harsh biochemical environment inside a mosquito.

For the vast majority of Canadians, irritating bites are the worst local mosquitoes have to offer. Upon landing, a female – the only sex that bites – drills into the flesh with several razor-thin stylets held within her long proboscis. She needs a few minutes of siphoning to get a full tank, which can double or quadruple her weight as her abdomen balloons red with blood. To keep it coming, she injects saliva containing an anticoagulant, as well as an anaesthetic. The body responds to such foreign compounds by surrounding the wound with histamine, a chemical that marshals white blood cells and other natural defences to sweep away and destroy toxins. Swelling, itching and redness around the bite are part of the allergic defence reaction.

As long-suffering mosquito magnets will attest, some people do get hit more than others. Mosquito antennae

pools, ditches; more than a dozen in tree holes, containers or water cupped in leaves; 11 mainly in wetlands; 11 mainly in weedy ponds, lake shallows and slow streams

Food: Nectar, honeydew, plant juices; blood to produce eggs; larvae filter algae, bits of decaying vegetation, protozoa and bacteria from the water

Average blood taken: 2–3 mg (0.001 of a tsp)

Maximum number of lifetime full blood meals for *Aedes vexans*: 8

Mating swarms: Clouds of flying males form at dusk or dawn over trees, watersides or other landmarks to attract mates

Time required to produce eggs after a obtaining a full blood meal: 1 to several days in warm weather

Number of eggs produced per blood meal: 60–400

Incubation period: 1–5 days in summer; some capable of lying dormant up to 5 years

Larvae: Aquatic, wormlike, beige, bristly, 1–2 mm (0.04–0.08 in) long after hatching, growing to 7–15 mm (0.3–0.6 in) after moulting 4 times over 1–4 weeks; a long tube at back of abdomen gets air at water surface; called wrigglers

Portion of Toronto storm-sewer catch basins found with mosquito larvae: 91%

Number of larvae per ha (2.5 acres) in wet fields: Up to 80 million

Pupae: Brown, comma-shaped, up to 6 mm (0.25 in) long; float, but can dive if threatened; after 1–4 days, pupal shells open and become launch pads for transformed winged adults

Full lifespan: 1–12 months, depending on species

Adulthood: 2–12 weeks, depending on species; 6–8 months for overwintering adults

Predators: Bats, swallows, nighthawks, swifts, flycatchers, warblers, frogs, toads, dragonflies, wasps, spiders; dytiscid beetles and other aquatic insects eat larvae

Temperature restraints: Become sluggish below 16°C (60°F), inactive at 10°C (50°F)

Winter whereabouts: Most as eggs in water or ground depressions; about 8 species hibernate as larvae in mud or tree holes and 8 as adults in storm sewers, buildings, animal burrows, tree holes and hollow logs

Occurrence of West Nile–carrying mosquitoes in Ontario during 2002 epidemic: Up to 15 per 1,000 among northern house and white-spotted mosquitoes; less than 2 per 1,000 among eight "bridging" species

Protection provided by repellents with 30% DEET: 5–6½ hours

Range: Throughout Canada

Number of Ontario mosquito species: 57

Number of mosquito species worldwide: More than 3,000

Also see: Crow, Dragonflies

lock on to the carbon dioxide exhaled by humans or animals and track increasing concentrations to the source. As the insects get closer, body heat, odour, moisture and sight also guide them. They're especially attracted by dark colours, such as brown, grey and navy blue, but also seem partial to certain chemical compositions or levels in sweat and skin vapours, such as lactic acid, that vary from person to person. Women are generally more appealing to them than men.

The key ingredient of most insect repellents, DEET, or N,N-diethyl-meta-toluamide, seems to block sensors in the mosquito's antennae, mouth and legs from detecting the lactic acid. Though DEET absorbed through the skin is shed in urine within 24 hours, without building up in body tissues, Health Canada recommends not using it on infants less than six months old and restricting children under 12 to repellents with concentrations of up to 10 percent. Alternatives containing natural repellents, such as the citronella, lavender or soybean oil, can keep mosquitoes away for 30 minutes to three hours.

Humans have probably been experimenting with ways of ridding themselves of biting pests since the dawn of time. Even wedge-capped capuchin monkeys – the famous organ-grinder variety – in Venezuela have been found to spread the caustic secretions of huge millipedes over their fur to protect themselves from mosquitoes in the rainy season. Most high-tech anti-bug gadgetry, on the other hand, has proven to be a flop. Electric bug zappers dispatch few mosquitoes or black flies, most of whom are not attracted to lights, instead frying large numbers of beneficial insects that prey on biting pests and garden despoilers. Window screens, introduced in the 1880s, were a far greater advance.

MOTHS
Night-Flying Insect Legions

MOTHS RARELY get the good press enjoyed by butterflies. Biologically, they are far more significant than their day-flying relatives, with about 10 times as many species. But their natural pervasiveness seldom sits well wherever humans dominate the environment.

In the city, as elsewhere, moths make the greatest impact on their surroundings during their ravenous youth as caterpillars. Virtually every kind of garden plant, tree or shrub is set upon by various species of moth larvae. Caterpillars known as sod webworms cause brown spots and patches in lawns by eating grass roots and stems.

Inside houses, **clothes moth** eggs hatch into dark-headed white caterpillars that nibble holes in wool sweaters, blankets and rugs stored in closets and chests. Residues of food, beverages or sweat also make unwashed cotton, linens and other fabrics appetizing for them. Under the cover of fabric fibres woven together with silken webs spun from spinnerets near their mouths, they feast for anywhere from 40 to 200 days, growing to a little more than a centimetre (0.4 in) long before pupating into fingernail-sized, yellowish-tan-winged adults.

Clothes moths are rarely seen because they keep to the dark, ducking into hiding places when lights are turned on. Small, dingy grey-and-brownish indoor flyers often assumed to be clothes moths are usually **Indian meal moths**, which do flutter around lights and TV screens. Their interest, however, lies mainly in the kitchen. Most often, their eggs arrive with the groceries on or actually inside packages and boxes of cereal, pasta, flour, crackers, nuts, dry pet food and many other products. After hatching, small yellowish-green or pink-tinted caterpillars gorge for up to six weeks, leaving

Biggest Ontario moth: Cecropia, wingspan up to 15 cm (6 in)

Cecropia caterpillar length: Up to 11 cm (4.3 in)

Moth wingbeats per second: Up to 20

Woolly bear caterpillar crawling speed: About 0.8 km/h (0.5 mph)

Amount eaten by polyphemus moth caterpillar in its 56-day development period: 86,000 times its own birth weight

Alias: Les mites, order Lepidoptera

Moth food: Nectar, sap, honey-dew, overripe fruit and carrion as adults; caterpillars eat leaves, buds, roots, stems, fruit, nuts, seeds, bark, beeswax, grain and processed foods

Caterpillar with the most varied tastes: Fall webworm samples 636 tree and plant species

Lifespan: Most about a year

Time spent in adult stage:
Several days to several months

Light attraction: Disoriented moths flutter around night lights because, it is thought, they normally navigate a straight course by keeping constant the angle of moonlight on their eyes

Other insects attracted to lights: Night-flying mayflies, midges, lacewings, beetles, flies and true bugs

Ontario moths that are daytime flyers: 2–5%

Only fully domesticated insect: Silkworm moth, which, unlike honeybees, cannot survive in the wild; domesticated in China 2,500 years ago

Number of cocoons needed to make a silk handkerchief: Hundreds

Biggest moth domestication flop: Gypsy moths imported from France to Massachusetts in 1869 in a failed attempt to use them to produce commercial silk; escaped gypsies have ravaged North American forests, reaching Ontario in 1970

Purpose of antennae: Used by males to detect chemical scent of female; each species has a unique scent, except those that use no scent at all

Distance a male cecropia moth can smell a female: Up to 11 km (7 mi)

Wingless moths: Wormlike females of species such as bagworms, cankerworms and white-marked tussock moths depend wholly on their scent to attract winged males

behind stringy webs, never a pleasant discovery in a bowl of munchies. They often pupate at the ends of silk strands hanging from walls and ceilings and can go through several generations in a year. Another species, known simply as the **meal moth**, has whitish caterpillars, up to 2.5 centimetres (one inch) long, that spin protective webbed tubes around themselves and drag them about as they gobble food grains in storage bins.

Outdoor moth caterpillars also employ a wide range of dining styles directed toward eating in anonymity. Some pull the edges of leaves up around them with their silk, or tie bunches of evergreen needles together into snack shacks. Bagworm caterpillars live and munch within small hanging sacks of webbing, twigs and other plant bits on a variety of trees and shrubs. Tiny leaf miners create splotches or trails in leaves that start out small, where the egg hatches, and grow wider as the caterpillar winds through the leaf, ending where it pupates and emerges as a moth. Other moth larvae hatch from eggs laid within plant tissues that cause some of the bulging galls common on goldenrods and oak trees. As the caterpillars eat away at a stem or acorn from the inside, the plant surrounds the area with hard, tumorlike gall tissue. The hidden inhabitants eat an exit hole out of the gall before transforming into adults.

Some moth larvae, such as tent caterpillars and fall webworms, live communally, spinning large silk nests in trees for refuge. Most moth caterpillars also use strands of silk as safety lines if they fall or get blown off their perch, and to encase themselves in cocoons.

For all their deprivations, moth caterpillars play an important part in ecosystems, even in cities. They concentrate nutrients from the incredible quantities of vegetation into their plump, juicy, bite-sized little bodies for birds and a huge assortment of other predators. Even mainly seed- and fruit-eating birds depend heavily on the high-protein caterpillar meals that allow their nestlings to reach adult size in a matter of weeks. While tent caterpillar outbreaks may plague apple, pear and other trees in the rose family, they can also swell the numbers of beautiful Baltimore orioles and rarely seen black-billed cuckoos in parks and even backyards.

Adult moths also play an important ecological role, taking over from butterflies at night in pollinating a wide array of flowers as they suck up nectar with their long, coiled tongues. Though some species, such as the colourful, early-summer flying **cecropia** and **luna** (illustrated) moths, do not eat at all as adults, many more flock to evening primrose, jimson weed, evening lychnis and other nocturnal bloomers, which are usually white or light toned and easy to see in the dark.

Some species are also active by day, though they may not be recognized as moths. **Clearwing moths** look like wasps, benefiting from bold colour patterns that predators associate with painful stings. **Hummingbird moths**, with a wingspan of up to nine centimetres (3.5 inches), resemble hummingbirds, but produce a softer buzz as they hover at garden flowers. Others, such as day-flying **eight-spotted foresters**, which sport bright-white-and-yellow spots on velvety black wings, are often mistaken for butterflies, though they lack the large knobs found at the ends of butterfly antennae.

Most moths, however, have dull wings, which they keep outspread while resting to blend with tree bark and other surfaces. Butterflies, in contrast, usually perch with their wings folded together, except for when basking in the sun to increase their metabolic rate.

When they lift off to fly, the large lunas, cecropias, polyphemus moths and some sphinx moths flash pairs of large spots on their wings that look like eyes, which may startle an attacking predator. The otherwise concealed bold colours on the hind flappers of midsized underwing moths serve the same purpose. Underwings, as well as other owlet and geometrid moths, also have thin membranes stretched over tiny air cavities on their abdomens or thoraxes for picking up ultrasonic sound waves screeched by bats for their sonar tracking of flying prey. On tiger moths, these special sets of "ears" also click to warn bats of their extremely distasteful flavour. The youngsters of the **Isabella tiger moth** are the well-known fuzzy reddish-brown woolly bears commonly seen along roadsides and sidewalks in autumn and early spring, among the few moth caterpillars for whom many people seem to express genuine affection.

Predators: Bats, birds, mice, beetles, wasps, ants, spiders

Winter whereabouts: Beneath bark, soil or leaf litter, in galls, wrapped in pine needles or amid other debris; most as eggs or pupae, some as caterpillars or adults

Common autumn caterpillars: Woolly bears and other tiger moth larvae, fall webworms

Cold-weather moths: Small, grey-brown fall cankerworm and Bruce spanworm moths mate and lay eggs between late Oct. and early Dec.; other pale geometrid family moths overwinter as adults and emerge early in spring

Inchworms: Very slender caterpillars of the geometrid moth family that loop their bodies into the air as they pull their back ends up toward their front to move forward

Oldest moth fossil: 180 million years old

Mexican jumping beans: Caused by movement of moth caterpillars eating into beans

Moth range: Throughout Ontario and all Canada to the Arctic

Number of species whose caterpillars eat clothes, fur and feathers: 3

Number of Ontario moth species: About 2,000

Number of species of foreign moths established in Canada: At least 15, including clothes moths and meal moths

Number of moth species worldwide: More than 150,000

Also see: Goldenrod, Red Oak, Big Brown Bat, Red-winged Blackbird, Monarch Butterfly

SPIDERS
Indispensable Sinister Spinsters

KILLING SPIDERS MAY not bring rain, but it does grant a field day to flies, moths and other insects around the house and garden. The old arachnicide weather superstition was one of the few to counter deep, age-old prejudices against spiders, the mere sight of which gives countless Miss Muffets the willies. Freud contended that spider phobias rise from a primal fear of a cannibal witch or ogre with long, pointy, bending fingers, subconsciously identified with the arachnids' legs.

Perched at the centre of classic, concentrically ringed vertical webs in sunny-but-sheltered spots in many backyards, big, sleek, long-legged black-and-yellow garden spiders are both scary and striking. They're members of the large spider family known as orb-weavers, which construct ornate, expansive bug nets up to 75 centimetres (2.5 feet) wide. The shamrock orb-weaver, with a huge, spherical, white-spattered brown abdomen, as well as the large brown cross spider normally lurk in recesses or curled leaves at the top or sides of their webs, often hung in gardens or on the sides of houses. They become more noticeable in late summer and fall as they reach full size and build their webs higher up off the ground.

Many orb-weavers rebuild their webs nightly, first gobbling up and recycling most of the old, tattered strands, which are made of protein, and then restringing the remaining frame in as little as half an hour. With select use and adjustment of each of their six back-end spinneret valves, they vary thickness, strength and elasticity of the silk as they spin. The strong girderlike strands that converge at the centre of orb-weaver webs are threaded with spiralled rings of special sticky silk that actually catches the flying insects.

Largest Ontario spider: Dock spider, *Dolomedese tenebrosus* (illustrated), with a legspan of up to 13 cm (5 in)

World's largest spider: Goliath bird-eating spider of South America, with a legspan of up to 28 cm (11 in)

Estimated mass of insects consumed annually by spiders in Canada: Equal to the weight of the country's entire human population in 2004

Alias: Arachnids, *les araignees*, Araneae order

Spider name origin: From Old English *spinthron*, meaning "spinner"

Cobweb name origin: Another Old English name for spider was *attorcoppe*, which became shortened to "coppe" or "cob"

Arachnid name origin: In Greek mythology, the maiden Arachne was changed into a spider by

The tangled cobwebs clumped in the corners of ceilings and window frames also contain select sticky lines that, when alighted upon, often detach at one end, wrap around and suspend hapless flies and moths. Small, salt-and-pepper-mottled house spiders hanging upside down nearby move in quickly to dispatch the victims.

But the works of many other eight-legged trappers contain no sticky silk at all. Funnel-web weavers and sheet-web weavers – both large families whose flat, silken mats glisten in the grass with early-morning dew – lie hidden beneath their webs until a passing insect becomes entangled. The long-legged cellar spider, originally from the tropics and probably inadvertently transported by early colonists, slings a messy, arched canopy from the ceilings of many houses, but often roams to catch its prey, which includes other house spiders. Its slight, almost translucent body is dwarfed by extremely long, bent, skinny legs, by which it hangs and characteristically shakes its web when disturbed.

Some 40 to 50 percent of all types of spiders don't even make webs, though all spin silk. Jumping spiders, such as the tiny zebra spiders often seen scaling walls and doorways, stalk and leap upon their prey, but remain anchored to silk safety lines in case they fall. Crab spiders too tie themselves off while lying in wait inside flowers to ambush pollinating insects. Nocturnal wolf spiders run down their quarry, but use silk to lash together shelters.

All spiders also possess venom. The paralyzing poison gives them the option of consuming their catch right away or wrapping it up and keeping it fresh and alive for later snacking. They actually drink, rather than eat, sucking their victims' bodily juices through a pump in their digestive system.

The minority of spiders that have big-enough chompers to break human skin bite only in self-defence, leaving an irritating, swollen red spot with a pair of tiny fang marks. Many stinging indoor bites are caused by black-footed sac spiders when they get trapped in bedding or clothes during nocturnal hunting forays. Residing in small silken sacs in nooks and crannies during the day, the yellowish, centimetre-long (0.4-inch-long) natives

Athena after defeating the goddess in a weaving contest; spiders were identified with Greek and Hindu goddesses who were spinners of fate

Name of a group: A smother of spiders

Food: Insects, other spiders, mites, daddy longlegs, tadpoles, tiny fish

Average clutch: 2 to several thousand eggs, depending on species

Lifespan: Most species less than a year; long-legged cellar spiders and a few other Ontario species live up to 3 years; tarantulas up to 30 years

Predators: Birds, toads, frogs, salamanders, shrews, snakes, ants, wasps, tiger beetles, centipedes, other spiders; eggs eaten by many insects and birds

Number of kinds of spider silk: 8, but no one species can produce them all; can be as thin as $1/100$ the diameter of an human hair, twice as strong, for its size, as steel and stretch up to 4 times its original length

Top wolf spider running speed: More than 50 cm/sec (20 in/sec)

Top dock spider running speed on surface of water: 75 cm/sec (30 in/sec)

Maximum time dock spiders remain submerged: At least 45 minutes

Number of eyes: 8 for most species; while orb-weavers and most other web-slingers have very poor eyesight, jumping spiders, wolf spiders, dock spiders and other roving hunters can see well

Winter whereabouts: Most species hibernate beneath bark, in logs or under dead leaves, grass or stones; eggs or hatchlings of others overwinter in egg cases; some spiders may remain active indoors and, during very mild spells, rouse outdoors

Birds that use spider silk in nests: Hummingbirds, vireos, flycatchers, tree-nesting warblers

Famous individuals: Inky Dinky, Charlotte, Boris, Shelob, The Spiders from Mars

Folk remedies: Because spiderwebs are coated with bactericides and fungicides to protect them from hungry organisms, they have been used as effective antibiotic dressings for wounds in many cultures

Portion of fatal venomous bites worldwide caused by spiders: 10–15%

Number of Ontario spider species: About 1,500

Number of known spider species worldwide: About 36,000

Daddy longlegs: Unlike true spiders, this type of arachnid can neither spin silk nor inject venom and has only 2 simple eyes; mostly forage for dead or small insects, decaying plant matter, spider and insect eggs

Other arachnids: Mites, ticks, scorpions, pseudoscorpions, horseshoe crabs

Also see: House & Home

of the Mediterranean region have become common house dwellers since turning up in southern Ontario in the early 1980s. The rare, retiring **northern black widow**, which haunts rocky crevices on the Bruce Peninsula, packs the most threatening bite in the province, causing fever, breathing trouble, paralysis and, in a small percentage of cases, even death. Most Ontario black widow sightings, though, occur when the dark little spider with the red hour-glass icon turns up in bunches of grapes or other fruit shipped from the southern United States. An actual bite hasn't been reported in decades.

Female black widows are also synonymous with the femme fatale because they're known to sometimes devour their mates after males have served their purpose. The practice actually occurs among many spiders. To avoid being eaten even before mating, the generally much smaller males may strum love notes on a strand of a potential mate's web, signal to her with his legs in a kind of sexual semaphore, or send a chemical message. If she appears receptive, he rushes in and fertilizes her. But fleet-footed males usually manage to hit the road before giving their hungry partners a chance to devour them heartlessly for a quick protein fix to nourish their eggs.

Most Ontario spiders mate in early summer and then wrap their eggs in yellowish cocoons, which they closely guard. Some, such as the **dock spider** (illustrated), tote their egg sacks around with them. Wolf spiders even carry their hatchlings on their backs for up to 10 days. Soon after hatching, most tiny spiderlings swarm to the tops of plants and shrubs and spin a thin strand of silk, which catches in the breeze and lifts them up into the air, sometimes thousands of metres. This "ballooning" spreads them out over wide distances, keeping their populations from becoming too concentrated in one area. As night falls, the silk becomes moisture-laden and the tiny paratroopers drop back down upon the Earth.

TERMITES
Blind, Wood-munching Home Wreckers

UNBEKNOWNST TO THE average urban surface-dweller, termite colonies in many southern Ontario communities form vast subterranean cities, sometimes with millions of inhabitants and stretching for hundreds of metres (or yards) across residential blocks. Tiny, white, eyeless insects throng through interlacing tunnels leading to widespread dormitories, nurseries, royal chambers and innumerable eateries in dead, damp wood. Rotting roots, stumps, fence posts, picnic tables, decks, indoor beams and floor joists are prime termite fare. To turn wood into a meal – something almost no other animals can do – the little lumber chompers tote gutfuls of microscopic protozoans. The symbiotic one-celled creatures break cellulose down into digestible carbohydrates and account for about one-third of a termite's total weight.

Though eastern subterranean termites may have been long established on the shore of Lake Erie near Windsor, others arrived in Ontario as Depression-era migrants, probably in crates or pallets from the eastern half of the United States. They first turned up in a Toronto waterfront warehouse in 1938 and spread through the city's east end over the next 20 years. Today, they reach into Brampton, Richmond Hill and Pickering, while most of Ontario's other infestations centre around the Kitchener-Guelph and Windsor areas.

Mature colony population: 10,000–10 million
Age of a colony when rapid growth begins: 4–7 years
Termite length: Workers and soldiers 6–7 mm (0.25 in); winged termites and kings 7–7.5 mm (0.3 in); queens 7–13 mm (0.3–0.5 in)
Markings: Workers creamy white; soldiers white, with orange heads; kings, queens and winged breeders black
Alias: Eastern subterranean termites, white ants, subs, *les termites à pattes jaunes, Reticulitermes flavipes*
Whereabouts: Yards with moist soil and dead roots or firewood, wood chips and wood debris; often live in stumps or garden-border logs; eat into houses
Food: Cellulose in dead wood, cardboard and paper; prefer pine, spruce, fir and light, fast-growing hardwoods, such as silver maple and tree of heaven
Annual consumption by a colony of 5 million: Equal to 40 two-by-fours, each 2.4 m (8 ft) long
Egg production: Dozens laid daily, during warm months, by queen, whose oversized, swollen abdomen makes her barely mobile; queen mates periodically with king, her constant attendant; secondary reproductive colony members collectively lay more eggs than queen
Hatchlings: About 0.5 mm (0.02 in) long, translucent, moult many times before becoming

full-grown workers, soldiers or reproductive adults

Lifespan: Workers 1–4 years; queens up to at least 10 years

Predators: Colonies attacked by ants, centipedes, spiders, red-backed salamanders, toads, shrews, moles, voles; swarming termites also eaten by birds, dragonflies, beetles, wasps and predatory flies

Winter whereabouts: In ground below the frost line or in stumps or logs; rather torpid, but revive and feed during mild spells

House attacks: Enter through cracks and seams in concrete foundations and basement floors and frames of basement windows and garage doors; wood dampened by leaky plumbing, air-conditioning condensation and water trapped behind siding most vulnerable

City blocks with termite infestations in Toronto: Probably more than 1,000

Trap, treat and release: Cheap, new control technique, using 1/5,000 as much chemicals as older methods, pioneered by University of Toronto entomologist Dr. Tim Myles, coats termites lured into cardboard traps with slow-acting substance; because of mutual grooming, a single treated worker can fatally contaminate about 100 others

Ontario Range: In at least 32 cities and towns from Windsor to Oshawa, Fergus and Kincardine

Musical contributions: Didgeridoos of Australia are made from termite-hollowed branches

Also see: Ants, House & Home

Though seemingly antlike, termites are of far greater antiquity and more closely related to cockroaches. With softer, thinner skin than ants they shun the open air and light to keep from fatally drying out. Within the dark, dank chambers and tunnels of termitaries, the walls of which are plastered with hardened termite dung, the humidity is above 90 percent, while carbon-dioxide levels from wood-processing flatulence are up to 100 times higher than in the open air. To venture above ground, termites build grey, snaking tubes, up to 2.5 centimetres (one inch) wide, of saliva-moistened dirt cemented with droppings, leading to cracks in the foundations of houses or up tree trunks to dead branches.

Unlike ant societies, termites also have gender equality, with castes of workers and soldiers made up of both sexes, and a resident founding "king," as well as a "queen." Workers take care of the building and upkeep of the colony, tend the eggs, young, soldiers and royal breeders and feed them regurgitated sawdust from wood-chewing forays. Soldiers (larger of the three illustrated) – which have armour-plated heads twice the size of those of workers and long, fearsome mandibles – comprise 1 to 2 percent of the population. They guard against ant attacks and, like bouncers, bar entrance to all lacking a distinctive scent spread among colony members from pheromone secretions by the queen.

Reproductive adult termites are black, equipped with long wings and functioning eyes. They fly in swarms on warm, sunny mornings in late winter or spring, most often around early May. After usually less than 10 minutes in the air, they land, snap off their wings and seek out the opposite sex. The very few that pair and survive crawl into an unoccupied crevice, dig out a honeymoon suite and start a new colony as the king and queen. But isolated small new colonies of termites usually can't survive northern winters. Ontario populations rely much more on select wingless breeders that are light-orangish or mottled and establish adjunct egg-laying chambers, like suburbs, near the edges of their home colonies. Most long-distance dispersal occurs through termite-infested soil, building materials or firewood being transported by humans.

WATER STRIDERS
Just Skimming the Surface

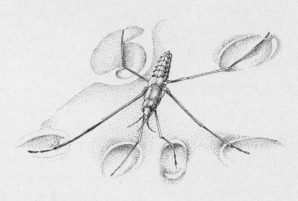

WATER STRIDERS are the most superficial of insects. The surface means everything to the torpedo-shaped, nimble-footed bugs, which are among the easiest of aquatic creatures to observe, their shadows gliding across the shallow bottoms of many urban creeks and ponds. They literally skate over the water on little dimples made in the surface tension by each of their sprawling legs, which are tipped with numerous, tiny hairs that push down, but don't break through, the film of closely packed molecules that forms at the top of any body of water. At the same time, they are supersensitive to information carried on ripples as subtle as one-thousandth of a millimetre high, using them to find both sustenance and each other.

Disturbances caused by other insects falling into the water, often dead or dying, or by submerged mosquito larvae coming up for air, bring water striders vaulting in furiously for a meal. Seizing prey with their two short forelegs, striders sink in their needlelike snouts and inject caustic digestive juices that dissolve their victims' insides into a liquid lunch within minutes.

After finding a floating plant or piece of wood to serve as an egg-laying platform, males attract mates by shaking their legs to send out high-frequency wave patterns in the water. Both sexes mate frequently throughout their adult lives. Young water striders look like small versions of their parents. They grow and moult five times within 40 to 60 days and before becoming ready to reproduce themselves.

Speed: Up to 1 m/sec (3.3 ft/sec)
Lifespan: About 6 months
Body length: 2–16 mm (0.1–0.6 in)
Markings: Various species are black, dark grey or yellow on top, with brown, grey or whitish markings; white on undersides
Alias: Pond skaters, Jesus bugs, *les patineurs*, Gerridae family
Whereabouts: Creeks, rivers, ponds, lake inlets, swamps
Food: Insects and their larvae, springtails, mites, spiders
Predators: Fish, birds, dragonflies, water spiders, water beetles
Winter whereabouts: Adults hibernate from Oct. to early spring beneath rocks, logs or leaves underwater or on land nearby
Range: All Ontario; all other provinces and territories
Number of Ontario water strider species: 11

Fish

MANY URBAN STREAMS and lakeshores have come a long way in a few decades, since the days when the only fish they harboured were carp and other murky-water bottom-feeders. Rainbow trout and salmon have begun swimming upstream through cities, jumping at weirs and rapids, to spawn. They're actually introduced west-coast fish whose populations are still heavily supplemented by the annual stocking of millions of fingerlings. But many homegrown species are also showing signs of recovery in urban waters. Aquatic ecosystems may never return to what they once were in pre-settlement times, but having wild fish swimming and spawning in the middle of the city is a heartening sign of a healthier environment for all.

CARP
Voracious Mud-grubbing Scavenger

EVER WAS THERE a fish more disposed to excel in the grubbiest of urban conditions than the thick-skinned, slime-revelling, bottom-feeding common carp. Rising to the surface of the murkiest of waters, its often leviathanian proportions, flesh-dangling mouth and prominent dorsal fin sometimes inspire tales of lurking monsters in the city's foulest drinks. Luckily, the creature from the black lagoon's gaping maw is all lip and no bite because the carp is, in truth, a gargantuan minnow, and like its tiny relations it packs only small teeth at the back of its throat.

Despite their lowly urban milieu, carp have been esteemed in many cultures through the ages for their size, power and good eating. Native to Asia and Eastern Europe, the unsightly fish are a traditional symbol of strength in the Orient. It was said that carp able to ascend the fastest-flowing rivers were transformed into dragons. Similarly, just before Chinese and Vietnamese New Year, the Kitchen God leaves the homes of families he watches over to make his annual report, riding to heaven on the back of a carp, which earns its dragon's wings upon arrival.

Probably the first fish to be "farmed," carp were stocked in royal ponds in both Asia and Europe and served during great ceremonial feasts. Today, they still take the place of turkey on many Eastern European

Average adult length: 30–60 cm (1–2 ft)

Weight: Usually about 2–5 kg (4.4–11 lb); sometimes 15 kg (33 lb) or more in Great Lakes

Record carp: 26.2 kg (57.8 lb) in Great Lakes; 37.3 kg (82.2 lb) in Europe

Markings: Usually an olive-green back, shading to a yellowish undersides, often with reddish lower fins

Fleshy feelers: Highly sensitive dangling "barbels" at the sides of the mouth and a smaller pair on the upper lip are packed with taste buds to help detect food on murky, muddy water bottoms

Alias: Common carp, mirror carp, German carp, European carp, *la carpe*, *Cyprinus carpio*

Whereabouts: Shallow, weedy bays and lake margins, slow stretches of rivers, marshes, ponds, reservoirs

Food: Bloodworms (midge larvae), caddis fly and other insect larvae, planktonic crustaceans, snails, clams, aquatic worms, decaying plant and animal matter, fish and amphibian eggs, aquatic plant roots and shoots, seeds, algae; fry eat plankton and algae

Eggs per female: 36,000–2.2 million, depending on her size

Egg development period: 3–6 days

Hatchling length: 3–5.5 mm (0.1–0.2 in)

Length after first growing season: 13–19 cm (5–7.5 in)

Age of first-time breeders: Males 3–4 years; females 4–5 years

Lifespan: Males often live 8–10 years; females 16–18 years; maximum 47 years

Predators: Pike, pickerel, muskellunge, largemouth bass, herons and other birds probably take young under about 1.5 kg (3.3 lb)

Range: Southern Ontario to Lake Superior; also in Quebec, Manitoba, Saskatchewan, British Columbia

Old Country cousins: Goldfish, which originate in China, are closely related to and sometimes hybridize with carp; feral goldfish populations in lakes, ponds and rivers revert to their original olive-green shades because selectively bred, brightly coloured individuals are picked off more quickly by predators

Number of Ontario fish species: 128 native, 31 non-native

Christmas dinner tables. Spurred by their Old World popularity, the United States Fish Commission began importing large numbers of carp for farm and mill ponds in the 1870s. Ontario's first were stocked in an impoundment near Markham in 1880. Within a couple of decades, however, burst mill dams on the Holland River, north of Toronto, and many other locations set captive carp free to spread and multiply in sluggish waters across North America.

Unfortunately, while carp can thrive in oxygen-poor, algae-clogged environs degraded by erosion and pollution where most other fish can't endure, they do much themselves to despoil healthier habitats. They're appallingly sloppy eaters, deriving much of their sustenance by sucking up huge mouthfuls of ooze from silty bottoms and spitting everything back into the water to pick out floating morsels of bloodworms, caddisfly larvae, snails, clams and rotting plant and animal material. They also stir up sediments as they uproot and devour aquatic vegetation, while all the nutrients they liberate from the muck are soon shot back out their other end in prodigious amounts into the open water in a form that feeds equally voluminous algae blooms. The clouding effect of all the mud, excrement and algae chokes off most kinds of submerged plants, reduces zooplankton, drives away other fish and buries their eggs. Carp weed-bed ravaging also destroys food and habitat for ducks, frogs and aquatic insects.

Between mid-May and early summer, carp really stir things up when they spawn in raucous aquatic orgies along weedy shorelines, usually in less than 50 centimetres (1.6 feet) of water. Splashing, thrashing and jumping wildly, with their dorsal fins and backs frequently breaking above the frothing surface, two or three males usually attend each female, though groups sometimes form of up to 18 egg- and milt-spewing fish. A single large female typically scatters hundreds of thousands of eggs over the submerged vegetation, where they hatch within days into an other generation of voracious, algae-gulping, mud-grubbing scavengers.

MINNOWS
Huge Family of Little Fish

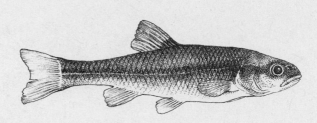

MINNOWS often seem to appear almost miraculously in some of the smallest suburban headwater creeks, shallow marshes and sometimes even in flooded drainage ditches. The outwardly inconsequential little fingerlings comprise the largest and perhaps most important single family of freshwater fish in the world. They form a vital link in the aquatic food chain, eating vast quantities of algae, plankton and aquatic insects and passing on their energy and nutrients to most of the other larger fish as well as fishing birds and other animals.

Ontario's three dozen minnow species occupy virtually every aquatic habitat, each finding its own niche. **Creek chub** (illustrated), which grow up to 10 centimetres (four inches) long and display iridescent silvery-purple sides, are one of the most common stream minnows and sometimes colonize seasonally flooded urban ponds. Dark olive-brown **fathead minnows**, only half the size of creek chub, are often the most abundant fish in small mucky lakes, ponds and ditches, where they persist by sticking their eggs to the bottoms of rocks, logs and branches. Large schools of **golden shiners** and **emerald shiners** inhabit river mouths and shallow, weedy lakeshores, where gulls, terns, cormorants and bait nets scoop up multitudes.

Though most tiny fish, including the fry of many large species, are commonly referred to as minnows, true members of the family are set apart by possessing just a single soft-rayed fin on their backs. They're also a lippy lot, with teeth located at the back of their throats rather than on their jaws.

Adult length: Most species 5–8 cm (2–3 in)

Biggest native Ontario minnow: Fallfish, up to 45 cm (18 in) long

Alias: Cyprinids, *les vairons*, family Cyprinidae

Food: Plankton, algae, aquatic insect larvae, fish fry

Eggs per female: Up to 3,000

Egg development period: 4–10 days

Maximum lifespan: 8 years

Popular bait minnows: Fatheads, golden shiners, emerald shiners, creek chub, common shiners

Range: Throughout Ontario; also in all other provinces and territories except Newfoundland

Number of Ontario minnow species: 34 native, 3 introduced, 1 recent natural immigrant

Number of minnow species worldwide: About 2,100

PUMPKINSEED SUNFISH
Glimmering from the Shallows

Average adult length: 18–23 cm (7–9 in) in lakes, 10–15 cm (4–6 in) in brooks and ponds
Adult weight: 28–340 g (1–12 oz)
Maximum size in Ontario: 25 cm (10 in), 480 g (17 oz)
Markings: Gold sides in alternating shades forming vertical bars, most noticeable on females, and covered with oval spots of olive, orange and red; golden-brown to olive top, bright-yellow, bronze to reddish-orange bottom; wavy blue-green lines on orange cheeks, distinct bright-red spot on gills; spiny fins, big golden eyes, small mouth; colours intensify in spawning territorial males
Alias: Common sunfish, yellow sunfish, sunny, punky, sun bass, pond perch, ruff, kivry, *le crapet-soleil, Lepomis gibbosus*
Whereabouts: Shallow, weedy rivers, ponds, bays, small lakes, marshes and muddy brooks

T HE FIRST TROPHY of many a budding angler, the colourful but generally less-than-wary pumpkinseed sunfish is a perennial, iridescent jewel of shoreside shallows in urban streams, ponds and weedy bays across the province. Thriving in warm waters, it has persisted in built-up areas where many other native fish that require cold, clear, gravel-bottomed rivers have perished. True to their name, schools of vibrantly hued sunfish venture into the shallows to feed only when the sun shines. The brief shadow of a passing cloud is enough to send them back into deeper water. "Pumpkinseed" alludes to their flat, pointed, oval shape, though their numerous oval spots are also reminiscent of the seeds.

Like other sunfishes and bass, many pumpkinseed males are hard-working homebodies, while females are absentee moms. When shoreside waters warm to near room temperature, in late June or early July, robust males, usually six or seven years old, begin sweeping away debris with their tails and pulling out roots from weed beds to form circular nests about twice their own length. Nurseries of 10 to 15 nests, about a metre (three feet) or more apart, are often established by groups of the maternally inclined bruisers.

Many male sunfish are young turks with no taste for the settled life. At least a third smaller than the established pumpkinseeds, they are fast-living, cheating, sneaky scoundrels. They stand back and observe as members of the opposite sex come to inspect nest colonies. The females are chased about by the eager residents until convinced by one to come back to his place. As a couple slowly circles around the nest, her body inclined toward his in the act of spawning, a young sneaker will dash in close and squirt a stream of his own milt into the mix and then try to make off before being detected.

The sneak-and-squirt strategy is a successful one. Nest-tending fathers often unknowingly raise more offspring of other fish than their own. Most of their real sons remain celibate until later in life, when they're big enough to hold down a good nesting spot and drive others away. Foster sons, however, mainly grow up to be shiftless, promiscuous cheaters like their biological daddies, sexually active by the time they are two. Putting more of their internal resources into sperm production, they never grow as big as the territorial males. All the fast living and being chased from one nest to another also burns them out more quickly. Few live more than five years. Many die from fungal infections of fin wounds inflicted by jealous homesteaders.

Often mating with several partners, territorial males can accumulate piles of more than 15,000 eggs. They fan them constantly, to keep them aerated in the warm water, and fiercely attack any other fish that intrudes, even biting human fingers. After the minuscule, transparent fry hatch, fathers watch over them in the nest for up to another 11 days, until the young swim off on their own. Many males then mate again and raise a second batch.

Bluegill sunfish are also common in many urban waters, especially in eastern Ontario. Pumpkinseeds sometimes either mate with bluegills or take over their nests. The two fishes are similar in most ways, with the bluegill having blue-green or olive colouring reflecting a purple iridescence.

Food: Dragonfly and mayfly nymphs, bloodworms and other insect larvae, snails, small crustaceans, salamander tadpoles, fish eggs and fry, clams, leeches, worms, algae

Nest: Shallow, saucer-shaped clearing in weeds and debris, 10–40 cm (4–16 in) wide, in less than 75 cm (2.5 ft) of water

Clutch: Females lay 600–5,000 light-amber eggs, each 1 mm (0.04 in) wide

Incubation period: 3–10 days

Age of first-time breeders: 2 years for "sneaker" males, 5–6 years for territorial males, 4–5 years for females

Maximum age: 10 years

Predators: Pike, pickerel, sauger, muskies, osprey and kingfishers; bass, perch, catfish, other sunfish and older pumpkinseeds eat young or eggs

Winter whereabouts: Largely inactive at bottom of deep water early Sept. to early May

Range: Southern Ontario to about Lake Temiskaming and Sault Ste. Marie; also west of Thunder Bay to north of Kenora and in southeastern Manitoba, Quebec, New Brunswick and introduced in southern British Columbia

Number of Ontario sunfish species (including bass): 9

Number of sunfish species worldwide: 32 (restricted to North America)

Also see: Smallmouth Bass

RAINBOW TROUT
Widely Famed West Coast Import

Average adult length: 41–60 cm (1.3–2 ft)

Average weight: 1.4–5.5 kg (3–12 lb)

Ontario record: 98 cm (3.2 ft) long, 13.2 kg (29.1 lb), caught in mouth of Nottawasaga River, 1975

World record: 19.1 kg (42.1 lb), caught in Alaska

Markings: Steel-blue to yellowish-green or brownish back and upper sides; black-spotted silvery to light-yellowish lower sides with a long faint-pink to red band; silvery, grey, white or yellowish belly; radiating lines of black spots on tail fin

Alias: Steelhead salmon, steelhead trout, silver trout, *la truite arc-en-ciel*, *Oncorhynchus mykiss*

Name origin: From Greek *troktes*, meaning "nibbler"

Whereabouts: Around shoals and mid-levels in larger lakes, usually less than 11 m (36 ft) deep, often near river mouths;

RAINBOW TROUT ARE such well-known and popular Ontario sport fish, many people don't realize that they are West Coast transplants, closely related to sockeye, chinook and coho salmon, rather than to native trout. They were first introduced in the Great Lakes watershed in the late 1800s, when the American government was trying to create a coast-to-coast anglers' paradise with specially outfitted railroad cars carrying sport fish across the country to stock every watershed lacking in any desirable species. Fish were often tossed from trestles into rivers and lakes while trains stopped to take on water. Though rainbows now reproduce in many streams, the provincial government and recreational groups maintain artificially high populations by continuing to stock hundreds of thousands every year to satisfy angling demand for the feisty, high-jumping, fighting fish.

Rainbow trout spend much of their adult lives around shoals and moderately deep water in the Great Lakes and other big water bodies feeding on freshwater shrimp, aquatic insects, plankton, minnows, alewives and other smaller fish. In October, however, they begin migrating up spawning rivers and streams, some of them running through even the largest cities. At rapids, or specially constructed stepped fishway chutes at dams, they display the same kind of athletic prowess that makes them such popular game fish, sometimes leaping one to two metres (3.3 to 6.6 feet) into the air to get past obstructions in their journey upstream.

Some rainbows spawn as soon as late December, but most wait until early spring. They can sometimes be seen near stream edges, hovering in groups above gravel-bottomed riffles, all facing into the current, their passions inflaming their sides a dark purple-red visible through the rippling water. Females create oval nest trenches, or redds, a little bit longer than themselves by swimming on their sides and slapping their tails into the gravel. Males jostle for position around the redds, with the biggest usually the most successful in courting nest holders, swimming alongside, nuzzling and pressing against them. Eggs and milt, released together over several seconds, sink into the trench below and are covered with gravel by the females, who may go on to dig and spawn in several more nests. In any one spot, however, spawning usually lasts only one or two days before the fish head back to the big lakes.

The Ministry of Natural Resources also stocks hundreds of thousands of European **brown trout** in Ontario rivers every year to provide quarry for fly-fishing enthusiasts and other anglers. Like rainbows, brown trout fare better than and outcompete native **brook trout** in streams altered by erosion, pollution and other human disturbances. Brook trout still persist in the upper reaches of many southern Ontario watersheds, as well as in rivers and lakes throughout much of the rest of the province.

Lake trout, however, once among the monarchs of the Great Lakes and backbone of the commercial fishing industry, have been much reduced from their former glory. Overfishing combined with industrial contaminants and the invasion of sea lamprey through the chain of freshwater seas nearly wiped out the big lakers by the late 1950s. Attempts by Ontario and neighbouring U.S. states to repopulate the lakes with stocks from Lake Superior and Haliburton have met with only limited success.

in smaller streams with gravel-bottomed riffles until as much as three years old and during spawning season; also stocked in many ponds and reservoirs

Preferred water temperature: 14.5–17°C (58–62°F)

Food: Freshwater shrimp, insects and their aquatic larvae, plankton, alewives, smelt, minnows and other small fish, worms, snails, leeches, clams, eggs of salmon and other fish

Eggs: 3–5 mm (0.1–0.2 in) wide, pink to orange

Average clutch: 800–1,000 eggs in each of several nests made by female

Egg development period: 4–7 weeks

Age of first-time breeders: Most 3–5 years

Lifespan: Up to 8 years

Predators: Young taken by walleye, pike, bass and most other predatory fish, terns, herons, cormorants, mink, sea lampreys

Winter whereabouts: Many in deep pools in streams

Range: Throughout Great Lakes, their surrounding hinterlands, including Lake Simcoe, and in northwestern Ontario to north of Kenora; also in all other provinces and the Yukon

Number of fish caught annually by anglers in Ontario: About 130 million, with two-thirds released back into water

Number of salmon family species in Ontario: 13 native, 5 introduced

Also see: Salmon, Minnows

RIVERS, CREEKS & WATERSIDES

After Long Neglect and Abuse, Cities Are Reconnecting with the Waterways and Lakes That Lie at the Core of Their Sense of Place

Origin of *Ontario*: Iroquoian for "beautiful lake" or "beautiful water"

Age of most rivers and lakes in southern and central Ontario: 10,000–13,000 years, left after the retreat of glaciers

Number of lakes in Ontario: About 250,000

World's biggest freshwater lake in surface area: Lake Superior, 82,100 km² (31,699 sq mi)

Ontario's biggest interior lake: Lake Nipigon, 4,848 km² (1,872 sq mi)

Ontario's deepest lake: Lake Superior, 405 m (1,329 ft)

Height of the CN Tower: 553 m (1,815 ft)

Maximum depth of Lake Ontario: 237 m (778 ft)

Maximum depth of Lake Huron: 229 m (750 ft)

THE USE OF urban waterways as conduits of waste and refuse was once so pervasive, junked machinery and hulks of old cars were heaved into the smallest neglected creeks and rivers as if they might somehow be carried away downstream and out of mind. In recent decades, however, a sea change in attitudes has brought local streams and waterfronts to the fore of public attention as people reconnect with the central geographic, ecological and even spiritual significance waterways hold in the landscape. Virtually all Ontario cities, in fact, grew up around important junctures of rivers or lakeshores. There's even a growing interest today in the meanderings through cities of long-buried streams, their presence stirring the imagination, representing a faint, underlying trickle from the past.

A legacy of buried creeks is part of the reason why even most above-ground urban streams continue to be in rough ecological shape. City drainage systems have traditionally been designed to flush rainwater from eave-stroughs to gutters, storm sewers and outfalls as quickly as possible. Water has much less chance of being absorbed and filtered through the ground and along winding feeder creeks before it ends up in larger streams.

The result is rushing torrents during and after storms that increase erosion, widen stream banks and bury river bottoms in mud and silt. Channelling of parts of streams in concrete, stones and wire only increases the problems farther downriver. In between storms, streams are more shallow, warmer and slower than they would be under more natural conditions. Many fish and other aquatic species can't abide by the widely fluctuating conditions, on top of poor water quality.

Yet, the health of many urban rivers and major Ontario lakes has significantly improved since the late 1960s through pollution abatement legislation, the building and upgrading of sewage treatment plants and phasing out of phosphates in detergents. Levels of many of the most clearly dangerous chemicals, such as PCBs, dioxin, mercury, DDT and mirex, have been greatly reduced. Lake Erie recovered from phosphate-fed algal blooms that nearly choked the life out of its ecosystem and caused the once-thriving commercial fishery to collapse. Fish such as rainbow trout and salmon are beginning to make spawning runs up many streams that were considered virtually dead 30 years ago. More than 40 fish species now inhabit Toronto's once murky harbour, including good numbers of large northern-lake angling icons such as pike (illustrated) and pickerel.

At the same time, consciousness has grown that every place and every backyard and city street is part of a watershed, affecting the state of the rivers and lakes within it. Conservation authorities, which are organized around major provincial drainage basins, and the development of new municipal watershed-management plans are helping to lead the way. Stoop-and-scoop bylaws, moves to reduce the use of pesticides and road salt and efforts to encourage the disconnection of eavestrough downspouts from storm-sewer systems all significantly contribute to minimizing the contamination of urban streams through runoff. Storm-water retention basins to slow down peak flows are being built in many new subdivisions. Volunteer groups adopting rivers and creeks in urban watersheds have made great strides in pulling all manner of junk out of the water, removing old dams and other obstructions and planting

Maximum depth of Lake Erie: 65 m (211 ft)

Portion of the world's fresh surface water found in the Great Lakes: About 20%

Average time taken by water flowing into upper Lake Superior to reach the St. Lawrence River: 329 years

Southern Ontario's longest river: Grand River, 270 km (165 mi)

Ontario's longest interior river: Severn and Albany Rivers, both 982 km (610 mi) long

Ontario's longest bordering river: Ottawa River, 1,271 km (790 mi)

Most popular sport-fishing lake in Ontario: Lake Simcoe

Fish that survive in warm, murky, oxygen-depleted urban waters: Carp, white suckers, sunfish, catfish, fathead minnows

Number of dams 2 m (7 ft) high or more in Ontario: About 2,000

Years when Lake Ontario completely froze over: 1934 and 1893

Frequency of Lakes Huron, Erie and Superior all freezing over: About once every 10 years

World's greatest freshwater ship graveyard: Lake Erie, with almost 3,000 wrecks

Number of municipal watershed-management plans in Ontario: About 130

Number of toxic chemical compounds detected in the Great Lakes: More than 360

Number of non-native species established in Great Lakes:

About 145, more than one-third since 1970

Zebra mussel density at bottom of Great Lakes: Up to thousands per m² (1.2 sq yd)

Daily amount of water filtered by a zebra mussel: 1 L (1.75 pt)

People who study lakes, ponds and streams: Limnologists

Reason water feels warm to swimmers in the rain: The body has already adjusted to coolness caused by rain, so blood vessels do not suddenly constrict upon submersion in water, as they do on a hot day

Also see: Carp, Rainbow Trout, Salmon, Smelt, Wetlands

trees along shorelines to prevent erosion and provide the shade needed for cool-water species such as trout.

In many cities, though, systems of combined storm water and sewage pipes still overflow into rivers and lakes during heavy summer rains, causing the closing of beaches to swimming. Illegal or accidental dumping of effluents and fuels from factories, gas stations and hydro-electric transformers continues. Old dumps and toxic waste sites still leach into ground water and streams, and the airborne deposition of persistent industrial contaminants into lakes remains a major problem.

One of the biggest threats to Ontario waters is the recurrent introduction of invasive species. Zebra mussels are the best-known invaders of recent years, filter feeding on vast quantities of plankton, redirecting much of the energy and nutrients in the Great Lakes system to the water bottom. The resulting changes to the ecosystem are wide-sweeping but still not fully understood. Like the thumbnail-sized mussels, tiny crustaceans known as spiny waterfleas and fishhook waterfleas were also released into the Great Lakes in recent years from the discharged ballast water of foreign freighters. The plankton-eating creatures have multiplied phenomenally, reaching up to 1,300 per cubic metre (35 cubic feet) in some parts of Lake Ontario. After much disruption from a newly introduced species, a new balance may eventually settle out, but in a changed ecosystem. In the meantime, government regulations on shipping and commercial activity have been tightened to try to stem the tide of new invasions.

SALMON
Running Rivers to Spawn and Die

EACH SEPTEMBER and early October, enormous fish can be seen making their way through cities around the Great Lakes, swimming just beneath the surface below footbridges and riverbanks and defying the currents at sets of riffles and rapids. Seemingly a long way from home, they are Pacific salmon, usually **chinook** or **coho** (illustrated), making their life-culminating spawning runs out of the big lakes, much to the delight of urban anglers. Swearing off even food in their single-minded drive to reproduce, they die within a month of spawning on gravel beds in fast-flowing river stretches. In a few places, the eggs they leave behind yield spring fry that later spend the prime of their lives feasting on smelt and alewives in the Great Lakes before returning to the streams of their beginnings to spawn and meet their ends. Most of Ontario's chinooks and cohos, however, begin life in artificial hatcheries – as have their forebears since the late 1960s – and are later released in streams and bays.

The Pacific salmon largely take the place of lake trout and the native Atlantic salmon of Lake Ontario and the St. Lawrence River. Once caught by the thousands in spawning runs, Atlantic salmon disappeared by 1896 after mill dams cut off spawning grounds and forests cleared to the stream banks caused massive erosion, siltation and warming of rivers.

Average adult length: Coho (illustrated) 45–60 cm (1.5–2 ft); chinook 80–90 cm (2.6–3 ft)

Average weight: Coho 2.7–5.4 kg (6–12 lb); chinook 4.5–13.6 kg (10–30 lb)

Chinook markings: Gold-flecked or tinted, iridescent- to bluish-green back and upper sides, silvery to white belly; spawners turn olive-brown to purple

Coho markings: Black-spotted, steel-blue to greenish back, silver sides, white belly; red side stripe on spawners

Alias: *Les saumons*; Pacific salmon in genus *Oncorhynchus*

Whereabouts: Cohos usually within top 12 m (39 ft) in open water, chinooks a little deeper

Food: Mostly smelt, alewives, minnows and other small fish

Eggs: Orangish-red, lentil-sized, 1,400–14,000 per female, laid in several nests

Lifespan: Usually 3 or 4 years

Range: Great Lakes, Lake Nipissing and tributaries; Yukon

SMALLMOUTH BASS
Crayfish-loving Twilight Feeder

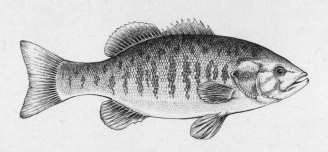

Adult length: Average 25–50 cm (10–20 in)

Average weight: 225–1,350 g (0.5–3 lb)

World record: 5.4 kg (11 lb, 15 oz), caught in Kentucky, 1955

Markings: Usually green, sometimes brown or yellowish, with dark hash marks along sides and dark spots on back; white belly; sunlight causes colours to temporarily lighten

Alias: Bronzeback, northern smallmouth, black bass, green bass, *l'achigan à petite bouche, Micropterus dolomieu*

Name of a group: A shoal of bass

Whereabouts: From steep shores to 6 m (20 ft) deep at the mouths and slower stretches of rivers and in clear, rocky lakes and bays

Food: Crayfish, minnows, perch, darters, fish fry, small frogs, mayfly nymphs and other insect larvae, leeches, tadpoles, snails

Water temperature needed for spawning: Above 15°C (60°F)

T HE SUDDEN APPEARANCE of saucer-shaped impressions in near-shore sand and gravel shallows in late May and June can look like evidence of extraterrestrials lured by intergalactic rumours of good fishing. The circles, however, are entirely aquatic in origin, the love nests of male smallmouth bass with an impressively maternal bent.

Smallmouths are the most abundant game fish in many parts of southern Ontario, including the lower stretches of rivers running through urban areas. Despite their reputation among anglers as feisty fighters, male bass are truly sensitive, dedicated family fish. They spend up to two days sweeping away sand and debris with their tails to form their distinct pebble-bottomed nests, usually a metre or two (3.3 to 6.6 feet) deep offshore. A male defends the site against all interlopers but steers fertile members of the opposite sex – whose background colours fade to contrast sharply with their dark markings – to the nest. After some fishy foreplay, with the he-bass rubbing and nipping, the passive female lays eggs in numerous four- to 10-second spurts over about two hours, interspersed with promenades around the nest. She then leaves him to care for them. Male and female may both spawn with several other partners, usually at night, over a period of six to 18 days.

The eggs, which stick to the gravel at the bottom of the nest, are fanned and guarded by the males from caviar-gulping predators. The feisty fish are even known to charge human swimmers and, on rare instances, to bite. All the while they eat only prey that comes within their nesting area. Black hatchlings, about the size of rice grains, are protected by their devoted dads for one to two weeks in the nest and another two to four weeks in open water, until the schools of tiny siblings begin to break up.

Young bass must eat well in their first months if they are to survive the winter, during which they fast. If spring and summer are cool, delaying their hatching and development, most are goners. Heavy storms also destroy nests, and bass fry are more susceptible to acid rain than just about any other major sport fish. Adverse weather often results in a bass-fishing drought three years later, when the lost generation would have reached the age when most smallmouths are caught.

Smallmouth bass spend hot summer days in shadows beneath steep banks, overhanging shoreline branches or in deeper water. They lie motionless most of the time around rocks, logs, submerged tree roots and other debris, waiting to ambush a swimming snack or two. Mealtime really arrives at dusk and dawn, when bass move into shallow rocky areas as crayfish, their favourite food, come out of their lairs to forage. After twilight fades, it's too dark for smallmouths to hunt.

The nearly identical **largemouth bass** prefer calmer, weedier, more shallow waters, often farther upstream. Tending to be a little bigger than smallmouths, they're prized by anglers more for their heft than their fight, as well as for the challenge of finding them. The **rock bass**, another relative, is more squat, bony and homely, with blood-red eyes. Like smallmouth bass and all other members of the sunfish family, they feature males with a nest-building, fry-rearing inclination.

Nest: Circular, rock- and gravel-bottomed depression, 30–76 cm (1–2.5 ft) wide, usually sheltered by a large rock or log, 1–6 m (3.3–19.7 ft) deep near calm shores; same sites often used for years

Clutch: Up to 10,000 tiny, yellowish eggs, often laid by several females

Egg development time: 3–10 days

Average number of hatchlings per nest: About 2,000

Nest failure rate: Often about 40%

Age of first-time breeders: Males 3–5 years, females 4–6 years

Lifespan: Often 5–7 years; up to 20 years

Predators: Pike, pickerel, muskies, cormorants and osprey eat adults; young also taken by perch, catfish, rock bass, loons

Water temperature at which bass become inactive: 13°C (55°F)

Winter whereabouts: Lying dormant in rubble and crevices at water bottom

Range: Southern Ontario to Kapuskasing, Lake Nipigon and Sioux Lookout; also in all other provinces except Newfoundland, Prince Edward Island and Alberta

Number of lakes with smallmouth bass in Ontario: 2,400

Fish that often lay eggs in bass nests: Common shiners, long-nosed gar

Other nest-tending fish: Largemouth and rock bass, sunfish, fathead minnows, creek chub

Also see: Pumpkinseed Sunfish

SMELT
Coming In from the Deep

Average adult length: 15–20 cm (6–8 in)

Maximum length: 36 cm (14 in)

Markings: Silvery, iridescent sides; light-green back, silvery-white belly, clear fins

Alias: Rainbow smelt, American smelt, freshwater smelt, l'éperlan arc-en-ciel, *Osmerus mordax*

Name origin: Has strong, "smelly" cucumber odour when caught

Whereabouts: On or near deep lake bottoms during the day; feeds near surface and closer to shore at night

Food: Planktonic crustaceans, aquatic worms, insect larvae, fry

Eggs per female: 10,000–30,000

Egg development period: 2–4 weeks

Lifespan: Very few more than 6 years; up to 17 years

Range: Great Lakes, Lake Simcoe and many smaller lakes north to about Parry Sound

A S DARKNESS FALLS, the dip nets drop on April and early-May evenings along lakeside concrete piers and urban river mouths across southern Ontario. The quarry of the flashlight-wielding nocturnal fishing folk and their broad-framed, fine-meshed nets are great schools of rainbow smelt making their nightly spring spawning runs from the benthic depths. Over a period of about three weeks, the slender, silvery little fish keep returning to release eggs and milt over gravel beds in fast-flowing waters.

Many male smelt die after spawning and sometimes wash up in great numbers along beaches, often mistaken as a sign of pollution. Along with alewives – even smaller, schooling silvery fish in the big lakes – they can also have mass die-offs in early summer with sudden water temperature changes, disease or population stress.

Though among the most abundant fish in the Great Lakes, smelt and alewives were originally coastal stream-spawning sea-goers. Alewives spread inland through the Erie and Welland Canals. Smelt were introduced in the early 1900s as forage for stocked salmon. But the little fish prey on the fry of lake trout, whitefish and cisco, contributing to their decline. Their wide population fluctuations have also made the lakes' ecosystem much more unstable.

Mammals

HUMANS, ACCOMPANIED BY THEIR PETS, seem to leave little room for other mammals within cities. Yet others do manage to survive and prosper on the fringes, in the night and just beyond our reach. Grey squirrels are the most visible among them, thriving wherever residential neighbourhoods offer plenty of trees. On grassy hillsides and fields, groundhogs also venture out by the light of day, but most other city mammals wait until dark to show their furry faces. Bats take wing over backyards and watersides, skunks emerge from ground burrows and raccoons, which have become icons of urban wildlife, climb down from dens in hollow trees, garages and attics.

The fringes in which urban mammals dwell range from wooded, deer-inhabited river valleys on the outskirts to our own homes, where house mice may set up shop, as they've done for thousands of years. Rats, also long-time citizens of settled civilization, occupy garbage dumpsters, derelict buildings, sewers and subway tunnels. Other city animals relatively new to Ontario include cottontail rabbits, which spread north from the United States, and opossums, which arrived more recently from the same direction. Small numbers of coyotes have also moved in from the west, their presence highlighting the reach of the wild even into the most human-centred of habitats.

BEAVER
Nation-building Rebounding Rodent

T HE QUALITY and denseness of the beaver's soft inner fur, needed for warmth in frigid winter waters, once proved the great rodent engineer's undoing in southern Ontario. In the mid-1600s, the Iroquois drove their Petun, Neutral and Huron rivals from the region to gain control of lucrative fur-trade routes to the interior, building large, fortified villages near the mouths of Toronto's Humber and Rouge Rivers. Fuelled by Europe's insatiable demand for wide-brimmed beaver-felt hats, in the days before umbrellas, the fur frenzy that dominated two and a half centuries of Canadian history had already virtually eliminated the national mascot from much of the land settled by Loyalist refugees from the American Revolution by the time they arrived in the late 1700s.

Even in rocky wilderness areas of central Ontario, the beleaguered beaver was rare until given some protection with the creation of Algonquin Park in 1893. Thereafter, numbers increased so rapidly, Algonquin beavers began to be live-trapped in 1908 and relocated to beaverless parts of the province. The released buck-toothed dam builders took quickly to prime, unused habitats, while the government introduced conservation and trapping management measures. With improving water quality in recent years in many urban rivers and streams, beavers have even returned deep inside some of Ontario's largest cities, though they've yet to make their debut in Windsor and most of the rest of the extreme southwest.

Today, beavers are so at home in settled areas, their activities are sometimes decried for ignoring all local ordinances, plugging culverts, flooding out roads, fields and bridges and cutting down trees in parks and backyards. Like people, they're driven by the urge and ability to change and control their environment. A native tradition holds that the Creator took the power of speech away from beavers to keep them from becoming superior to humans. The Ojibway said that beavers could change form into birds or other animals. They were highly respected and an important food source, especially their rich, fleshy tail. It was taboo to throw a beaver's bones to the dogs, for fear of insulting its spirit.

A pair of beavers can build an incredibly solid dam in three or four days, with branches stuck diagonally into the mud so that the wall slopes downstream, fully braced against the force of the constrained water. They scoop up mud with their paws to fill in the structure once all the branches are woven in place.

By controlling the water level, beavers ensure their impoundment won't freeze to the bottom in winter and their lodge won't be flooded out or left high and dry by seasonal watershed fluctuations. The inundated area, often covering several hectares, is like a farm, growing the succulent, nutritious water plants. As well, it's a conduit for reaching and transporting felled hardwoods. Wherever the ground is soft, beavers may dig thin, shallow canals and tunnels into the woods and across peninsulas. Flooded areas behind beaver dams create rich habitat for a succession of plants and animals, both in the water and in the dead and dying trees.

But beavers don't always build dams if they occupy a deep water body with easy access to nearby trees, especially aspens, birch, willows and cottonwoods. Urban beavers also often forgo constructing domed lodges if they live in rivers and lakes with steep, sandy banks in which they can dig burrows, with entrances hidden below the waterline.

Colony territory: 0.6–2.2 km (0.3–1.8 mi) along a stream or shoreline

Home: Bank burrow with a hidden, underwater entrance, or a domed lodge of branches and mud, about 2 m (6.6 ft) high and 4–8 m (13.3–14.6 ft) wide above waterline, built at the centre of ponds or at side of deep lakes

Food: Duckweed, cattails and other aquatic plants, grasses, sedges, leaves, berries and ferns in summer; bark and twigs of aspen, willow, cottonwood, birch, poplar, red maple, mountain ash and aquatic plant roots in winter

Average daily food helping: 0.5–2.5 kg (1–5.5 lb) of bark and twigs in winter; about 330 g (12 oz) of green plants in summer

Size of winter larder of tree stems and branches submerged beside lodge: Up to 7 m (23 ft) long, 2.5 m (8.2 ft) wide and more than 1 m (3.3 ft) high

Foraging distance from water: Up to 200 m (650 ft)

Gestation period: 3 1/2 months

Average litter: 2–4

Birth weight: 230–680 g (0.5–1.5 lb)

Age at which young beavers leave home: Usually 1 year, some stay for 2 years

Age of first-time breeders: 2–3 years

Lifespan: Average 4–5 years; up to 20 years in wild, 23 years in captivity

Predators: Occasionally dogs, coyotes, foxes, mink

Best senses: Smell and hearing

Capacity to hold breath under-water: Up to 15 minutes

Heart rate underwater: As low as 20% of normal rate

Swimming speed: Usually about 4 km/h (2.4 mph), up to 10 km/h (6 mph)

Tracks: Front feet 6–10 cm (2.5–4 in) long, handlike, with 5 fingers; back feet webbed, 13–16 cm (5–6.3 in) long

Famous beaver hot spots: Montreal (Hochelaga, Iroquoian for "where the beaver dams meet"), Albany, New York (formerly Beaverwyck)

Number of beaver pelts traded for a musket in 1700s: 10–12

Number of hats made from one large beaver pelt in 1700s: About 18

Mad hatters: Ungloved hatmakers often experienced mental deterioration from mercury used to help separate a beaver pelt's soft inner fur from longer guard hairs and break it down into felt

Debut of beaver on Canadian nickel: 1937

Debut of first Canadian beaver stamp: 1851

Mega-beaver: 46,000-year-old bones of a bear-sized beaver were dug up near the banks of Toronto's Don River in 1890

Range: All of Ontario, except parts of southwest; also in all other provinces and territories

Also see: Trembling Aspen

Throughout much of the spring and summer, Canada's paragons of industry actually spend most of their time lazing and grazing on aquatic plants. They're active mostly from dusk to dawn, occasionally warning each other to dive for safety with a loud tail slap on the water when danger approaches. Come the shorter days of September, though, they begin to live up to their reputation, attacking shorelines like crazed lumberjacks, often extending their nocturnal toilings into the day. By November, they usually have a large-enough pile of tasty branches and saplings submerged beside the lodge to keep them comfortably holed up for most of the winter.

Amid all the lounging and snacking, winter's main event comes in January or February, when beaver couples exit their lodgings to consummate their relationships in the water. After swimming attentively together for a while, the male clasps his partner, moves aside her paddled tail and slides around her so they are both turned slightly sideways. They mate for anywhere from 30 seconds to four minutes. After catching a breath of air, grabbing a bite, perhaps making small talk and resting for 20 to 60 minutes, they may repeat their love plunge three or four times.

Newborns arrive between late April and early June, fully furred and with their eyes open. Females spend more time feeding than their mates in spring and early summer to ensure an ample milk supply, while males do most of the maintenance around the house. Beaver families are essentially matriarchies. According to some experts, when one- to two-year-olds leave home for good in search of new horizons, females choose their mate for life and determine where they will live. If her partner dies, a widow beaver recruits a replacement and life goes on. If a matriarch passes away, however, the colony usually breaks up.

BIG BROWN BAT
Good Fortune in the Night

Frequency of bat sonar calls:
40–100 kHz

Upper limit of human hearing:
16.7 kHz

Average frequency of human
conversation: Less than 5 kHz

Other big brown bat calls:
Audible chattering, clicking and
squealing

Heartbeats per minute: More
than 1,000 in flight, 200–450
at rest, 10–15 in winter torpor

Flying speed: 16–41 km/h
(10–25.5 mph)

Wingspan: 32–39 cm
(12.6–15.4 in)

Total length: 9–14 cm (3.5–5.5
in), including 2–6 cm
(0.8–2.4 in) webbed tail

Average weight: 13–25 g
(0.5–0.9 oz)

Markings: Glossy light- to dark-
brown fur, often with golden
hue on back; lighter undersides;
black, sparsely haired face,
ears, wings and tail membrane

Alias: Flittermouse, reremouse, le
grande chauve-souris brune,
Eptesicus fuscus

Name origin: From Old Norse
bakke, meaning "flutter"

Whereabouts: Throughout city,
especially around trees and
watersides

Food: Prefers June bugs and other
beetles, leafhoppers, planthop-
pers and stinkbugs; also eats
flying ants, flies, mosquitoes,
bees, wasps, moths and cockroaches

Number of times bats chew per
second: 7

NEXT TO HUMANS, bats form the world's biggest mammal colonies, with caves in Texas holding roosts of up to 20 million. Among the ranks of Ontario's furry flyers, big brown bats are the most accomplished urbanites. With wings almost as wide as a clothes hanger, they're actually tinier than house sparrows and can squeeze into cracks and spaces as thin as a pencil, giving them access to day roosts inside attics and eaves and behind shingles and shutters. Older buildings offer the most nooks, crannies and entry points, particularly where walls meet roofs. The bat boarders themselves cause no structural damage and most hosts don't even know they're there, often despite years of seasonal reoccupancy.

Even if uninvited, bats do much for the neighbour-hoods in which they reside. Taking to the air at twilight, they sweep over treetops, open spaces and street lights, intercepting juicy June bugs and other beetles and night-flying, lawn-and-garden-despoiling insects. Most big brown bats scarf equal to half their weight in insects every night, scooping them up in their tail membranes and flipping them into their mouths. Nursing females commonly consume the equivalent of their entire weight nightly.

Bats have excellent night vision, but their sense of hearing is their meal ticket. Using sonar, or echo location, they emit a steady stream of high-pitched squeaks that bounce off nearby objects and insects. A big brown bat can detect an airborne June bug up to five metres (16.4 feet) away. Their large ears and tiny brains interpret the distance more accurately than human sonar devices. They also utter lower-frequency buzzes – though still too high for human hearing – that can pick up whole swarms of insects at least 600 metres (656 yards) distant.

With the benefit of bugs attracted around night lights, city bats can sometimes have their fill within two hours of sunset. Most retire by 1 a.m. to digest their dinners, hanging upside down at night rests beneath porch roofs or garage eaves. They usually fly again for a bedtime snack before dawn and then return to more-sheltered day roosts.

Big brown males usually bunk alone or with a couple of buddies behind loose boards and fraying slabs of bark. Females more often come indoors or use hollow trees, forming close-packed nursery colonies that usually swell to anywhere from 20 to 100 bats after the young are born around late June or early July. Occasionally, they may pack in 200 or 300, and houses sometimes host more than one maternity ward. In a growing number of backyards, bats are being enticed into their own specially built abodes, with a single open-bottomed bat house the size of a large tool box – divided into multiple compartments by slats inside – able to accommodate a nursery colony large enough to devour tens of thousands of insects a night.

Adult males begin visiting maternal colonies in early autumn, when both mothers and most of their offspring are ready to mate. Sleepy bats also sometimes seek carnal company when they rouse from torpor during mild winter spells, when some even rarely take wing to change quarters. Big browns are hardier than most other bats and commonly forage well into autumn, feasting upon Indian summer's last flying-insect bounties. Most hibernate alone or in loose groups of up to four inside walls – where they can sometimes be heard moving around, scratching and squealing – or in basements, garages, sewers and derelict buildings. Lowering their heart rate, body temperature and metabolism to just a fraction of their normal levels, they only very slowly use up their body fat, which accounts for about a third of their weight going into the season. Most emerge in spring about one-quarter lighter, though long, cold winters can reduce some to half of their former weight, leaving them too weak to fly and doomed.

A grounded bat can also have rabies. Unlike many other animals, rabid bats are timid and usually die quickly. But if picked up, they will, like healthy bats, bite and often draw blood, which is the way most potential exposures to bats occur. Because bat bites can also be too small to be detected, authorities recommend that anyone sleeping in a room where a bat is discovered should seek medical advice. Rabies, though, are not common among bats, infecting well under 1 percent of their population.

Like the myths of bats being blind or becoming entangled in long hair, most fears in general about the flying spectres of the night are baseless. Yet their association with the dark side in the popular mind reaches back past the witches, vampires and devils of the Middle Ages even to ancient Babylon, where ghosts were believed to take the form of bats. In Mayan civilization, the underworld deity Zotz bore the head of a vampire bat.

In an Ojibway tale, however, the bat was originally a squirrel that was burned, deformed and blinded while heroically freeing the Sun from the tangled branches of a tall tree. The Sun rewarded its seriously singed rescuer with the power of flight and the ability to see in the dark. On the other side of the world, the Chinese greeted bats as omens of good luck. The Wu Fu charm, traditionally hung above the doors of Chinese homes, depicts five bats circling the tree of life, representing the top-five human blessings – virtue, wealth, children, longevity and a contented death.

Great Lakes region in United States and Canada: At least 300,000–400,000

Big brown bat range: Southern Ontario to North Bay, Sudbury and around Lake Superior west to Lake of the Woods; also in all other provinces except Nova Scotia, Prince Edward Island, and Newfoundland

Portion of bats found sick, acting strangely or suspected of biting a person or pet in Ontario that test positive for rabies: Less than 2%

Oldest bat fossils: 60 million years

Ontario species that migrate to the United States in fall: Eastern red bat, hoary bat, silver-haired bat

Number of Ontario bat species: 8

Number of bat species worldwide: More than 1,100

Portion of world's mammal species that are bats: About 25%

Other animals that use echo location: Shrews, dolphins, whales, cave-dwelling birds

Also see: Moths, Mosquitoes, Raccoon, Lawn & Garden

CHIPMUNK
Hoarding Hermit Warrior

Cheek holding capacity: Up to 32 beechnuts or 48 wild cherry pits

Body temperature: 35–41°C (95–106°F) when active, 5–7°C (41–45°F) in hibernation

Breaths per minute: More than 60 when active, less than 20 in hibernation

Average adult body length: 14–16 cm (5.5–6.5 in)

Weight: 70–125 g (2.5–4.4 oz)

Tail length: 6.5–11.5 cm (2.5–4.5 in)

Markings: Tawny brown back and sides with 9 black-and-whitish stripes; two stripes on face; white undersides and chin

Alias: Eastern chipmunk, chipping squirrel, *le suisse, Tamias striatus*

Name origin of *chipmunk*: Algonquian word meaning "head first," after the manner it descends trees

Calls: "Chip," "chuck," trills, whistles, squeals, chatter

Whereabouts: Open woods and forest edge with lots of logs, stumps and rocks; large suburban yards

Home range: Average 0.1–0.2 ha (¼–½ acre); up to 1.3 ha (3.2 acre)

Food: Acorns, beech and hazel nuts, maple keys and other seeds, berries, cherries, mushrooms, buds, root bulbs, snails, slugs, insects; occasionally frogs, bird eggs and nestlings, young mice, snakes

Winter food stores: Up to 6.7 L (7 quarts)

RENOWNED INCORRIGIBLE mooches at picnic grounds and provincial parks, chipmunks have a more tentative pawhold in the big city. While they'll climb to pick seeds, nuts and berries, they're primarily ground-dwellers and can't as easily rise above the hustle and bustle as tree-loving squirrels. Yet they do find accommodation in unhemmed spaces such as large wooded parks, untamed ravines, cemeteries and expansive, well-treed suburban yards.

Key to their enthusiasm for handouts, chipmunks are obsessive hoarders. After filling their considerable cheeks, instead of sitting down and enjoying their meal, they stash it away in underground burrows and then return for more. Their winter survival depends on building up a vast cache of seeds and nuts. Unlike squirrels, chippies sleep most of the winter away, but don't pack on fat that gets hibernating groundhogs and bears through the season. Instead, they stir every few days and grab a bedtime snack from the larder.

With so much riding on their stash, chipmunks are exceedingly testy about any of their own kind getting near it. They live alone and harbour a keen dislike for each other, like warrior hermits. When they meet, there are almost always strong words, scraps and chases. Chip and Dale could never have been pals.

Accordingly, woods abounding in chipmunks ring with chattering discord. Yet, in a moment of common peril, they pull together in a kind of neighbourhood watch. Whenever a fox, raccoon or other large mammal is spotted, they join in a chorus of sharp, repeated warning "chips." For hawks and other big birds, the alarm call is a distinctly different, lower series of "chucks." When hordes of nervous, inexperienced six- to eight-week-old youngsters set off on their own looking for refuge in June, the pickings are prime for carnivores and the chips and chucks can reach fever pitch. The waifs that survive their troubled youth usually find sanctuary in old, empty chipmunk burrows anywhere from five to more than 700 metres (five to 750 yards) from their original homes within a few weeks of leaving.

When excavating new quarters, chipmunks finish them off by ingeniously digging a second entrance tunnel and transferring the dirt from it to seal the opening of the original three- to 15-metre-long (10- to 49-foot-long) working shaft, hiding any obvious evidence of their occupation. The new entrance hole is often hidden beneath a log, rock or brush pile.

After four to six months in the darkness of their well-stocked, leaf-lined chambers, male chipmunks resurface in March in a lustful state, as patches of bare ground emerge in the melting snow. Breaking with antisocial conventions, they go calling on still-slumbering neighbourhood females, only to be thrashed and rejected until the time is finally right. Then, love briefly conquers chipmunk belligerence and a couple will nuzzle, play, lounge and squeak together for hours before and after mating. Beyond that, the relationship's over and the single moms deliver their litters between mid-April and late May.

Home: Burrow, about 45–85 cm (1.5–2.8 ft) underground, football- to watermelon-sized; entrance hole neat, round, 4–5 cm (1.6–2 in) wide

Gestation period: 31 days

Average litter: 4–6

Birth weight: 3 g (0.1 oz)

Weaning age: 5–6 weeks

Age upon reaching adult size: 2–3 months

Age of first-time breeders: Females as young as 10 weeks; males 1 year

Annual adult survival: 50% or less

Adult lifespan: Average 1–2 years, with few living more than 3 years; up to 12 years

Predators: Hawks, foxes, coyotes, raccoons, weasels, cats, dogs, snakes

Top running speed: 12 km/h (7.5 mph)

Swimming speed: 11 km/h (7 mph)

Best sense: Hearing

Winter whereabouts: In light hibernation beneath ground

Famous individuals: Chip and Dale; Simon, Alvin and Theodore

Range: Southern Ontario to tip of James Bay, Lake Nipigon and a little north of Kenora; also in Manitoba, Quebec and Maritime provinces

First appearance of chipmunks: 25 million years ago

Number of Ontario chipmunk species: 2

Number of chipmunk species worldwide: 21 in North America, 1 in China

Also see: Grey Squirrel

COTTONTAIL RABBIT
Easter Star an American Immigrant

Maximum jumping distance:
4.6 m (15 ft)

Top running speed: 29 km/h
(18 mph)

**Number of hare or rabbit taste
buds:** 17,000

Number of human taste buds:
9,000

Average adult body length:
36–41 cm (14–16 in)

Weight: 0.9–1.8 kg (2–4 lb)

Tail length: 4–7 cm (1.6–2.8 in)

Markings: Reddish- to greyish-
brown back with black-tipped
guard hairs; more greyish on
lower sides; white undersides
and bottom of tail

Alias: Eastern cottontail, *le lapin à
queque blanche, Sylvilagus
floridanus*

Calls: Screams and grunts in dis-
tress, squeals during mating;
young squeak faintly

Whereabouts: Forest edges, thickets, riversides, hedges and
nearby tall-grass areas or woods
with thick ground cover

TOGETHER with the United Empire Loyalists and Vietnam draft dodgers, cottontail rabbits count among the storied ranks of those who have hopped north across the border to make a life in Canada. The rabbits arrived around 1860, perhaps crossing the St. Clair or Detroit Rivers while frozen over, and found a cottontail-friendly patchwork of newly cleared land, hedgerows and remnant woodlots. While relishing all manner of grassy growth and clover, the diminutive bunnies never like to be far from a thickly tangled refuge. Unlike larger, long-legged snowshoe hares, which are rare south of the Canadian Shield, cottontails do not bound great distances in a flash to elude danger. Instead, they dash for cover in a zigzagging, hopping run. After the commotion of their initial flight, upon reaching a well-hidden place, they creep silently away without detection, so that they always seem just to disappear from the spot where they stopped.

Rabbits and hares differ even more fundamentally when it comes to baby bunnies. As hinted by their name, hares are born fully furred, eyes open and able to run within hours. Rabbits, on the other hand, come into the world helpless, naked and blind. Unlike hares, cottontail mothers make warm, bowl-shaped nests for their little ones by scraping out shallow depressions, 13 to 25 centimetres (five to 10 inches) wide, in meadows or thickets and lining them with soft grass and fur plucked from their own undersides. They keep a veil of grass and fur over top of the nest as well, and return only a couple of times a day to nurse, often at dusk and dawn, though they're never far away.

A mother sometimes mates again within 24 hours of giving birth, so that by the time her first charges are four or five weeks old and can take care of themselves – two or three weeks after first emerging from the nest – she brings forth yet another bevy of bunnies. Cottontails commonly produce three and sometimes four litters in a breeding season that runs from March to September.

Although rabbits are active mainly at night, their elaborate courting hoedowns can carry on into the grey light of dawn, sometimes even in the open space of backyards abutting ravines or other brushy areas. Female pheromones often draw several bucks, who fight and compete amongst themselves. A mating pair, after a perfunctory chase, face each other and periodically rise up and play footsie with their front paws. Then they make head-on runs at each other, with one jumping high straight into the air at the last moment while the other passes below. They may repeat the nuptial manoeuvres a number of times before they finally mate.

The seemingly crazy behaviour that kicks off the long-eared mating season at the end of winter inspired the old expression "as mad as a March hare." Such exuberance, and the impressive numbers of offspring that result, is undoubtedly at the heart of the Easter Bunny's pre-Christian fertility-symbol origins. A rabbit- or hare-headed supernatural teacher also figures prominently in the lore of most northern Algonquian-speaking peoples. The Ojibway called the spirit Nanabush. He remade the world after the great flood, stocked it with game animals and gave humans fire, hunting weapons and the sacred pipe for communicating with the spirits. Of all the animals, rabbits and hares were especially important in feeding hunting bands in winter, when other game was scarce.

Home range: Average 0.5–4 ha (1.2–10 acres)

Food: Grass, leaves, shoots, fruits and flowers of many plants; in winter, bark, buds and twigs; spilled birdseed

Gestation period: 28–30 days

Average litter: 5–6

Weaning age: About 3 weeks

Age of first-time breeders: 10–36% of females in their first summer; the rest mate the following spring

Annual adult survival: About 20%

Adult lifespan: Average 15 months; up to 5 years in wild, 9 years in captivity

Predators: Foxes, coyotes, dogs, cats, weasels, hawks, owls; nests raided by raccoons, skunks, opossums, red squirrels, rats, crows, snakes

Tracks: Front feet, 2.5–3.8 cm (1–1.5 in) long, usually land one in front of the other, but behind the two back feet, 7.6–8.9 cm (3–3.5 in) long

Scats: Size of plump Smarties

Range: Southern Ontario to about Parry Sound and Renfrew County; also in Quebec, Manitoba, Saskatchewan and introduced in British Columbia

Famous bunnies: Bugs Bunny, Peter Cottontail, Thumper, Roger Rabbit, Harvey, Flopsy and Mopsy, Fiver, Bigwig, Brer Rabbit, The White Rabbit, Fletcher Rabbit, Raggylug, Blackberry

Number of Ontario rabbit or hare species: 4

Number of hare and rabbit species worldwide: About 50

COYOTE
Far from Home on the Range

Running speed: Usually about
40–50 km/h (25–31 mph);
maximum more than 64 km/h
(40 mph)

Average adult body length:
0.9–1.1 m (3–3.6 ft)

Tail: 28–40 cm (11–15.7 in)

Shoulder height: 58–66 cm
(23–26 in)

German shepherd shoulder height:
71–74 cm (2.3–2.6 ft)

Average weight: 11–18 kg
(25–40 lb)

Maximum weight: More than 27
kg (60 lb)

Markings: Greyish salt-and-pepper
back and sides, often with a
buff or reddish hue; throat,
chest and undersides white or
light grey; yellow eyes

Alias: Eastern coyote, brush wolf,
prairie wolf, song dog, *le
coyote, Canis latrans*

URNING UP with increasing regularity along
busy expressways, in large urban parks and even
on school grounds, coyotes seem to be a long way
from their proverbial home on the range. Primarily
native to the prairies, they spread east with the clearing
of forests and settlement in the 19th century and crossed
into Ontario at Sarnia, Sault Ste. Marie and along
railway corridors from Manitoba in the early 1900s. By
the 1940s, they were well established even in eastern
Ontario.

It wasn't until more recent years, however, as ever-
expanding suburbs blurred the lines between town and
country, that the bushy-tailed wild canines became bold
enough to follow river valleys and other natural corridors into the core of many cities. Though they number
fewer than any other furry urban predator, coyotes
maintain a shadowy presence, coming out to hunt as
night falls, steering well clear of humans and largely
refraining from their well-known proclivity for atten-
tion-grabbing howling.

Supreme adaptability is the key to the coyote's
expanding horizons. Unlike wolves, which are big-game

specialists that shrink from any sign of human settlement, coyotes evolved to maximize their opportunities in marginal hunting grounds not occupied by their more stout-snouted brethren. They became omnivorous, developed very flexible reproductive abilities and learned to adjust their ways to meet almost any situation. Necessary for such powers of adaptability is an elevated intelligence. The Navajo were so impressed with the cagey canine, they called it "God's dog." Coyote was the trickster deity for many western native peoples – as the rabbit or hare was in the east – responsible for placing people on Earth and providing for many of their needs and teachings.

In the east, the coyote has actually adjusted to the point of becoming a slightly different animal than it was back on the range. There's more than a grain of truth in its oft-used alternative name "brush wolf." The coyote's spread coincided with the persecution and extirpation of wolves from southern and much of central Ontario, with the provincial government paying wolf bounties from 1793 to 1972. Though wolves normally drive off or even make lunch of their smaller cousins, it's believed that the vanguard of eastbound coyotes and remnant wolf holdouts made a marriage of convenience when the presence of others of their own kind was wanting. Studies show that when forest densities drop below the threshold of one wolf per 40 square kilometres (15.4 square miles), coyotes move in. The crossing is invariably between a male wolf and a female coyote.

Today, eastern coyotes are noticeably larger – about the size of a collie or small, lean German shepherd – and darker than their western counterparts because of mixing with wolves. Recent genetic evidence reveals that even before the hybridization, the wolves of south-central Ontario and coyotes were actually kissing cousins, much more closely related to each other than to the larger northern grey wolf, whose ancestors migrated to Asia about one to two million years ago and developed separately before returning over a Bering Sea land bridge some 1.7 million years later. Meanwhile, the ancestral canids that remained in North America split off 150,000 to 300,000 years ago into coyotes and

Pronunciation: *Coyotl*, meaning "barking dog" in the Aztec language, was pronounced by the Spanish, and later in the U.S. southwest, as "ky-o-tee," shortened in other areas to "ky-oat"

Call: High-pitched whines, yips, barks, howls, growls

Whereabouts: Scrubby river valleys and ravines, forest edge, open woods, meadows, wetlands, Hydro corridors, large parks, golf courses

Home range: Average 13–65 km^2 (5–25 sq mi), but spends most of time in territory of 5–8 km^2 (2–3 sq mi)

Portion of population without territories: 8–20%

Food: Voles, mice, rabbits, groundhogs, chipmunks, squirrels, rats, fawns, carrion, ducks, geese and other birds and their eggs, frogs, grasshoppers and other insects, berries, cherries, acorns, grass; adult deer most often taken in deep snow in late winter; occasionally kill cats and small dogs

Natal dens: Most often in enlarged fox or groundhog burrows, about 3 m (10 ft) deep, with entrance about 30 cm (1 ft) wide, in brushy ravine slopes, streamsides and sandy embankments; also in brush piles, hollow trees or logs; a family usually has several den sites and sometimes moves their pups between them

Gestation period: 60–63 days

Average litter: 5–7

Weaning age: About 6 weeks

Age of first-time breeders: 10 months for some, nearly 2 years for most

First-year survival: 20–60%

Annual adult survival: 50–70%

Lifespan: Few live more than four years in wild; up to 19 years in captivity

Predators: Wolves and bears in wilderness areas

Peak activity periods: Dusk and dawn

Tracks: Oval, 6–8 cm (2.5–3.5 in) long; back feet commonly land in tracks made by front feet

Scat: Like dog droppings, but usually dark grey with hair, bone fragments and pointed at ends, averaging cigar thickness

Portion of Algonquin Park wolves found to have some coyote genes: 50–60%

Range: Southern Ontario north to about Kirkland Lake, Lake Nipigon and Red Lake; also in all other provinces and territories except Nunavut

Also see: Red Fox, White-tailed Deer

eastern Canadian wolves, known as red wolves in the United States, where they survive mostly in captivity.

Regardless of their bloodline, coyotes have not pleased everyone with their success. From farmers worried about their livestock to pet owners in the city, many view their presence as an imminent threat. Determined eradication efforts throughout North America, however, have invariably failed. The U.S. Fish and Wildlife Service has directed the killing of millions of coyotes for decades without succeeding in reducing the population. When hunted and trapped intensively, coyotes become ever more wily and increase their birthrate by 30 to 100 percent, breeding younger and producing litters of up to 19 pups.

Coyotes mate in the dead of winter, late January and February, so that when the pups arrive two months later, the melting snow makes for good mousing to nourish the litter. Emerging groundhogs also supply plenty of take-home meat. Fathers provide for both the young and their nursing partners, with whom they remain for life.

Though coyotes hunt much of the time on their own, or sometimes in pairs, youngsters begin accompanying their parents in August or September. By that time, rising adolescent petulance may set some off on their own, usually dispersing from 15 to 25 kilometres (9.3 to 15.5 miles), but sometimes more than 480 kilometres (300 miles). Others remain with the folks into winter, when they often scavenge or hunt as a family pack, especially if there's deer around. One of the young may even stay behind to help raise the following spring's litter.

In contrast, coyotes also occasionally mate with dogs, but the "coydog" strain doesn't persist in the wild because hybrid males lack the instinct to help feed their young. Coydog females also usually mate in late fall and give birth in midwinter, when chances of pup survival are lowest.

GREY SQUIRREL
Most Outgoing of Furry Burghers

U NLIKE THE PIGEON, house sparrow, house mouse, honeybee, cockroach, dandelion and daisy, the city-going grey squirrel is an Ontario native through and through. The most conspicuous of mammals about town, it has the speed, agility, nerve and panache to live cheek by jowl among humans and thrive in the urban forest overhead.

Following three-dimensional thoroughfares of regularly used branches, squirrels move seamlessly from tree to tree across the green canopy enshrouding shady neighbourhoods and parks. Their specialized vision makes instant trigonometric computations using vertical objects, mainly trees, to judge leaping distances, while four sets of whiskers and other sensing hairs guide them to twist and contort around obstacles at hyperspeed. Their signature, sumptuously plumed tails, in addition to providing shade, warmth, distraction and serving as emotional barometers, are also used for balance and, in a pinch, as parachutes. Grey squirrels have been known to survive falls from as high as 30 metres (98 feet).

Despite their unicoloured name, the majority of grey squirrels in many Ontario cities are actually black. As evident in any backyard, differently attired individuals make no distinctions among themselves, with the same litter often including both black and grey siblings, though sometimes from different fathers. The species, however, was first named in the United States, where

Maximum jumping distance: 2.4 m (8 ft)

Running speed: Up to 25 km/h (15.5 mph)

Record number of males counted in a mating chase: 34

Average adult body length: 22–27 cm (8.7–10.6 in)

Tail length: 21–24 cm (8.3–9.5 in)

Weight: 350–700 g (0.8–1.5 lb)

Markings: Usually all black or with salt-and-pepper grey back and sides and white or light-grey undersides; sometimes shaded light- to dark-brown or with cinnamon tints on head, back and tail; usually a prominent white eye ring and white-tipped tail with grey summer coat and white tufts behind ears with grey winter coat; some cities, such as London, also have significant numbers of black squirrels with reddish tails

Moults: In spring and fall, sometimes making squirrels appear to be missing half their fur; also a separate tail moult in summer; mange can cause fur loss in winter and early spring, sometimes fatal in cold

Alias: Eastern grey squirrel, black squirrel, silvertail, *l'écureuil gris, Sciurus carolinensis*

Name origin: From the Greek *skia*, meaning "shadow," and *oura*, "tail"

Calls: A loud, raspy, repeated "churr"; harsh or soft barks; a rapid, clicking "kut, kut, kut" alarm call; females make repeated mating quacks

Whereabouts: Tree-lined streets, backyards, parks, woods, cemeteries

Home range: Most squirrels are seldom more than 100 m (110 yd) from their nest trees

Food: Buds of silver maple, oak and elm and maple sap in late winter and early spring; tree catkins, flowers, new shoots, silver maple and elm seeds later in spring; berries, wild cherries, mushrooms, horse chestnuts, hazelnuts in summer; acorns, beechnuts, hickory nuts, walnuts, hawthorn fruits, wild grapes, crabapples and seeds of evergreens, ash, Manitoba, Norway and sugar maple in autumn and winter; goldenrod gall larvae, twigs and inner bark if cached nuts and seeds run out in winter; also bulbs, roots, leaves, caterpillars, acorn weevils, grasshoppers, birdseed, human food scraps and hand-outs and occasionally carrion, bird eggs and nestlings

Average daily food helping: 60–130 g (2–4.5 oz)

Homes: In winter, usually in a leaf-lined tree cavity, at least 30 cm

black squirrels are rare in most areas and virtually unheard of in regions that get little or no snow. Kent State University in Ohio even has an annual Black Squirrel Festival to celebrate the population of novel dark beasts it imported from London, Ontario.

Though grey-coloured squirrels have the edge in parts of southern Ontario, such as the Niagara Peninsula, north of around Waterloo and Guelph the balance shifts. Black predominates in central Ontario, and in some places is worn by virtually the entire population. Studies suggest that sun-absorbing dark fur has the advantage in winter at the northern edge of the squirrels' range, allowing blackies to burn 20 percent less energy than their grey brethren to stay warm at -18°C (0°F). Thunder Bay's grey squirrels, however, belong to a separate western subspecies that lacks black genes.

Whatever their shade, squirrels don longer, thicker coats in autumn, sprucing up their appearance in time for the winter mating season, which usually lasts for about three weeks in late January and early February. A female begins to release fragrant pheromones about five days before she's ready to mate, setting eager members of the opposite sex to following her around. On the morning of the big day, she announces that she's game by uttering loud, repeated ducklike quacks and then promptly races off with her suitors in tow. The quacks and commotion of the ensuing chase attract still more males to the contest from up to 500 metres (547 yards) away. Five to a dozen pursuers commonly squabble and scrap amongst themselves as they jockey for position, until one is ready to claim the prize when the dashing damsel finally lets up and demurs to accept the winner's affections. After all of that, the moment of truth usually lasts less than 30 seconds. The pair may mate again after a break, but then it's the end of the affair.

Mothers give birth in March, but their babies don't start peering from nest holes until after their eyes open about five weeks later. In May, the half-grown youngsters begin venturing about and learning to forage, and can usually fend for themselves within a month. Meanwhile, mothers that are two years or older often mate again in late spring and establish new nests before delivering a second litter in July.

Most young squirrels, especially males, hit the road in September or October, commonly relocating a kilometre (0.6 miles) or more from the home of their birth. They're often convinced to leave by mothers who want to ensure that there aren't too many paws vying for limited food stores in one area come winter. Grey squirrels are "scatter hoarders," each of them digging hundreds or thousands of shallow holes in autumn and burying a single acorn, nut or seed in each one. They also stash food under rocks and roots, inside tree holes and other hiding places. In the cold months afterwards, they sniff out the little treasures, even through the snow, to stay alive. They're not very territorial, following a finders-keepers ethic, regardless of who buried a particular stash. Anywhere between 15 and 40 per cent of the nuts and seeds, in fact, are usually not found again, which in the wild is responsible for the dispersal and planting of many trees, especially oaks, beech, hickory and walnut.

While urban squirrels also have a knack for coaxing handouts from kind-hearted souls, they're notorious for their ingenuity and persistence in foiling many of the best-laid designs for excluding them from bird feeders. They dig up bulbs and decapitate garden flowers in spring as well. Worst of all, squirrels looking for winter dens and natal quarters eagerly take the opportunity offered by cracks or slight holes in the wood beneath eaves or in dormers to chew their way into attics, where they can cause considerable damage with their constant gnawing. It's enough to make even the most gentle urban tree-hugger fantasize about the right to bear squirrel rifles in the city. A call to professional pest removers and preventative home repairs – aluminum or vinyl – is usually the best course of action.

(1 ft) wide, with entrance hole at least 8 cm (3 in) wide; in warmer months, may also make a succession of spherical, waterproof nests, 30–60 cm (1–2 ft) wide, of tightly woven twigs and leaves in a tree or in forked branches near tree trunks; lined inside with shredded bark, leaves, grass, fur and feathers; also make smaller, more rudimentary leaf nests farther out on branches for resting

Gestation period: 40–45 days

Average litter: 2–4

Weaning age: 7–10 weeks

Age of first-time breeders: 11–15 months for females; 15–18 months for males

Annual survival: About 35–50% in first year and 50% for adults

Lifespan: Very few live more than 6 years; up to 13 years in wild and 23 years in captivity

Predators: Dogs, cats, foxes, coyotes, hawks, owls; nests raided by raccoons, crows

Tracks: Trail 10–15 cm (3.9–5.9 in) wide, with front paws, 2.5–4.6 cm (1–1.8 in) long, landing behind back paws, 5.8–7.6 cm (2.3–3 in) long

Famous squirrels: Rocky, Nutkin, Goody and Timmy Tiptoes, Slappy, Skippy

Range: Southern Ontario to around North Bay and a little north of Sault Ste. Marie; also between Thunder Bay and Rainy River and in Manitoba, Quebec, New Brunswick and Nova Scotia; introduced in British Columbia and Alberta

Also see: Chipmunk, Blue Jay, Red Oak, Silver Maple, Woods

159

GROUNDHOG
Fabled Furry Forecaster

WHILE BIG-CITY GROUNDHOGS remain comfortably numb deep in their burrows every year on February 2, far away on the icy shores of Georgian Bay, a lone albino woodchuck squints into the limelight in Wiarton, Ontario. Coaxed in front of banks of cameras by formally attired civic officials on Groundhog Day, Wiarton Willie is perhaps the most famous weather forecaster in the province. If it's a typically crisp, sunny, midwinter day there's a good chance he will see his shadow, bidding six more weeks of winter. On a mild, overcast day, the shadowless rodent holds out the proposition of imminent spring.

Ontario's most infamous Groundhog Day came in 1999 when Willie was found dead just before his big day. Amid weeklong festivities that usually bring 10,000 celebrants to Wiarton, the star attraction's demise was kept secret until his much-anticipated scheduled appearance. At the moment of truth, his handlers staged a surprise state funeral, bringing out a tiny pine coffin surreptitiously containing the more presentable taxidermied body of one of the half-dozen predecessor Willies employed by Wiarton since 1956. A shocked and duped nation mourned.

Groundhog Day is based on the old European folk belief that badgers and hedgehogs could predict the weather. February 2 used to be a holiday, called Candlemas in Christian times, though originally it was the pagan festival of Brigid, celebrating the first stirrings of spring. It was one of the many days farmers gathered to, among other things, guess the weather for the coming growing season. In Ontario, however, where winters seldom end even six weeks after their namesake day, groundhogs remain tightly curled in their subterranean chambers in a largely uninterrupted, deep, five- to six-month-long slumber.

Bleary-eyed woodchucks, or freshly dumped dirt outside their burrow entrances, can be seen along roadside and highway embankments and wooded or brushy hills when the Rip van Rodents finally begin emerging in March or early April. Males are the first to arise, and immediately go knocking at the doors of the opposite sex in hopes of a spring fling. They're usually sent packing by the wakened, grouchy bachelorettes, but with any luck eventually find agreeable mates, who give birth in late April or May and raise their charges alone.

Plump, inquisitive groundhog pups begin viewing the surface world when four to six weeks old. By the latter half of June, they weigh about half a kilogram (1.1 pounds) and crowd the natal burrow. Mothers often set up some in old dens nearby or dig new burrows for them, which she continues to visit. A month or so later, however, the young strike out on their own, journeying anywhere from a few hundred metres (yards) to much farther away before either finding an abandoned burrow or quickly digging their own. Older animals usually have a summer burrow in an open area and a winter home in or at the edge of a forest or fence row.

Around early June, groundhog metabolism begins to slow, permitting considerably faster weight gain. Much of it is laid down as energy-rich brown fat, which yields twenty times as much heat as the white fat possessed by humans. Stuffed and sleepy by the time much of their remaining food withers with early frosts, the whistle pigs block off their sleeping chambers before turning in, allowing other animals to use the rest of the burrow through winter. The young of the year, eating longer to catch up with larger, older groundhogs, like true teenagers both go into hibernation and wake up later than their elders.

Home range: Up to 100 m (109 yd) wide

Home: Ground burrow, often on a hillside or gully; usually about 4–7 m (13–23 ft) long, 1–2 m (3.3–6.6 ft) deep, with 2 entrances, plus plunge holes that drop straight down, bathrooms and a bed chamber, 30–45 cm (12–18 in) wide and 30 cm (12 in) high, lined with grass and leaves

Soil excavated for a burrow: Up to 320 kg (700 lb)

Food: Grass, clover, leaves and stems of many other herbs, flowers, seeds, berries, occasionally insects, snails; bark, buds and twigs in early spring

Gestation period: 30–32 days

Average litter: 4–5

Weaning age: 5–6 weeks

Age of first-time breeders: 2 years for most

Average annual mortality: First-years about 75%; adults 30%

Adult lifespan: Commonly 2–3 years; up to 6 years in wild; up to 10 years in captivity

Predators: Foxes, coyotes, dogs, mink, hawks, great horned owls

Top running speed: 16 km/h (10 mph)

Famous forecasters: Wiarton Willie, Punxsutawney Phil, Shubenacadie Sam, Dunkirk Dave, Penniechuck Chuck, General Beauregard Lee

Range: All of Ontario; also in all other provinces and territories except Nunavut, Newfoundland and Prince Edward Island

HOUSE MOUSE
The Walls Have Very Little Ears

High jumping ability: Up to 30 cm

Top running speed: 12.5 km/h (7.8 mph)

Heartbeats per minute: 320–860

Average number of naps per day: 20

Adult body length: 7–10 cm (2.8–3.9 in)

Tail length: 6–10 cm (2.4–3.9 in)

Weight: 14–25 g (0.5–0.9 oz)

Markings: Grey to brown back and sides, lighter-grey undersides, grey or beige tail

Alias: Grey mouse, common mouse, domestic mouse, granary mouse, *la souris commune*, *Mus musculus*

Calls: Squeaks, ultrasonic murmurings

Whereabouts: Houses, other buildings, yards, nearby fields

Territory: As small as a few square metres (or yards)

Population density: Up to 10 per m² (1.2 sq yd) in badly infested places

NEXT TO DOGS and cats, no other mammal lives so closely with humans as the much-storied, little-loved, sneaky, plundering house mouse. The diminutive grey-brown rodent is believed to have originated as a rock-crevice dweller in central Asia who found a better living by moving into early farm-valley settlements and oasis trade centres. Hitching rides in caravan carts travelling east and west along the Silk Road and boarding grain ships in the Mediterranean, house mice spread throughout the ancient world. Stories of mouse plagues figure prominently in both the Bible and Homer's *Iliad*. One of the manifestations of the Greek god Apollo was Smintheus, who had the power to send or put an end to grain-threatening mouse infestations. Rare albino mice were considered sacred to Apollo Smintheus and when found were collected and raised at temples dedicated to him.

Love them or hate them, house mice have been the constant companions of explorers, traders and colonists to the ends of the Earth. Today, they continue to catch fast rides on trucks, boxcars and air-cargo containers to cities and towns everywhere, employing skills of stealth honed over millennia to take up profitable residence in modern homes. At the same time, their captive-bred albino brethren still hold a place of vital importance in human affairs, accounting for more than one-third of all animals used in scientific research in Canada. In 2002, the house mouse became the first mammal, after humans, to have a rough draft mapped of its full DNA sequence, which is close enough to the human genome to serve as an invaluable "Rosetta stone" in unlocking the genetic secrets to scores of afflictions, from heart disease to inner-ear defects. In recent years, hundreds of different strains of genetically modified lab mice have been created to push such research forward.

Given a chance, however, apparently domesticated white mice can still return to the free-booting ways of their ancestors. In 1976, they squared off against the most powerful man in the world – at the time U.S. President Gerald Ford – when eight albinos escaped captivity and infested the White House.

House mice seem to be most abundant in the densely packed older neighbourhoods of larger cities, where they scurry easily between duplexes, row houses and apartments. They can squeeze through spaces as thin as six millimetres (0.25 inches) wide and commonly gain entry where plumbing and wires go through walls. Mice also climb pipes and rough vertical surfaces and chew into cupboards, baseboards, furniture, wires, plastic, clothes and cardboard. Though they operate mostly by night, they may be afoot at any time of the day, as long as the coast is clear and there's food to be had.

Most mice rarely forage more than 15 metres (49 feet) from their nests, which may be shared by up to 40 relatives. They usually form fiercely territorial family groups consisting of a rough-and-ready patriarch, several wives and their young. They mark their turf with pee and droppings along regular runs and chase away trespassing non-clan members. Combat between martial males is fairly common.

With access to unprotected food stores, house-invading mice can breed year-round and build up very quickly in numbers. Females may have five to 10 litters a year, if they live that long. When only three or four weeks old, shortly before becoming able to breed themselves, youngsters are forced to leave home by the older generation. Some may settle in another part of the house or move next door, while others may find quarters under a backyard woodpile or ramble more than 400 metres (437 yards) away into a park or field. House mice, however, do not survive temperatures below -10°C (14°F). Many infestations start in autumn when outdoor nesters move into houses to avoid the growing cold.

Food: Most household foods, seeds, stems, leaves, roots, insects, carrion, glue, soap

Homes: 10–cm (4–in) ball of shredded paper, rags, grass or fibreglass insulation inside walls, under floors, in cupboards, boxes, drawers, old mattresses, rolled-up carpets; outdoors in ground burrows, under rocks, logs and stumps

Gestation period: Usually 18–21 days; up to 30 days if female already nursing young when she conceives again

Average litter: 4–8

Weaning age: 16–21 days

Age of first-time breeders: 5–8 weeks

Lifespan: Few live more than a year; up to 6 years in captivity

Predators: Cats, dogs, skunks, raccoons, foxes, opossums, hawks, owls, garter snakes

Best senses: Hearing, smell; can detect sugar or salt levels as low as 1 part per million

Famous mice: Mickey, Minnie, Mighty, Itchy, Jerry, Speedy Gonzalez, Topo Gigio, Appley Dapply, Algernon

Range: Southern Ontario to about Timmins and Kenora; also in human habitations in all other provinces and territories

Mouse, vole and lemming species in Ontario: 14

Also see: Rat, House & Home

MINK
Slinking by the River

Adult body length: 33–52 cm
  (12–20 in)
Tail length: 16–20 cm (6–8 in)
Weight: 0.7–1.6 kg (1.5–3.5 lb)
Markings: Light brown to black,
  darkest on the back, white chin
  patch, often a white chest spot
Alias: American mink, *le vison
  d'Amérique, Mustela vison*
Calls: Snarl, squeak, bark, hiss
Whereabouts: Streams, lakes,
  marshes, forest edges
Food: Voles, muskrats, rabbits,
  squirrels, crayfish, fish, frogs,
  ducks, small birds, eggs, garter
  snakes, mussels, worms, insects
Gestation period: 40–79 days
Average litter: 4–6
Lifespan: Up to 8 years in wild;
  14 years in captivity
Predators: Coyotes, foxes, great-
  horned owls
Dive durations: Usually 5–20
  seconds, up to 2 minutes
Range: All Ontario; also in all
  other provinces and territories

ASIDE FROM THE heedless skunk, few of the many Ontario members of the weasel family often show their faces in urban environs. Mink are occasionally spotted in or along wooded or scrubby stretches of rivers in many cities, though not as often as they're seen on the backs of well-heeled patrons at chichi boutiques and restaurants. The rich, luxurious fur, underlain by a dense, supersoft inner layer, is designed for a semiaquatic lifestyle in sometimes frigid waters.

Mink hunt on long circuits that may take up to a week to complete, finding prey both along tangled stream banks and at the bottom of deep, watery dives. They're mainly nocturnal, but relentless hunting often keeps them going into daylight. The deceptively cute, prized furbearers often attack and eat animals larger than themselves, wrapping their serpentine bodies around bunnies and muskrats and killing with a bite to the neck.

While normally solitary, lovelorn mink seek each other out between late February and early April for brief, raucous encounters. Females give birth in late April or early May and raise their litters alone. After they're weaned, when about five weeks old, the youngsters tag along with their moms on the hunt until around late August, when they head off on their own, travelling up to 18 kilometres (five miles) before finding a waterside territory unoccupied by another of their kind.

OPOSSUM
Canada's Own Marsupial

UNBEKNOWNST TO MANY, shadowy nocturnal marsupials are spreading through southern Ontario even into the reaches of its largest cities. Usually associated with the rural American south and queasy hillbilly cuisine, opossums are among the newest and certainly most unusual wild creatures in the province. Among their many anatomical oddities, they possess pouches, like kangaroos and other marsupials, for carrying their young. Also unlike any other mammal north of the Rio Grande, opossums have grasping, almost monkeylike tails and handlike hind feet with opposable thumbs, making them expert tree climbers, though they're most often on the ground.

Opossums are traditionally looked upon as plodding, slow-witted evolutionary relics. They have a low, sloping brain case with a cerebral cortex only about one-sixth as big as in similarly sized non-marsupials. But to persevere, what they lack in smarts, they make up for with cast-iron stomachs, thespian survival instincts and explosive fecundity. Biologists liken opossums to weeds because they take advantage of marginal and disturbed habitats where other species have been knocked off balance. The omnivores gladly eat the poorest quality foods that other animals avoid, heedless of taste and toxicity. They snap up poisonous red efts and will make a meal of a rattlesnake, whose bite seems to be no worse to them than a bee sting. The tubby-cat-sized marsupials can reportedly withstand up to 60 times the dose of

Gestation period: 12–13 days, shortest of any mammal on Earth

Number of teeth: 50, more than any North American mammal

Average adult body length: Females 37–42 cm (14.6–16.5 in); males 41–45 cm (16.1–17.7 in)

Tail length: 27–33 cm (10.6–13 in)

Average weight: Females 1.3–2.3 kg (3–5 lb); males 1.7–3.3 kg (3.7–7.3 lb)

Markings: Grizzled whitish grey with black-tipped guard hairs; white face; pink nose; black legs, eyes and ears; scaly grey or pinkish tail

Alias: Virginia opossum, common opossum, possum, l'opossum, Didelphis virginiana

Opossum name origin: From the Algonquian word apasum, meaning "white animal"

Scientific name origin: Didelphis derives from the Greek words di, "two," and delphys, "womb," noting the fact that the female opossum has a double uterus, matching the male's two-pronged penis

Calls: Growls, snarls, hisses, screeches, clicks; young chirp

Whereabouts: Wooded or brushy river valleys, ravines, lakesides and large parks; suburban neighbourhoods; swamps

Food: Insects, snails, earthworms, roadkill, mice, moles, young rabbits, rats, bird eggs and nestlings, frogs, toads, salamanders, snakes, crayfish, fish, fruits, nuts, grass, mushrooms; garbage scraps, pet food, birdseed

Homes: Dens in old groundhog, skunk or fox borrows; hollow trees, logs or stumps, rock piles, crevices, brush piles, culverts, under porches, window wells, garages, sheds, basements

Litter: 3–25

Age of first-time breeders: 7–12 months

Adult lifespan: Very few live more than 15 months; up to 7 years in captivity

Predators: Great horned owls, hawks, foxes, coyotes, raccoons, dogs; many hit by cars while feeding on roadkill

Range: Southern Ontario to around Barrie and Wiarton and Kingston; sometimes as far north as Parry Sound (probably truck or train hoppers that don't survive the winter); also in British Columbia

First appearance of opossums: 71–87 million years ago

Number of opossum species worldwide: 76, all but the Virginia opossum in Latin America

snake venom lethal to other mammals their size. They also often survive injuries that would kill most other animals and are resistant to many diseases.

When threatened by an animal larger than themselves, opossums fiercely brandish their abundant teeth and snarl, spit and hiss. If push comes to shove, they release a smelly green fluid from two glands beneath the tail, sometimes defecating as well, and then famously flop to the ground, tongue hanging out, eyes open, giving every impression of being dead as a doornail. Most predators, especially foxes and coyotes, usually lose their appetites for the apparently instant, stinking corpse. The motionless marsupials usually drop the act after the danger disappears, though some have been known seemingly to lie in this state for up to four hours.

The opossum's abilities were ideally suited for the opportunities created by the widespread habitat disturbance that came with European settlement, allowing them to push north from their home in the southeastern United States. After several earlier abortive invasions of Ontario – swimming, waddling over ice flows or taking bridges across the Niagara River – they finally established a firm beachhead around Fort Erie in the late 1960s. With the steady trend of mild winters in the 1980s, they spread abundantly from Windsor to Toronto. Opossums, however, cannot go as long without eating, holed up in their dens, as can raccoons and skunks, and severe winters can still devastate populations along the leading edge of their range. Most in Ontario have frostbite-mangled ears and tail tips.

As the worse of winter's privations draw to a close, opossums mate in March and April. Less than two weeks later, often well over a dozen pink, blind, only partially developed newborns, each smaller than a kidney bean, emerge from their mother's womb and crawl along a saliva trail left by her to her stomach pouch, containing 13 nipples. Seven to nine opossumlets usually survive to emerge from the nursery pocket two to three months later to ride on their mom's back and sides. By June, they're independent and mothers mate again.

RACCOON
Icon of Urban Nightlife

T HE ICONOGRAPHIC FACE of urban wildlife in Ontario wears a black mask and appears when the sun goes down, calmly tripping the light fantastic along thick telephone cables above patio barbecue parties, even in dense downtown neighbourhoods. More often than not, there's three or four widely spaced little ones tagging along behind. The scene is repeated in countless variations in backyards across the province, especially in the south, where winter is less cruel and raccoons live the high life, raiding garbage cans and dumpsters, rolling up newly laid sod for grubs and earthworms and taking in all the big city has to offer. Toronto's tony Rosedale, in fact, boasts some of the biggest, best-fed bandits found anywhere.

By day, raccoons secret away in comfortable illicit squats inside attics and sheds, or beneath garages, decks and porches. The most impetuous of their lot are even given to home invasions, entering through a cat door or slashing the screen of an open window on a hot, muggy night and making for the kitchen, with results that could put a rampaging rock band to shame. They're of the same ilk that has made their country cousins the biggest despoilers of vegetable farms and cornfields in the province.

Guiding their marauding is an acclaimed intelligence, topping dogs, cats and foxes in animal IQ tests.

Urban raccoon population density: Average 8–20 per km^2 (0.4 sq mi), up to 100 per km^2 in choice ravines below residential neighbourhoods

Average rural population density: 4–11/km^2 (0.4 sq mi)

Estimated Ontario raccoon population: About 1 million

Toronto population: Despite wild claims of up to 600,000, Ministry of Natural Resources estimates are 6,400–16,000

Adult body length: 40–75 cm (1.3–2.5 ft)

Tail length: 20–33 cm (8–13 in)

Shoulder height: 23–25 cm (9–10 in)

Average weight: Females 5–8 kg (11–17.6 lb); males 8–10 kg (17.6–22 lb)

Heaviest raccoon ever found: 28 kg (62 lb)

Markings: Two-tone grey or brown-and-tan fur, with black mask over eyes, black-and-tan striped tail

Alias: Coon, bandit, ring-tailed bandit, *le raton laveur, Procyon lotor*

Name origins: The Algonquian-language name, *aroughccon,* meaning "hand scratcher," derives from the raccoon's dexterous use of its handlike paws; the Latin *lotor,* or "washer," similarly refers to the raccoon's habit of dipping food into water; *Procyon* comes from the Greek words "before" and "dog," pointing to a distant common lineage with the canine family

Calls: Chattering trills; low growls, snarls, hisses, whines; a hoarse, staccato whimpering when afraid; cubs purr when content

Whereabouts: Residential neighbourhoods, parks, forested ravines, streamsides and cemeteries

Home range: 0.05–0.1 km² (0.02–0.04 sq mi) in prime urban areas; 0.4–4 km² (0.15–1.5 sq mi) in rural and wilderness areas

Food: Fruit, berries, acorns, nuts, seeds, garden vegetables, beetle grubs, bee and ant larvae, grasshoppers, crickets, earthworms, snails, toads, frogs, crayfish, bird and turtle eggs, birds, snakes, fish, mice, squirrels, rabbits, garbage food scraps, roadkill, pilfered pet food and birdseed

Pet threat: Occasionally kills cats and known to, in confrontations, wound or kill dogs twice its size

Home: 6–12 m (20–40 ft) up in tree crooks, hollow trunks, large abandoned bird or squirrel nests; attics, sheds, garages, chimneys, culverts, old groundhog, fox or skunk burrows; under porches; decks and large rocks

Gestation period: 63 days

Average litter: 3–7

Birth weight: 50–85 g (1.8–3 oz)

Weaning age: 2–3 months

Age of first-time breeders: 40–60% of females mate when 10 months old, most others and males when 22 months old

Adult lifespan: Average 3–5 years; up to 10 years in wild, 16 years in captivity

Raccoons are infamous for quickly figuring out how to untie knots, unscrew jars and turn door handles. There are even reports of them learning how to press the button to open automatic garage doors.

Like humans, raccoons can put their superior thoughts to action with extremely dexterous handlike paws and a very fine sense of touch. Their front paws, in fact, have many thousands more nerve endings than do human hands. Driven by keen curiosity, they explore the nocturnal world with their fingers, constantly picking up objects and thoroughly feeling their food before eating. Biologists believe their sense of touch is actually enhanced by water, which is why raccoons often seem to be washing their food in creeks or bird baths.

Raccoons are thoroughly omnivorous, like bears, and grow most corpulent in autumn, gorging on acorns and other bounties of the season, building up heft for warmth and nourishment in winter dens. A thick layer of fat may account for half their weight by the time the snow flies. Still, raccoons are not real hibernators and cannot survive the season without eating. Many may starve during hard winters. During mild spells, they resume their garbage-raiding ways and during the day often bask in the sunlight high in a tree or wedged in an eavestrough perch.

Between late January and early March, weather permitting, black-masked male Casanovas are also on the make. If invited into the quarters of the opposite sex, they mate repeatedly, often staying over for a week or more before moving on to the next address in their little black books. Females, however, indulge in just one fling per year and don't accept any callers afterwards.

Most raccoon cubs are born around early May, but don't emerge from the den until they're six or seven weeks old. In the summer, they begin following their mother on her nighttime foraging rounds, trooping into backyards and climbing up and down trees and drainpipes behind her, their eyes glowing orange-red in the beam of a flashlight. These are halcyon days for raccoon public relations, when few can help but find the curious little Rockies thoroughly engaging. Though not fully grown, some become independent in the fall, setting up in digs and a territory of their own. Others stick with Mom through their first winter and don't move out until she's ready to give birth again in spring, sometimes not without some night-splitting, raucous persuasion.

Concern about southern Ontario's thronging raccoon population has risen in recent years with the approach of a new strain of rabies from the south to which they are particularly susceptible. So far, a massive vaccination program along the border by the provincial Ministry of Natural Resources – involving both live-trapping raccoons and dropping vaccine-laced baits – has kept the numbers of rabid raccoons extremely low since the first animals infected with the new strain were found in eastern Ontario in 1999. Even apparently healthy bandits, though, are best never fed or closely approached.

The messes raccoons leave behind, too, require caution. In backyards and on decks, their droppings should be carefully removed and disposed of as soon as possible because some 60 to 70 percent of all raccoons carry a roundworm parasite in their intestines that can, at worst, fatally infect humans, though cases are exceedingly rare. Roundworm eggs hatch after incubating for 30 days in the scat, which by that time may become dry and powdery and, if disturbed, potentially release dust-like particles that could be inhaled.

Predators: Coyotes, foxes, dogs and great-horned owls sometimes prey on cubs

Top running speed: 25 km/h (15 mph)

Swimming speed: 5 km/h (3 mph)

Tracks: Handlike, 5–9.5 cm (2–3.7 in) long, 4.5–6.5 cm (1.7–2.5 in) wide

Scat: Small irregular piles or single, sausage-shaped, shotgun-shell-sized, brown-to-greyish droppings; also sometimes black, reddish, yellow or with blotches of white

Winter whereabouts: Hole up for long periods inside dens, coming out on mild nights to forage

Number of rabid raccoons found annually in Ontario: 9–45

Date of the last human rabies fatality in Ontario: 1967

Range: Southern Ontario to about Lake Abitibi and far north of Lake Nipigon and Kenora; also in other provinces except Newfoundland and Labrador

Famous raccoons: Rocky, Rascal, Bobby Coon

Closest relatives: Coatis and kinkajous of Latin America

Number of raccoon family species worldwide: 18, all in New World

Also see: Striped Skunk

RAT
Most Feared of Rodents

FROM THE BLACK DEATH to harrowing dungeon scenes and Room 101 in the dystopian novel *Nineteen Eighty-Four*, rats are the stuff of worst nightmares and deepest fears. The scaly-tailed, secretive rodents are bywords in repulsion, filth, viciousness, desperation, maleficence, betrayal, rapacity, affliction, decay and anarchy. No other fur-bearing spectre commands more vigilance from city health departments or looms so ominously over even the threat of garbage strikes.

The beast behind the reputation is a canny scavenger, generally well over 10 times as big as a house mouse, that has learned to survive and thrive in the underbelly of urban civilization. Though very seldom actually seen, rats are said to equal the human population in most large North American cities. By some estimates, up to 70 million rats feast on their piece of the Big Apple in New York City. Because the burly rodents form their own complex, stratified societies, they're the favourite test subjects of behavioural scientists, who usually use domesticated albino strains. Rats are also reputed to make intelligent, affectionate pets. Breeds of "fancy rats," such as Dalmatian, blue Agouti and chocolate Irish, are judged for aesthetics and personality at international competitions. The University of Nebraska also holds annual Rat Olympics, with twitchy-nosed athletes squaring off in rat races, tightrope walking and weightlifting.

Though the occupants of labs, pet cages and city sewers in Ontario are known as Norway rats, they hail originally from Asia. After spreading west, they apparently boarded Norwegian timber ships in Russian Baltic ports in the early 1700s and travelled to Britain, from whence they later sailed to North America. Surprisingly, their arrival in Europe is credited with helping to end the recurrence of bubonic plague epidemics in most of the continent after the 1600s. The explosively contagious disease, responsible for killing untold millions, was commonly spread by fleas on the backs of black rats, earlier invaders from south Asia with a penchant for climbing and living in the thatched roofs of peasant homes. The larger, more aggressive Norway rats displaced the roof-infesting rodents, taking over their spoils in both town and country. Though Norways too, like many other rodents, can harbour plague and a bevy of other diseases, including salmonella, murine typhus and rat-bite fever, they generally avoid living in close contact with humans.

Urban rats are active mainly at night, when they emerge from hidden places beneath garages and crawl spaces in the vicinity of back-alley dumpsters, poorly maintained composters and other food sources. The best foraging grounds are claimed and staunchly defended by social groups headed by a single large, battle-proven male who commands the loyalty and affections of several Amazonian mates. Females commonly deliver five litters a year, with breeding peaking in spring and autumn. Under ideal conditions, living indoors year-round with unlimited food, they can have up to 12 litters, mating again in as little as 18 hours after giving birth.

After they mature, when about three months old, young rats may ramble up to eight kilometres (five miles) from their original homes. Unruly rat packs of mostly unmated males often form at the periphery of family-group territories, leading to frequent border skirmishes. Shut out of prime feeding areas, such non-territorial rats are occasionally driven to forage in the light of day.

shrubby or debris-strewn backyards and fields

Home range: Usually 25–150 m (27–164 yd) wide

Food: Garbage scraps, pet food, birdseed, carrion, insects, birds and their eggs, mice, snakes, fish, fruit, vegetables, grass, new shoots, leather, paper, soap, book-binding glue

Home: Nest about 30 cm (1 ft) wide, lined with leaves, grass, paper or rags, at end of a tunnel, may be 45 cm (1.5 ft) long, sometimes connected to others, in ground under a shed, garage, bushes, boards or inside walls of a derelict building

Gestation period: 21–23 days; up to 30 days for females that are already nursing

Average litter: 7–9; up to 22

Weaning age: 3–4 weeks

Age of first-time breeders: About 3 months

Lifespan: Only about 5% live more than 1 year

Predators: Great horned owls, red-tailed hawks, dogs, cats, skunks, foxes, coyotes

Winter whereabouts: Often In disused buildings or sewers; unable to survive outdoors below -18°C (0°F)

Famous rats: Ben, Templeton, Ratty, Samuel Whiskers, Anna Maria, Mr. Jingles

Range: Southern Ontario to Sudbury and Sault Ste. Marie; also in Thunder Bay and in all other provinces except Alberta

Number of rat species worldwide: 51

Also see: House Mouse

RED FOX
Crafty Catlike Canine

FABLED AS SWIFT, sly and secretive, foxes have captivated human imagination from Aesop to Kafka. Watching one bound lightly across a cemetery or streamside urban meadow in the blink of an eye, there's little wonder why.

As wild as they seem, foxes are no strangers to the city. Spared from the hunting and trapping that claim most at an early age in the countryside, they prosper within the shadows of high-rise apartments and the sound of heavy traffic. Given enough cover, the rusty predators can abound in creeks, ravines, scrubby fields and hillsides. One Mississauga golf course has had up to 15 residing in one square kilometre (0.4 square miles) on its grounds. A broad palate and keen talent for adapting to new settings, in fact, has enabled the red fox to become the most widespread carnivore on Earth, native to North America, Eurasia, North Africa and introduced in Australia.

Stealth and nocturnal habits, however, keep the terrier-sized canines largely out of the public eye. Like many night stalkers, their night vision is enhanced by a special reflective layer behind the retina of the eyes, doubling the light available to photoreceptors, causing a greenish eye-shine. They're the only canids whose

Top running speed: 48 km/h (30 mph)

Maximum jumping distance: 4.6 m (15 ft)

Adult body length: 60–70 cm (2–2.3 ft)

Tail length: 30–46 cm (1–1.5 ft)

Shoulder height: 35–41 cm (14–16 in)

Weight: 3–7 kg (6.6–15.4 lb)

Markings: Orange- or yellow-red back and sides, white chin, chest and tail tip, black legs

Alias: *Le renard roux, Vulpes vulpes*

Name of a group: A skulk or den

Calls: A shrill, barking yelp, high-pitched howls, whines

Whereabouts: Forest edge, open woods and meadows along creeks, ravines, riversides, shorelines, hills, Hydro corridors and in nearby parks, cemeteries, golf courses and occasionally backyards

pupils turn into catlike vertical slits during the day to protect their light-sensitive eyes.

Striking parallels with cats extend to hunting. Meadow voles are staple fox fare, captured by first listening with sensitive ears for scurrying in long grass or beneath as much as 10 to 12 centimetres (four to 4.8 inches) of snow, and then making a precision pounce upon the unseen prey. The master mousers can reportedly hear a squeak up to 45 metres (150 feet) away. Similarly, feline-style stalking – including the silent footing of semi-retractable claws – is used to get as close as possible to larger quarry before making a fast, deadly dash.

Despite their sneaky, nighttime proclivities, foxes do sometimes appear in broad daylight. Such seemingly abnormal behaviour often raises fears of a possibly rabid animal. A determined aerial-drop vaccine-bait campaign by the Ministry of Natural Resources, however, has reduced rabies among foxes in Ontario from once-epidemic proportions to an extremely rare occurrence. Occasional daytime rambles by foxes, rather, are quite normal, especially in winter, when food scarcity can extend hunting forays well past sunrise. On sunny, mild days, they also like to come outside to luxuriate in the warm rays.

The search for a mate in late January and early February also often brings foxes into the light of day. The larger male may follow a vixen around for a couple of weeks before she finally lets him nuzzle up to her. If there are competing suitors, they may go nose to nose in screaming matches until one backs down. The celebrated bushy tails are also brandished with effect, with the owner of the biggest plume often intimidating his rivals. The winner of a vixen's heart sticks around to help her raise the young, whose arrival in the second half of March coincides with shrinking blankets of snow, creating excellent vole-hunting conditions in the long, matted grass beneath. Cubs remain in the den for about a month, nourished on a puppy chow of regurgitated meat. They usually leave home in the autumn, keeping on the move in search of unoccupied hunting grounds, a journey that sometimes takes the inexperienced canines onto streets and bridges, even into downtown neighbourhoods.

Home range: 5–20 km^2 (2–8 sq mi)

Food: Meadow voles up to 50% of diet; rabbits most important when snow deep in winter; gulls, ducks, bird eggs and nestlings, grasshoppers, crickets, adult beetles and grubs, worms, crayfish, snakes, berries, cherries, apples, nuts, carrion, garbage scraps, occasionally cats

Average daily food helping: 5–40 mice or voles

Home: Ground burrows usually about 8 m (26 ft) long, often on dry, sandy south-facing hillsides, or under dense brush or tree roots; also in old groundhog burrows; with several entrances, 25 cm (10 in) wide

Gestation period: 51–53 days

Average litter: 4–8

Weaning age: About 2 months

Age at first breeding: 10 months

Adult lifespan: Rarely more than 4 years; up to 12 years in wild, 19 years in captivity

Predators: Coyotes, dogs; cubs taken by great horned owls

Best senses: Hearing, smell

Tracks: Front foot 4.5 cm (1.8 in) wide and 5–6 cm (3–3.4 in) long, with 4 toes

Scat: Like small dog droppings, about 5–8 cm (2–3 in) long, dark grey with hair and bone chips

Range: All Ontario and throughout Canada to Baffin Island

Estimated fox population in Toronto: About 1,000

Number of Ontario fox species: 3

Number of fox species worldwide: 13

Also see: Coyote, Groundhog

STRIPED SKUNK
Night Prowling with Impunity

Maximum spraying range: 6 m
(20 ft)

**Amount of spray in a pair of
fully loaded scent glands:**
About 30 ml (2 tbs)

Running speed: 10–16 km/h
(6–10 mph)

Adult body length: 35–51 cm
(1.1–1.7 ft)

Adult tail length: 17–30 cm
(7–12 in)

Weight: 1.8–4.5 kg (4–10 lb)

Markings: Black body with two
wide white bands running
down the back, joining at the
bushy tail and top of the head;
thin white vertical line between
eyes

Alias: Canada skunk, wood pussy,
big skunk, line-backed skunk, *la
mouffette rayée, Mephitis
mephitis*

Calls: Grows, screeches, hisses,
but usually silent

Whereabouts: Parks, yards, cemeteries, golf courses, fields,
forest edges, railway embankments, Hydro corridors, dumps

Average home range: About 0.6
km^2 (0.25 sq mi) in the city,
1–3 km^2 (0.4–1.2 sq mi) in
rural areas

**Number per km^2 (0.4 sq mi) in
cities:** 13–26

Food: In summer, mostly beetle
grubs, bees, wasps, grasshoppers, crickets, caterpillars and
other insect larvae; also spiders,
worms, snails, carrion, bird and
turtle eggs, nestlings; in colder
months, more mice, rats, chipmunks, squirrels, berries,

S KUNKS OFTEN GO about their nocturnal business with such impunity, they can be mistaken
from a distance in the dark for fat pussycats waddling across the street. They may show up unannounced
on doorsteps and patio decks looking undeniably cute
and cuddly. But more often than not, they're smelled
rather than seen, signalling an unfortunate encounter
has taken place somewhere in the dark, and ensuring
the sweet-faced stinkers' infamous reputation.

The skunk's not-so-secret weapon is a double-
barrelled spray that squirts from two nozzlelike glands
below its tail. To fire, the potent beast tightens its sphinc-
ter, popping the nozzles out, and lets fly an oily yellow-
green fluid. About 30 centimetres (one foot) out, the two
streams merge and turn into a fine misty spray. A skunk
can shoot three to four metres (10 to 13 feet) with accuracy. The stream is usually aimed at an enemy's eyes,
causing blinding pain for 15 to 20 minutes unless washed
out. The active ingredient, butylmercaptan, contains
sulphuric acid, bearing a stench that can wreak, or reek,
havoc on noses over more than six square kilometres
(two square miles). A skunk, however, stores only
enough musk for four or five sprayings and takes several

174

weeks to replenish an empty tank. The spray is a defence of last resort. If threatened, the night prowler first lifts its tail, stamps its feet, arches its back and growls. Finally, it forms a horseshoe – face and bum toward the assailant – flips up the tip of its tail and squirts.

All members of the weasel family have musk glands, used for marking territory and attracting mates. Skunk musk is so odious that it evolved as a perfect defence mechanism, allowing skunks to forgo the sleek, swift body design of their weasel brethren (some zoologists contend skunks should be placed in a separate family). Instead, with their malodorous reputation preceding them, they saunter casually about, seldom running from anything. The white stripes are a warning none can mistake in the night. Their fearlessness, however, and penchant for roadkill, also makes getting run over the leading cause of death among city skunks.

Yet skunks, like raccoons, are so at home in the city, urban populations generally outnumber those in the surrounding countryside. Digging little holes in lawns and gardens, they find bountiful pickings of beetle grubs, earthworms and ground-nesting bees and wasps. Garbage nights offer unlimited feasts. Many are also happy to bed down beneath porches or garages, or in disused sheds and buildings.

When temperatures drop to freezing, females and young nestle together for long periods in their nests and live off their fat. Adult males may brave the cold down to -10°C (14°F). But torpid skunks are not true hibernators and their temperatures, heart and breathing rates are little altered. They may lose up to half their weight by late winter.

During mild spells between late February and mid-March, skunks usually come out of their winter sleeps to mate. A male may have multiple partners, sometimes overwintering with harems of 10 or more. He doesn't assist any of his mates, however, when the newborns, called kits or skunklets, arrive in May. After about two months, the kits follow their mother, single file, on nightly food-gathering journeys, their own musk glands fully functional. Many wander off on their own in late summer or fall, roving sometimes even in the daylight.

grapes, nuts, roots, fungi, carrion, garbage scraps

Portion of diet made up of species considered pests to humans: 70%

Home: May have 2–20 dens under porches and garages and in disused sheds, culverts, hollow logs, under rock piles; also dig burrows, about 60 cm (2 ft) deep, and use old groundhog or fox holes; lined and plugged with leaves and grass

Gestation period: 62–64 days

Average litter: 5–7

Weaning age: 6–8 weeks

Age of first-time breeders: Females as young as 9 months

First-year survival: 30–50%

Lifespan: Few longer than 3 years; up to 12 years in captivity

Predators: Great horned owls, rarely foxes, coyotes, dogs

Average number of rabid skunks found annually in Ontario: 30–60 (12–46% of total animal cases)

Range: Most of Ontario, except large area in far northwest; also in all other provinces and territories except Nunavut, Yukon, Newfoundland and Labrador

Famous individuals: Pepé Le Pew, Flower, Mess Mam'selle Hepzibah, Jimmy Skunk

Skunk spray remedies: Mixture of 1 L (1 qt) of 3% hydrogen peroxide, 50 ml (1/4 cup) of baking soda, 5 ml (1 tsp) of dish soap; vinegar and detergent; tomato juice

Number of skunk species worldwide: 13

Also see: Mink, Lawn & Garden

WHITE-TAILED DEER
Speed, Grace and Tension

Top running speed: About 70 km/h (42 mph)

Swimming speed: About 7 km/h (4 mph)

Maximum jumping distance: 8.8 m (29 ft)

Maximum jumping height: At least 2.1 m (7 ft)

Average adult height at shoulder: 0.7–1.1 m (2.3–3.5 ft)

Adult body length: Females 1.6–2 m (5.3–6.6 ft); males 1.8–2.2 m (6–7.2 ft)

Average adult weight: Females 55–80 kg (120–175 lb); males 90–135 kg (200–300 lb)

Markings: Reddish-brown back in summer; dull grey-brown in winter; white undersides; fawns with white-spotted backs in first summer

Alias: Long-tailed deer, bannertail, Virginia deer, American fallow deer, le cerf de Virginie, Odocoileus virginianus

CATCHING SIGHT of a white-tailed deer is an exhilarating wildlife experience anywhere, let alone in an urban setting. Yet, the fleet-footed herbivores do reside both on the fringes and in large remnant wooded areas within the borders of many Ontario cities. But they're usually too fast, wary and quiet to be easily spotted. Deer often venture into more open areas to graze around dusk and dawn, hiding afterwards in safe, sheltered spots in deep woods to ruminate, like cows, summoning their cud back up into their mouths to chew before swallowing it again for further processing in their four-chambered stomachs. On occasion, however, they follow natural corridors, such as river valleys and ravines, deep into town, sometimes emerging on busy waterfronts or nearby neighbourhoods where, to say the least, they can't help but be noticed.

The reason deer encroach upon cities is that they're exceedingly abundant in the surrounding countryside. Agricultural land – offering delicious fields of clover and alfalfa, apple orchards and crisp vegetables – mixed with at least 25 percent forest cover, is white-tail Nirvana, much preferred to heavily treed wilderness. The combination of dense forests and severe winters was once too much for deer in most of Ontario before European settlement and logging created vastly increased foraging opportunities, allowing them to push much farther north.

Even before the coming of the French and English, though, land-clearing by agricultural Iroquoian peoples allowed white-tails to thrive in parts of southern Ontario. Deer were hunted when they concentrated to feast on acorns and nuts in stands of oak and beech in autumn and in cedar swamps and hemlock groves where they took shelter from deep snow in winter. The Neutral, who numbered some 40,000 people in about 40 settlements in the Niagara, Hamilton and Brantford areas, called themselves "People of the Deer" and actually kept white-tails in large pens to ensure a steady supply of hides could be sent overland to Chesapeake Bay to trade for seashells used to make wampum beads, highly coveted for ceremonial artworks throughout northeastern North America. Iroquoian tribes even crowned their chiefs with antlers, saying they were like antennas, making them supersensitive to their surroundings.

Deer are indeed keenly alert beings, their huge ears and sensitive nostrils constantly scanning far beyond the field of vision for every rustling or whiff of danger. When a threat is detected, a raised, waving tail of one deer is a flag to all the others, signalling them to flee. They're sneaky, and often circle around to get upwind of a predator or someone taking a hike in the woods. Nervous vigilance, stealth and speed are key to their survival, but as a last resort, their sharp hooves can disembowel an assailant.

The cold grip of winter, however, is the biggest threat of all. With food mostly limited to unnutritious buds, bark and twigs, deer rely on their fat reserves for up to a third of their energy needs through the season. Some 15 to 20 percent of the herd commonly perishes in an average winter, a third or more in severe years. With the steady march of climatic warming, though, the mostly mild winters in recent years have generally kept Ontario's white-tail population at peak levels.

The often haggard, hungry deer that survive winter may increase their numbers by 30 to 40 percent when

Call: Light squawks, snorts, grunts; fawns bleat

Whereabouts: Wooded ravines and river valleys with abundant clearings and scrub; woodlots and fields on the urban fringe

Food: Grass, clover, flowers, tree seedlings, fresh shoots, especially on aspen, chokecherry and birch in spring; leaves of aspens and other trees, plants, berries and other fruit in summer; acorns, beechnuts, grass, clover, evergreen herbs, mushrooms, berries in fall; buds, twigs, conifer needles and bark, especially cedar, red maple, yellow birch, white pine, dogwood, aspen, hazel and hemlock in winter

Daily food helping: 2.5–4.1 kg (5.5–9 lb)

Summer home range: 0.8–8 km^2 (0.3–3 sq mi)

Gestation period: 6½ months

Average litter: 1–2

Birth weight: 1.6–3.6 kg (3.5–8 lb)

Weaning age: About 6 weeks

Average fawn survival in first 5 months: 60–80%

Age of first-time breeders: Does mate at six months in low-density populations, 2½ years in high densities

Fat reserves in late fall: 10–25% of body weight

Winter mortality: 10–50%

Adult lifespan: Usually 2–8 years; up to 13 years in wild, 20 years in captivity

Predators: Coyotes, dogs; wolves and bears in wilderness areas; rarely bobcats, lynx, red foxes

Best senses: Smell, hearing

fawns are born in May and June. Up to 70 percent of newborns, though, may not survive their first few weeks after a hard winter. A week or two before giving birth, does secret themselves away in search of hidden, secluded spots in deep forests or grassy thickets. Their fawns remain well-concealed for several weeks, until they can run fast enough to escape coyotes and keep up with the herd. If twins are born, they're kept in separate hiding places averaging about 150 metres (164 yards) apart. The baby deer betray almost no odour and their white-spotted coats blend with their sun-dappled surrounding. Mothers visit them only briefly, every few hours or so, when it's time for milk.

While groups of a few does and their young travel together along regular deer trails throughout the summer, bucks lead more reclusive, solitary lives. Males start growing antlers in April – budding, horny manifestations of their rising testosterone levels. The largest, strongest deer in their prime, between four and six years old, boast the biggest racks, signifying their status to both potential mates and rivals. Growth stops in September and bucks rub off the once-soft velvety linings. As the November rut approaches, their necks swell to twice their normal size and they become gripped with a mixture of lust and rage, perfuming themselves by peeing on the ground and wallowing in the spot, challenging rivals in head-to-head pushing matches and constantly searching for mates, while eating little. About 60 percent of car collisions with deer occur during this period, when bucks are thus distracted and on the move.

Successful bucks may strike up mating liaisons with a dozen or more does, each lasting a day or two, coupling with them frequently and passionately during their brief time together. After the nuptial season ends around early December, antlers form a separation layer and break off later in the winter, providing a vital source of calcium and salt for mice, rabbits and other gnawing vegetarians.

Reptiles & Amphibians

MOST REPTILES AND AMPHIBIANS – collectively known as herpetiles – have a tough time of it in built-up areas because they are among the most environmentally sensitive groups of animals. Frogs and salamanders breathe through their permeable, moist skins and are therefore especially susceptible to environmental adversities of all kinds. Snakes, on the other hand, have always been heavily and irrationally persecuted by humans. Turtles, too, have been left with little habitat with the development of watersides and wetlands in urban confines.

The hardiest few, however, soldier on in the city. Toads are probably the toughest of all, needing standing water only during the spring breeding season and their brief development period as tadpoles. Tiny chorus frogs, too, require only temporary ponds and ditches in or near woods and thickets. Garter snakes, the most adaptable of Ontario's serpents, also persevere in ravines, woodlots, watersides and occasionally slither into nearby, well-appointed backyards. Where remnant wetlands and other undisturbed waters do persist, painted turtles and even snappers may continue to lurk, basking on logs and rocks on warm, sunny days. There are also trends toward greater accommodation for amphibians and reptiles within urban and suburban areas, with improving water quality, waterside naturalization, the restoration of wetlands and creation of backyard ponds.

CHORUS FROG
First Frog of Spring

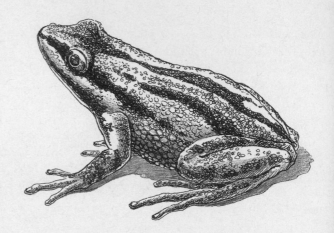

RISING FROM THE cold meltwaters of leafless ravine woods, flooded fields and remnant suburban wetlands, loud, creaking frog choruses give irrefutable voice to the sudden arrival of spring. Wherever frogs manage to persist in and around most Ontario cities, chorus frogs are usually the first to pipe up. Warm spells as early as mid-March in southern realms such as Hamilton or London can set them off, their voices commonly likened to the amplified sound of a thumb flicking the teeth of a stiff comb.

While their calls carry for hundreds of metres (or yards), chorus frogs are tiny beasts, barely the length of a loonie. Sitting on floating debris or in branches of willow and dogwood just above the water, males sing night and day at first, their throats expanding like balloons. When approached, though, they clam up and dive, making them always hard to see. As the weather warms, their clicking serenades speed up and they only perform evening concerts, which gradually fade out in May.

Female chorus frogs arrive at the aquatic karaoke about a week after the singing begins. They enter a pond in large numbers only for a few nights, then leave after laying their eggs, with each mother producing several batches. The resulting tadpoles graze and grow for about eight or nine weeks before transforming into centimetre-long (0.4-inch-long) froglets between mid-June and late July. They stay near pond edges at first, wolfing down tiny springtails and eight-legged mites. Many froglets are themselves soon eaten by garter snakes attracted by their pondside aggregations, which later break up and spread out over the land.

Through the summer, chorus frogs are active mainly at night in fields and open woods, usually within 100 metres (109 yards) of their breeding ponds. They're very rarely noticed, though some may call again briefly in September or October. Members of the tree-frog family, they have small, round sticky toe disks for climbing, but usually remain on or near the ground, seldom ascending more than 25 centimetres (10 inches) up grass stems and other low plants. By day, they take cover under logs, rocks and fallen leaves around forest edges.

Unlike many other amphibians, chorus frogs remain in their daytime hiding places, above the frost line, for the winter. They can withstand temperatures as low as -3°C (27°F) before freezing, and can actually freeze and thaw repeatedly through winter. Remaining close to the surface allows them to rouse for breeding with an early-spring thaw.

In some areas, **spring peepers** begin calling within a week or so of chorus frogs tuning up. The two species are closely related. While peepers are generally more common in the countryside, chorus frogs predominate in built-up areas because they are more tolerant of forest clearing and other habitat disturbances by humans. Chorus frogs develop more quickly from tadpoles into adults and therefore are better adapted to the smaller and faster dissipating ponds of urban areas. The paving over and digging up of even these refuges, however, is reducing chorus frog abundance in some cities.

Around Thunder Bay and other northern Ontario communities east to Chapleau, the **boreal chorus frog** is nearly identical to the chorus frog of the east, but has a slower, shorter trill. Though some experts class them as a subspecies, most authorities award each with separate species status.

caterpillars, mosquitoes, mites, springtails; tadpoles mostly eat algae

Eggs per female: 500–1,500 laid each spring, in gooey clumps, each up to 2 cm (0.8 in) long and usually containing 5–100 eggs, around underwater twigs and leaf stems 5–20 cm (2–8 in) deep in water

Egg development period: 10–14 days

Tadpoles: Dark-brown to black back flecked with gold; bronze sides and undersides; translucent tail fins; up to 3 cm (1.2 in) before transforming

Length of newly transformed froglets: About 1.3 cm

Age at first breeding season: 1–2 years

Lifespan: Few live more than 3 years

Predators: Garter snakes, water snakes, raccoons, shrews, kingfishers, herons, blue jays and other birds; tadpoles eaten by other frogs, dragonfly nymphs, fish, turtles

Winter whereabouts: Under logs, rocks and leaf litter in fields and woods

Range: Southern Ontario north to Algonquin Park and about Magnetawan, but scarce in eastern and central Ontario; also in southwestern Quebec and introduced in Newfoundland

Number of treefrog species native to Ontario: 5

Number of treefrog species worldwide: 630

Also see: Leopard Frog, Toad

GARTER SNAKE
Holding Up Under Pressure

E VEN NEAR THE centres of many Ontario cities, garter snakes lurk along riversides, ravines, lakeshores and anywhere else that offers a little cover and a steady supply of earthworms, toads or leopard frogs. Most of the time they go undetected, their black-and-yellow lines – resembling the old-fashioned garters used to hold up men's socks – blending well with their surroundings.

Garters are the most familiar of snakes primarily because they are more adaptable than any of their legless kin. They're generalists, hunting anywhere and eating almost any prey they can get their expandable jaws around. If anything, they probably expanded their reach as the natural habitats of more specialized species were destroyed and replaced by farmlands and towns.

In rainy weather in late September or early October, garter snakes may migrate a kilometre (.06 miles) or more across roads and yards from their hunting grounds to distant hibernating sites, sometimes at the foundations of old houses and buildings. Finding choice moist digs below the frost line, a metre (3.3 feet) or more beneath the surface, is critical. A third to a half of all overwintering garters often perish because they're not well situated or don't have enough starch and protein reserves to get them through their long sleep. Losses are highest among youngsters in their first winter. More experienced snakes find good, deep hibernation chambers, often shared with a dozen or more other garters, and return to them year after year, navigating their way there by landmarks, the pheromone trails of other snakes and by using the sun as a compass, possibly through the ability to detect polarized light.

Garters awaken in a lustful mood on warm, sunny days in early spring, often in late March in southern Ontario. At group-hibernating spots, called hibernacula,

Average adult length: Males 30–50 cm (12–19 in); females 40–75 cm (16–30 in)

Maximum length: 137 cm (4.5 ft)

Markings: Usually 3 yellow stripes on a black, brown or dark-green background, sometimes with a reddish tint; undersides greenish-white or yellow; populations of completely black garters occur along Lake Erie, Toronto Islands, Leslie Street Spit and in smaller numbers elsewhere

Number of times adults shed skin annually: 2–4

Alias: Eastern garter snake, common garter snake, grass snake, *la couleuvre rayée*, *Thamnophis sirtalis*

Whereabouts: Moist ground around creeks, ponds, lakes and rivers, woods, meadows, parks and large suburban yards

Home range: Up to 0.8 ha (2 acres)

"mating balls" of many randy, writhing, tongue-flicking serpents form for up to several hours at a time. As each cold, bleary female emerges from her winter sleep, she's joined by numerous waiting males, whose collective body temperature swiftly raises her own from about 4°C (39°F) to about 20°C (68°F), leaving her no longer sluggish and vulnerable to predators. Some emerging males also derive the thermal benefits of this group hug by producing a female pheromone that dupes other fellows to their side until they've warmed up. As with all snakes, males have a choice of two penises, which pop up from the base of their tails.

As well as producing many young at a time, females can store sperm from a single mating in their bodies to fertilize future eggs for up to five years. Thus one snake can slither far and wide to populate new areas without needing to find a male. Like many Ontario snake species, they give birth to live young, usually around the end of August. Mothers may stay near the little ones for several days afterwards, and siblings often stick together for a few weeks, growing by frequently shedding their skin, including the clear scales that protect their unblinking eyes. Even as adults, snakes continue to grow, though much more slowly.

All snakes lack apparent noses or ears, are nearsighted and probably don't have a sense of taste. Anything more than about a metre (3.3 feet) away is a blur. To focus close up, one must move its head back and forth like a magnifying glass, because the lens of its eye cannot change shape. Yet a snake's senses are finely honed for survival. Its entire retina is sensitive to movement, which can be detected in a very wide field of view because the eyes sit on the sides of the head. It smells by constantly darting its tongue out to pick up odours from particles in the air or whatever it touches. When the serpent withdraws its tongue, the forked tips touch a set of twin sensory sacks at the roof of the mouth, called Jacobson's glands, which transmit the odours to the brain for identification. Snakes are also extremely sensitive to vibrations, which are relayed via the jawbone to an inner ear. They can judge from an animal's vibrations whether it's small enough to be eaten.

Food: Toads, frogs, earthworms, salamanders, insects, mice, voles, bird eggs and nestlings, fish, tadpoles

Saliva: May contain toxins and enzymes that help immobilize amphibians and other small prey; not venomous to humans, but may cause swelling or burning rash for some

Digestion: Large meals take 4–10 days (depending on body temperature), during which garters remain inactive, hiding beneath rocks, logs, boards or debris; slow metabolism allows them to survive weeks without food

Average litter: 10–20

Length at birth: 12–20 cm

Age at first breeding: 2–3 years

Annual survival: 20–40% in first year; 35–50% for adults

Lifespan: Up to at least 9 years in wild; 14 years in captivity

Predators: Raccoons, cats, skunks, foxes, coyotes, mink, crows, kestrels, hawks, herons, owls

Main activity period: Midday in spring and fall; early morning and late afternoon in summer

Winter whereabouts: Commonly hibernates in groups, often with other species, in rock piles, crevices, tree-root masses, mammal burrows, ant mounds, raised road and railway beds, old building foundations and quarries

Largest known garter colony: Estimated 75,000 snakes in several Manitoba limestone-crevice hibernacula, site of famous snake-pit scene in Indiana Jones movie *Raiders of the Lost Ark*

Snakes themselves betray almost no body scent, and their heads appear tiny and harmless when poking through the grass. They strike like lightning, lunging up to half the length of their bodies, and usually eat prey headfirst and whole, the easiest way to both restrain and swallow still-struggling food. The double-hinged jaws can open almost 180 degrees. A garter has six rows of tiny, sharp, backwards-curving teeth for drawing its mouth over prey rather than for chewing. To keep from being eaten itself, the snake releases a bad-tasting, pale greenish-brown liquid from a gland at the base of its tail when caught by mammals. The defence is not as effective against birds, which usually have a poor sense of taste.

Snakes have long engendered fear, reverence and wonder the world over. The ancients viewed a snake's shedding of its skin as a symbol of rebirth. Hindu, Norse and Egyptian cosmology all featured a great snake supporting or enfolding the world. The polar star, upon which the Earth's axis seems to spin, was said to be the eye of a serpent that fertilized the land. Similarly, China's snakelike dragons were powerful but beneficial beings that brought summer rains with their thunder. Zombie was a West African snake god and Quetzalcóatl, the great deity of the Aztecs and other Central American peoples, was a feathered snake.

Long ago, a now vanished agricultural people that lived in large towns in the Ohio Valley left giant snaking earthworks. A much smaller version, probably made by the same people, overlooks Rice Lake at Serpent Mounds Provincial Park, near Peterborough. The enemies of Nanabush, the central figure of Ojibway lore, were serpent people that lived beneath the water. But the creator, Kitche Manitou, also gave snakes the job of protecting plants from overindulgent browsers.

GREEN FROG
Singing with a Wetlands Twang

G IVEN THE PROPER accommodations, the green frog willingly makes its home in the city. Specifically, the big green hopper needs calm but permanent waters. Most of its youngsters overwinter as tadpoles and don't transform into air-breathing froglets until their second summer. If they live in a pond that dries up or freezes to the bottom, they will never know what it is to sprout legs and hop onto land.

After they metamorphosize, however, dispersing little green frogs do sometimes show up in smaller backyard ponds or creeks as they journey up to 600 metres (650 yards) from their natal waters over the course of the summer. They're usually only passing through en route to deeper waters. It's one of few times green frogs move far from the water's edge, allowing them to colonize new areas, including recreated wetlands in ravines and other urban areas.

Young frogs feed close to the shore during the day, then lie low to keep from being eaten by adults, who swim into the shallows to hunt and sing under the cover of night. While older frogs go into hibernation in early autumn, the young tend to follow them somewhat later, probably because they're still working on building up enough fat to get through the long sleep.

Food: Mostly beetles, flies, grasshoppers, ants, spiders, snails, slugs; sometimes crayfish, little fish and smaller frogs; tadpoles eat algae, bacteria and decaying vegetation

Male breeding territory: 1–6 m (3.3–20 ft) along water's edge

Eggs per female: 3,000–5,000 black-centred eggs laid each spring in a floating mat 15–30 cm (6–12 in) wide

Incubation period: 3–7 days

Tadpole: Green-brown with mottled tail, creamy, red-tinted belly; fat-bodied; 6–10 cm (2.4–4 in) long before transforming, in 2nd summer for most, 1st summer for earliest hatchers

Newly transformed froglet length: 3–4 cm (1.2–1.6 cm)

Age at first breeding: Males 1–2 years; females 2–3 years

Lifespan: Some more than 5 years; up to 10 years in captivity

Predators: Snapping turtles, snakes, raccoons, foxes, mink, herons, pike, bass; tadpoles eaten by fish, dragonfly nymphs, giant water bugs

Famous frogs: Kermit, Jeremy Fisher, Jeremiah

Winter whereabouts: In mud between rocks and sunken logs at water's bottom

Range: Southern Ontario to the midboreal forest region; also native to southeast Manitoba, Quebec, the Maritimes and introduced in Newfoundland and British Columbia

Also see: Leopard Frog, Wetlands

The frogs usually rouse from the mud in April, after the ice melts and days regularly hover around 10°C (50°F). After mostly eating and building up their strength in early spring, males inaugurate the long breeding season with deep, twanging choruses in late May or June. Their verbal declarations continue well into summer, gradually trailing off in August.

It takes two or three weeks for males to carve out shoreline territories and establish dominance hierarchies. Especially at dusk and into night, the biggest and toughest call from log tops and other prominences where they can display the yellow veterans badge on their throats. The bigger the frog, the deeper its voice and brighter the yellow on its chin. With all the time spent calling, patrolling, threatening, chasing and fighting each other, some males may lose up to a third of their weight during the mating season. Subordinate frogs without their own territories are not harassed by property holders as long as they keep low in the water, like females, and call little attention to themselves.

Once things are fairly settled, toward the end June or beginning of July, females inspect the breeding territories, looking for warm, shallow water and lots of veggie cover for their eggs. Once satisfied with a particular spot, a willing lass gives the local property holder a nudge. He responds by grabbing her. As she releases her eggs, he gathers up 30 to 50 at a time with his hind legs, fertilizes them with his sperm and then pushes them away. Each egg is a tiny incubator, with a clear, porous membrane that swells like a balloon on contact with the water. In warm weather they hatch in just a few days.

Large green frogs are often taken for bullfrogs, but may be told apart by two distinct ridges running down both sides of their backs, which the bulls lack. **Bullfrogs** are generally rare or entirely absent in most urban landscapes. They require large bodies of clean, weedy waters, which are not common in large cities. Their big, meaty legs have also long been sought by fancy restaurants. Commercial and sport licences for collecting bullfrogs, however, were suspended in southern Ontario in 1997 over concern for their populations in settled areas.

LEOPARD FROG
Master of Camouflage

COMMON ON both land and water, leopard frogs are among the most oft-seen of amphibians. In fact, they're the most widespread frog species in North America. With their classic spotted markings, they blend well with the green grass and shadows of summer meadows or with algae beneath the water, in which they lie stretched out, their eyes just breaking the surface. Their main defence is in sitting still or hopping only a short distance to a new hiding spot when detected.

But frogs are better at perceiving movement than focusing on objects. A slow-moving heron may easily sneak up on one. Leopard frogs especially are set upon by all manner of predators, from garter snakes and cruel little boys to bass anglers. Indeed, one of the most common urban haunts for leopard frogs may be high-school biology classes, with millions giving their lives annually across North America as the cadaver of choice for learning basic anatomy. Fortunately, high-quality computer simulation software has made virtual frog dissection an alternative to older fatal teaching methods in an increasing number of schools.

Between late March and early May, depending on the weather and latitude, leopard frogs rise from mucky

Adult length: Average 5–9 cm (2–3.5 in), up to 11 cm (4.3 in)

Markings: Black, irregular, raisin-shaped spots on bright-green or sometimes light-brown or grey back; white undersides

Alias: Northern leopard frog, meadow frog, grass frog, *la grenouille léopard, Rana pipiens*

Call: Deep staccato snore or chuckle about 1–3 seconds long (often described as the sound made by rubbing a balloon), usually followed by grunts; a piercing scream when attacked

Whereabouts: Ponds, slow streams, lakes, swamps, marshes and moist meadows near water with grasses 15–30 cm (6–12 in) high

Summer home range: 15–600 m^2 (18–700 sq yd)

Food: Grasshoppers, crickets, beetles, flies, spiders, worms, snails, smaller frogs; algae, plankton and decaying vegetation eaten by tadpoles

Average egg batch: 3,500–6,000 eggs in spherical globs of jelly, about 15 cm (6 in) long and 5 cm (2 in) wide, often stuck to stems or twigs in shallow water

Tadpole: Up to 9 cm (3.5 in) long, speckled olive back, white belly

Age at first breeding: 2–4 years

Average time between skin sheddings for amphibians: 1 month

Tadpole mortality in first 6 weeks: 95–99%

Annual adult mortality: Fluctuates greatly, averaging 60%

Lifespan: Up to at least 4 years in wild; 9 years in captivity

Predators: Garter snakes, water snakes, raccoons, coyotes, foxes, skunks, crows, kestrels, great blue herons, kingfishers, turtles, green frogs, bass, trout, pike and many more species; tadpoles eaten by dragonfly larvae, fish, frogs, aquatic insects, leeches

Winter whereabouts: In silt, mud or gravel of lakes, ponds, streams and wetlands with moving water

Range: Southern Ontario almost to James Bay, southern half of northwestern Ontario, but scarce or absent in large areas north of Lake Superior in recent years; also found in all other provinces and around Great Slave Lake in Northwest Territories

winter resting beds beneath the water, where they draw oxygen through their permeable skins. Air temperatures rising to about 10°C (50°F) warm the cold-blooded creatures enough to give them the jump they need for overland migrations to breeding sites in flooded wetlands and shallow ponds where there are few or no fish to eat their eggs and offspring. Most of these nuptial treks cover a few hundred metres (or yards), though some can be up to three kilometres (1.9 miles). Where their routes cross well-travelled roads, hundreds or even thousands of frogs can meet their ends on a single rainy night in the spring, or when they're returning to wintering sites in October.

Once in breeding pools, leopard frogs soon join the choir of chorus frogs and others already singing. Males, calling from under the water as well as above, make a snoring or chuckling noise to attract the opposite sex, followed by grunts to warn other suitors to back off. By late May, most have mated and spread out to summer hunting grounds in moist, grassy areas around streams, ponds and wetlands.

Leopard frog eggs, laid in a gooey mass about the size of a beer can, hatch in 10 to 20 days, yielding tadpoles that are like pieces of clay, constantly being remoulded by metamorphoses to become something completely different. The temperature of the water controls the speed of their changes. At first tadpoles are tiny sluglike larvae, blind and with no mouth, hanging on to their egg jelly or to vegetation by sticky structures under their heads. They're nourished by absorbing their egg yolk. Gills filter oxygen from the water. Soon the polliwog's eyes clear, a mouth breaks open on its head and it grows a tail, enabling it to swim and scrape up algae and decaying plant material to eat. All frog or toad tadpoles are mainly vegetarians.

Over time, tiny hind legs begin to sprout and flaps of skin grow over the gills as lungs form. Front legs develop inside the covered gill chambers, breaking through the skin about a week before the amphibian uses them to crawl onto land. During the last stages of rapid change, the polliwog is like an awkward adolescent and cannot eat. Instead, it lives off the reabsorbed tissue of its shrinking tail, losing about 25 percent of its tadpole weight. Bones harden, true teeth form, eyes rise up from the head, a long tongue develops and the intestine shortens to that of a meat eater. Nine to 13 weeks after hatching, the once fishlike creature has become a froglet, two to three centimetres (0.8 to 1.2 inches) long. Before it goes into hibernation with the first cold days of fall, it may double its weight again.

Long winters can be hard on hibernating leopard frogs, causing those resting beneath smaller ponds and creeks to use up all of their oxygen. Large local die-offs are also caused by viral epidemics and other diseases, which may be spread by anglers when they dump left-over young bait frogs from one stricken area into the water to infect another, otherwise isolated, population.

Frogs in general are suffering from declines variously attributed to habitat loss, pesticide poisoning, acid rain, global warming and the thinning ozone layer. Because they are so sensitive both on land and in water, they're regarded as vital indicators of ecosystem health. Their permeable skin, which is protected only by gland secretions, easily absorbs impurities. High acidity in lakes and ponds in spring kills eggs and tadpoles, with leopard frogs having a lower tolerance than most other Ontario species. Pesticides, including most brands used on lawns and gardens, have also been linked with population crashes. Runoff is absorbed through the soft membranes of both eggs and the skin of tadpoles, causing deformities, slowed development, nervous system disorders and a host of other fatal consequences. Pesticides also wipe out the insects eaten by frogs, while herbicide runoff kills the algae tadpoles imbibe and chemical fertilizers burn holes in amphibian skin. Declining populations in some areas, especially in northern and southwestern Ontario, have prompted the provincial government to restrict commercial collection of leopard frogs for bait to only eastern portions of the province.

Estimated number of leopard frogs sold for bait annually in eastern Ontario: 300,000–500,000

First appearance of frogs on Earth: 150–190 million years ago

Number of Ontario frog species: 11

Number of frog species world-wide: 2,770–3,500

Also see: Green Frog, Wetlands

WETLANDS
Once Scorned as Worthless, Marshes and Swamps Are Among the Richest of Habitats

Portion of southern Ontario's original wetlands that still remain: About 20%

Portion of Ontario covered by wetlands: 33%

Portion of Canada covered by wetlands: About 14%

Largest marshland area in southern Great Lakes region: Lake St. Clair wetlands, 170 km² (66 sq mi)

World's smallest flowering plants: 2 free-floating duckweeds, Columbia watermeal and dotted watermeal, both common in Ontario swamps and

IN THEIR EARLY DAYS of settlement, Ottawa, Toronto and many other future Ontario cities were often derided as little more than miserable outposts in the middle of pestilential swamps. In the same era, it's said, Luther Marsh was named by a Catholic surveyor who took great delight in christening what he considered a wasteland after the protestant patriarch Martin Luther. The 65-square-kilometre (25-square-mile) wetland west of Orangeville remains one of the largest inland marshes in southern Ontario, but most of the similarly soggy real estate within urban environs has long since disappeared.

Wetlands have only relatively recently been widely recognized for the vital role they play in purifying water and providing nurseries, food and habitat for a vast array of wildlife. At one time it was believed that the vapours and gases that sometimes rose from them were the cause of many of the contagions that long plagued humanity. Even after the discovery of microbial pathogens in the later 1800s, however, the popular bias against swamps, marshes and bogs generally held sway. What was left of Toronto's Ashbridges Bay marsh – once one of the biggest coastal wetlands in the Great Lakes and a major migratory waterfowl staging area – was filled in after 1912 to create a modern port. Oshawa's grand First Marsh suffered the same fate. But when expansion-hungry harbour authorities turned their eyes to Oshawa's smaller Second Marsh in the early 1960s, local citizens rebelled in the first stirrings of what has since become a tide of support for the protection and even restoration of wetlands in and around cities across the province.

Considering all the draining and filling of the past, it's amazing what remains intact. Aside from Second Marsh, important shoreline wetlands formed behind sandbars at river mouths and bays have survived at Whitby's Cranberry Marsh, Mississauga's Rattray Marsh, Toronto's Rouge River and in a number of other cities along Lake Ontario. A little farther from the lake, Kingston overlooks the vast Cataraqui Marshlands and Hamilton has Cootes Paradise. Barrie, Midland, Peterborough and many other Ontario communities have large wetland complexes within a stone's throw of town.

Under natural conditions, marshes and swamps are undefined collecting basins in which water levels may fluctuate significantly. They slow down the flow of water, helping prevent flooding and erosion. During dry spells, they are reservoirs, their soaked soils keeping the water table close to the surface, while releasing water slowly into outflowing streams or lakes.

Marshes are the richest of all habits, forming where silty, organic sediments collect in calm water. They teem with life. The still water, filled with insects, pollen, algae and bits of organic matter, allows cattails (illustrated) and other water plants to sink roots and take advantage of the superconcentration of nutrients in the muck. Fast-growing marsh plants are far more efficient than most others at capturing nutrients and quickly turning them into living tissue. The plant life in turn

ponds, with only a single leaf 0.5–1.5 mm (0.02–0.06 in) long

Common marsh vegetation: Cattails (illustrated), grasses, sedges, bulrushes, smartweed, pickerelweed, slender willow, water lilies, water-shield, water-arum, arrowhead, pondweed, wild iris, milfoil

Marsh nesters: Red-winged blackbirds, common yellowthroats, swamp sparrows, marsh wrens, Canada geese, ducks, bitterns, pied-billed grebes, Virginia rails, soras, moorhens, black terns

Other marsh dwellers: Tree swallows, herons, song sparrows, yellow warblers, muskrats, frogs, toads, turtles, water snakes, pike, largemouth bass, bofin, minnows, clams, lung snails

Swamp vegetation: Red maple, silver maple, black ash, white cedar, white elm, tamarack, speckled alder, red osier dogwood, willows, duckweed, jewelweed, marsh marigold, skunk cabbage, turtlehead, bitter cress, wood nettle, enchanter's nightshade, ostrich fern, marsh fern

Swamp nesters: Great blue herons, wood ducks, swamp sparrows, grackles, alder flycatchers, barred owls, turkey vultures, northern waterthrushes, woodpeckers

Other swamp dwellers: Mink, muskrats, frogs, turtles, pike

Wetland invasive aliens: Purple loosestrife, phragmites, mute swans, carp, zebra mussels

Ontario wetland nesters listed as at risk: King rail and prothonotary warbler endangered; least bittern threatened; yellow rail vulnerable

Bogs: Found mainly in north and parts of central Ontario, are acidic, nutrient-poor, stagnant wetlands with no drainage outlets, many formed 10,000 years ago by chunks of glacial ice that left depressions as they melted; dominated by sphagnum moss, which accumulates in barely decomposed layers as it dies, forming peat, because the bog's cold, acidic, low-oxygen conditions are inhospitable to bacteria and most fungi

Fens: Similar to bogs, but less acidic and with some moving water; dominated by sedges (grasslike plants with unjointed, three-side stems); rare in southern Ontario

Muskeg: Large areas of interspersed bogs and fens, covering much of far northern Ontario

Carr: A swamp thicket of shrubs, such as speckled alder, red osier dogwood, willows and sweet gale

Ontario's southernmost bog: Wainfleet Bog, 1,000 ha (2.5 acres), outside of Port Colborne

Also see: Red-winged Blackbird, Canada Goose, Dragonflies, Carp, Skunk Cabbage; Rivers, Creeks & Watersides

supports high densities of insects, snails, fish, frogs, birds and mammals.

With their dense colonies of absorbent plants, marshes effectively filter silt and other contaminants. Bacteria in the ecosystem further purifies the water by removing nitrates and breaking them down into nitrogen gas that is returned to the air. For such services, marshes have been dubbed "Mother Nature's kidneys." In an effort to both restore natural habitat and lessen the impact of contaminant-laced storm runoff into urban streams, community groups and government agencies have successfully created or restored a rash of small marshlands in many cities since the start of the 1990s. The new Spadina Quay Wetland in Toronto provides northern pike spawning habitat at the foot of the CN Tower.

While marshes can take hold fairly quickly, swamps take more time and are much more rare in urban areas. They specifically feature trees and are normally located along the edges of rivers. Usually sitting on top of clay or other nonporous material, swamps are flooded or wet all year long, though standing water sometimes dries up in summer. Abundant dead trees are mined for food and shelter by woodpeckers, which in turn provide nest cavities for many songbirds. The relative inaccessibility of swamps also makes them favoured locations for heron rookeries.

PAINTED TURTLE
Creature of Climate Control

IN THE COSMOLOGY of southern Ontario's Iroquoian peoples – the Huron, Neutral, Tobacco and Six Nations – the Earth rested on the back of a great turtle. The turtle had rescued the goddess Antaentsic after she fell from the sky into a vast ocean below. Mud scooped from the bottom of the sea by a muskrat or toad was placed over the turtle's back, forming her new realm, the Earth, Turtle Island. In a similar Hindu story, the world was started on the back of Vishnu, transformed into a turtle after a great flood. In northern and central Ontario, among some Algonquian-speaking peoples who also had flood creation stories, the great turtle Makinak was the symbol of fertility.

Along quiet, weedy stretches of urban riversides, muddy lakefront coves and marshes, the most familiar domed reptiles are painted turtles, which are particularly fond of sunning themselves above the water on logs and rocks. Basking is vital for these cold-blooded armoured creatures, whose body warmth rises and falls with that of their surroundings. They can't eat if their body temperature falls below 15°C (59°F). With a sun-powered metabolism, the more they bask, the faster they digest and the more they can eat and store fat for the winter.

Temperature even determines gender, both for painted and snapping turtles. After mating, usually earlier in the spring, female painted turtles crawl onto land on June afternoons in search of sandy stream banks or open hillsides, generally within 180 metres (197 yards) of water, in which to lay their eggs. They spend about 45 minutes digging out 10-centimetre-deep (four-inch-deep) nests with their back feet, dropping their eggs, covering them up and patting down the dirt with

Lifespan: Some live more than 40 years

Adult shell length: Average 11–18 cm (4–7 in), maximum 25 cm (10 in)

Markings: Olive, black or brown shell, with sections divided by pale-yellow lines; bright-red dabs around the edge of shell; red-and-yellow streaks on dark-grey skin of head and neck; red streaks on front legs; plastron (underside) usually yellow with a dark centre blotch

Alias: Midland painted turtle, mud turtle, pond turtle, *la tortue peinte, Chrysemys picta*

Name for a group: A bale

Whereabouts: Shallow, mud-bottomed rivers, bays, ponds and marshes with plentiful aquatic plants and lots of logs or rocks for basking

Food: Duckweed and other aquatic plants, algae, snails, caddis fly nymphs, beetles, tadpoles, fish, crayfish, fish eggs, salamanders, carrion; young mostly eat aquatic insects

Call: Squeak or sigh

Average clutch: 5–10 capsule-shaped, wine-cork-sized white eggs; some females lay a 2nd clutch about 10 days after 1st

Incubation period: 60–100 days, depending on the temperature

Nests lost to predators: Usually about 70%

Hatchling length: About 2.5 cm (1 in)

Annual adult survival rate: Up to 99%

Age in first breeding: Males 5–12 years; females 6–16 years

Predators: Eggs and hatchlings eaten by raccoons, skunks, foxes, mink, weasels, muskrats, crows, gulls, herons, snakes, fish and other turtles

Winter whereabouts: Up to 91 cm (3 ft) deep in mud beneath water, or in bank burrows

Range: Southern Ontario to about North Bay and Sault Ste. Marie; also in southern portions of northwestern Ontario and in all other provinces except Prince Edward Island and Newfoundland

Famous turtles: Yertle, Churchy La Femme, Brer Tarrypin, Makinak, Kumaa, Michelangelo, Donatello

Number of turtle species native to Ontario: 8

Number of turtle species worldwide: 257

Also see: Snapping Turtle

their plastrons before leaving. The nest's location, whether it has a northern or southern exposure, or is partially shaded, and the summer weather then dictate the sex of the developing embryos. Eggs that warm under fairly steady temperatures of 22–26°C (72–79°F) yield male turtles. At temperatures several degrees above or below that, Yertle becomes Myrtle.

Regardless of their gender, if there's already a chill in the ground when they burst from their egg shells in September, hatchlings have to wait till spring to see the light of day. To survive the winter, they remain in their subterranean nests, living off their egg yolk. During cold snaps they literally turn into turtcicles. Ice crystals form in their blood, their hearts slow to less than a beat per minute and breathing stops altogether. Their temperature can drop to -8°C (18°F), and up to 58 percent of their body fluids can freeze without harming them. Within shrunken blood and tissue cells a portion of unfrozen fluid remains. Though some frogs and insects have similar abilities, the painted turtle is the only reptile able to maintain this semi-freeze-dried state. A prolonged deep freeze, however, is fatal if there is not a deep-enough overlying layer of snow to insulate the nest.

Once spring does arrive, hatchlings head straight for the water and stay there for the rest of their lives, save for brief sojourns by egg-laying females or occasionally by turtles relocating between feeding ponds and deeper water bodies for winter. Painted turtles eat, sleep and hibernate underwater. Like all submerged turtles, they breathe by filtering oxygen from the water through special tissues in their mouths and in the cloaca, an all-purpose excretory and reproductive opening beneath the base of the tail. Even if all a pond's oxygen is used up during their muddy winter slumbers, the turtles can go without for up to 150 days, longer than any known vertebrate species. Such abilities, together with their protective shells, help give adult painted turtles perhaps the highest annual survival rate of any animal species ever studied, offsetting the heavy predation on their nests and young.

RED-BACKED SALAMANDER
Keeping a Low Profile

IN DECEMBER 1986, several hundred red-backed salamanders were dug up 1.3 metres (4.3 feet) below the ground during construction behind Hamilton's St. Joseph's Hospital along the Niagara Escarpment. The slippery little creatures are seldom seen, but take refuge within the moist, undisturbed shady spots of many remnant urban woods. They spend almost their entire lives in small hunting territories under fallen leaves, rocks and logs. To maintain the coating of moisture essential to their survival, they keep to the damp earth, surfacing only on moist nights or, very occasionally, on rainy days.

Without moist skin, salamanders would be unable to breathe. Red-backs do not even have lungs. They use their skin and the roof of their mouths to filter oxygen from the air and to release carbon dioxide. The ancient Greeks gave salamanders their name, which means "fire animal," because they believed their skin allowed them to crawl through flames unscathed.

In some instances, salamanders' permeable skin can actually be a liability. Most species are rare in cities partly because they are very vulnerable to high acidity and pollutants common in the early-spring urban meltwater ponds in which they mate and lay eggs. Red-backed salamanders persevere because they are completely terrestrial. They go through their gilled aquatic stage inside the fluid of their egg cases, which a mother red-back hangs in a bunch from the ceiling of her nest cavity, usually in a rotting log, in June or early

Lifespan: Up to 30 years

Adult length: Average 6–10 cm (2.5–4 in), including tail; maximum 12.7 cm (5 in)

Markings: Reddish-brown back, dark-grey sides, mottled with light grey near salt-and-pepper belly; "grey phase," with solid dark back and sides, rare

Alias: Eastern red-backed salamander, *la salamandre rayée*, *Plethodon cinereus*

Whereabouts: Mature deciduous, white pine or hemlock woods with deep, moist soil strewn with logs and rocks along hillsides, ravines and waterfronts

Population density in prime habitat: 1–4 salamanders every 4 m^2 (5 sq yd)

Food: Beetles, flies, ants, earthworms, spiders, mites, snails, slugs, sowbugs, centipedes

Sense of smell: Acute; grooves between mouth and nostrils detect scent of prey and other salamanders marking territories

Territory: Usually stay within 0.2–0.3 m^2 (22–3.5 sq ft), but may travel more than 90 cm (3 ft) on wet nights

Average clutch: 6–10 eggs, hanging in bunches like grapes

Incubation period: 30–60 days

Hatchling length: 2–2.5 cm (0.8–1 in)

Age at sexual maturity: About 2 years old

Predators: Snakes, owls, shrews, robins, herons and other birds, bigger salamanders

Winter whereabouts: Underground below frost line

Range: Southern Ontario to Temagami, Chapleau and around Lake Superior to Quetico Provincial Park; also in Quebec and the Maritime provinces

Age of oldest amphibian fossils: 370 million years

Cloaca: All-purpose excretory and reproductive opening at base of tail in most amphibians, reptiles and birds

Largest Ontario salamander: Mudpuppy, 25–50 cm (10–20 in)

Ontario salamanders listed as at risk by provincial or federal authorities: Northern dusky salamander endangered; Jefferson and small-mouthed salamanders threatened

Number of salamander species native to Ontario: 10

Number of salamander species worldwide: About 350

Also see: Leopard Frog, Earthworms, Woods

July. She stays with the eggs for up to two months, wrapping her body around the egg cluster, guarding it and keeping it moist but not mouldy with her skin secretions. The young look like miniature versions of adults when they hatch in August or September. They may stay in the nest with their mother for another one to three weeks before heading out on their own.

Until setting up permanent residence on good hunting grounds, young salamanders are "floaters," and can have a tough time of it. Especially so during dry summer weather, when larger, older salamanders occupy and fiercely defend territories in shrinking pockets of moisture within rotting logs and deep mineral soil. Up to 30 red-backs may stake out turf beneath or inside a large deadfall. Spring and early autumn, on the other hand, are times of plenty, when salamanders chance open-air adventures on rainy nights. Such conditions serve up a bountiful buffet because the salamanders can cover more ground and imbibe in the vast selection of other little creatures beckoned to the wet surface.

Female red-backs, who breed once every two years, also release pheromones – chemical scents – that attract mates on wet nights in September or early October. Male salamanders court by doing intricate dances, each species with its own unique style. They release their sperm on the ground in a small capsule of jelly, which the female picks up with the muscles of her cloaca. Some subterranean mating and feeding can also proceed during mild spells in winter, though red-backs generally spend the season in rock crevices or passages left by decaying tree roots below the frost line, living off fat reserves stored in their tails.

SNAPPING TURTLE
Dragon-tailed Reptile of Renown

WITH ITS long, jagged-ridged dragon's tail, the snapping turtle is a living relic from the age of dinosaurs 70 million years ago and perhaps the closest thing Ontario gets to having Godzilla tramping through its cities. Effective, protective shells have given turtles little need to change through the ages. The snapper, though, is actually one of the few turtles that cannot fully retract its limbs into its dome when in danger. A small plastron, or underside shell, and very thick, meaty legs prevent the classic turtle defence.

A renowned razor-sharp beak and powerful jaws – capable of a painful, flesh-ripping bite – are instead the snapper's salvation. When threatened on land, snapping turtles can lunge quickly and accurately, up to 20 centimetres (eight inches), with their long necks outstretched. Once they bite, they can hang on tenaciously. Some have had to have their jaw muscles cut before they let go. They also ooze a foul-smelling, syrupy musk.

But snapping turtles almost always retreat swiftly when larger animals approach them in the water and normally don't chance being trapped on land. They spend most of their time underwater, often partly buried in mud, poking their hooked snouts and eyes just above the surface. Active mainly at night, the fearsome-looking reptiles have pronounced vegetarian tastes. They're most carnivorous in spring, before aquatic plants are abundant, when they sniff out water-bottom nooks and crannies for insect larvae and crayfish, and suck up small, slow fish or frogs. Larger victims are dragged down to the depths to drown before being ripped apart by the turtles' huge claws.

Occasionally, especially in spring, the hard-topped codgers sun themselves on rocks, logs or water's edge, just

Adult lifespan: Commonly more than 30 years; maximum more than 70 years and possibly more than 90 years

Oldest definite recorded age of a turtle: 152 years, for a Marion's Tortoise

First appearance of turtles: 200–250 million years ago

Adult shell length: Average 20–35 cm (8–14 in), up to 50 cm (20 in)

Length from beak to tail tip: Up to 1 m (3.3 ft)

Weight: Average 4.5–9 kg (10–20 lb), largest kept in captivity reached 39 kg (86 lb)

Markings: Black, brown or olive shell, often covered with algae; dark grey or brown skin; underside dull yellow or black

Alias: Common snapping turtle, snapper, la chélydre serpentine, Chelydra serpentina

Call: Sometimes hisses when threatened

a dive away from safety. Otherwise, their submerged, nocturnal tendencies keep them largely out of the public eye. But given a good weedy stretch of water, they can turn up in good numbers, even in urban environs. One study found 650 snappers in a 10-hectare (25-acre) pond fed by nutrient-rich outflow from a sewage treatment plant near Hamilton's Royal Botanical Gardens.

The most likely time to see a snapping turtle on land is from June to early July, when females look for dry, sandy places to lay eggs. Some have been known to return to the same backyards near watersides year after year to dig out nests. Working most often in the morning, they scoop out dirt with their hind feet, deposit their eggs, cover them up and leave. Some 50 to 90 percent of all nests are cleaned out by predators. Most of the tiny turtles that do hatch in September or early October have fairly soft shells and are soon eaten by birds and fish. To survive, they probably quickly bury themselves in underwater mud and hibernate before even having their first meal.

While very few snappers make it to adulthood, those that do are longer-lived than any other animal in Ontario. Little wonder many cultures regarded turtles as symbols of longevity, tranquility and happiness. Their reproductive lives are far longer than those of humans. Females play the odds by producing a new clutch almost every spring, even those living into their seventies. A few offspring are bound to make it through.

However, the fine balance between low reproductive success and long-lived fecund adults is easily upset by excessive roadkill, especially where open, gravely roadsides offer tempting nest sites. Turtle-crossing signs mark some notorious stretches in Ottawa, Hamilton, Brampton and a number of smaller Ontario communities. Snappers are also the turtles in turtle soup and the only one allowed to be captured by fishing-licence holders in Ontario. Commercial hunting took 5,000 to 8,000 a year until the province banned it in 1990. Near settled and agricultural areas, snappers have also been found with PCB and pesticide levels up to five times the safety limit, resulting in deformed hatchlings and even lower reproductive rates.

TOAD
Most Citified of Amphibians

TRUE TOUGH and crusty city dwellers, toads have adjusted better to urban life than any other amphibian. Less aquatically oriented than frogs, they can adapt to a wide variety of terrestrial haunts. Toads need only temporary spring pools of standing water to remain flooded for as little as seven weeks to mate, lay eggs and allow their offspring to transform into tiny toadlets. Shallow creeks, small backyard ponds, marshy ditches and even accumulated rainwater and snowmelt on top of swimming pool covers will all do.

Before mating, toads dig themselves out from winter slumber chambers a metre (3.3 feet) or more deep in sandy ground in early spring. They retrace their steps over the following days or weeks back to almost the exact spot where they first emerged from the ponds of their youth. It's a particularly perilous time for urban toads because many must cross busy streets. The warty migrants are slower than frogs, limited by smaller legs to short hops or outright walking. Some populations suffer heavy traffic tolls.

Once in the water, males call out at first with slow trills, which speed up with their metabolism as the weather grows warmer. Some people mistake the call for that of crickets. These breeding overtures peak around late April and early May in the south and may continue through June in central and northern Ontario. Toad socials, though, can be very brief on any one pond, the males eating little for the duration and their appreciably larger mates leaving as soon as they lay their eggs.

Hatching just days later, tiny black toad tadpoles soon school in dark, darting clouds. Sun-warmed waters in their shallow nursery pools allow them to develop faster than any other amphibians in Ontario, sprouting

Average adult length: Males 5–7.5 cm (2–3 in); females 6–10.5 cm (2.5–4 in)

Maximum length: 20 cm (8 in)

Markings: Mottled brown, tan, rust or green on back and sides bearing numerous, bumpy "warts"; grey-white undersides; male's throat darker than female's; able to change colour slightly, becoming darker when nestled in moist, brown earth

Alias: American toad, eastern American toad, *le crapaud d'Amérique, Bufo americanus*

Name for a group: A knot

Call: High, musical trill in 15- to 30-second bursts

Whereabouts: Moist woods, meadows, ravines, creeks, vacant lots, backyards, under porches; in spring in shallow ponds, marshes, stream margins and flooded ditches

Food: Beetles, ants, earwigs, grasshoppers, spiders, flies, earthworms, insect larvae, slugs, moths; tadpoles eat algae, plankton and bacteria

Nightly serving: Up to 100 insects

Spring emergence: Usually early Apr. in southern Ontario, as late as May farther north

Eggs per female: Average 4,000–7,000 each spring, up to 12,000, released like a double-strand, gooey string of beads around submerged vegetation, rocks or sticks

Egg development period: 3–12 days

Tadpoles: Fat, black, with short wiggling tails

Newly transformed toadlet length: About 1 cm (0.4 in)

Age at first breeding: Males 2 years; females 3–4 years

Lifespan: Few live past 4 years; up to 10 years in wild, 36 years in captivity

Predators: Raccoons, skunks, garter snakes, hognose snakes, water snakes, crows, herons, owls, hawks; tadpoles eaten by dragonfly nymphs, diving beetles, turtles, fish, herons

Winter whereabouts: Below the frost line in sandy ground or compost heaps

Range: All Ontario except extreme northwest; also in the other eastern provinces and Manitoba

Only other Ontario toad species: Fowler's toad, scattered along Lake Erie shoreline

Number of toad species worldwide: More than 300

Also see: Raccoon, Wetlands

legs in six to nine weeks, just in time to escape the summer disappearance of many small ponds. Tiny enough to perch comfortably on a finger, the toadlets remain around the muddy, weedy water's edge for a time and then fan out on rainy nights, some travelling more than a kilometre (0.6 miles) into ravines, meadows, vacant lots and backyard gardens. Most toads noticed by people are the two- to three-centimetre-long (0.8- to 1.2-inch-long) variety, still in their troubled youth stage, through which few survive. Those that do, continue to grow throughout their lives and may reach the size of bullfrogs.

Moisture requirements keep toads mainly in soft dirt depressions – which they can dig quite quickly with their back feet – or under debris during the day. At night, they feed on worms, slugs, bugs and the city's other creepy-crawlies until they go into hibernation around early October. In fact, herpetologists insist toads are far more effective at keeping down garden-harming creatures than pesticides, which also kill the toads themselves.

If, in turn, confronted by predators, toads can puff up their bodies with air to nearly twice their normal size, a defence especially handy for convincing snakes that they're too big to be swallowed. Their survival is also enhanced by poison-packing "warts" and parotid glands behind their heads. The bitter white liquid exuded from the glands irritates the mucous membranes in the mouth, eyes and nose of dogs, cats and many other assailants, causing them to foam at the mouth. Though the substance does not, in fact, cause warts, it has been used by poisoners through history as noted by the witches in Shakespeare's *Macbeth*:

Toad, that under cold stone
Days and nights has thirty-one
Swelter'd venom sleeping got,
Boil thou first i' the charmed pot.

PLANT KINGDOM

Plants

ADORNED WITH A WIDE assortment of exotic, cultivated plants, grasses, shrubs and trees, cities stand in stark contrast with the areas, primarily forests, still clothed in native vegetation. Even most of the plants considered weeds in yards and the wildflowers proliferating along roadsides and in urban fields and meadows are mostly non-native in origin, constituting a large part of the untamed life of the city. Goldenrods, asters and other native wildflowers also flourish in open areas, while relatively intact native plant communities can still be found in the least-disturbed remnant woods. The following pages feature some of the most common and easily recognized of these many wildflowers, both introduced and native. For convenience, an entry on urban fungi is also included in this section, though strictly speaking fungi are not part of the plant kingdom, forming instead their own separate category of life.

As in our previous books, the entries feature the lore surrounding the various plants and note some of their traditional uses as food and medicine. We strongly recommend, however, consulting detailed medicinal references and wild-food guides or experts before trying them out. The same active ingredients that have curative powers in many plants can also be toxic in high concentrations or if not prepared properly.

ASTERS
Floral Stars of Autumn

> The scarlet of the maples can shake me like a cry
> Of bugles going by.
> And my lonely spirit thrills
> To see the frosty asters like smoke upon the hills.
> – Bliss Carman, "An Autumn Song"

VIBRANT PURPLE SWATHS of **New England asters** (illustrated) highlight urban meadows and hillsides illuminated with white asters and goldenrod in the year's last spectacular wildflower display. Asters start blooming in August, but come to the fore in September and October, flowering in vast multitudes while most summer beauties are fading fast. The galaxies of fall flowers are aptly named: *aster* means "star" in ancient Greek, a reference to the starlike bursts of rays spreading from their flowerheads. In past ages, when fate was commonly believed to be guided by the stars, an ill-starred event was literally a "disaster." In Greek mythology, asters were created when Virgo, the celestial virgin, wept tears of stardust that fell to Earth. As such, the flowers were sacred to the Greeks, who made them into altar wreaths for festivals.

But the Old World's handful of relatively drab asters pale in comparison to North America's huge array of brightly coloured species. There are more kinds of asters on the continent than any other genus of flowers. At least a dozen bloom in most southern Ontario cities.

Not surprisingly, asters are members of the highly evolved and successful composite family, the world's largest, accounting for about 10 percent of all flowering plants. Unlike plants that retain the older design of a single, large-petalled blossom, composite flowerheads are composed of many individual miniature flowers. The long, petal-like rays that surround each aster flowerhead are sterile flowers that have evolved primarily to catch the attention of pollinating insects with their colour.

Height: 20–244 cm (0.7–8 ft)
Alias: Michaelmas daisies, starworts, frost flowers, *les asters*, Asteraceae family
Whereabouts: Meadows, woods, roadsides, vacant lots
Flowers: Composite flowerheads, 1–4 cm (0.4–1.6 in) wide, composed of light-blue, violet, reddish-purple, pink or white rays around a usually yellow centre of tiny, tubular fertile florets, which turn brown, red or purple after pollination
Blooming period: Purple-stemmed and flat-topped asters may begin blooming in late Jul.; most others start in Aug. and continue into Oct., some reaching early Nov.
Seeds: Very light and tiny, attached to silken fibres, with

Numerous minute fertile flowers form the asters' yellow centres, together pooling much nectar.

By massing so many flowers so closely together, asters guarantee a high percentage of their population will be fertilized. As hardy late bloomers, they virtually monopolize the services of pollinating bumblebees, butterflies and other diehards making their last rounds for the year. The huge number of flowers also helps ensure great genetic variability and adaptive potential.

Each tiny, pollinated floret produces a single seed, with long, wispy fibres, a few weeks after fertilization. As the colour fades from the landscape and the first snow falls, the fluffy aster seedheads are broken up by the wind. The dead stalks often remain standing into winter. Dispersed far and wide, the seeds of most species germinate in spring. They first form small ground-hugging whorls of leaves, called rosettes, and then flowering stalks. However, small, white frost asters – such as calico and heath aster – have seeds that germinate and produce rosettes in the autumn before going dormant.

Once established, an aster persists for years, its long, tough rhizome continually spreading and sending up numerous new stalks. Their perennial nature and impressive late-season blooms have made asters increasingly popular in many naturalized home gardens.

Several varieties of asters also grow in urban woods. Forest asters have much bigger, broader leaves than those of their meadow relatives, gathering as much light as possible. They grow in large, lush patches, usually not too deep into the woods. Just those growing close to forest edges get enough sunlight to bloom, displaying only a small number of light-blue flowerheads.

many together forming spheres of fluff, spread by the wind

Leaves: 1–20 cm (0.2–8 in) long, narrow and grasslike on most meadow asters; somewhat heart-shaped, up to 15 cm (6 in) wide and 25 cm (10 in) long, with widely toothed edges, on woodland asters

Roots: Long, thick rhizomes

Common meadow species: New England aster, heath aster, calico aster, panicled aster, flat-topped white aster

Common forest species: Large-leaved aster, heart-leaved aster

Wetland and shoreline species: Purple-stemmed aster, panicled aster, flat-topped white aster

Frequent diners: Flowers pollinated by bees, butterflies, moths, wasps, flies and beetles; seeds eaten by mice, chipmunks, chickadees, goldfinches, tree sparrows, swamp sparrows, ruffed grouse; leaves browsed by rabbits and deer

Native uses: Ojibway hunters camouflaged their human scent by smoking aster rootlets, said to resemble the smell of the scent glands in the clefts of deer's hooves

Range: Throughout Ontario; also in all other provinces and territories

Number of asters native to Ontario: More than 30

Number of aster species worldwide: At least 250, most in North America

Number of flowering plant species in Ontario: About 3,000

Also see: Goldenrod, Goldfinch; Bees, Wasps & Hornets

BUTTER-AND-EGGS
Served Up in Summer Meadows

Alias: Toadflax, wild snapdragon, common toadflax, *la linaire vulgaire, Linaria vulgaris*

Whereabouts: Meadows, fields, roadsides, vacant lots

Height: 20–90 cm (8–36 in)

Flowers: 2–3 cm (0.8–1.2 in) long, light-yellow spur topped by a dark yellow-orange spot on the lower lip; blooming from Jun. to Oct.

Seeds: Black, flat, smaller than confetti; many held within two-chambered oval capsules 8–12 mm (0.3–0.5 in) long

Leaves: 2–6 cm long, very narrow, straight, pointed

Range: Throughout most of Ontario, around towns and roads; also in all other provinces and territories except Nunavut

Number of Ontario snapdragon family species: 41 native, 31 introduced

WELL NAMED FOR its pale-yellow, yolk-spotted flowers, butter-and-eggs is a garden escape that has become thoroughly wild. Originally an Asian beauty that was captured by European plant hunters and brought back home, it was later taken with settlers to grace gardens in the New World, where it promptly jumped its bounds and proceeded with its own colonization. Butter-and-eggs, also commonly known as toadflax, spreads quickly with root runners that send up numerous clones, forming dense patches of yellow-flowered spires. It thrives on ground that is often too dry for many other meadow plants and is protected from browsers by bitter-tasting sap.

Most people are quick to recognize butter-and-eggs' kinship with cultivated snapdragons. Like many other members of the same family, its distinctive, ornate flower, when gently squeezed at the sides, opens its loped, flaring lips like the figurative mouth of a dragon. The tight-lipped mouth bars small bugs that would rob the rich pools of nectar at the bottom of the flower's cone-shaped spur without brushing its reproductive parts. Only the largest, long-tongued insects, such as bumblebees and sphinx moths, have the brawn to push through the lips to lap up the nectar, their hairy girth necessarily picking up pollen in the process and spreading it from one flower to another.

BUTTERCUP
Pretty but Not So Sweet

Name of buttercup sap poison: Protoanemonin

Other common plant defence toxins: Nicotine, caffeine, tannins, alkaloids, terpenoids, cardiac glycosides

Number of plant toxins known to science: Tens of thousands

Alias: Tall buttercup, common buttercup, field buttercup, meadow buttercup, tall crowfoot, butter rose, yellow gowan, *la renoncule âcre, Ranunculus acris*

Scientific name meaning: *Ranunculus* means "little frog" in Latin, so named by Roman nature writer Pliny because he found buttercups growing in wet, froggy places; *acris* is Latin for "acrid," describing the plant's bitter, poisonous juice

Whereabouts: Fields, meadows, parks, vacant lots, roadsides, railway embankments, lawn and garden edges, along fences and other spots difficult to reach with a lawn mower

Height: 30–100 cm (1–3.3 ft)

Flower: Bright, shiny yellow, 1.5–3 cm (0.6–1.2 in) wide, with 5 petals and many stamens around a cluster of pistils; many flowers per plant, each blooming for 4–9 days on a long, slender stalk

Seeds: Light brown, 2–3 mm (0.125 in) wide, flat, with a curved beak; in small round clusters; germinating in spring and fall

Leaves: 2.5–10 cm (1–4 in) wide, those rising from base of

BUTTERCUPS SEEM TO be best appreciated in childhood, when their golden reflections illuminate the chins of those promptly declared to be true butter connoisseurs. A reflective white layer of cells underlaying the outer half of the glossy-coated yellow petals makes the whimsical jest possible. The true purpose of the buttercup's play on light, however, is seen through the ultraviolet vision of pollinating insects. To them, the shiny yellow outer zone appears pink, vividly contrasting with dark purple-red toward the centre of the flower, creating a bull's eye guiding them to pots of nectar at the base of the petals.

It's fortunate buttercups don't produce berries that might further entice children. All parts of the plants are poisonous and have a burning, bitter taste. Most browsers steer clear of them. In well-grazed farm pastures, buttercups stand out as tall, prominent leftovers. Even the juice of their leaves and stems can cause blisters on sensitive skin. The chemical defences also effectively protect their roots against soil bacteria. Preparations of the caustic roots were once used to dissolve warts and

stem on long stalks divided into 5 narrow, deeply cut parts (sometimes 3 or 7), each with many irregular points or large teeth; those higher up on stem gradually become smaller, simpler and stalkless, divided into just a few straight blades near top of plant

Stem: Light green, softly haired, strong, hollow, branched near top; 1 to several per plant

Roots: Short, thick rootstock with many coarse rootlets

Common diners: Seeds eaten by chipmunks, meadow voles, snow buntings and other birds

Companion plants: Grasses, daisies, tansy, asters, goldenrod, thistles, chicory, red clover, white sweet clover, milkweed, bird's-foot trefoil, knapweed, catnip, sow thistle

Range: Throughout most of Ontario, mainly around towns and roads in north; also in all other provinces and extreme southern Northwest Territories

Forest relatives: Kidney-leaved buttercup, early buttercup, hooked buttercup

Relatives in moist open areas: Creeping buttercup, swamp buttercup

Wetland relatives: Cursed buttercup, curly white water crowfoot

Number of species in buttercup genus in Ontario: 19 native, 7 non-native

Number of buttercup genus species worldwide: About 300

Also see: Queen Anne's Lace; Meadows, Vacant Lots & Roadsides

corns and raise blisters in the days when doctors also prescribed bleeding and leeches for difficult ailments.

Thus armed, the common tall buttercup spread fearlessly throughout North America after it was introduced along with the many other European plants that now comprise the majority of wildflowers growing in southern Ontario's meadows and fields. Doing best in moist open ground, the sun-loving perennial blooms from late May into September, its flowers opening each morning and closing again in late afternoon. Toward the end of summer, small rosettes of new leaves sprout around the bases of dying stems and persist through the winter before giving rise to new flowering stems in spring.

Among Ontario's many other buttercup species, another foreigner, **creeping buttercup**, is probably the most common in residential areas, often growing in well-watered parks and lawns. Its flowers look much like those of tall buttercup, but even if left uncut reach only 20 to 30 centimetres (eight to 10 inches) high, rising from thin stems that snake and root along the ground in wide-spreading colonies. In urban woods, a native species, **kidney-leaved buttercup**, is also abundant, but little noticed because its flowers are only two to three centimetres (about one-tenth of an inch) wide, dwarfed even by the small green sepals upon which they rest.

Marsh marigold, on the other hand, looks a lot like a large, very showy buttercup, blooming in vibrant yellow clumps and patches in muddy creeks and wet forest edges from late April to early June. Though not a true buttercup, it's a native member of the same family, one of several dozen in Ontario. Other relatives include lavender-hued **hepatica**, one of the first forest flowers of spring, large-blossomed white **anemones** and the wild red **columbine** that blooms along rocky forest edges in June. The leaves of anemones and most buttercups are deeply divided and pointy, like birds' claws, lending the buttercup family its other common name, crowfoot.

CINQUEFOIL
Five Is the Magic Number

FOR ALL ITS varying forms, abundance and rich history as a heavyweight herb of medicine and magic, cinquefoil is largely anonymous in the city. When noticed at all, its bright-yellow flowers are often mistaken for buttercups. A signature set of serrated-edged leaflets tells the difference. They're most often arranged in groups of five – hence the French *cinquefoil*, "five leaf" – spreading out from a central point like the fingers of a hand.

The leaves themselves, especially the long slender leaflets of sulphur cinquefoil, bear more than a passing resemblance to the iconographic marijuana leaf, for which the plant is sometimes persecuted by weed-ripping authorities. Similarly botanically challenged hemp enthusiasts happening upon a field of cinquefoil would find their euphoria misplaced upon sparking up. Yet, cinquefoil is a famously potent herb. Its Latin name, *Potentilla*, literally means "little potent one." Its high-tannin roots and leaves are powerful astringents, helping to constrict the flow of blood and other bodily fluids when needed. For hundreds of years, into the 19th century, it was one of the most important ingredients in medicines for stopping internal bleeding, inflammation and digestive disorders, and was used in mouthwashes for sore throats, toothaches and cankers. In Ontario, the Ojibway also traditionally used the mashed or dried and

Lifespan: Commonly 6–20 years for sulphur cinquefoil; up to 30 years

Alias: Five-finger, five-finger grass, *la potentille*, *Potentilla* genus

Whereabouts: Fields, meadows, parks, lawns, vacant lots, dry woods, roadsides, railway embankments

Height: 10–90 cm (4–36 in), depending on species

Leaves: Compound, most often composed of 5 tooth-edged leaflets on most species, though commonly ranging to 7 on some and up to 25 on silver-weed; covered with fine hairs on most species; undersides of silvery cinquefoil, silverweed and shrubby cinquefoil are downy white

Species limited to only 3 leaflets: Rough cinquefoil, three-tooth cinquefoil

Flowers: Yellow on most species, 0.6–2.5 cm (0.25–1 in) wide, with 5 petals, many stamens and tiny pistils at centre; most bloom mainly from Jun.–Aug., common cinquefoil blooms Apr.–Jun.; individual flowers of some species last only about a day, dropping their petals in late afternoon after pollination by bees and other insects

Other colours: Tall cinquefoil and three-tooth cinquefoil have white flowers, those of marsh cinquefoil are reddish-purple

Seeds: About 1 mm (0.0625 in) long, yellowish to dark brown, released gradually throughout summer, fall and winter through small openings in enclosing bracts and sepals when stems swayed by the wind

Roots: Taproots range from slender to thick, deep and woody, depending on age and species

Winter state: Most species start sprouting rosettes of overwintering leaves at the base of their dying stems in late summer, with an outer circle of large, long-stemmed leaves surrounding smaller ones filling in circle

Species that grow from colonial, ground-running stems: Common cinquefoil (illustrated), silverweed, creeping cinquefoil

Cinquefoils of moist, sandy watersides and wetlands: Silverweed, marsh cinquefoil

Species that also grow in dry woods: Common, tall and rough cinquefoil

Range: Throughout Ontario; also in all other provinces and territories

Other rose family members: Roses, strawberries, raspberries, gooseberries, currants, apples, crabapples, cherries, plums, pears, hawthorns, mountain ashes, serviceberries, spiraea, avens

Number of Ontario cinquefoil species: 16 native, 4 introduced

Number of cinquefoil species worldwide: About 500

Also see: Buttercup; Meadows, Vacant Lots & Roadsides

powdered roots of native cinquefoils on cuts, wounds and many other ailments.

In the Middle Ages, the powers of cinquefoil were so highly regarded, it was said to be a key herb in magic love potions and divination. It was also apparently useful in helping witches get airborne.

More than half a dozen cinquefoil species flourish in southern Ontario's cities. Sulphur cinquefoil is likely the most noticeable, its sturdy, branching stems bearing profusely blooming butter-coloured summer flowers with contrasting dark-yellow centres. The flower, about the size of a quarter, resembles a miniature wild rose, but for its colour. Cinquefoils, in fact, are probably the most ubiquitous members of the rose family in urban fields and meadows. Some, though, such as silvery cinquefoil – like sulphur cinquefoil an immigrant from Europe – have barely noticeable flowers, half the size of Aspirin tablets.

Many cinquefoils thrive on dry ground, outcompeting and topping over less hardy wildflowers. But common cinquefoil (illustrated) keeps low, sprouting along dusty road shoulders and dry, worn park grounds and lawns, and spreading along the ground on fine, wire-thin creeping stems, called stolons. A native species, it sends up its leaves and dime-sized, lemon-yellow flowers on individual threadlike stalks, beneath which it grows new roots capable of producing more stolons. It too is often the subject of mistaken identity, since colonies of wild strawberry spread in the same fashion. The size and shape of the leaves are similar, but strawberry holds out leaflets of three, rather than the trademark cinquefoil five.

MEADOWS, VACANT LOTS & ROADSIDES
A Wide Array of Wildflowers Adds Colour to the City's Open and Neglected Spaces

HAVENS FOR WILDFLOWER lovers and home to groundhogs, rabbits, foxes and coyotes, urban meadows are refreshing oases of unordered space. Broad meadowlands may occur along riversides and ravine bottoms or in parts of large parks and other public lands that are cut back only every few years. These include wide swaths beneath Hydro lines, above buried pipelines or along railway embankments, all of which form valuable corridors for wildlife moving between green spaces in the city. Meadow flowers also bloom along many uncut roadsides and quickly colonize vacant lots and construction sites, adorning even the edges and splitting asphalt in downtown parking lots.

While hundreds of different species of introduced plants grow in urban meadows, many native wildflowers also abound, especially goldenrod and asters. Some classic flowers, such as daisies and buttercups, are widely recognized. Many others, though, are largely anonymous to the multitudes that pass them every day, unaware of their storied backgrounds in folklore, medicine and history that have been celebrated through the ages.

Common Mullein   60–200 cm (2–6.6 ft) tall

Like a picturesque cactus in a western movie, mullein grows straight and tall on dry, sandy, open ground, often near dusty roadsides and railroad tracks. In its first year, however, the plant produces only a dense, low clump of many large, very fuzzy, pale-lime-green leaves that remain alive in winter. In the second or third growing season, a thick spire shoots up bearing yellow flowers that bloom sparsely but continuously through the summer and beyond. The whole plant dies with the first killing frosts of autumn, but it remains standing and spreading up to 170,000 seeds for another year or two. The dried spires were dipped in tallow and used as torches in Roman times. Among a number of traditional mullein folk remedies, smoke from the leaves was inhaled to relieve asthma and bronchitis and the

Networks of vole runways in meadows: Up to 18 km/ha (4.5 mi/acre)

Average meadow vole lifespan: 2–3 months

Period mullein seeds remain viable in soil: More than 100 years

Number of dormant seeds per m² (1.2 sq yd) of meadow: Up to 100,000

Sow thistle root depth: As deep as 3 m (10 ft)

Portion of plants in urban meadows and roadsides that are non-native: About 85%

Common non-native medicinal plants that have escaped into the wild in Ontario: Coltsfoot, catnip, mullein, heal-all, motherwort, chamomile, tansy, climbing nightshade, celandine

Other alien garden escapes: Viper's bugloss, creeping bellflower, dame's rocket, ground ivy

Meadow plants first introduced for livestock fodder: Red and white clover, bird's-foot trefoil, purple vetch, white sweet clover, alfalfa

Other common meadow alien species: Sow thistle, goat's beard, spotted knapweed, orange hawkweed, prickly lettuce, wild mustard, bladder campion, musk mallow, bouncing bet

Western North American range plants that have moved into urban Ontario: Black-eyed

Susan, ragweed, pineapple weed

Common native meadow flowers: Goldenrod, asters, yarrow, Joe-pye weed, yarrow, daisy flea-bane, wild bergamot, wild lettuce, pussytoes, cow parsnip, pearly everlasting, boneset

Common non-flowering meadow plants: Bracken fern, sensitive fern, field horsetail

Meadow ground nesters: Killdeer, savannah sparrows, field sparrows, meadowlarks, bobolinks, horned larks, common snipes

Meadow nesters in shrubs or isolated trees: Song sparrows, goldfinches, yellow warblers, kingbirds

Other birds that dine on meadow seeds or berries: Chickadees, chipping sparrows, mourning doves, robins, juncos, brown-headed cowbirds, red-winged blackbirds

Birds that catch insects or other prey in meadows: Tree swallows, barn swallows, purple martins, crows, red-tailed hawks, kestrels

Ontario grassland nesters listed as endangered: Loggerhead shrike, northern bobwhite, Henslow's sparrow

Also see: Asters, Butter-and-Eggs, Buttercup, Cinquefoil, Daisy, Goldenrod, Queen Anne's Lace, Thistles, Forest Edge, Lawn & Garden

velvety leaves were applied to soothe the pain of sunburns. The flowers were used to make yellow dye.

Chicory   30–120 cm (1–4 ft) tall

Bright-blue, long-rayed flowers, blooming a little ways down from the tips of numerous, stiff, almost leafless branches, set chicory apart. Each flower blooms for only one morning and usually closes by around noontime. While the wide-branching plant continues to produce flowers from July to October, chicory is most noted for its thick, deep taproot, which has long been roasted and ground as a coffee additive or substitute. Like its sister species, endive, the plant's early-spring rosettes of jagged-edged, dandelionlike leaves have also been picked since ancient times in Europe for salads.

Evening Primrose   50–150 cm (1.6–5 ft) tall

As the name suggests, evening primrose opens its light-yellow, long-necked flowers and wafts sweet scents in the late afternoon or early evening, enticing pollinating moths to its side. The four-petalled blossoms fade and close by the following midday, but there's always new blooms near the densely budded top of the same plant's lofty, leafy stem to take their place from July to September. A native inhabitant of dry, sandy soils, evening primrose usually lives two years, appearing as a symmetrical starburst of narrow, pointy leaves splayed on the ground in its first growing season. The oil of the plant's seeds is one of the most popular herbal extracts used today, shown in studies to be anti-inflammatory. It's taken for headaches, hyperactivity, asthma, rheumatoid arthritis and many other ailments.

Common Milkweed   90–150 cm (3–5 ft) tall

Nodding pink or purple spheres of fragrant milkweed flowers offer great quantities of nectar for pollinating butterflies, moths, bees, flies and other insects from mid-June to August. Usually one or two of the flowers in each cluster yields a large, bumpy green pod containing thousands of seeds attached to soft, silky fibres that carry them aloft in the air. Best known as the food plant of monarch butterfly caterpillars, the dry-meadow native perennial is also fed upon by the equally colourful black-and-orange milkweed bug. While milkweed's toxic milky sap protects its long, broad leaves from most nibblers, monarch caterpillars and milkweed bugs munch with impunity, storing the toxins in their bodies, which in turn makes them unpalatable to larger predators.

St. John's Wort   30–60 cm (1–2 ft) tall

Because its starry yellow flowers begin blooming around late June, St. John's wort was associated in pre-Christian Europe with the summer solstice and worn in garlands during its celebrations. In later times, the Catholic Church tried to change the focus of attention to June 24, the feast day of John the Baptist, from which the flower takes its present name. *Wort* was the Old English word for "plant." Magical powers continued to be ascribed to the flower of Midsummer Day in subsequent years, and it was widely used as a medicinal herb. Oil extracted from its leaves and flowers has been identified as an antidepressant and is today used to treat insomnia and stress. However, it also contains a chemical that makes light-skinned people and animals more susceptible to sunburn.

Tansy   40–120 cm (1.3–4 ft) tall

With its flat-topped bouquets of multiple petal-less flowerheads, resembling little yellow buttons, and the strong, spicy scent of its fernlike leaves, tansy is unmistakable both to the eyes and nose. In ancient Greece, the deep-green aromatic leaves were placed with dead bodies during funerals and associated with immortality, having transformed, it was said, the cup-bearer of Zeus, Ganymede, from a mere mortal so that he could wait table atop Mt. Olympus. Because tansy's scent also seems to protect the plant from insects, its leaves were strewn across the floors of medieval homes to repel fleas, lice and ants. Early colonists brought it as a medicinal herb to the New World, where tansy remains especially abundant in urban meadows, flowering from July to September.

Burdock (illustrated)
60–180 cm (2–6 ft) tall

Though not popularly thought of as a wildflower, burdock initially presents attractive pinkish-purple summer flowerheads that only later turn brown and become the troublesome clinging burrs all too familiar to anyone who's been off of a beaten

211

path. The seed-bearing burrs are so good at surreptitiously sticking to passersby, European settlers inadvertently brought them to North America. Observing under a microscope the tiny hooked ends of burrs removed from his dog's fur in the late 1940s, Swiss inventor George de Mestral came up with the idea for Velcro.

Teasel   60–200 cm (2–6.6 ft) tall

The spiny brown seedhead at the top of a tall stem of teasel looks a little like a huge, egg-shaped burr, but its bristles are very long, stiff and meant for defence. In England, cultivated teasel seedheads were once collected and fixed to rollers in textile mills to raise, or "tease," the nap on woollen cloth. Between July and September, tiny, lavender tubular flowers can be seen blooming on the initially green prickly heads, starting in the middle and progressing toward the top and bottom. Shorter, stouter spines also line teasel stems and are scattered over the surface and mid-ribs of the oppositely paired, long, pointy leaves. Like many tall meadow species, the dead, dry stalks remain standing through winter.

Catnip   30–100 cm (1–3.3 ft) tall

Rich-soiled urban meadows abound in the stuff of feline euphoria. A typically aromatic member of the mint family, catnip contains a chemical called nepeta lactone that repels insects but seems to have the opposite effect on cats when the square-stemmed plant's tissues are bruised or if it's picked and dried. Humans, on the other hand, have long sipped catnip tea to calm nerves, settle upset stomachs and relieve colds. Like many other common Eurasian meadow immigrants, the summer-flowering plant spread to the wild from domestic herb gardens. Its upreaching branch tips hold pink-dotted, white or pale-purple clusters of tiny, wide-lipped florets. Unfortunately, with no flowers present, its spade-shaped, round-toothed leaves can sometimes be confused with those of stinging nettle, which are generally more sharply toothed and narrowly tapered.

CLOVER
Lucky Leaf of Prosperity

BELOVED OF BUMBLEBEES, renowned for its aberrations and revered for enriching the earth, clover abounds in high accolades and associations of luck. Only the most fastidious of lawn enthusiasts cries foul when the sweet-flowered fabled fodder mingles with their own turf grass. First planted by settlers in Ontario in the 1800s to graze their livestock and fallow their fields, clover is a flourishing rural legacy that has become that part of the urban fabric.

Clover's practical importance lies in its membership in the legume family, one of the most important groups of plants for humankind. Beans, peas, soybeans, peanuts and alfalfa are all card-carrying legumes, packing enough protein to keep vegetarians on the straight and narrow. Legumes owe their high-nutritional status to bacteria-filled knobby chambers, called nodules, on their roots. The bacteria take nitrogen – needed to make proteins and enzymes in all life forms – from air passages in the ground and turn it into ammonia, which plants can absorb. Most other plants rely on a less-concentrated supply of nitrates produced by free-living bacteria that decompose vegetation in the soil.

Planting farm fields with clover dramatically improves fertility and the yields of other crops rotated there in subsequent years, especially if the nitrogen-rich clover is ploughed back into the soil. Originating from

Best species for finding 4-leaved clovers: Red clover (illustrated)

Alias: Cowgrass, peavine, *les trèfles*, *Trifolium* genus

Name meanings: The Old English name *clafre* probably came from the Latin *clava*, meaning "club," because of the clover leaf's resemblance to the three-lobed club of Hercules, just as the black clover-leaf suit in a deck of cards is called "clubs"; the scientific name, *Trifolium*, is Latin for "three leaf"

Whereabouts: Lawns, parks, gardens, roadsides, vacant lots, fields, meadows

Average height: White clover 3–25 cm (1.2–10 in); red clover 5–40 cm (2–16 in); alsike clover 25–80 cm (10–31.5 in)

Leaves: In groups of 3 small leaflets, each 0.5–2 cm (0.2–0.8 in) long on white clover, broadly rounded, with a pale V mark near middle and finely toothed edges; red clover leaflets each 1–3 cm (0.4–1.2 in) long, tapered to a blunt point, smooth edged, usually with a pale V; alsike clover leaflets 2.5–4 cm (1–1.6 in) long, oval, unmarked, with finely toothed edges

Flowers: Purple-pink to rose-coloured on red clover; white clover sometimes tinged with pink; alsike clover creamy white to pink, often showing both; flowerheads 1.5–3 cm (0.6–1.2 in) wide, composed of 30–275 individual tiny florets, each with 5 petals forming a flaring tube; flowerheads bloom from bottom up over 6–10 days, with individual florets wilting within hours of being pollinated, turning brown

Seeds: About 1 mm (0.04 in) long, green to black, 1–4 per pod, ripening in 3–4 weeks

Frequent diners: Leaves eaten by groundhogs, rabbits, deer, skunks, raccoons, opossums and ruffed grouse; seed pods eaten by chipmunks, voles and many birds

Traditional uses: Dried red clover flowers long brewed in Europe as a medicinal tea, serving as a tonic, sedative and treatment for many other ailments

Range: Settled areas throughout most of Ontario and Canada, except Nunavut

Number of true clover species growing wild in Ontario: At least 9, all introduced

Number of clover species world-wide: About 250

Also see: Lawn & Garden

around Turkey and Greece, cultivated clover helped transform British agriculture after it was introduced in the mid-1600s and was then taken with colonists to the New World. Its value as the best pasture was reflected in the expression "in the clover" to describe general prosperity or luxury.

White clover is the most common species on lawns, sidewalk strips and manicured parks. Like other clovers, it flowers from May into October, but is perhaps most prominent in June, topping green expanses with a white glaze before its first big bloom falls to the blade. White clover grows in quick-spreading patches, one plant sending out up to a dozen wiry, ground-hugging stems, each stretching as far as a metre (3.3 feet) in different directions. They root at nodes along their length where separate stalks of either single leaves or flowers rise.

Growing so low to the ground, white clover is generally crowded out in areas of longer grass and wildflowers. **Red clover** (illustrated) is more common in such places, since its stem stands erect, or at least leans, bearing leaves and flowers aloft together. It usually grows alone, or a few plants in one spot, rather than in colonies. The individual floral tubes in red clover flowerheads are so long and narrow, only the bigger species of bumblebees, and some butterflies, have long-enough tongues to reach their rich pools of nectar with ease. Still, honeybees often do make the extra effort. White clover's shorter florets, on the other hand, are one of the biggest sources of commercial honey.

Honeybees are also the main pollinators of **alsike clover** flowers, which can be creamy white, pink or both. Alsike grows on erect, branching stems and lacks the pale chevrons usually on the leaves of the other two common species. Unlike red clover, its flowerheads rise on long stalks well spaced from the leaves below them. It's often planted along roadsides and highway medians to bind the soil, but also makes its own way to unkept meadows and the city's other welcoming green fields of clover.

DAISY
The Petal-plucking Favourite

FIGURING IN popular allusions to love, death and happy abandon, daisies are for many the most familiar wildflowers. They seem, for city folk at least, to strike just the right balance between simple beauty and abundance to invite picking. Accordingly, the yellow-centred flowers are associated with idyllic summer days of impromptu bouquets, daisy-chain garlands and petal-plucking divinations of affection.

In truth, each daisy "petal" is really an individual ray flower, with a tiny yellow Y-shaped female stigma at its base. The daisy's yellow centre is also composed of hundreds of tubular mini-flowers, or "florets," each with both male and female parts. Florets at the edge of the compound flowerhead open first, with their pollen-bearing male structures rising up, followed later by a Y-tipped stigma. Nectar-lapping bees work the flowerheads systematically, first circling around the fuzzy edge where flowers bear protruding female parts, and spiralling inward toward the male-dominated florets, so that they leave with pollen sticking to their hairy bodies and cross-pollinate the next daisy they visit.

Like most common open-field wildflowers in settled areas, daisies are newcomers to North America. They probably spread from stray seeds mixed in with grain or packing straw brought to the colonies by early supply ships from Europe.

Alias: Ox-eye daisy, field daisy, *la marguerite blanche*, *Chrysanthemum leucanthemum*, *Leucanthemum vulgare*

***Daisy* name origin:** From Old English *daegas eag*, meaning "day's eye"

Whereabouts: Meadows, fields, roadsides, vacant lots, gardens

Height: 30–100 cm (1–3.3 ft)

Flowers: Compound flowerhead, 2.5–5 cm (1–2 in) wide, composed of 20–30 white petal-like ray florets surrounding hundreds of tiny yellow tubular disk florets; blooming mainly from Jun. to Aug.

Leaves: 4–15 cm (1.6–6 In) long; with long stalks, tapered bottoms, wide tops, round-toothed or lobed margins; higher stem leaves narrow, sword-shaped, edged with projecting teeth

Range: Throughout most of Ontario, also in all other provinces and the Yukon

DAME'S ROCKET
June Beauty of Forest Fringes

Whereabouts: Low, damp forest edges, shady streamsides, flood plains, wet meadows, roadside ditches

Alias: Dame's violet, mother-of-the-evening, *la julienne des dames*, *Hesperis matronalis*

Average height: 30–90 cm (1–3 ft)

Flowers: Purple, pink or white, 1.5–2.5 cm (0.6–1 in) wide, with 4 petals; in small clusters at top of stems and branches; blooming mainly from mid-May to early Jul.

Seeds: Brown, 2–4 mm (0.08–0.16 in) long, lying in a row within slender, pointy pods, 2.5–14 cm (1–5.5 in) long, held upwards below the blooming flowers

Leaves: Spearhead-shaped, 5–20 cm (2–8 in) long, tooth-edged

Range: Mainly in southern Ontario; also in all other provinces

ALONG THE borders of urban woods, especially in creek and ravine bottom-lands, dame's rocket is hard to miss in June, its tall bouquets of flowers fringing the forest in varying shades of purple, pink and white. Refusing to be ignored even as the light fades on the season's long days, the showy flowers fill the evening air with fragrance, likened by some to the spicy, sweet aroma of cloves. The nocturnally aromatic plant's scientific handle, *Hesperis matronalis*, translated from Greek and Latin respectively, means "mother of the evening," hence the dame of the name. "Rocket" is a term used for a number of mustard family plants, originating from the Latin name for rapeseed, *eruca*.

Dame's rocket has perfumed early summer evenings in European country cottage gardens for hundreds of years. It was brought to Ontario in the 1800s and commonly planted around farmhouses. Long after the farmsteads disappeared in urban areas, their orphaned flowers persist in wild, renegade patches. Dame's rocket has been so successful on its own, in fact, it's now considered an invasive species, crowding out native wildflowers that are hard-pressed to get a foothold beneath the shade of its dense, lofty stalks. In most urban woods, however, the plant's far-less-alluring alien cousin, garlic mustard, is a much greater problem.

ALIEN INVADERS

Some Foreign Species Are Benign, but the Worst Are Like Vikings Falling Upon Rich Shores, Spreading Rapidly Until Native Species Are Vanquished

CITIES ARE cosmopolitan by nature, the gathering places of disparate and exotic elements. Even the green spaces of Ontario's cities have been settled by hundreds of kinds of plants, shrubs and trees from beyond North America. Most are mild-mannered residents taking advantage of the living opportunities created by human intervention and have little known widespread impact on native plant and animal communities. The worst alien invaders, on the other hand, are like Vikings falling upon rich, undefended shores, free from key elements that kept them in check back home, such as specialized insect browsers or pathogens. They spread rapidly even into largely undeveloped areas, dominating the space and resources and displacing native species. After habitat destruction by humans, which usually gives them their start, invading scourges are considered the next leading cause of the widespread disappearance of plants and animals worldwide.

Urban woods are often particularly impoverished by alien invaders. In place of fabled carpets of blooming white and red trilliums, yellow trout lilies, purple violets and other spring ephemerals, forest floors commonly sport little but straight-stalked expanses of rangy garlic mustard (illustrated). The European import initially forms mats of small, roundish leaves that have a garlic aroma when crushed and remain green through the winter. Usually early in its second year, each plant sprouts a metre-tall (3.3-feet-tall) stem, bearing tiny, white, unimpressive flowers in May and June. It dies

> Portion of invasive alien plants in North America originally brought for gardens and landscaping: About 85%
> Portion of established alien plants and animals found in U.S. studies to cause severe harm to native ecosystems: About 15%
> Invasive alien forest species: Garlic mustard (illustrated), goutweed, Himalayan balsam, periwinkle, scilla, moneywort, European stinging nettle, English

217

ivy, common buckthorn, Japanese honeysuckle, European barberry, Norway maple, tree of heaven, Siberian elm

Invasive aliens of forest edges: Dog-strangling vine, Canada thistle, dame's rocket, multiflora rose, autumn olive, Tartarian honeysuckle

Invasive alien meadow species: Dog-strangling vine, Japanese knotweed, Canada thistle, crown vetch, spotted knapweed, Kentucky bluegrass, white bedstraw, white poplar

Invasive aliens of wetlands and riverbanks: Japanese knotweed, common reed, purple loosestrife, flowering rush, rough manna grass, glossy buckthorn, European black alder, European birch

Invasive aliens of open waters: European frog-bit, curly pondweed, Eurasian watermilfoil, floating heart

Alternative native ground cover plants for yards with deep shade or poor soil: Herb Robert, Virginia creeper, foam flower, wild strawberry and native ferns

Number of native Ontario plant species that have been extirpated or not seen in past 20 years: 71

Number of alien vascular plants established in the wild in Ontario: About 700

Number of native vascular plants in Ontario: About 1,900

Also see: Dame's Rocket, Thistles, Norway Maple, White Elm, Green Ash, Ladybugs, Termites, Mosquitoes, Smelt, House Sparrow, Starling, Woods

back in summer but remains standing, brittle, brown and dry with upright forking seed pods, for another winter.

Garlic mustard was originally grown in 19th-century gardens as a medicinal herb and tangy salad green, but like many other foreign mustards escaped into the wild. For some reason, it reached a critical mass and began exploding in the 1970s, spreading from disturbed forest edges into the hearts of woodlands across southern Ontario, especially in moist flood plains and ravines. It usually takes over completely within 10 years of becoming established in a given area, crowding and shading out most native herbaceous plants.

Goutweed, periwinkle and scilla also create dense ground covers in urban woods, usually after spreading from residential yards and gardens nearby. Common buckthorn, however, is a spiny ornamental hedge tree that ended up in forests because birds eat its clusters of black or red berries and spread the seeds in their droppings. While shade-tolerant itself, buckthorn forms densely branched understory thickets that cut off the light to native tree seedlings and everything else growing beneath. The foreign interloper also apparently releases toxins in the soil that further keep out the competition. In autumn, buckthorn stands out by retaining its dark-green leaves late into the season. It's thin greyish-brown bark also curls at the edges like birchbark.

Along forest edges and stretching over fields, meadows and riverbanks, dog-strangling vine has become one of the most serious invasive aliens in southern Ontario since the mid-1990s. Also known as swallowwort, it twines around and over the tops of other meadow plants and up tree trunks, forming thick, impenetrable, smothering masses. Similar to milkweed, to which it is related, the exotic strangler produces long, slender seed pods that split open to release downy-fibred seeds that spread far and wide in the wind. Once established, it sends out deep, suckering roots, like many other invasive species, producing colonies of clones that can seldom be either mowed away or burned out.

Japanese knotweed is another alien with an otherworldly rate of growth. Its thick, hollow, rubbery stems rise like bamboo up to three metres (10 feet) out of the ground before dying back again each year. Originally used in screen-forming ornamental plantings, it propagates readily from small fragments of its reddish-purple mottled stem, even when buried a metre (3.3 feet) deep in loads of fill. Dense, jungle-like stands of knotweed spring up in wet meadows and along urban streams and ditches, spreading by thick horizontal rootstocks that can extend up to 20 metres (66 feet) from one plant.

Toward water's edge and in wetlands, Japanese knotweed gives way to phragmites, narrow foreign reeds up to four metres (13 feet) tall, topped by large, feathery plumes. Like other invasives, they grow so thickly they leave little room for other plants. Phragmites are so effective at taking over shorelines, they're the most widespread plant species on Earth.

Another waterside spreader, purple loosestrife, became the poster plant for alien invaders in the early 1990s. Recent, if controversial, studies, however, suggest the purple-flowered beauty may not be as bad as it was made out to be, rarely actually displacing other species. Most often, wide swaths of loosestrife spread and thrive along developed shorelines where most of the natural vegetation has already been removed.

Nonetheless, several hundred thousand European beetles that feed exclusively on purple loosestrife were released in Ontario in the mid-1990s to prune back the plant in heavily colonized areas. Researchers are also looking at several kinds of beetles that help control garlic mustard on its home turf in Europe. Even in the recent past, however, many intentionally introduced foreign insects, such as multicoloured Asian lady beetles, have had major unforeseen negative consequences for native species.

Most of the voracious vegetarian alien bugs that have become threats to native plants and trees in recent years have come with ever-increasing volumes of world trade and the use of large, enclosed cargo containers that can be transferred from ship to train to trucks and transported to factories and warehouses almost anywhere. In September 2003, a major infestation of Asian longhorned beetles, which could potentially devastate maple, birch and aspen forests across the province, was discovered in an area centred around an industrial zone at the northwest edge of Toronto, prompting the felling of thousands of trees in a six-square-kilometre area. The trunk-boring beetles, native to China and Korea, were believed to have arrived in wooden shipping crates from Asia. Overall, about 80 percent of invasive exotic species that have arrived in North America in recent decades have come with trade goods.

DANDELION
Dug In for Lawn Warfare

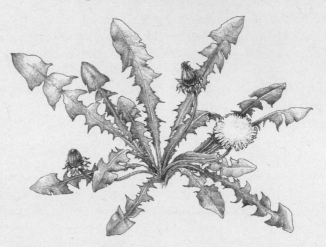

Alias: Common dandelion, blow-ball, lion's tooth, fairy clock, monk's head, *le pissenlit*, *Taraxacum officinale*

***Dandelion* name origin:** French *dent de lion*, meaning "lion's tooth," a reference, according to most sources, to the dande-lion's sharp, toothlike, jagged-lobed leaves; other sources credit the long, fanglike taproot for the name

Whereabouts: Lawns, gardens, parks, fields, roadsides

Height: 5–45 cm (2–18 in)

Flowers: Yellow flowerhead is made up of 100–300 individual ray florets that bloom gradually over several days, starting at the outer edge; flowerhead gradually opens early in morning, starts contracting in early afternoon and is completely closed by sunset; may remain closed on overcast and rainy days

Seeds: Slender, 3–4 mm (0.125–0.166 in) long, brown

DANDELIONS ARE MOTHER NATURE'S elite commandos in the never-ending battle for the perfect lawn. Their airborne fluff-tufted seeds parachute into open, sunny places and sink deep, intractable taproots wherever they find a sparse spot in the grass. Once dug in, they spread out circular rosettes of leaves that hunker low to the ground, invariably sur-viving repeated mechanized assaults. Flower buds, too, form at ground level, at the centres of the rosettes, and when ready to bloom rise rapidly on expanding hollow stems in a bid to attract air support from pollinating insects. Those that succeed close up and duck for cover again for several days, while their seeds develop, and then shoot up even higher than before, offering their expanding spherical seedheads to the breeze.

Even decapitated flowerheads can produce viable seeds within a day or so of a lawn mower's passing. In most cases, the only successful methods of quickly rooting out dandelions is hand-to-hand combat or chemical warfare. Mounting evidence of the innocent casualties caused by the latter is prompting a growing number of municipalities to ban herbicides on residen-tial lawns and public parks.

The bitter turf war is a relatively recent development in humankind's long relationship with the dandelion. Many centuries before the coming of lawn mowers and spacious suburban yards, the same deep taproot that is reviled today was considered a godsend from western Europe to China. Juice squeezed from the highly nutritious root probably helped save many lives in the days when scurvy and other diseases caused by winter vitamin deficiencies were common. Tender spring dandelion leaves are similarly nutritionally superior to broccoli and spinach, have more beta carotene than carrots, more potassium than bananas and 25 times as much vitamin A as tomato juice. The golden-flowered plant's value as a salad green, spring tonic and medicine for many ailments earned it an important place in ancient and medieval gardens and a berth aboard ships to the New World with European colonists.

Culinary enthusiasts collect early-spring dandelions before they flower and the leaves become too bitter to eat. Dandelions bloom in greatest profusion in mid- to late May, turning some city parks into oceans of yellow and becoming the main focus of most pollinating insects. They also flower in smaller numbers from early spring to late autumn, and the buds of a few hardy souls sometimes even peek open during snowless mild spells in winter in some southern Ontario cities.

The quick transformation from yellow flower to delicate puffball, upon which children blow to make a wish, has always been a big part of dandelion lore. In the play *Cymbeline*, Shakespeare likens the fluffy seedheads to chimney cleaning brushes, noting:

Golden lads and girls all must,
As chimney sweepers, come to dust.

In an Algonquian story, the slothful, portly South Wind, Shawondasee, catches sight of a beautiful, golden-haired maiden in the form of a flower, but is too lazy to cross the meadow to meet her. When he returns a few days later, she has turned into an old woman with white hair, and he breathes a sigh of regret, which blows all her hair away. Every spring he sighs again in memory of her. If the story dates to pre-contact times, the subject could have been a native hawkweed or wild lettuce species, which have dandelionlike flowers and puffball seedheads.

to olive, attached to wispy white fibres, with many forming a spherical seedhead of fluff, 3.5–5 cm (1.4–2 in) wide, breaking apart and floating in air with wind or disturbance; viable in soil for up to 5 years
Leaves: Highly variable, 4–40 cm (1.6–16 in) long, 1.3–8 cm (0.5–3 in) wide, usually with sharp, deeply cut, downward-pointing lobes, toothed margins and narrow base
Root: Fleshy taproot usually 5–30 cm (2–12 in) long, 0.6–1.3 cm (0.25–0.5 in) thick, with rootlets capable of reaching more than 3 m (10 ft) deep
Frequent diners: Seeds eaten by house sparrows, house finches, goldfinches, chipping sparrows, pine siskins; leaves browsed by rabbits and deer
Traditional medicinal uses: Roots, leaves or flowers used in teas and medicines for liver and kidney problems, arthritis, fever, heartburn, insomnia
Range: Throughout most of Ontario; also in all other provinces and territories
Number of Ontario dandelion species: 3 native, 2 introduced
Number of dandelion species worldwide: About 40
Also see: Asters, Ladybugs

FERNS
Lush Stalwarts of Shady Refuges

B OTH IN MOIST, undisturbed pockets of urban woods and in shady, naturalized yards in downtown neighbourhoods, clusters of gracefully arching ferns lend a cool, lush primeval air. Fortunately, the most widely planted ornamental, **ostrich fern** (illustrated), is also a native species and often grows in thick colonies of lofty fronds along muddy suburban creeks and wooded ravine bottomlands. In many parts of eastern Canada and the United States, collecting succulent ostrich fern fiddleheads, which emerge around early May in southern Ontario, is considered a traditional rite of spring. Defence toxins, however, begin building in all ferns as they sprout and authorities warn against eating large amounts of even the youngest fiddleheads. They also warn against illegally picking them in city parks and conservation authority lands.

Ferns in general have not done well in urban areas, where usually only about half a dozen of Ontario's 75 different species are common. The most versatile, **bracken fern**, forms thigh-high canopies in both open woods and dry, sandy utility corridors. The less-intricately cut, light-green fronds of **sensitive fern** can also be found in a range of semi-open to thickly treed areas, but usually on wet or very moist ground. Circular clusters, or "crowns," of various wood ferns, which remain green through the winter, keep to rich, damp woods. Hamilton, Owen Sound, St. Catharines and other cities along the Niagara Escarpment enjoy the bonus of a number of intriguing, limestone-loving species, such as fragile fern, maidenhair spleenwort, smooth cliffbreak and walking fern, which are rare elsewhere.

Lifespan: Up to 100 years

Tallest Ontario fern: Ostrich fern (illustrated), up to 2 m (6.7 ft)

Smallest Ontario fern: Wall rue, usually about 6 cm (3 in)

Spore casings: Many species have "fruit dots" containing spores on the undersides of fronds, others have separate sterile and markedly different fertile fronds or spikes bearing dense clusters of spore casings; spores travel on air currents

Number of spores produced by a single frond: Millions

Alias: Fiddleheads, order Filicales, *les fongères*

Name origin of *fern*: From proto-Indo-European *porno,* meaning "feather"

In European folklore, fern seeds were believed to have the power to make people invisible and open locked doors, but were only produced on the night of Midsummer's Eve. No one ever could find a fern seed to test the theory. Ferns actually reproduce by dustlike spores. Unlike a seed, which contains a minute, inflatable, rolled-up plant and a supply of protein to nourish it, a spore is a single cell. It grows by dividing once it lands in a suitable site. After several weeks, it produces a tiny, heart-shaped plant called a prothallium, usually less than a centimetre (0.4 inches) wide, lying flat on the ground.

The prothallium is short-lived and, unlike its parent, reproduces sexually. As with primitive water plants, sperm travels through a film of rain or moisture from male parts on the underside of one plant to the female organs of another nearby. The fertilized egg grows into a tiny fern, drawing nutrients from the prothallium until it sinks its own roots. The rhizome, or underground stem, that develops sends up more fronds.

Long before seed-bearing and flowering plants evolved, all vegetation on Earth reproduced by spores. But unlike spore-spewing fungi, lichens and mosses, which depend on the slow diffusion of water and nutrients through their tissues to grow, ferns have vascular canals, like veins, to transport its supplies much more quickly, allowing it to grow both higher and faster. The world's first steamy jungles, in fact, were dominated by tree-sized ferns and horsetails during the Carboniferous period some 300 million years ago. As the Earth's climate cooled, giant ferns perished in temperate zones, leaving behind only species that buried their woody trunks underground as horizontal stems. The visible ferns that appear above the ground are the plant's leaves, called fronds. There are still some tree ferns in the tropics that reach heights of 25 metres (80 feet) and are easily mistaken for palm trees.

Name for fern enthusiasts: Pteridologists, or ferners

Self-proclaimed fern capital of Ontario: Owen Sound

Native remedies: The Ojibway boiled lady fern and sensitive fern into a tea for relieving pain and to help nursing mothers produce milk; fresh, moistened lady fern was also slapped onto scrapes and bruises to ease pain; natives wore bracken ferns on their heads to ward off black flies, used rattlesnake fern in a poultice for snake bites and brewed maidenhair fern tea for respiratory ailments

Common wetland species: Sensitive, ostrich, royal, lady, New York, marsh, cinnamon, oak and crested shield ferns

Species of mainly hardwood forests: Maidenhair, bulblet, New York, Christmas, rattlesnake and silvery glade ferns

Species of rocky, limestone areas: Maidenhair spleenwort, smooth cliffbreak, polypody, fragil, bulblet, marginal shield, hart's tongue, walking and Clinton's wood ferns

Range: Throughout Ontario; in all other provinces and territories

First appearance of vascular spore-producing plants: 400 million years ago

Number of fern species native to Ontario: 75

Number of fern species worldwide: 9,000–10,000

Also see: Wetlands, Fungi

FUNGI
Bursting Out All Over

NEITHER PLANTS nor animals, fungi form their own separate kingdom of life that is mostly unseen, but all pervasive, even in the gritty city. On occasion, large, white shaggy manes and sidewalk mushrooms push right up through the asphalt in downtown parking lots and laneways, powered by hydraulic pressure. More often, common little white or tan mushrooms such as smooth parasols, haymaker's mushrooms, puffballs and tiny, flimsy-topped mica cap mushrooms appear fleetingly on residential lawns, especially during or after rainy weather.

Late-season rains summon the hidden kingdom of fungi to the surface in a great profusion and explosion of form and colour. Mushrooms and their intricate inner structures develop in a matter of days. Just as yeast, one type of fungus, makes bread rise, minute, rain-saturated fungal filaments grow at a phenomenal rate, intertwining and merging like animated strands of Plasticine. Most mushrooms flourish only long enough to produce and disperse their spores, perhaps a week or so, before decomposing into pulp. Some of the smaller species last just a few hours.

Thick, fleshy, brown-mottled **dryad's saddles**, on the other hand, may emerge from backyard stumps and old tree trunks in either spring or fall and flourish for weeks. Other polypores, also known as bracket fungi, last considerably longer. In the woods, fallen logs bear rows of flaky-thin **turkey tail**, which persists throughout the year. Normally hard and dry, it becomes rubbery with moisture, sharpening its sand-and-rust concentric rings to resemble the fanned tail feathers of its namesake gobbler. Larger woody polypores grow on tree trunks for years. The grey-and-brown bands of an

Ontario's biggest mushroom: Giant puffball, up to 51 cm (20 in) wide and weighing 22 kg (48.5 lb)

Number of spores or microscopic fungal colonies in 1 g (0.03 oz) of soil: 300,000–3 million

Number of spores in a single mushroom: Billions

Time spores can remain dormant: Up to 20 years

Rate of growth: Under ideal warm, moist conditions, a new fungus can sprout several kilometres (miles) of strands in a few days

People who study mushrooms: Mycologists

People who fear mushrooms: Mycophobes

People who are addicted to mushrooms: Mycophagists

Mushroom sex: Strands of two fungi grow and fuse together, uniting nuclei of the opposite

224

artist's conk can reach more than 50 centimetres (1.6 feet). The big polypore's smooth white underside, which stains dark brown where scratched, has long been used for handicraft etchings.

Mushrooms and tree-clinging polypores are only the external, spore-producing fruiting bodies of extensive fungal organisms. Aside from tree roots, networks of microscopic fungal fibres comprise an estimated 90 percent of the subterranean biomass in forests. Fungal threads, called hyphae, weave through every nook and cranny of the upper soil of most habitats, forming a mesh on the underside of decaying leaves, intertwining with roots and entering rotting logs, live trees, dead animals and droppings, forming an immense living web literally tying everything together. A thimbleful of soil can have two kilometres (1.2 miles) of microscopic fungal strands running through it. A single honey mushroom organism – an edible, yellow-brown species that can be found in many autumn urban woodlots – has been discovered in Oregon covering almost nine square kilometres (3.5 square miles), sprouting mushrooms throughout, and is believed to be at least 2,400 years old.

Fungal networks are like veins and capillaries in the soil, keeping ecosystems alive. Fungi cannot produce chlorophyll, so must get their energy mostly from plants. Latching on to dead vegetation to reclaim nutrients back into the life cycle, fungal strands secrete enzymes that dissolve the organic material into food molecules they can absorb. A succession of different fungus species is usually involved in breaking down the sugars, cellulose, lignins and hemicellulose that form leaves, wood and other organic material, like the process of a pulp mill breaking down wood fibre.

Unfortunately, the decomposition process can also begin in houses when fuzzy yellow or pinkish spots of dry rot fungus form on softwood in damp spaces, sending out thick black or brown fibres as it spreads. Other unwanted household colonies of fungi include moulds growing on old cheese, bread, fruits and other foods, and mildews in bathrooms and on damp walls.

Some fungi are parasites, rather than decomposers, responsible for most plant and many insect diseases.

sex to create a reproductive spore-producing organism

Fairy rings: Rings of dead grass, left in fields by mushrooms produced by a spreading central underground fungus; usually less than 10 m (33 ft) wide, one 700-year-old fairy ring in France is more than 1 km (0.6 mi) across; a large ring near Ottawa once garnered international media attention as the possible site of a UFO landing

Fairy steps: Long-lasting, woody bracket fungi on trees

Common poisonous mushrooms: Fly agaric (illustrated), poison pie, destroying angel, red-tinged parasol, death cap; most have gills on the undersides of caps

Number of poisonous mushroom species in Ontario: More than 40

Origin of "toadstool": Folklore held that the whitish flakes on the caps of fly agaric were poisonous warts left by toads after sitting on the mushroom

Fly agaric name origin: In Europe, bowls of milk with pieces of the mushroom were left out to poison house flies

Maximum lifespan of underground portion of fly agaric mushroom organism: More than 100 years

Mycorrhizal name origin: From Latin myco, "fungus," and Greek rhiza, "root"

Ontario mushrooms symbiotic with trees and plants: About 15%

Common Ontario mycorrhizal mushrooms: Fly agaric,

destroying angel, boletes, *Tricholoma, Hebeloma, Inocybe* and *Laccaria* species

Most expensive mycorrhizal fungi: Edible truffles from France and Italy, sold for up to $4,000/kg (2.2 lb)

Puffball **scientific name meaning:** *Lycoperdon* is Latin for "wolf flatulence," after the clouds of dustlike spores sent up by bursting puffballs

Spore dispersal: By wind, rain, insect and mushroom-eating animals

Most important animal dispersers of spores: Mites, both on their bodies and in their droppings

Species that glow in the dark: Jack-o'-lantern, luminescent panellus, honey mushroom (only its fibre network)

First appearance of fungi in ancient oceans: Probably about 2.5 billion years ago

Number of mushroom species that grow on lawns in southern Ontario: At least 100

Number of mushrooms and other fungi with fruiting bodies visible to the naked eye in Ontario: Probably more than 5,000

Estimated number of fungi species worldwide: At least 1.5 million; more than 100,000 named

Many others engage in an interspecial chemical trading network with 95 percent of all plants and trees. By entwining their filaments around rootlets, these "mycorrhizal" fungi transfer water and nutrients, most notably nitrogen and phosphorus, to their trading partners. In return, trees and plants pass about 10 percent of their high-energy carbohydrates, created through photosynthesis, on to the fungi. Fossil evidence of the relationship dates back 400 million years. Mycorrhizal species even transport important materials from one plant to another, block the intake of toxic compounds, such as heavy metals, and produce chemicals that protect plants from microbial diseases and parasitic fungi.

Fungi also manufacture a stew of other chemicals for their own protection and competition. Some produce antibiotics to make it difficult for bacteria and other organisms to grow near them. In 1928 in Britain, Alexander Fleming isolated one of these substances from *Penicillium* mould and produced the first modern medical antibiotic, penicillin.

Defence chemicals are probably the active ingredients in most poisonous mushrooms, known as toadstools. Ancient shamans and oracles learned ways of taking small doses of toxic mushrooms to achieve a state of ecstasy and enter the spirit world. The Roman writer Seneca called such mushrooms "voluptuous poison." **Fly agaric** (illustrated), the speckled mushroom depicted in *Alice in Wonderland* and many other children's storybooks, was used ritually throughout much of Asia and Europe and is also common in North America, even in wooded urban areas. Soma, the sacred elixir of Indo-European peoples more than 4,000 years ago, is believed to have been made from a deadly mushroom, possibly fly agaric, that grew on the steppes of central Asia. It induced a battle rage among warriors that made them fearless and heedless of pain. Many of the rites involving wine in Christian churches come from the soma ceremony, via Zoroastrianism in ancient Iran.

GOLDENROD
Falsely Accused Beauties

FOR ALL ITS goodness and beauty, goldenrod is unjustly badmouthed and reviled like few other wildflowers. In many people's minds, it is the poster plant for hay fever. Yet, goldenrod's rich plumes of yellow flowers, which dominate urban meadows and roadsides in August and September, produce large, sticky grains of pollen that are picked up by insects rather than the wind. The only way someone could likely breath it in would be to grab a flowering stem of goldenrod and shove it up their nose.

The true culprit of late-summer red eyes, sniffles and sneezing is **ragweed**, an inconspicuous plant with deeply cut compound leaves and multiple spires of tiny, nodding green flowerheads, like little bobbles, that send out vast clouds of dry, dustlike pollen at the same time that goldenrod blooms. It affects 85 percent of Ontario's more than 1.5 million hay-fever sufferers. The problem is worse during dry weather and compounded by urban smog. While the name "ragweed" is infamous, many insist it applies to the tall yellow "weeds" that are so prominent at the height of hay-fever season.

The castigation of goldenrod as a noxious weed is especially misguided given that its scientific name, *Solidago*, means "make whole" or "solid" in Latin, a tribute to its ancient use in healing wounds. The Ojibway, too, called it *geezisomuskiki*, meaning "sun medicine." They, as well as many other native nations and settlers after them, brewed the flowers into a tea for a wide assortment of ailments, from fevers and chest pains to ulcers, kidney problems, even excessive flatulence. The Ojibway also added the flowers to a pipe

Lifespan: More than 100 years for some colonies in the prairies

Alias: Woundwort, Aaron's rod, *la verge d'or, les bouquets jaunes, Solidago* genus

Whereabouts: Meadows, fields, roadsides, vacant lots, streamsides, railway embankments

Height: 20–200 cm (8–80 in)

Flowers: Each tiny yellow flowerhead has numerous female ray flowers around its edge and at least 20 disk flowers at its centre with both male and female organs; numerous flowerheads form a plume, with those on top blooming first

Seeds: Minute, with fluffy fibres that carry them on the wind; emerge from split, dried flowerheads through fall and winter

Leaves and stem: Many different forms, depending on species; die back in autumn, but remain standing through winter

Roots: Some of the deepest taproots of any native herb, Canada goldenrod reach 3.3 m (11 ft) below ground in prairies; also spread horizontal rhizomes

Development: Usually no flowers produced in first year; 4 or 5 rhizomes spread beneath ground from stem base in second autumn, each sending up a new stalk the following spring; colonies of clones may grow to several metres wide

Common dry meadow species: Canada (illustrated), grey, early and tall goldenrods

Common forest edge species:
Blue-stemmed, early, late and
Canada goldenrods

Open forest species: Zigzag goldenrod

Shoreline species: Tall, Canada
and grass-leaved goldenrods

**Wetland and wet meadow
species:** Grass-leaved, bog,
rough-stemmed and Canada
goldenrods

Non-medical uses: Leaves brewed
as a tea substitute; flowers long
used for homemade yellow
dyes; rich, golden honey produced by goldenrod-addicted
honey bees; diviners once used
stems to find water

**Number of pollen grains shed by
1 ragweed plant:** 1.5 billion

Goldenrod range: Throughout
Ontario; also found in all other
provinces and territories

**Number of goldenrod species
native to Ontario:** 28

Number of species worldwide:
About 100, most in North
America

Also see: Asters, Ants; Bees,
Wasps & Hornets

blend smoked to bring success in hunting, and applied the boiled roots as a poultice for burns and sprains. Many modern herbalists still consider it a panacea.

In recent years, goldenrod has even been used to heal the earth. It's planted, along with species such as poplar, cattail and duckweed, in polluted habitats because it has enzymes that break down organic toxins contaminating the soil and water. Various goldenrods are also important elements in most urban wetland recreation projects.

Wherever they grow, goldenrods are of vital importance to an incredible assortment of tiny inhabitants, forming veritable multitiered cities. Offering immense quantities of nectar and pollen, the flowers dominate the attentions of bees, butterflies, flies and other pollinating insects during late summer. Meanwhile, golden-rod beetles and their larvae eat the plant's leaves, and tree hoppers siphon off sap. Amid all the activity, predators such as ambush bugs, crab spiders and even praying mantises select from the bounty of inhabitants, like lions on the Serengeti. The offspring of at least one species of tree hopper, however, enjoys the protection of organized bands of *Formica* ants, who in return sup on the waste sap exuded by the larvae.

Even in winter, when goldenrod stalks stand dry and lifeless, the young of many insects lie sleeping within the plant's derelict tissues. These winter quarters are created when small flies use their pointy ompositers to inject eggs into goldenrod stems during the growing season. When a maggot hatches and begins nibbling at its natal chamber, the plant responds by rapidly constructing new tissue around the irritant, resulting in the characteristic spherical bulges, called "galls," found on many goldenrod stems. More oval-shaped galls are also caused by minute moth caterpillars, while midge larvae create black blister-galls on leaves and bunchy, flower-like galls at branch tips. Ambush bugs, as well, leave their eggs in the overwintering leaves and stem.

POISON IVY

"Leaves of Three, Let It Be"

NO OTHER PLANT in Ontario is more often cited for steering city folk away from the great outdoors than poison ivy. One need not brave the wilds of Algonquin Park, however, to risk its itchy wrath. The infamous shrub is far more common in southern cities than in the forest fastness of the Canadian Shield, imperilling innocent riverside strollers and illicit late-night frolickers in the park alike. Even within parts of the continent's greatest metropolis, New York City, poison ivy is reported to be among the 10 most abundant wild plants.

One of the few northern members of the mostly tropical cashew family, poison ivy is not particularly fussy about where it takes up residence. It can spread along dry, open Hydro corridors, old, rocky fencerows or heavily shaded swamp margins. At the same time, the plant itself is a shape shifter. It can grow as herblike ground cover, a low woody shrub or – in areas along Lake Erie, Lake Ontario and Lower Ottawa Valley – as a vine running along the ground or up trees, with long rootlets clinging to bark crevices. Even poison ivy's oft-noted warning signature of three pointed leaves, or leaflets, is maddeningly variable. The leaflets may be wide or narrow, smooth-edged, toothed or sometimes slightly lobed. They tend to droop in the spring, but straighten up later in the summer. There are also many other

Amount of poison ivy resin needed to cause a rash: As little as 1 nanogram (1 billionth of a gram), but usually about 100 nanograms

Remedies for relieving itching: Soap and water, calamine lotion, wet compresses of equal parts whole milk and ice water, baking soda in cold water, plain cold water, juice from crushed jewelweed

Alias: Poison creeper, markweed, three-leaved ivy, climbing sumac, picry, climath, poison vine, *l'herbe à la puce, Rhus radicans, Toxicodendron radicans*

Whereabouts: Forest edges, along paths, weedy roadsides, fence-lines, Hydro corridors, railway embankments, open woods, meadows, swamps

Height: Shrub form usually 10–80 cm (4–31.5 in); vine form usually 6–10 m (20–33 ft), up to 15 m (49 ft)

Leaves: Branching into 3 slightly asymmetrical, pointed leaflets, each 5–15 cm (2–6 in) long, with the two lower leaflets meeting close together, separated from the third by a small space; edges highly variable, often with a slight notch and/or a few irregular teeth or smooth; unfold reddish or purplish in May and early Jun., shiny green in summer, bright red in early fall, yellow in shaded areas

Flowers: Tiny, waxy, greenish white, clustered along a 5-cm-long (2-in-long) stalk beneath leaves; blooming Jun. to Jul.; pollinated by bees

Berries: White or dull greenish yellow, about 5–6 mm (0.2 in) wide, dry, each containing one white seed; in a cluster; appear in mid- or late Jul., some remaining on plant all winter; eating berries can cause severe irritation to digestive system and even death

Roots: Long, woody, spreading rhizomes, running just below the ground, send up new plants, establishing clonal colonies

Frequent diners: Berries eaten by robins, crows, starlings, chickadees, cedar waxwings, woodpeckers, juncos, catbirds, yellow-rumped warblers, phoebes, white-throated sparrows, purple finches, ruffed grouse, wild turkeys

Range: Southern Ontario to about Cochrane and Kenora; also in all other provinces except Newfoundland

Also see: Queen Anne's Lace, Forest Edge

plants, such as raspberry, with leaflets growing in threes.

Poison ivy contains a pernicious oil, called urushiol, that can cause a painfully itchy red rash, usually within a day or two of contact. Beadlike blisters often follow a couple of days later. The reaction usually lasts less than two weeks.

Even in winter, when it has lost its leaves, the plant's blackened twigs and white berries are hazardous. Sweet-smelling smoke and vapour from burning poison ivy branches can also cause a rash and inflame respiratory passages. The oil can remain active on pets' fur or on shoes, unwashed clothes and garden shears for weeks or even years. One botanist got a rash after examining dried, 100-year-old leaf specimens. Little wonder urushiol was once used as the base to make indelible ink. The oil derives its name from the Japanese word for lacquer, *urushi*, made for more than 4,000 years from the Japanese lacquer tree, a sister species in the same genus as poison ivy.

Depending on the dose, it can take minutes or hours for the plant's resin to bond with the skin. It can sometimes be washed off with soap and water before that happens. Not everyone is affected to the same degree. Somewhere between 15 and 50 percent of people have no reaction at all after contact. Others may acquire only a mild itch. Lighter-skinned people are more prone than those with dark complexions. But any one person's susceptibility may change with time, depending on her or his body chemistry, diet and exposure to the sun. The chance of an allergic reaction generally increases with repeated contact.

There's actually nothing toxic about poison ivy. Humans bring the trouble on themselves with a defence reaction by their immune systems. Most animals don't seem to be bothered by it at all. Rabbits, deer and mice eat the leaves and stems with relish. Many species of birds and rodents gorge on the shrub's berries with no ill effects, spreading its seeds in their droppings. Poison ivy leaves exposed to sunlight turn bright red, like their close sumac relatives, literally waving a red flag to migrating birds that berries are available below to fuel their flights.

LAWN & GARDEN
Yards Are the Meeting Places of Our Own Outdoor Handiwork with the Wider Forces of Nature

RESIDENTIAL NEIGHBOURHOODS constitute a greatly varied and shifting patchwork of different, if simplified, habitats, from plush, golf-green perfect lawns to postage-stamp vineyards and patches of restored native forest floor. They're both personal expressions and the closest everyday connection most residents have with the outdoors. Yet, however much we may order our personal spaces to our liking, yards are still parts of a larger, dynamic continuum of natural forces that can never be completely shut out. Attempts to create the least diverse habitats, particularly monocultures of turf grass, generally entail the greatest efforts to keep those natural forces at bay. Amid growing ecological awareness and restrictions on pesticide use, many city folk are opting to go with the flow, accepting a few weeds and letting the yard's multiplicity of tiny inhabitants sort things out for themselves.

Of the scores of plants commonly considered weeds in lawns and gardens, the vast majority are non-natives that excel in exploiting the constantly disturbed spaces created by humans. While generally unappreciated, they have become integral parts of urban ecosystems, providing pollen and nectar for bees and butterflies, seeds for birds and fodder for groundhogs, rabbits and any number of other creatures.

Lamb's Quarters   20–200 cm (8–80 in) tall

Though lamb's quarters lives only a year, no matter how many of its sprouts are dug out of the garden, more pop up throughout the growing season. One of the most familiar yet anonymous of weeds, the persistent, pale-green plant spreads out triangular, wavy-toothed leaves, often with a whitish cast, and develops tiny beads of inconspicuous greenish flowers clustered along its upreaching limbs. It can produce up to 100,000 seeds, which are eaten and spread by birds and can remain viable in the soil for almost 40 years. Also known as pigweed, the rich-soil habitue is a relative of spinach

Number of wild plant species growing in front lawns and along the street in the average city block: 20–40

Grass name origin: From ancient Germanic *gro,* meaning "thing that grows"; also the root of "green"

Lawn name origin: From Old French *launde,* originally meaning "forest clearing"

Most common Ontario lawn grasses: Kentucky bluegrass, perennial ryegrass, red fescue

World's most widespread grass species: Kentucky bluegrass, originally from northern Eurasia

Number of grass species in Ontario: More than 600, about 25% non-native

Number of grass plants in a lawn measuring 7 m x 12 m (25 x 40 ft): About 1 million

Invention of the hand mower: 1830, by Edwin Budding in England, perfected over the following 50 years, replacing the scythe and spurring the widespread introduction of front lawns in new urban developments, emulating the parklike expanses of English country estates, on which grazing cattle and sheep once kept the grass short

Average time spent annually on lawn care by adults in North America: 30 hours

Minimum grass length commonly recommended for retaining moisture, excluding weeds

and beets and was brought from Europe by settlers as a nutritious garden pot herb. People seem to have lost their taste for the plant, but lamb's quarters has never lost its taste for gardens.

Broad-leaved Plantain   8–30 cm (3–12 in) tall

A prominently veined, ground-hugging circle of leaves and stiff seedhead spires make plantain one of the most noticeable plants growing in the grass. Perfectly happy on well-trodden, compacted ground, the deep-rooted perennial is especially common in schoolyards and parks. Because broad-leaf plantain came and spread with European settlers, natives referred to it as whiteman's foot. Like most common lawn and garden plants that arrive on their own accord, it continually produces flowers – though tiny and little noticed – and seeds through summer and early autumn.

Prostrate Knotweed   30–40 cm (12–16 in) long

While also extremely common in high-traffic areas, including around the edges and cracks of sidewalks, prostrate knotweed is largely unknown to most. Its tiny leaves and barely visible, pink-fringed flowers do little to distinguish it. Sparrows, pigeons and other birds, however, love the stuff. Flocks often pick away feverishly for tiny seeds in loosely tangled mats of low-lying, wiry knotweed stems in parks and along roadsides. Birds also strip the seed-ball-packed spikes of taller members of the same family commonly growing in and around yards and fences, including lady's-thumb, smartweed and sheep sorrel.

Black Medick   Up to 80 cm (32 in) long

Spreading with ground-trailing stems, black medick is especially abundant in roadside strips of grass. It has three-parted, club-shaped leaves, like clovers but smaller, and rounded, little flowerheads bearing both tiny yellow flowers and twisted black seed pods from early spring to late fall. Like other members of the pea and clover family, black medick is good for the soil because it fixes nitrogen from the air. Another clover relative that sometimes grows in lawns and gardens, yellow wood sorrel, has perfect, heart-shaped leaflets and three- and five-petalled yellow flowers.

Shepherd's Purse   10–60 cm (4–24 in) tall

Of the many mustard family plants that sneak into yards, shepherd's purse is one of the most delicately elegant. Lawn mowers usually keep its sparsely leaved, branching stems from being well noticed. But even when cut repeatedly, its branch tips keep producing Lilliputian bouquets of white flowers that leave behind long-stalked, heart-shaped seed pods as the branches grow upwards. The tiny, purselike valentines open to scatter minute, windblown seeds, from which sprout low rosettes of dandelionlike leaves in autumn or early spring.

Ground Ivy   10–30 cm (4–12 in) tall

Flourishing in sparse patches of grass and gardens, ground ivy sends up clumps of rounded or kidney-shaped, wavy-edged, light-green leaves that seem to always look like they need water. Sometimes called creeping charlie and gill-over-the-ground, the perennial trailing vine is part of the mint family, though its crushed leaves are fairly stinky. Small, tubular, blue or violet flowers bloom at the base of leave stalks on its rising, square-sided branches throughout the summer. Other free-ranging mints that often turn up in yards include heal-all, henbit and motherwort.

Crabgrass   5–120 cm (2–48 in) tall

Reviled as the ugly duckling among grasses, crabgrass grows in knotty clumps of sprawling stems tipped with distinctive, multi-pronged, purplish seedheads spreading out like fingers from a central point. It takes root in poor soil and bare patches of ground and thrives on crew-cut lawns. Appearing in late spring or early summer, the hay-fever contributor grows extremely quickly, but unlike turf grasses, its roots do not survive the winter.

whiteflies, thrips, mealy bugs, scale insects, leafhoppers, tree hoppers, spittlebugs, cabbage fly maggots, spider mites

Sowbug lifespan: Usually 2 years; up to 5 years

Ground beetle lifespan: Commonly 3–4 years; rarely 5 years

Other beneficial garden creepy-crawlies: Spiders, parasitic wasps, paper wasps, ladybugs, lacewings, hover flies, tachinid flies, flower flies, robber flies, long-legged flies, bee flies, rove beetles, tiger beetles, earwigs, ants, dragonflies, praying mantids, predatory mites

Also see: Ants; Bees, Wasps & Hornets; Cicada, Earthworms, House Fly, Moths, Spiders, Cardinal, Robin, Clover, Dandelion, Goldenrod, Thistles, Bird Gardens, Butterfly Gardens, House & Home; Meadows, Vacant Lots & Roadsides

Chickweed   5–50 cm (2–20 in) long

As its name suggests, chickweed is another seed-snack source for many birds. Sprouting in a clump of limp, leaning stems soon after the ground thaws, the extremely common lawn squatter blooms from early spring until well into fall, but its starry white flowers are so small, they're barely apparent among the bright-green, spade-shaped little leaves.

Climbing Nightshade   1–3 m (3–10 ft) tall

Although bright-red nightshade berries are said to be poisonous, at least to children, birds gobble them and spread the seeds to many yards, where the tough-stemmed vines climb fences and grow into gardens. Also known as deadly nightshade and bittersweet night shade, it has highly variable leaves but singular yellow-beaked, purple-petalled little flowers. The leaves contain poisonous natural insecticides, as do those of other members of the nightshade family, including potatoes, tomatoes, eggplant and tobacco.

Living on, in and beneath the grass, plants, shrubs and trees in any yard is a vast assortment of fauna, most of it much smaller than the birds and squirrels that catch our attention. A cubic metre (35 cubic feet) of soil in most backyards has thousands of earthworms, beetle grubs, root maggots, cutworms and other insect larvae, as well as millions of mites and nematodes. Though such numbers of crawling things might make some gardeners and patio loungers uneasy, experts credit the declining popularity of pesticides with a rise in urban populations of butterflies, bees and other beneficial insects that help ensure the health of plant life.

Sowbugs (illustrated)
1–1.5 cm (0.4–0.6 in) long

The brown or grey armadillolike creatures uncovered from rocks in the garden, or when the lid is lifted on the composter, are sowbugs, nocturnal scavengers of decaying matter. They're crustaceans, related to crabs and crayfish, and breathe through gills, so they need moist surroundings. Related night-crawling garden scavengers known as pillbugs are similarly armoured and equipped with 14 tiny legs, but have the distinction of rolling into a tight ball when threatened.

Snails and Slugs   up to 15 cm (6 in) long

Like the most common urban sowbug species, many of the abundant slugs and snails munching holes into garden plants in Ontario have been inadvertently introduced from Europe. They, too, are nocturnal, though the familiar large, beige-and-chocolate-swirled shell of the European garden snail can often be seen on the undersides of leaves during the day. Slugs generally do the most damage in the garden, especially the grey garden slug, which is brown to yellowish and flecked with light grey.

June Beetles   1.8–3.5 cm (0.7–1.4 in) long

Attracted to lights on hot summer nights, June beetles often make their presence known by whacking into screen doors and windows. The hefty, dark- or reddish-brown bombers, which are also called June bugs, spend their first two or three years of life as white, subterranean, root-gnawing grubs and resting pupae before becoming adults. Shallow-rooted lawns, resulting from grass that is kept very short and overfertilized with nitrogen, are especially susceptible to grub damage. Emerging as adults in late spring, June beetles sleep beneath the ground by day and fly up to feed on the leaves of trees and shrubs after dark. White grubs of the closely related, tan-coloured European chafer assault urban yards as far north as the Kitchener-Waterloo and Toronto areas, while those of the metallic-green and bronze Japanese beetle have made inroads across the Niagara Peninsula and into Hamilton.

Ground Beetles   1–25 mm (0.04–1 in) long

Healthy yards have lots of predatory beetles to keep their root- and leaf-eating relations in check. Ground beetles are among the most prominent of several hunting families prowling in residential neighbourhoods. Most ground beetles are shiny-black, large-eyed and active mainly at night, hiding out under rocks and other debris during daylight. Besides the grubs of other beetles, the fast-moving predators seize large numbers of snails, slugs, earthworms, root maggots, tent caterpillars and grass-eating cutworms. They're also highly territorial, with individual beetles living in the same spaces for up to two years.

Stinkbugs   6–20 mm (0.2–0.8 in) long

Like many other members of the true bug order, such as grass-stem-sucking chinch bugs and herds of tiny aphids, some stinkbugs feed on the juices of garden plants. However, about half of the varieties of colourful, shield-shaped stinkers that frequent backyards are fearsome predators of aphids, caterpillars and other insects. The family gets its name from the reeking scent they emit when confronted. A number of other true bug families, with appropriately ominous names such as assassin bugs and ambush bugs, are also effective garden hunters.

QUEEN ANNE'S LACE
Castle Beauty to Noxious Weed

Roots: Long, strong, white, fibrous taproot, like a slender carrot

Alias: Wild carrot, bird's-nest, crow's-nest, devil's-plague, *la carotte sauvage, Daucus carota*

Whereabouts: Meadows, fields, roadsides, vacant lots, railway embankments, construction sites, garden edges

Height: 30–100 cm (2–3.3 ft)

Flowers: Many small, single-stalked clusters of tiny white, sometimes slightly pinkish, florets together form a flat flowerhead, 4–12 cm (1.6–4.7 in) wide, at top of stem or branches; usually with a single dark-purple floret at centre of flowerhead; up to 100 flowerheads, or "umbrells," produced per plant through summer; pollinated by bees, wasps, flies

Seeds: 2 held within each oily, grey-brown, mini-burrlike case, 3–4 mm (0.125–0.166 in) long; average of about 10,000 seeds per plant; dispersed through summer, fall and winter

Seedhead occupants: Often used as nest by some species of bees and spiders; ants take shelter inside during rainstorms

Leaves: 5–20 cm (2–8 in) long, divided into many finely cut leaflets, branching in opposite pairs; distinct carrot scent

Lifespan: Usually 2 years, producing a bushy rosette of leaves, 10–15 cm (4–6 in) high and up to 46 cm (18 in) wide, the first year and flowering stems in the second; in ideal conditions,

REGALLY spreading its saucer-sized, frilly white flowerheads above weedy roadsides and patches of urban meadow, Queen Anne's lace is one of the most elegantly named of common wildflowers. The lithe summer beauty's eponymous sovereign was the wife of England's James I, a Danish fashion plate whose extravagance in court festivities and dazzling finery helped nearly bankrupt the royal household in the early 1600s. Elaborate lace neck-ruffs, cuffs, aprons and handkerchiefs were the rage among royalty and the nobility, the only ones who could pay for the hundreds of hours of intricate threadwork that went into creating such items. Well-healed ladies also dabbled in lacemaking as a gentile hobby, and according to legend, Queen Anne challenged her retinue to a contest to replicate the ornate pattern of the decorative palace-garden flower that now bears her name.

From its deep, finger-thick taproot, Queen Anne's lace sends up numerous stems that bloom and shed seeds continuously from June to September. After pollination, each embroidered flowerhead – composed of many individual florets – closes up, turns green and then brown as it dries out, forming a characteristic "bird's nest." When ready, these nests open again in dry, sunny weather to disperse tiny, barbed seeds, which are picked up and spread on the fur or clothes of passersby, or carried away in the wind. A single plant can yield up to 40,000 seeds, which is probably why garden patches sown with wildflower seed mixes often become completely dominated by Queen Anne's lace within a year or two.

The doily-topped plant's fecundity, vigour and disfavour among cattle have earned it a place on Ontario's noxious weeds list alongside poison ivy and ragweed.

Yet, Queen Anne's lace was brought to North America by early colonists as a valued garden vegetable and medicinal herb. Also known as wild carrot, it's literally the same plant as Bugs Bunny's favourite fodder. Carrots were probably first domesticated around Afghanistan and later grown in ancient Greek and Roman farming communities. In the New World, feral carrot plants spread from the seeds of colonial gardens soon reverted back to their original tough, scrawny-rooted form, selected by nature for survival in unpampered conditions. Even cultivated carrots didn't become the popular large, crisp, orange vegetables of today until the nutritional value of vitamin A, or carotene, was recognized and plant breeders set to work in the 1920s.

The carrot's herbal traditions are less well-known today. Various parts of the plant were used in folk remedies, including a medicinal tea for digestive and kidney problems. But birth control was probably the most important usage. Hippocrates, the reputed father of modern medicine, reportedly prescribed the seeds for that purpose almost 2,500 years ago. Even today, ethnobotanists report that countrywomen from Appalachia to Rajasthan, India, consume the seeds of Queen Anne's lace either before or after lovemaking to prevent pregnancy.

The contraceptive powers of Queen Anne's lace and many other plants are more than coincidence. Many protect themselves by producing hormones identical to or aping those of their leaf-munching assailants, interfering with their reproduction and thereby keeping numbers down. Some of the wild carrot's relatives, such as **cow parsnip**, also have defence chemicals that react with ultraviolet light, causing rashes on people with sensitive skin. The carrot family in Ontario includes deadly **poison hemlock** and **spotted water-hemlock**, both of which can be mistaken for Queen Anne's lace.

life cycle occasionally completed in 1 year, in poor conditions up to 5 years

Range: Throughout most of Ontario; also in all other provinces except Alberta and island of Newfoundland

Number of plants worldwide known to have substances that interfere with human reproduction or reduce fertility: About 450

Other common wildflowers on Ontario's noxious weeds list: Milkweed, coltsfoot, goat's beard, knapweed, sow thistle

Most poisonous plant in Ontario: Spotted water-hemlock, as little as one mouthful of root fatal

Tallest herbaceous plant in Ontario: Probably giant hogweed, a member of carrot family, up to 5 m (16.4 ft)

Number of carrot family species growing wild in Ontario: 22 native, 19 introduced

Number of carrot family species worldwide: About 3,000

Also see: Starling, Buttercup

SKUNK CABBAGE
A Flower with a Furnace

THE FIRST WILDFLOWER of spring is no shrink-ing violet. Heedless even of winter's lingering white blanket, skunk cabbage awakens around the same time the sugar maples begin to run. Rising in clumps and patches in shadowy forest sloughs, its gar-gantuan terrestrial buds often start to expand and open by mid-March. The snow seems to fall back from around them, revealing their eerie, purple pointed hoods nodding above the leaf litter on the cold, mucky ground.

To make its bold appearance through the snow, skunk cabbage actually generates its own warmth, like a bird or mammal. For about two weeks, before the early-spring sun is strong enough to do the job, the plant fires up its internal heater, an oval, flower-packed knob, or "spadix," held within its purple cowl. Sparked by a chemical reaction involving salicylic acid, the spadix draws in oxygen from the air and burns large reserves of starch from its thick rootstock at about the same meta-bolic rate as a similar-sized shrew or small bat, raising its temperature to 22–23 °C (71.5–73.5 °F). The spongy, air-pocketed hood, or "spathe," that surrounds it further insulates the warm knob from the cold outside. Even when the thermometer drops as low as -15 °C (5 °F) outside, the plant maintains a comfortable room tem-perature by redoubling its fuel and oxygen intake.

In addition to melting the snow, the floral furnaces

serve up bounties of pollen while warming the wings of the year's earliest-stirring pollinating insects, such as honeybees and beetles. For fruit flies and orb-weaver spiders, the skunk cabbage's sheltering spathe is a centrally heated love shack in which to meet and mate. The plant's meaty colour and scent also lures carrion flies, which cross-pollinate the tiny flowers as they are duped from one spathe to another. To the human nose, though, the scent is faint and almost sweet.

When broken or crushed, skunk cabbage leaves produce a stronger smell, more deserving of the plant's malodorous name. The aroma is often likened to a mixture of garlic and perhaps rubber or more rank scents. The Mi'kmaq used to crush bundles of the leaves and inhale the pungent fumes to clear headaches.

Initially tightly curled in long, pointy buds, bunches of huge, rhubarblike leaves unfold only after the plant's flowers are pollinated and the spathe begins to wilt. By late spring, they form a lush, low canopy over the muddy ground, grabbing every inch of available sunlight to manufacture and store enough carbohydrates to feed the furnace the following spring. As succulent as they look, the bright-green leaves are avoided by large herbivores because, like the related jack-in-the-pulpit and other members of the arum family, they contain minute, needle-shaped calcium oxalate crystals that burn and blister mammalian mouths.

The leaves decay through summer, their place often taken by rising stems of jewelweed. Beneath them, next year's long, pointy green skunk cabbage buds of leaves wrapped around closed spathes push up as much as 15 centimetres (six inches) above the ground by the end of the summer. Meanwhile, maturing fruit clusters droop onto the mud and start to break apart around August. Some of the heavy, pea-sized seeds germinate on the ground beside their parents while others are carried away by seeping surface water or by squirrels and mice. Those not eaten right away by the rodents may be buried and sometimes forgotten, allowing them to sprout. Young skunk cabbages only send up one or two leaves and may take seven years to build up enough carbohydrate stores to produce and heat their first flowers.

Companion plants: Marsh marigold, jewelweed, turtlehead, sensitive fern, greenbrier

Frequent diners: Squirrels, mice, wood ducks and ruffed grouse eat seeds; garter snakes, red-backed salamanders and spring peepers forage under cover of leaves

Range: Southern Ontario to about Wawa; also in Manitoba, Quebec, New Brunswick and Nova Scotia

Other ill-smelling flowers that deceive insect pollinators: Red trillium, jack-in-the-pulpit

Other Ontario arum species: Jack-in-the-pulpit, water arum, sweet flag, arrow arum

Common tropical arum house plants: Philodendrons, dieffenbachias

World's largest arum: Titan arum of Sumatra, with a 3-m-high (10-ft-high) flowering structure wafting an overpowering reek akin to a mix of rotting fish and brown sugar

Number of arum family species worldwide: Probably more than 3,500, mostly in the tropics

Also see: Sugar Maple, Wetlands

SOLOMON'S SEAL
Mystically Marked Herbal Healer

Height: 50–100 cm (1.6–3.3 ft)

Alias: Hairy Solomon's seal, true Solomon's seal, conquer-John, *le sceau-de-Solomon, Polygonatum pubescens*

Whereabouts: Rich soil in hardwood forests, often mixed with white pine

Flower: Greenish white or white, bell-shaped, 1–1.5 cm (0.4–0.6 in) long, usually hanging in pairs, sometimes single or in threes, beneath arching stem

Berries: Bluish-black, containing several seeds

Leaves: 5–15 cm (2–6 in) long, 1.3–7.5 cm (0.5–3 in) wide, pointed at both ends; pale bottoms with conspicuous veins; turning yellow in autumn

Roots: Knotted horizontal rhizome, 1–2 cm (0.4–0.8 in) thick

Range: Southern Ontario to about Temagami and Sault Ste. Marie; also in Quebec, New Brunswick and Nova Scotia

RISING ON STURDY arching stems along many forest paths, Solomon's seal seems to persevere in remnant urban woods a little better than many other native forest wildflowers. It also blooms a little later than most, its tiny pairs of bell-like flowers dangling in a long row beneath the stem into June and early July. Later in the summer, birds bob for the smooth dark berries that replace the flower bells.

While Solomon's seal stems and leaves die back each autumn, the plant's deep, knotted rootstock lives on, sending up a new sprout every spring. After they're gone, the stems leave distinctive, scrawling circular scars on the rootstock, which, on the Old World version of the plant, early Greek scholars likened to Hebrew letters. Legend grew that they were a pharmacological seal of approval from the ring of King Solomon. A long tradition esteemed the wise king as the first learned botanist because the Bible mentions his fascination with trees of all kinds.

Solomon's seal roots, indeed, have long been used for treating a wide sweep of maladies on both sides of the Atlantic. Many native groups on this continent applied it as a poultice for bruises, sores, wounds and black eyes. The Ojibway brewed the roots into a tea to treat coughs and inhaled the steam from a preparation that was placed on hot stones. The Iroquois ate the root raw, cooked or pounded into flour.

THISTLES
Purple-flowered Pernicious Pricker

A S "WEEDY" PLANTS go, thistles are as tough as they come. Fearsomely spined and heedless of the blade, the pernicious prickers rise up from deep taproots and ground-hugging leaves almost no matter how many times they're cut down to size. Of the several species that jab unsuspecting fingers and toes in countless gardens, lawns and fields, **bull thistle** (illustrated) is the most heavily armed. It's the only thistle with sharp prickles on the surface of its dark-green, angular leaves in addition to the longer spines around the margins. In meadows bull thistle draws itself up to its full martial might, with striking, purple-flowered summer crowns hoisted shoulder high on long-branched stems lined with jagged, razor-wire-like ridges of spikes.

Another species, **Canada thistle**, is not as intensively protected, but has greater strength in numbers. It blooms from June to October in large clusters of smaller, lighter-purple flowerheads and sends out numerous clone-sprouting root runners, each spreading up to six metres (20 feet) a year. Despite its name, Canada thistle, like bull thistle, is an inadvertent import from Europe, its wispy, airborne seeds probably having stowed away on ships sailing to the New World. After arriving in Canada, it spread south, where farmers in Vermont and New York declared it an invading Canadian menace in the late 1700s, taking over whole fields in a few years. Ontario's Weed Control Act was passed in 1866 specifically to combat Canada thistle, which remains on the act's noxious weeds list, as it does on similar most-wanted lists in states and provinces across North America.

Height: 0.3–2 m (1–6.6 ft)

Alias: Prickers, pricker plants, *les chardons*, *Cirsium* genus

Whereabouts: Fields, parks, yards, fencelines, roadsides, vacant lots, forest edges

Leaves: 3–18 cm (1.2–7 in) long, 0.5–6 cm (0.2–2.4 in) wide, stiff, spined, sharply lobed

Flowers: Bull thistle (illustrated) flowerheads reddish-purple, 2.5–7.5 cm (1–3 in) wide, on top of oval, green, heavily spined knobs; Canada thistle flowerheads light purple, occasionally white, 1–2 cm (0.4–0.8 in) wide, on narrow green knobs with short spines

Seeds: Greyish brown to yellowish, 1.5–5 mm (0.0625–0.2 in) long, thin, attached to silky white or light-brown branched fibres that carry them in slightest breeze

Range: Throughout Ontario; in all other provinces and territories

VIOLETS
Sweet, Nutritious Flowers of Love

A SIMPLE FLOWER with a romantic past, the common garden pansy is the descendant of a small wild European violet. It derives its name from the French word *pensée*, meaning "thought" or "remembrance," after the once-common custom of offering violets as a courting gift. Violets were equated with modesty, chastity, love and loyalty and have been worn by brides or thrown in their bouquets since the days of Helen of Troy. In Greek mythology, the flowers were created by Zeus as sweet fodder for the cow goddess Io, after whom they were named, rendered in Latin as *viola*.

Humans, too, have long browsed the plants' sugary blossoms and vitamin-rich leaves. Violets were widely used by both Europeans and North American natives as ingredients for medicines, food dyes, soups, jams, syrups, candies and liqueurs. The flower decorations topping cakes today imitate the old practice of placing sugar-coated violets on desserts. The essential oils of Mediterranean violets are also one of the oldest sources of perfumes.

While pansies and other foreign violet cultivars have long been grown in Ontario gardens and flower plots, the growing popularity of naturalized yards is bringing many native violets back into urban neigh-bourhoods. Species such as **northern blue violet** (illus-trated) and the white **Canada violet** make ideal ground covers, flowering abundantly from April into July. In remnant urban woods and meadows, a wide variety of wild violets abound as well, coming in varying shades of purple, blue, yellow and white, blooming in greatest profusion in June.

In their highly varied colours and sizes, different violets share a very similar design and layout. All feature a specialized lower, central petal that forms an organ- and nectar-bearing tube stretching toward the back of the flower. The front of the petal also serves as a landing platform for incoming flying insects, complete with runway markings in the form of brightly coloured veins. Drawn by the flower's delicate scent, insects follow the veins straight to the rich payload of nectar. Violets also display (appropriately enough) ultraviolet patterns, visible to bees and other pollinators but not to humans, which must make the veined petals even more striking in appearance.

Most violet species actually reproduce mainly without their flowers, spreading thin underground runners that send up many clones instead. In addition, while cold weather or other mishaps often prevent insects from pollinating many, the plants still produce seeds with a second set of smaller flowers that never actually bloom. These "cleistogamous" buds are usually formed below or near the ground in summer and polli-nate themselves without opening.

runners; species with leafy flower stalks have thick, branch-ing woody roots

Forest species: Woolly blue, downy yellow, northern blue (illustrated), sweet white and Canada violets

Meadow species: Dog, Canada, and smooth yellow violets

Shoreline and forest edge species: Lance-leaved, marsh blue, north-ern white, northern blue, dog, shore and Canada violets

Wetland species: Marsh blue, sweet white, downy yellow, woolly blue and northern white violets

Green violet: Rare, 30–60-cm-tall (12–24-in-tall) plant, with small green flowers at leaf axils, growing in southern Ontario woods and bottom-lands; in a separate genus from most violets, but in violet family

Common diners: Bees, butterflies, mice, mourning doves, juncos, grouse, woodcocks

Tiny nibblers: Cutworms, fritillary butterfly caterpillars, slugs

Range: Throughout Ontario; in all other provinces and territories

Ontario violet officially listed as threatened: Bird's-foot violet, growing in oak savannah rem-nants in far southern Ontario

Number of violet species native to Ontario: About 24 (much hybridization and debate on species status)

Number of violet species world-wide: About 500

Birthplace of *Viola* genus: Andes Mountains, South America

Also see: White Trillium, Ants; Bees, Wasps & Hornets

WHITE TRILLIUM
Monarch of Spring Woods

Height: 20–45 cm (8–18 in)

Alias: Great white trillium, snow trillium, large-flowered trillium, white wake-robin, trinity lily, bath flower, white lily, *le trille blanc*, *Trillium grandiflorum*

Name origin: From Latin *tres*, meaning "three," in reference to the number of petals, leaves, and sepals on each plant

Whereabouts: Rich soil in mature broadleaf woods

Flowers: 3 white, pointed petals, 2.5–8 cm (1–3 in) long, fading to pink before they die; yellow organs at centre; 3 narrow, sharply pointed, green sepals beneath petals; individual flowers bloom for about 2–3 weeks

Pollinators: Bees, especially bumblebees; also beetles, flies

Seeds: 9–10 contained in a single, dark-red, hexagonal capsule, about 1.3–2.5 cm (0.5–1 in) wide, ripening around late July; go through 2 winters before germinating

Leaves: Wide, pointed, smooth-edged, 3.5–15 cm (1.5–6 in) long; 3 per plant, meeting together at stem below flower; wither by mid- to late summer

Roots: Short, thick, tuberlike rootstock; rootlets reach at least 13 cm (5 in) below surface

Companion plants: Trout lily, bloodroot, spring beauty, mayapple, red trillium, jack-in-the-pulpit, blue cohosh, Dutchman's breeches, toothwort, violets

ONTARIO'S PROVINCIAL FLOWER is a good measure of the health of urban woodlots. In undisturbed stands of sugar maple, beech, black cherry and basswood, expansive carpets of white trilliums flourish in late April and May, mixed with a myriad of other blithe, fleeting spring wildflowers. All too often, however, trilliums and other spring ephemerals are choked out by dense, invading colonies of straw-stemmed alien garlic mustard, or succumb to the heavy traffic of too many feet and thick-treaded mountain-bike tires. Air pollution also burns the tender leaf tissues of spring flowers and inhibits their insect pollinators and the subterranean fungus partners that supply them with nutrients and water. Heavy-metal contamination on the ground, as well, slows the decomposition of dead leaves, which replenish soil nutrients.

Yet for generations, white trilliums have been treasured as the essence of Ontario. During the First World War, when the public longed for an official flower to mark the graves of soldiers, federal bureaucrat James Burns Spencer proposed the popular flower as a national emblem for Canada. He said the white petals bespoke purity, while their number represented the Holy Trinity and the foundations of the British Empire – England, Scotland and Ireland. Though a national flower was never named, Spencer's arguments, and the votes of thousands of high-school students, led Queen's Park to name the trillium Ontario's floral emblem in 1937.

In the spring woods, white trillium's reign is brief. Most forest flowers base their lives around their moment in the sun between early spring thaw and leaf-out. Preformed in tightly packed bundles at the tips of their rootstocks the previous growing season, they sprout rapidly and bloom in quick sequence, protected by the trees from the chill of April's winds. Trilliums take over from trout lilies, bloodroot and hepaticas and flower two to four weeks, until cast in the Victoria Day shade of freshly unfolded leaves overhead. Meadow flowers, on the other hand, with the benefit of the full sun all the time, bloom throughout summer into early autumn.

With the limited sunlight they receive in spring, trilliums usually take about six years from the time their seeds sprout until they produce their first flowers, all the while storing energy captured by their leaves in their thick roots. If the leaves are picked, the plant usually dies. Like the world's first flowers, which premiered at least 140 million years ago, trilliums have a simple, unspecialized design, their large petals offering a broad landing pad for incoming pollinating insects.

Furry foragers tend to leave most flowers alone because many contain bitter-tasting psychoactive chemicals. Deer and groundhogs, though, delight in trillium leaves. Birds, chipmunks and other small animals also eat the plant's mealy, berrylike red capsule, probably spreading its seeds with their droppings. Many more of the sticky brown seeds are dispersed by much-tinier creatures as the capsules rot. Like up to 40 per cent of all herbaceous plants in deciduous forests, trillium seeds have large, whitish oily appendages, called elaiosomes, that exude a chemical aroma that brings ants running. Dragging the seeds back to their underground community larders, up to 60 metres (200 feet) away, the diligent insects later feast on the nutritious attachments and chuck the hard-shelled seeds into refuse tunnels that serve as fertile, protective seedbeds.

Summer light levels in mature broadleaf forest: 1–5% of full sunlight

Green striped trilliums: Mutation caused by micro-organisms spread by sap-sucking insects

Native remedies: The Ojibway spread the juice of ground, boiled trillium roots on rheumatic joints and then punctured the skin with thorns or bone needles; though the root is considered poisonous, many native peoples also brewed tea from it for menstrual cramps, or made it into a poultice for sore eyes

Range: Southern Ontario to about North Bay and Sault Ste. Marie; also in Quebec

Other wildflowers with seeds spread by ants: Trout lily, hepatica, wild ginger, bloodroot, Dutchman's breeches, spring beauty, fringed polygala, violets and other trilliums

Name for someone who studies ant-seed relationships: Myrmecochorigist, from the Greek words *myrmex*, meaning "ant," and *chore*, meaning "farm"

Number of trillium species native to Ontario: 5

Number of trillium species worldwide: 43–48

Also see: Woods, Alien Invaders, Fungi; Bees, Wasps & Hornets; Sugar Maple

Trees

FROM THE CN TOWER, or similar lofty perches in many other Ontario cities, forests of green seem to obscure much of the surrounding urban landscape almost as far as the eye can see. The "urban forest" canopy commonly covers about one-third of the older sections of the province's cities and is treasured by most citizens.

Beyond shade and aesthetics, urban trees freshen and purify the air, pumping out oxygen, taking up pollutants and collecting particles of dust, pollen, ash and smoke. They absorb noise, prevent erosion, shield from the wind and provide habitat for birds, mammals and insects. A mature tree beside a house can reduce air-conditioning and heating costs and raise property values by up to 15 percent.

Yet the urban forest may not be as mighty as it first appears. On top of constant pressure for development and more parking spaces, many cities have relatively few mid-aged trees growing up to take the place of whole neighbourhoods of older monarchs nearing the end of their lives. A relatively small number of species also accounts for a large percentage of city trees, decreasing ecosystem diversity and leaving many streets in danger of losing their entire canopy to species-specific epidemics or invasive pests. Reliance on large numbers of foreign imports, especially Norway maple, itself threatens urban woods with invasions of trees that shade and choke out native understory plants, leading to erosion and taking away food and habitat from birds and other animals. Fortunately, many municipalities, groups and individuals are seeking change, increasing tree planting and stocking streetsides, yards, parks and natural areas with more native saplings.

CRABAPPLE
The Belle of Spring

PASSED BY AS small, unassuming ornamental trees for most of the year, crabapples have their moment of glory in May when their squat crowns fill city streets and parks with a spectacular explosion of sweet-scented blossoms. Many of the trees are descendants of tough, profusely flowering species found on the cold expanses of Siberia and northern China that were brought to England in the late 1700s to bestow a little beauty to gritty urban streets. Later, in the following century, similarly impressive Japanese crabapple trees arrived in the West. Nurseries have made hundreds of selections from the original imports, focusing on their blossoms, which can come in purple, red, pink or white. Great numbers of crabapples were planted on Ontario's city and suburban streets in the 1960s and 1970s, but later complaints about sidewalks slippery with rotting fruit, and problems with insects and fungal diseases, caused many municipalities to discontinue routine plantings.

As many know from their youthful days of crabapple wars, the hard little fruits also ripen in the wild around creeks, ravines, fencerows and unkept fields. Some are from the seeds of cultivated trees spread by foxes, robins and other fruit eaters. Around cities such as Windsor, London and Hamilton, some are true **wild**, or **sweet**, **crabapples** (illustrated), Ontario's only native apple tree. Not growing much farther north than Burlington

Average mature height: 1.8–10 m (6–33 ft)

Average trunk width: About 30 cm (1 ft)

Lifespan: Average 20–30 years, maximum about 70 years

Alias: *Le pommier sauvage, Malus* genus

Name origin: "Crab" may come from the ancient Germanic word for "scrub," denoting small, stunted trees; the Old English word *aeppel* originally referred to any fruit

Whereabouts: Streetsides, yards, parks and around public buildings; sometimes escapes into unkept fields, thickets and railway embankments

Flowers: 1.5–5 cm (0.6–2 in) wide, with 5 purple, red, pink or white petals, depending on species or variety; growing in small clusters; flowers of some varieties have extra petals

Fruit: Red, orange or yellow apples, 1–5 cm (0.4–2 in) wide; ripening in autumn

Leaves: 3–10 cm (1.2–4 in) long, shiny green, purple-red or bronze on top, lighter below, turning yellow in autumn; sleekly oval with pointed tips and edged with tiny teeth

Bark: Smooth and grey on young trees, becoming flaky, mottled grey and brown, with age

Wood: Reddish-brown to light-yellow heartwood, thick yellowish sapwood, fine-grained, hard, 20 kg/m³ (44 lb/cu ft)

Specialty products: Wild crabapple and domestic apple wood used for carvings and furniture because of its fine grain patterns and colours

Common nesters: Robins, starlings, catbirds, cedar waxwings, goldfinches, mourning doves

Frequent diners: Skunks, deer, coyotes, opossums and many birds eat fruits

Range: Planted in most Ontario cities; also planted in all other provinces

Famous Ontario apple trees: Newton Apple at National Research Council in Ottawa, a descendant of tree whose falling fruit inspired Sir Isaac Newton; 5 McIntosh trees near Dundela, first grafts of the original Mac; 2 Tolman sweet apple trees on Yonge St. in Toronto, remnants of orchard of David Gibson, a leader in 1837 Rebellion

Number of crabapple species native to Ontario: 1

Number of crabapple species worldwide: About 60

Also see: Cinquefoil, Forest Edge

or Grand Bend, wild crabapple has blunt thorns and large-toothed, triangular leaves, often with small lobes at the base. Wood from the tree's strong, flexible branches was once used by native groups for spear shafts and digging sticks, and by earlier settlers for tool handles and moving parts in mills.

Crabapples are thinly fleshed and generally sour unless eaten when very ripe. Eating one, though, is said to be thirst quenching. Cooked and sweetened, they make a tasty jam, alone or mixed with other fruits. Iroquoian peoples mashed and dried the mini-apples for later winter use mixed with cornbread or as a sauce. Leftovers were made into cider and syrup in the spring.

Common orchard apples themselves are descended from a wild crabapple species that originated in Kasakstan that has been cultivated since ancient times. Millennia of selecting and crossbreeding gradually produced thousands of varieties of bigger, sweeter apples. Like non-native crabapple species, domestic apple trees sometimes spring up in the wild from the dropping of apple-eating animals, but their fruits are usually not as big or tasty because trees grown from seeds generally put more of their resources into roots, leaves and branches. Orchard trees are clones, grown from the buds of high-yielding trees grafted on to the cut-back rootstock trunks of specially selected seedlings. All McIntosh apples, Canada's most widely grown variety, come from grafts of a sapling found in the wild by John McIntosh in Dundela, northeast of Brockville, in 1811. The original tree died in 1906, shortly after being damaged by a fire.

Together with the domestic apple, all crabapple species are members of the rose family, which is probably the most important fruit-bearing group in temperate lands for humans and wildlife. Pears, plums, cherries, peaches, apricots. almonds, hawthorns, strawberries, raspberries, serviceberries and mountain ash are all included within its ranks. The juicy pulp of most wild fruits is an enticement to birds and other animals, which then spread the seeds. In the city, crabapples, hawthorn fruits and mountain ash berries may persist well into winter, providing an important food source for birds toughing it out through the cold months.

GREEN ASH
Golden Vail Dropped on Cue

A DISPROPORTIONATE NUMBER of native trees growing along city streets are riverbank, floodplain and wetland species. Green ash is one of them. Like the others, it's adapted to life in the relatively open, unstable conditions that come with fluctuating water levels. That flexibility and toughness suits it well for urban roadsides, where it puts up with smog, road salt and often droughtlike conditions in small patches of beaten-down turf. More shade-tolerant trees, such as sugar maple and beech, are much more fussy, having evolved to thrive in the nutrient-rich humus, even moisture and dependable microclimate that develops with a maturing forest.

Though generally smaller than many traditional urban trees, green ash grows quickly, often reaching eight metres (26 feet) within seven or eight years of being placed as a sapling. Spreading a wide, rounded crown, the feisty tree leafs out a little later in spring than most others. In the autumn, it turns a uniform shining hue of gold for a week or so and then, as if on cue, drops virtually all its leaves within a couple of windy or rainy days.

Green ash was extensively planted in Ontario cities in the late 1950s and 1960s to help replace the vast numbers of street elms wiped out by Dutch elm disease. The tree was considered a prudent choice because it was

Average mature height:
10–20 m (33–66 ft)
Average trunk width: 30–60 cm
(1–2 ft)
Ontario giant: 23.5 m (77 ft)
tall, 1.3 m (4.3 ft), Moullnette
Island, west of Cornwall
Lifespan: Commonly to 100 years
Alias: Red ash, soft ash, *Frêne
vert, Fraxinus pennsylvanica*
Whereabouts: Streetsides, parking
lots, yards, parks, river valley
flood plains and around swamps
Leaves: Compound, composed of
5–9 leaflets, each 8–15 cm
(3–6 in) long, 2–3 cm
(0.8–1.2 in) wide, pointed at
both ends, edged with tiny
teeth and joined in opposite
pairs along a 23–35 cm
(9–14 in) central stalk; glossy
dark green on top, lighter on
undersides, turning bright
yellow in autumn
Bark: Light greyish-brown, developing low, thin, interlacing ridges

Sex: Tiny male flowers without petals in small, round, dense, green-and-brownish clusters, like little heads of broccoli; smaller raggedy bunches of red-tipped, greenish females on separate trees; appear before leaves; wind pollinated; most planted trees are males

Seeds: Attached to paddle-shaped wings, 3–6 cm (1.2–2.4 in) long, light green fading to yellow, then brown, hanging in thick clusters, falling from late fall through the winter

Roots: Widespread, up to 1.4 m (4.6 ft) deep

Wood: Pale grey-brown heartwood, whitish sapwood, with straight, wide grain, 20 kg/m³ (44 lb/cu ft), hard, tough, hot-burning

Heat equivalent of 1 m³ (35 cu ft) of wood: 146 L (32 gal) of oil

Frequent diners: Squirrels, mice, cardinals, house sparrows, house finches, cedar waxwings, wood ducks and evening grosbeaks eat seeds

Range: Southern Ontario to just north of North Bay, Sault Ste. Marie and Kenora; also in Saskatchewan, Manitoba, Quebec, New Brunswick, Nova Scotia and planted in Alberta and British Columbia

Number of hockey sticks made annually in Canada: About 5 million

Number of ash species native to Ontario: 5

Number of ash species worldwide: 60–70

Also see: Silver Maple, Sugar Maple, White Elm, Woods

known to be resistant to most insects and diseases. Unfortunately, the rush to green ash brought the same risks implicit with street-tree monocultures, to be realized decades later. In 2002, with ashes comprising one-third of all Windsor's street trees, thousands began to die with the sudden appearance of the emerald ash borer, an east Asian beetle that was already devastating trees in Michigan. Authorities responded by throwing up a "fire wall" against the invader, cutting down more than 60,000 ashes in a 10-kilometre-wide (six-mile-wide) swathe across Essex County from Lake St. Clair to Lake Erie in the winter of 2004.

Small numbers of **European ash** also grow in Ontario cities. Its compound leaves usually bear twice as many leaflets as those of green ash, but they're less than half the size. The Norse world tree, Yggdrasil, which held Heaven and Earth, was a European ash. In fact, ancient tales about ash trees strike similar chords on both sides of the Atlantic. The Romans, Greeks, Vikings and others all had legends of the first people coming from a tree often described as an ash. A common story among Algonquian-speaking peoples in North America, as well, tells of the first humans emerging from a hole made in an ash by an arrow shot by the supernatural culture hero Gluoscap.

Ash boughs were widely used by native groups for bows, spear shafts, axe handles, lacrosse sticks, snowshoes and canoe ribs because of the wood's strength, elasticity and shock absorbency. **White ash**, which was especially favoured, holds a hallowed place in Canadian culture as the source of most hockey sticks. Unlike other native ashes, it's an upland species, often growing in remnant urban woods and ravine slopes, and is planted in many parks. The tree tends to grow taller than green ash, has less tapered leaflets and is wrapped in a beautifully finely furrowed, more regularly patterned light-grey bark.

Unlikely as it seems, ash trees, along with lilacs and forsythia, both introduced from the Old World, are among the few temperate climate members of the olive family.

HONEY-LOCUST
Thorned Menace Disarmed in Town

WITH ITS FLAT-TOPPED, open crown of delicate, lacy leaflets filtering dappled light to sidewalks and lawns below, the sweetly named honey-locust has become one of the most ubiquitous of small to midsized street trees. It subsists in the harshest urban surroundings, commonly growing up out of raised cement boxes and small sidewalk pits along busy downtown avenues and paved-over areas, where it's often draped with lights during the Christmas season and other festivals. Honey-locust is also very lawn-friendly. Turf grass and flowers grow happily beneath its light shade and the tree's tiny leaflets crumble and decompose rapidly in the autumn.

Yet, in its native habitat, in moist river valleys, along creeks and ravine bottoms, the slender tree is decidedly inhospitable, its trunk and branches armed with dense clusters of long, multi-pronged thorns that command respect from passersby. Up to 30 centimetres (one foot) long, the hard, strong spines are second to none north of the tropics and were once fastened on weapons and animal traps and used as nails and pins. Thorned honey-locusts are sometimes pruned into impenetrable farm hedges. However, thornless selections are propagated and planted along city streets.

Most urban honey-locusts have also lost their feminine touch. Nurseries have selected only trees that don't

Average mature height: 8–20 m (26–66 ft)

Average trunk width: 30–50 cm (1–1.6 ft)

Ontario giant: 25.3 m (83 ft) tall, 1.3 m (4.3 ft) wide, south of Niagara-on-the-Lake

Lifespan: Up to 125 years

Average lifespan of sidewalk trees on busy streets: 10 years

Alias: Thorny locust, sweet-locust, three-thorned acacia, sweet bean locust, le févier épineux, Gleditsia triacanthos

Name origin: Mediterranean carob tree bears similar pods, for which it is also called a locust because of their resemblance to the insect

Whereabouts: Streetsides, yards, parks, parking lots, paved plazas, highway verges, open or scrubby areas in river valleys, ravines and along creeks

Leaves: Compound, some composed of 14–30 narrow leaflets, each 2.5–5 cm (1–2 in) long, slightly alternating along a central stalk, 15–20 cm (6–8 in) long; others divided again into 8–14 secondary stalks, each with many leaflets; bright yellow in autumn

Bark: Smooth, shiny and brownish with hatch marks when young, later developing narrow fissures between long, flat, wide, flaky strips, lifting at the edges

Flowers: Light greenish-white, 5 mm (0.2 in) wide, with 5 petals; males in dense dangling bunches, 2–5 cm (2–2.8 in) long; sparser, slender clusters of females 7–9 cm (2.8–3.5 in) long; bloom in Jun.; sweet-scented and pollinated by bees

Seeds: Flat, twisted pods, 15–40 cm (6–16 in) long, 2.5–3.5 cm (1–1.4 in) wide, containing hard, beanlike seeds; pods turn from light green to purplish-brown and drop in late autumn and winter; first pod borne when about 10 years old

Roots: Thick, widespread, with deep taproot

Wood: Bright reddish-brown heartwood, wide yellowish sapwood, hard, very strong, rot-resistant, 20 kg/m^3 (44 lb/cu ft)

Range: Native to southwestern Ontario and planted north to the Ottawa Valley; also grown in Quebec, British Columbia and Nova Scotia

Number of tree species considered rare in Ontario: 40

Number of rare Ontario trees that are Carolinian species: 33

Closest Ontario relatives: Kentucky coffee-tree

Also see: Green Ash, White Elm

litter the ground with seed pods. In the wild, while thorns fend off browsers from the tree's limbs and bark, the fallen pods have quite the opposite effect. The "honey" of the tree's name comes from the sweet white pulp inside the pods, which is enjoyed by many birds and mammals and was once dried and used as a sweetener by native cooks. The pulp is basically a bribe that turns critters into effective seed dispersers, with new trees sprouting in open spaces from droppings containing the hard, indigestible seeds. Given the eagerness of cows to eat the pods, some botanists believe migrating herds of buffalo may have once played a key role in hoofing the tree over vast areas. Others suggest mastodons, before they disappeared in North America about 11,000 years ago, could have been the main dispersal agents, based on the close relationship between elephants and similar heavily-thorned, large-seeded trees in Africa.

Honey-locust was originally only found in southwestern Ontario, around Essex and Kent Counties. As such, it is probably the most common Carolinian tree growing in the province's cities, representing a forest region that stretches from northern limits around Toronto all the way to the deep south in the United States. Only a small fraction of Ontario's Carolinian forest remains and many of its species, including such trees as sassafras, pawpaw, shellbark hickory and Kentucky coffee-tree, are rare or threatened. Yet honey-locust has become so popular in cities, it is commonly overlooked and even considered overused in many cases. Fast-growing, thornless and seedless varieties of the tree became widely commercially available in the 1950s, just in time to help fill the gaps left by the massive die-off of street elms to Dutch elm disease.

Black locust is distantly related to honey-locust. It grows wild in urban pockets along old backroads, unkept fields and open woods, rising high on a narrow, sinewy trunk deeply furrowed with thick, chunky, twisting ridges of bark. It has compound leaves of little oval leaflets, short seed pods and pairs of stubby thorns at the base of its leaf stalks. In June, it blooms with showy, fragrant dangling clusters of white pealike flowers.

HORSE CHESTNUT
Alluring Conkers Forbidden Fruits

HORSE CHESTNUTS ARE distinctive in any season. In winter, they'd be perfect beside a haunted house, their narrow crowns a stormy mass of dark, curling limbs with stout, blunt branch tips reaching out like thick, upcurved fingers. Their huge, sticky buds burst in spring into clutches of moist, expanding leaflets, initially hanging like roosting bats. Later in spring, as the large, palmlike leaves spread out, the trees bloom with tall, candlelike spires of frothy, red- and yellow-spotted white flowers. Spiky green balls develop on the branches through the summer and then split and rain glossy reddish-brown chestnuts onto city streets as schools reopen in September.

The tree's deep-domed canopy and impressive flowers have attracted keen botanical interest since at least the late 1500s, when horse chestnuts began to be transported from their homeland in the mountains of northern Greece and the Balkans to great estate and palace gardens in western Europe. Later, planted in early parks and along grand boulevards, they proved highly resilient

Average mature height:
10–25 m (33–82 ft)
Average trunk width: 30–90 cm
(1–3 ft)
Maximum height: 38 m (125 ft)
Average lifespan: 80–100 years
Alias: Chestnut, common horse chestnut, European horse chestnut, candle tree, *le marronnier d'Inde, Aesculus hippocastanum*
Whereabouts: Streetsides, parks, golf courses and other spaces with rich, moist soil and not too crowded by other trees; escapes into ravines
Leaves: Compound, composed of 5–9 leaflets, each 10–25 cm (4–10 in) long, tooth-edged, joined at a central point; dark green on top, pale below, dying

back and turning crispy brown on branch in fall; leaf stems appear in opposite pairs along branch

Flowers: White with dark-pink and yellow spots, bell-shaped, 2–3 cm (0.8–1.2 in) long, with long, curved protruding stamens; 100–200 clustered on 20–30 cm (8–12 in) spire at branch tips; mainly pollinated by bumblebees

Nuts: Round, lumpy, 3–4 cm (1.2–1.6 in) wide, glossy, mahogany brown with a large, irregular tan patch; usually 1–2 contained within a spine-covered, spherical green husk

Bark: Dark grey, smooth when young, becoming scaly with age, with fissures often twisting upwards to the right

Buds: 2–5 cm (0.8–2 in) long at branch tips, dark brown, pointed, sticky

Wood: Almost white, light, weak, with fine, even grain

Specialty uses: Carving; made into toys and artificial limbs in past because it does not splinter

Range: Planted as far north as Ottawa and Orillia; also planted in other eastern provinces and British Columbia

Only member of horse chestnut genus native to Ontario: Ohio buckeye, found in extreme southwestern Ontario

Number of species in horse chestnut genus worldwide: 13

Also see: Grey Squirrel, Pigeon

to the stresses of urban living. The still-renowned rows of stately horse chestnuts lining a broad avenue in London, England's, Bushy Park were established in 1699. Similar, the spectacular spring blossoms of the famous horse chestnut trees along the Champs Élysées were rhapsodized in the 1930s hit tune "April in Paris."

Notwithstanding the popularity of the tree's shade and blossoms, its bountiful nuts are poisonous and bear only a superficial resemblance to true chestnuts, which are borne by trees in a completely different family. Squirrels are one of the few animals that can stomach horse chestnuts, also known as conkers, but they only eat the light-coloured "embryo stalk" portions. The unpalatable nut mush was even once used as a binding to deter bookworms and other insects hungry for literature.

The toxin in the nuts, esculin, is also found in the tree's leaves and bark, from which it's extracted and applied to the skin for ailments such as varicose veins, phlebitis and ulcers. For hundreds of years, the nuts were also crushed and applied in salves for sunburns, backaches and rheumatic joints, or in medicines for colds and fevers. The Turks used them in a cure for shortness of breath and colds in horses, though other sources claim variously that the tree gets its name from a horseshoe-shaped scar left on the twigs by the fallen leaf stalk, or from the large tan patch on the nut resembling a horse's eye.

True chestnuts are members of the beech family. The commonly sold edible ones, "roasting by an open fire," are from the European chestnut tree, also called sweet or Spanish chestnut. The closely related **American chestnut** was once common in Ontario south of Lake Simcoe and was highly esteemed for furniture panels. However, an east Asian canker fungus known as chestnut blight was accidentally introduced by foreign trees brought to Long Island in 1904 and spread to Ontario in the early 1920s, virtually wiping out the province's estimated two million native chestnut trees within a couple of decades. Aside from a scattered handful of disease-resistant individuals, sprouts sometimes grow from the stumps of some once-great trees, only to be struck down by the fungus upon reaching several metres (or yards).

LITTLE-LEAF LINDEN
The True Honey Tree

THE SWEET FRAGRANCE that linden trees lend to early-summer city streets has been esteemed for more than 2,000 years. In Greek mythology, the trees were said to be the husbands of the dryads, the wood nymphs, and were commonly associated with sweetness, modesty, gentleness and conjugal love. Later folklore held that it was good luck for pregnant women to hug linden trees, as well as ashes or elms.

The endearments of love also evoke the sweet essence of linden trees. Honey is intrinsically associated with lindens and lies at the base of their age-old popularity. During the two or three weeks they're in bloom, the trees attract droves of bees and become one of their prime sources of honey. Distinctive, clear linden honey is one of the most prized varieties cultivated by beekeepers and is also used in liqueurs. The sweet flowers themselves are dried for use as a popular, age-old herbal tea, touted for its powers to calm imbibers, aid their digestion and boost resistance to infections.

People have long had plenty of other reasons to appreciate lindens. Before hemp was introduced to western Europe from the east around A.D. 500, the long, strong fibres of the tree's inner bark were woven into rope, twine and even garments. "Otzi," the 5,000-year-old ice mountaineer found preserved in a glacier in the Alps in

Average mature height: 9–15 m (30–50 ft)

Average trunk width: 40–80 cm (1.3–2.6 ft)

Maximum height: 24 m (79 ft)

Lifespan: In Europe up to 500 years old; new sprouts readily grow from old stumps, some root systems may be more than 1,000 years old in Europe

Alias: Small-leaf European linden, small-leaved linden, small-leaved lime, *tilleul à petites feuilles*, *Tilia cordata*

Whereabouts: Streetsides, parks, yards, sometimes escapes into open natural areas

Leaves: 4–8 cm (1.6–3.2 in) long, squat, slightly lopsided, tooth-edged, dark green and shiny on top, lighter on undersides, turning light yellow to tan in autumn

Bark: Dark grey-brown, narrowly fissured with flat, wavy ridges

Flowers: Greenish-yellow, about 1 cm (0.4 in) wide, with

5 petals; bunches of 5–8 together on a stalk extending from midpoint of a 3.5–8-cm-long (1.4–3.2-in-long), narrow leaflike blade

Seeds: Each held in a hard, pea-sized, light-yellow to grey capsule covered with soft rusty hairs, usually several in a cluster; ripen in autumn, but may remain on trees in winter, eventually falling with attached leaflike blades acting as para-chutes; first produced when tree 20–30 years old

Roots: Deep, widespread, well anchored

Wood: Soft, smooth, light, whitish, with fine, straight, even grain, 560 kg/m^3 (35 lb/cu ft)

Nibblers and ailments: Japanese beetles, basswood leafrollers, lacebugs, leaf gall mites, sooty leaf mould; aphids suck sap from leaves and often coat the ground and objects beneath the trees with the sticky "honey-dew" of their droppings

Range: Planted in cities as far north as Sudbury and Thunder Bay and in all other provinces

Closest Ontario relative: Basswood, has huge lopsided leaves, grows in urban woods and ravines; the Iroquois carved masks depicting fierce images of the spirits that protect against disease and crop blights from living basswood trees and wore them during Iroquois False Face Ceremonies before the start of each growing season

Number of *Tilia* species world-wide: About 30

Also see: Bees, Wasps & Hornets

1991, had with him both cords and shoes partly made out of linden bark.

The tree's soft, smooth wood, with a straight, even grain, has also been traditionally favoured for carving and lathing. It can be worked thin and can be bent without cracking. Since the Middle Ages in Europe, it was widely used for much of the fine woodwork and intricately carved religious motifs inside churches. Linden wood is also made into the sound boards and keys of pianos and organs, venetian blinds and drawing boards because it does not warp.

It's the aesthetics of the trees themselves, though, that have won them a place on streets and in yards since ancient times. Some in British parks are more than 350 years old. Appreciated as much for the deep shade and tidy appearance of their densely leaved, rounded canopies as for their summer fragrance, lindens were brought with Europeans for their settlements in North America to remind them of home. They're also as tough as they are sweet, taking well to modern urban life, withstanding pollution, rock salt and limited soil and moisture. Among the landmarks famously graced with lindens are Washington Square in Manhattan's Greenwich Village, the main avenue of Cambridge University's Trinity College and the grand Berlin boulevard Unter den Linden.

Even one of the main criticisms of urban lindens may, in fact, be a mixed blessing. In late summer, lindens often host hordes of tiny, leaf-sucking aphids, whose sweet droppings, called honeydew, sometimes candy-coat everything beneath the trees. According to one theory, the honeydew may spur the growth of nitrogen-fixing bacteria in the soil, explaining why the ground beneath lindens, as well as their leaves, have higher levels of nitrogen than nearby trees. Though the element comprises about 80 percent of the atmosphere, leaves can't absorb the nitrogen from the air as they can carbon. Bacteria, however, does absorb airborne nitrogen and turns into ammonia in the soil, which tree and plant roots can absorb. High levels of nutrients in linden leaves make them ideal mulching and composting material.

MANITOBA MAPLE
Greening the Grittiest Spaces

LITTLE NOTED, often dismissed and sometimes reviled, the Manitoba maple is perhaps the most unsung stalwart of the urban forest. It is labelled a weed tree because it can, given the chance, shoot up and prosper almost anywhere. The resourceful rogue is most noticed when it grows where it isn't wanted. Yet, the tree is seldom given credit for volunteering to green up the most unlikely and otherwise stark and gritty locales – back alleys, parking lots, vacant properties and other neglected and abandoned places. Manitoba maple, together with the tree of heaven, will sprout from the narrowest cracks and crevices in asphalt and pavement and rise up faster than almost all other city trees, reaching beyond three metres (10 feet) in a few years. Its trunk can thicken by up to two or three centimetres (0.8 to 1.2 inches) every year in its first couple of decades.

Like the gangly oddball of the family, the Manitoba is usually not recognized as a maple. It stands alone among its cousins as the only North American maple with a compound leaf, with the lobes of the classic maple shape pulled apart into three to nine highly variable individual pointy leaflets, growing in pairs like an ash leaf. The tree itself strikes an unmaplelike pose, usually with a divided, often leaning trunk and splayed, uneven branches covered in drooping leaves, giving it a ragged, scrubby look little loved by horticulturalists.

The species is more appreciated on the tree-challenged prairies, where it was once tapped by natives and sugar-short pioneers and often planted for windbreaks and shade, bearing up through droughts and bitterly cold winters. Unable to live long in shade, Manitoba maple evolved to tough it out in places where

Average mature height: 8–15 m (26–49 ft)

Average trunk width: 30–60 cm (1–2 ft)

Ontario giant: 16 m (52 ft) tall, 1.4 m (4.5 ft) wide, Zorra Township, Oxford County

Lifespan: Often 50–75 years, up to 100 years

Alias: Box elder, ashleaf maple, plains maple, three-leaved maple, maple ash, l'érable negundo, Acer negundo

Whereabouts: Alleys, back lanes, vacant properties, edges of parking lots and property lines, yards, fringes of woods, along streams and lakeshores

Leaves: Compound, highly variable, usually with 3–5 leaflets, sometimes up to 9, each 5–12 cm (2–4.7 in) long, with irregularly jagged edges, sometimes slightly lobed, often asymmetrical; dull green on top, greyish-green beneath, turning greenish-yellow in autumn, sometimes tinted with red

Bark: Light grey streaked or flecked with brown when young; darker, with thin ridges on older trees

Sex: Flowers without petals, in clusters, appearing before or while leaves open in spring; reddish-brown tipped males hang on long, limp, greenish-yellow stalks; spiky bunches of pale-green females dangle on separate trees; mainly wind pollinated, but also visited by bees

Seeds: In winged pairs joined at a very sharp angle, each side 3–5 cm (1.2–2 in) long; green at first, turning brown; hanging on long, thin stalks; seed production can start when tree about 6 years old

Roots: Usually shallow, widespread, sometimes with a short taproot in deeper soil

Wood: Whitish, close-grained, soft, porous, weak, 12 kg/m³ (27 lb/cu ft)

Heat equivalent of 1 m³ (35 cu ft) of Manitoba maple wood: 129 litres (28 gal) of oil

Common nesters: Robins, yellow warblers, Baltimore orioles, mourning doves, kingbirds

Range: Southern Ontario to Ottawa Valley and Manitoulin Island; Thunder Bay and far western Ontario; also in all other provinces except Newfoundland

Number of maple species native to Ontario: 7

Number of maple species worldwide: About 150

Also see: Tree of Heaven, Green Ash, Sugar Maple

most other trees have trouble. In Ontario, it's a tree of the margins, once restricted mainly to lakesides, streams and flood plains where seasonal inundations kept most other species away. But with European settlement, the marginal maple took quickly to the open, harsh conditions in the new cities, spreading out from its original range west of London, around the east end of Lake Ontario and west of Lake Superior. Springing up before street trees were widely planted, it has never surrendered the niche it carved out in the cityscape's unattended spaces.

One reason Manitobas seem to find every tiny nook and cranny from which to grow is the sheer number of extremely vigorous winged seeds they shed continually from September into spring. The profuse masses of brown seeds in winter often look from afar like the trees have failed to drop their shrivelled, dead leaves. Squirrels and many birds eagerly gobble many of the keys. They're a staple for evening grosbeaks, originally birds of the western boreal forest that became permanent Ontario residents in the mid-1900s with the proliferation of Manitoba maples and bird feeders.

Once rooted, the trees are determined squatters. If they are cut or fall down, even in late summer, new shoots spring up from the trunk or roots within a few weeks. During the Dustbowl drought of the 1930s, most of the mature Manitoba maples on the Great Plains seemed to die off, only to re-emerge with new sprouts from their resilient roots once the rains returned.

But like many trees growing up in a hurry, Manitoba maple has weak wood and a short life. Broken branches and fallen trunks are a common malady as the aging tree becomes brittle and vulnerable to strong winds, heavy snows or ice. As firewood, it burns fast. As lumber, it's good for little more than crates and boxes, hence the other common name for the tree, box elder (which also refers to its elderlike compound leaves).

NORWAY MAPLE
Top Preforming Foreign Import

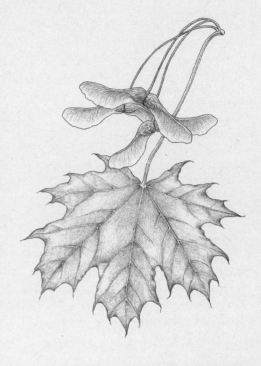

NORWAY MAPLE HAS become so common in Ontario, it is widely confused with Canada's national tree. In fact, it was the first Scandinavian draft pick to do spectacularly well in the land of the Maple Leafs. Shading innumerable neighbourhood roadsides, the foreign tree's leaves look very much like the sugar maple leaf on the Canadian flag. But upon closer inspection, they actually possess at least one pair of extra pointed lobes near the stem. They're also darker green, tend to be bigger than sugar maple leaves and ooze a unique milky white sap when their stalks are broken. Norway maple seeds are more obviously different, with the wings of the paired keys spreading straight out from one another, rather than forming a U shape like sugar maple seeds. In autumn, Norways also don't come close to the brilliant colours of the national tree, managing at best some muted yellow-reds.

Yet, with its attractive, finely furrowed trunk dividing into graceful, artistically posed limbs, and its lush, dense foliage that casts deep shade, Norway maple is by far the most common street tree in many cities. It's much more tolerant than sugar maple and many other trees of car exhaust, urban heat stress and drought, damage to roots from digging, and poor, compacted soils. It's also more resistant to harmful insects. In midspring, the tree begins to leaf out a week or two earlier than native maples and flourishes tiny bouquets of yellow flowers, which later carpet sidewalks as they're shed. Norways also retain their leaves about two weeks longer into autumn than their Canadian counterparts.

Despite its name and northern hardiness, Norway maple is not only native to Scandinavia but to much of

Average mature height: 10–21 m (33–69 ft)
Average trunk width: 30–75 cm (1–2.5 ft)
Maximum height: 41.8 m (137 ft)
Alias: L'érable de Norvège, Acer platanoides
Whereabouts: Streetsides, yards, parks; often spreads into urban woods
Leaves: 8–16 cm (3–6.3 in) long, 10–18 cm (4–7 in) wide, with 5–7 lobes tapering to long, narrow points; smooth edged, dark green on top, lighter green below, turning dull yellow, amber, light purplish-red

or just fading and browning from the edges in autumn, depending on the variety

Flowers: Greenish-yellow, about 1 cm (0.4 in) wide, with 5 petals, in small, outspread clusters at branch tips in early to mid-May

Seeds: Pairs of joined keys with wings pointing in opposite directions, each 3.5–5 cm (1.4–2 in) long, green at first, turning brown as they ripen in autumn; used as the logo for the Canadian Television Fund, presumably mistaken for a sugar maple seed

Bark: Light grey and smooth when young, becoming dark grey, with distinctive pattern of thin, even, interlacing ridges

Roots: Shallow, often reaching surface

Wood: Light coloured, with an even, straight grain

Nibblers and ailments: Cottony maple scale insects, bladder gall mites, leafstalk borers, aphids, verticillium wilt fungus, tar spot of maple

Range: Southern Ontario to Sudbury and Thunder Bay; also planted in other eastern provinces and British Columbia

Other commonly planted non-native maples: Japanese maple, sycamore maple, Amur maple, hedge maple

First appearance of maples: More than 90 million years ago

Also see: Sugar Maple, White Elm, Alien Invaders

Europe south to Turkey as well. Sturdy maple saplings once furnished spears for Roman legions, which is why, according to some authorities, the Latin word for maple is *Acer*, which means "sharp" and still serves as the scientific name for the genus. From the 1500s onwards, the density of Norway maple wood provided the ideal resonance and strength for the backs and sides of finely crafted, tightly strung violins.

Grown in North America since at least the mid-1700s, Norway maple began to be extensively planted in Ontario's cities in the 1930s. More than 80 varieties are now known, with varying shapes, sizes, leaf types and colours. The popular crimson king, with dark purple leaves, is often called a red maple by many people. True **red maple**, however, is a native tree with smaller green leaves and is named for the red hues of its buds, twigs, flowers, seeds and autumn foliage. It's planted much less often in cities, usually growing in parks.

The biggest criticism of Norway maple is its very success. Often accounting for more than a third of all species in many neighbourhoods, it's now considered overplanted. The brash foreign maple also often spreads into nearby woods, to the detriment of many native species. Norways, already resistant to most insects and diseases, also tend to beat out the competition by producing sizable seed crops every year, rather than every few years like native maples. Diversity decreases on the forest floor below, as well, with the trees' deep shade being too much even for native plants that have evolved to grow in dark sugar maple woods. Studies have found that 85 percent of all forest plants growing beneath invasive Norway maples are younger Norway maple seedlings. Cities such as Toronto now prohibit new Norway plantings from areas beside parks and ravines and actively root out the invasive trees from urban woodlands, replacing them with native species.

FOREST EDGE
Life Is Usually Richest Where
Two Habitats Meet and Overlap

JUST AS MUCH of nature is most active during the transitory hours of dawn and dusk, the place where two habitats meet and overlap, known as an ecotone, is incredibly rich in life, packed with plants and animals from both realms. Forest margins are among the most diverse of all ecotones, whether bordering meadows, watersides or other surroundings. In cities, treed fencerows and roadside fringes connected to remnant woods, parkside groves and ravine or valley green belts are also essentially extensions of forest edges. In fact, most of the native wildlife that has adapted best to the city, including raccoons, foxes, skunks, groundhogs, blue jays, robins, flickers and mourning doves, are, by their nature, denizens of the woodland margins.

Forest edges offer a place to root for many trees and shrubs that need full or ample sunlight. Besides aspens, white birch and the tree of heaven, they include:

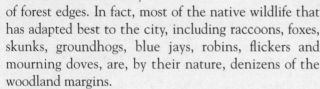

Hawthorns (illustrated)   5–10 m (16–33 ft) tall

A varied group of squat, closely related trees, hawthorns, like prickly raspberry canes and wild rose bushes, often form nearly impenetrable tangles along forest margins. Their strong, sharp thorns, up to 8 centimetres (three inches) long, ward off many of the browsers that frequent high-forage open areas. Together with black locust, another forest-edge species with smaller thorns, they're about the last trees to leaf out in late May and June, when their dense tangles of branches also sprout off-smelling white flowers. In September, they become heavily laden with red, crabapplelike, edible fruits, called haws, which often persist well into winter.

Portion of bird, mammal, amphibian and reptile species in southern and central Ontario that frequent forest margins: Almost half

Thickets: Very dense stands, sometimes colonies, of small, sunloving trees and tall shrubs that often form wide transition zones between forests and fields, including species such as hawthorn, staghorn sumac, tree of heaven, speckled alder, red osier dogwood, wild rose, buckthorn, honeysuckles and willows

Common forest edge vines: Virginia creeper, river grape

Forest edge warblers: Yellow warblers, redstarts, common yellowthroats, Nashville warblers, yellow-rumped warblers, mourning warblers

Forest edge butterflies: Mourning cloaks, tiger swallowtails, question marks, spring azures, fritillaries

Number of flycatcher species nesting in Ontario: 10

Number of Ontario hawthorn species: About 30–40 (much hybridization and disagreement on species definitions)

Number of Ontario serviceberry species: 7

Also see: Chorus Frog, Song Sparrow, Red-tailed Hawk, Poison Ivy, Honey-Locust, Woods; Meadows, Vacant Lots & Roadsides

Chokecherry   2–8 m (6.5–24 feet) tall

A very common shrubby tree, chokecherry has fragrant white blossoms in May and bright-red to purple-black, pea-sized cherries in late summer. Though not actually poisonous (if the pits aren't swallowed), the cherries are harsh and astringent, causing the mouth to pucker and dry. They become sweeter with age, especially after a frost, but birds and other animals get most before then.

Alternate-leaf Dogwood   2–4 m (6.5–13 ft) tall

Because alternate-leaf dogwood grows in progressively smaller layers of widespread branches with upward-bending tips, it's also known as pagoda dogwood. Like other dogwoods, its leaves, which turn dark purple-red in autumn, have prominent veins that curve lengthwise toward their pointed tips. It bears clusters of small, frothy white flowers in June and, as early as late July, profuse dark-blue to black, bitter, dry berries on short, bright-red stalks.

Serviceberry   2–10 m (6.5–33 ft) tall

Typically growing in small clumps of several thin trunks, serviceberry has white blossoms, opening with its leaves in April and May. They yield sweet red or purplish berries that ripen in late July and early August.

Elder   usually well under 3 m (10 ft) tall

Growing as multi-stemmed shrubs, elder bear compound leaves of five or more narrow, opposite leaflets. Red-berried elder has long, rounded clusters of tiny, yellow-white flowers in late May and June and bright-red, inedible berries, the size of BB-gun pellets, in July and August. Canada elderberry's flat-topped, white-flower clusters bloom in July, producing purple-black berries in late August and September.

Staghorn Sumac (illustrated, page 263)   2–5 m (7–16.5 ft) tall

Best known for the purple-red plumes that persist on its sparse, crooked limbs through winter, staghorn sumac forms dense, colonial thickets. The plumes, composed of fuzzy-coated seeds, ripen in summer, but are most often sought as an emergency food by overwintering birds, as well as by early-spring migrants such as robins.

Many woodland flowers, from trout lilies in early spring to large-leaved asters in late summer, also bloom more profusely with the extra sunlight near forest edges. Dame's rocket, white wood anemones, orange day lilies and yellow celandine all seem to take greatest comfort along such margins. Where the ground is wettest, bright-yellow marsh marigolds thrive, while dry, rocky places harbour beautiful, five-spurred, red-and-gold wild columbine flowers. Among other noteworthy forest edge wildflowers:

Coltsfoot   15–46 cm (6–18 in) tall

One of the first flowers of spring, coltsfoot sometimes blooms along roadside woods and other sunny spots as early as late March in southern Ontario. An introduced species, its yellow dandelionlike flowerhead, borne on a fuzzy, reddish-scaled stem, appears well before its large, rounded leaves unfold.

Wild Geranium   30–60 cm (1–2 ft) tall

Blooming in small colonies in late spring, wild geranium has showy, pinkish-purple, five-petalled flowers. Its leaves also divide into five widespread fingers. The closely related alien herb-robert also blooms along rocky forest edges, from May to October, but its pink flowers are only half as big as wild geraniums.

Helleborine   30–80 cm (1–31.5 in) tall

A tough foreign garden renegade, helleborine is generally the most common orchid in and around urban areas. It has prominently veined, stem-clasping, pointed leaves and a spire of tiny, intricate, nodding, purple-veined, greenish flowers that bloom through the summer.

Spotted Jewelweed   50–150 cm (20–59 in) tall

Dense patches of succulent-stemmed jewelweed grow on mucky ground along creeks and ravine bottoms. Their dangling, horn-shaped orange flowers appear from mid-July until the first frosts of early autumn.

As most birders know, woodland margins are usually the best places to find the greatest variety of feathered wildlife. In addition to those that exploit the concentrations of fruits, seeds and insects clustered there, many birds that forage mainly in open areas roost and nest in the safety of nearby trees. Some that may not frequent residential neighbourhoods in large numbers but can be abundant on nearby forest fringes include:

Baltimore Oriole   18–21 cm (7–8.5 in) long

Stunning black-and-orange oriole males, about the size of red-winged blackbirds, are most often heard singing their deeply whistled, melodious songs high in the trees in the first few weeks after they return from the south in mid-May. They're most common near riversides. Females, with olive-brown backs and orange-tinged yellow undersides, weave baglike nests that hang from the tips of thin, pendulous outer branches.

Rose-breasted Grosbeak   18–21 cm (7–8.5 in) long

Returning around the same time as orioles, loquacious rose-breasted grosbeak males with their namesake marking set off against a white belly and jet-black head sound somewhat like a robin, but with a richer, more accomplished voice. Their mates look like large, streaky-brown sparrows with a white stripe above the eye and a thick, cardinal-like beak.

Indigo Bunting   13–15 cm (5–6 in) long

Another sweet-voiced, thick-beaked, mid-May arrival, the indigo bunting is about the size of a house sparrow. In the right light, the male shines a deep, iridescent blue unlike the colour of any other Ontario bird. The female is brown with a pale, faintly streaked breast.

Warbling Vireo   13–15 cm (5–6 in) long

Like indigo buntings, the warbling vireo sings from May until well into summer. The male, however, is as plain olive and grey as his mate. Keeping high in the canopy, he's hard to make out, save for his slow, long-drawn warble.

Catbird   20–23 cm (8–9 in) long

Returning from the south around early May, catbirds are dark grey and black-capped, with both sexes alike. Males commonly ensconce themselves in low, densely branched trees, such as hawthorns, and sing long medleys of widely varying, jumbled phrases, often incorporating the imitated songs of other birds and distinct, catlike whines.

Least Flycatcher   13 cm (5 in) long

Tiny birds, the size of goldfinches, least flycatchers are very plain, with both sexes having an olive-grey back and dirty-white undersides. A sharp, repeated "che-bek!" is its calling card. First arriving from Mexico and Central America around late April, it frequents small trees and shrubs, such as red-osier dogwood and willows.

RED OAK
Mighty Monarch of City Parks

WHEREVER THEY GROW, oaks are held in awe, respect and affection. Throughout history, their strength, great size and longevity have made them both sites and symbols of spiritual and temporal importance. Sacred oak groves were the scenes of oracles by ancient Greek priestesses, ceremonies by the Druids and of Roman women beseeching oak nymphs for safe births. Magnificent golden oak panels lined royal chambers and holy chapels. In the tale of King Arthur, the Round Table was a cross section from a huge oak trunk. A great oak that once stood in Niagara-on-the-Lake was long honoured for shading the sweaty Loyalists of Upper Canada's first parliament, who convened beneath it for an open-air session during the intolerably hot summer of 1793 to pass the new colony's first anti-slavery act.

The age-old fascination with oak is believed to lie, in part, with the propensity for the tall, wide crowns of the trees to be struck by lightning, as noted in the old rhyme: "Beware of an oak, It draws the stroke." Even in predominantly beech forests, oak is estimated to be hit by lightning 10 to 20 times as often as beech. When hit, it often bursts into flame. The ancient Europeans saw in this spectacular phenomenon a direct connection with

Average mature height: 16–25 m (52.5–82 ft)

Average trunk width: 30–90 cm (1–3 ft)

Ontario giant: 31.1 m (102 ft) tall, 1.9 m (6.4 ft) wide, in Harwich Township, Kent County

Lifespan: Commonly 150–300 years

Alias: Northern red oak, eastern red oak, grey oak, champion oak, mountain red oak, *le chêne rouge, Quercus rubra*

Whereabouts: Grows best on sandy soil in parks, spacious grounds around schools and other institutions, large yards in quiet neighbourhoods, woods

Leaves: 10–23 cm (4–9 in) long, 7–15 cm (3–6 in) wide, with 7–11 pointed lobes between rounded notches; unfold later than maple and many other trees in spring, turn rusty red in autumn; not good for compost because they take long to decay

Bark: Smooth and dark grey when young; wide furrows between long, flat, light-grey ridges on older trees, intersected higher up on trunk by slight horizontal bulges

Sex: Dangling, greenish-yellow male catkins 10–13 cm (4–5 in) long; tiny, reddish female flowers at base of leaf stalks on new shoots; wind pollinated; blooming in mid-May; first flowers appear when tree 20–25 years

Acorns: 1–3 cm (0.4–1.2 in) long, woody, holding 1 seed, green at first, turning reddish-brown, with brown cap of scales; very bitter tasting, contain 8% protein, 37% fat; take 2 summers to ripen; 100–4,000 per tree, with big crops usually every 2–5 years; puberty at about 25 years

Roots: Deep, widespread, often with taproot

Maximum daily water uptake by roots of a mature oak: More than 1,000 L (220 gal)

Wood: Reddish-brown to pink heartwood, whitish sapwood, coarse-grained, very strong, hard, porous, 690 kg/m³ (43 lb/cu ft), very warm burning

Heat equivalent of 1 m³ (35 cu ft) of red oak wood: 181 L (40 gal) of oil

Companion trees and shrubs in wild: White pine, red maple, aspen, beaked hazel

Common nesters: Red-tailed hawks, great horned owls, pewees, white-breasted nuthatches, scarlet tanagers

the gods. The oldest classical Greek traditions depicted Zeus, the thunder god, as an oak or at least living in one. Oaks were sacred to Thor and Jehovah, both thunder-and-lighting deities. The tree was similarly the supreme god of the Gauls, and the name of the Finnish thunder god was Ukko, meaning "oak." Even the oak tree's parasite, mistletoe, was deified and is still hung at Christmas. Unable to shake pagan reverence for sites of sacred oaks, where sacrifices were made to older deities, the Christian Church eventually took their sites by blessing them and erecting crucifixes and images of Mary.

In Ontario, red oak is one of the monarchs of the mixed and hardwood forests. Though its strong, wide-grained, golden-hued wood is highly valued for furniture, floors, trim and veneers, the big red was also embraced by the early settlers as a beautiful farmstead and small-town shade tree. It's easy to transplant and develops huge, thickly furrowed trunks, often with low, wide-spreading, level limbs when grown in open spaces. While it's fussy about soil and doesn't deal as well with modern urban stresses as some street trees, it thrives in city parks and spacious residential neighbourhoods.

Wherever oaks rise up, come autumn their fabled acorns make them the centre of activity for squirrels, blue jays and all manner of other birds and beasts. Acorns are one of the most nutritious of wildlife foods. In wilderness areas on the Canadian Shield, bears plant themselves in oak trees for prolonged serious pigouts before going into hibernation. Populations of animal diners in some areas may rise and fall from year to year with acorn production cycles. Squirrels, jays and white-footed mice in turn help spread the seeds by storing acorns in various locations. Those they fail to retrieve have a high germination rate. Millions of migrating passenger pigeons, which once blackened the skies over Ontario, were dependent on acorn and beechnut crops. Their extinction is believed to have greatly limited the oak's ability to spread.

Native groups also sometimes ate the seeds inside red oak acorns, but only after prolonged boiling, days of soaking in running water or burying them for the winter to leech out their bitter-tasting tannin. An acidic defence compound, tannin is responsible for the red colour of the tree's leaves in spring and autumn. The acorns of white oak, on the other hand, are sweeter and edible even raw, though Native peoples usually dried and ground them to make into cakes and to add to soups.

White oak, with its round-lobed leaves and more flaky-ridged bark, grows mainly south of the Canadian Shield and in the Ottawa Valley. But it is less common in most cities than red oak. Bearing the strongest, densest, best-quality wood of any oak, it was widely used for the strong, sturdy beams of wooden ships. England had already cut down most of its own once-great oak forests in order to rule the waves, with up to 3,500 trees going into the building of one warship. Vast white oak stands in eastern Ontario were ranked next to white pines in importance to the loggers of the early 1800s. Because the wood was so heavy, early river drives had to lash timbers of pine to it keep it from sinking. White oak wood, because it is not porous like red oak, is also used for wine and whisky casks, contributing a singular flavour to their contents.

A much rarer species, **black oak**, is found in a handful of small but very significant natural spots in southern Ontario's cities. It has dark-glossy-green, deeply notched leaves and dark, thick-ridged bark broken into irregular blocks. Keeping mainly to dry, sandy ground, it once grew scattered amid the prairie grasses, wildflowers and shrubs of the province's pre-settlement oak savannahs. More than 10,000 hectares (25,000 acres) of oak savannah, together with tens of thousands of hectares more of related prairies, once flourished in pockets across the southern Carolinian forest zone. Today, it's almost all gone. Windsor's Ojibway Prairie and Toronto's High Park, however, contain two of Ontario's best remnant savannahs, now protected and being restored with plantings of native species and occasional prescribed spring burns to recreate the conditions that kept surrounding forests from encroaching on the semi-open habitat.

Frequent diners: Squirrels, chipmunks, raccoons, foxes, deer, blue jays, crows, flickers, nuthatches, grackles, ruffed grouse and wood ducks eat acorns; deer and rabbits browse leaves

Nibblers and ailments: Gypsymoth and forest tent caterpillars, filbert worms, oak-leaf shredders, acorn weevils, wood-boring beetles, oak-leaf rollers, sap beetles, gall-causing wasps, flies, beetles, aphids, oak wilt and shoestring root rot fungi

Accolades: Official tree of Prince Edward Island

Range: Southern Ontario to a little north of Sault Ste. Marie, Sudbury and Lake Timiskaming, and in a thin band between Thunder Bay and Quetico Provincial Park; also in southern Quebec, the Maritimes and planted in British Columbia

Other commonly planted urban oaks: White oak, pin oak, bur oak, scarlet oak, English oak

Definition of a savannah: Tallgrass vegetation with 25–35% tree cover

Largest oak remnant savannah in North America: About 1,500 hectares (3,700 acres), in Pinery Provincial Park, near Grand Bend, Ontario

Portion of North America's original 13 million hectares of oak savannah that remains: 0.02%

Number of oak species native to Ontario: 9

Number of oak species worldwide: 500–600

Also see: Blue Jay, Pigeon, Grey Squirrel, Thunder & Lightning

SILVER MAPLE
From Riversides to City Streets

Average mature height:
18–25 m (59–82 ft)

Average trunk width:
50–100 cm (1.6–3.3 ft)

Ontario giant: 32.4 m (106 ft)
tall, 2.1 m (6.9 ft) wide, in
Southwold Township, Elgin Co.

Lifespan: Commonly 70–130
years, rarely over 150 years

**Annual diameter growth for
young trees on good sites:**
About 1.5 cm (0.6 in)

Alias: Soft maple, river maple,
swamp maple, l'érable argenté,
Acer saccharinum

Whereabouts: Streetsides, yards,
parks, along lakes, streams,
swamp edges, flood plains

Leaves: 8–15 cm (3–6 in) long,
deeply and narrowly notched,
sharply toothed, light green on
top, silvery pale green on undersides; dull yellow, amber, red-
tinted, or brownish in autumn,
depending on variety

Sex: Clusters of tiny, petal-lacking
flowers appear well before

LEGEND HOLDS IT was a leaf from a silver maple tree falling on Alexander Muir's sleeve near the east Toronto school where he was principal that inspired him in 1867 to compose "The Maple Leaf Forever," for many years English Canada's unofficial national anthem. Muir wrote the words for a patriotic poetry contest marking the Confederation year, drawing upon a Canadian symbol used since the days of New France. The habitants carved their farms from vast forests dominated by various species of maple, which yielded quality building material, firewood, spring syrup and stunning autumn colours. Though the maple leaf remains the quintessential Canadian icon, Muir's song was eventually superseded by "O Canada!" which premiered in French in 1880, was translated, not literally, into English in 1908, but not officially adopted by Parliament as the country's anthem until June 27, 1980.

Silver maples were very popular in the young Ontario cities and towns of Muir's day. Fast-growing trees of rich, moist watersides, flood plains and swamps, they were ideal for quickly greening newly laid-out residential streets, reaching up to 15 metres (50 feet) in as little as 20 years. Developing thick, shaggy trunks dividing into two or more big main stems, they form vase-shaped canopies with their namesake silvery-bottomed leaves shimmering in an open lacework of fine branchlets, which often dangle and hook upwards toward their tips.

But just as silver maples are reaching their full magnificence, when about 70 years old, they begin dropping large branches in high winds, ice storms and wet snowfalls, allowing spores of wood-rotting fungi into the wounds left behind. The trees also have fast-growing roots to match their wide-spreading branches and are notorious for invading cracks and breaks in old clay drainage pipes. By the mid-1900s, silver maples were falling out of favour as cities turned to hardier species, such as Norway maple, which needed less space to thrive along side increasingly busy city streets. Meanwhile, falling branches (and smashed cars parked below), rotting trunks and blocked drains have brought the sorrowful demise of great numbers of old neighbourhood silvers, often to be replaced by small honey-locusts, crabapples or nothing at all.

In recent years, some municipalities have started planting silver maples again, especially in cooler, moist sites in parks and ravines. Tree breeders have also come up with a smaller silver hybrid, crossed with the closely related red maple, which is proving popular. Known as the Freeman maple, it is less wide-spreading, tends to hang on to its branches and dons reddish-tinted autumn colours.

In very early spring, silver maples furnish city streets with one of their first signs of the season. Conspicuous, fat clusters of round, red winter buds swell during mild spells in late March and soon turn fuzzy with the sprouting, petal-lacking flowers. Some trees may bloom much earlier than others. Male flowers form bursts of soft, yellow-tipped, green tendrils. Their dusty yellow pollen kicks off the hay-fever season, exploding in little puffs when the branches are jostled and marking the sidewalk when the blossoms fall. Tiny female flowers, mostly borne on separate trees, sport V-shaped pairs of purple-red filaments and develop rapidly into winged seeds that are already raining down in strong winds by the time the trees are fully leafed out in May and continue falling through June.

leaves open; males with 12 or more long yellowish-green tendrils with bright-yellow tips; females with smaller pairs of red filaments; pollinated by the wind and, to uncertain degree, by bees; flowers appear when tree as young as 11 years old

Seeds: Winged keys, 4–7 cm (1.6–2.8 in) long, joined in pairs at roughly right angles, but often with only one side fully developed; take just 3 weeks to mature, turning from red to green and then yellowish or reddish-brown; abundant crops almost every year

Bark: Grey and smooth on young trees, fissuring with age into broad, flaking, often shaggy vertical strips

Roots: Soft, very fibrous, shallow, widespread, fast growing

Wood: Light-brown heartwood, thick creamy white sapwood, with straight, fine grain, 510 kg/m^3 (33 lb/cu ft), hard, brittle, rot-prone; usually used for veneer, cheap furniture, crates and pulp

Heat equivalent of 1 m^2 (35 cu ft) of silver maple wood: 144 L (32 gal) of oil

Range: Southern Ontario to about New Liskeard and Sudbury, and close to U.S. border in north-western Ontario; also in all other provinces except Newfoundland

Famous silver maple: Tree planted in 1820s and said to have inspired "The Maple Leaf Forever" still stands, 1.5 m (5 ft) wide, on Laing St. in Toronto

Also see: Sugar Maple, Norway Maple, Green Ash

SUGAR MAPLE
Glowing with National Pride

CANADA'S MOST famous tree, whose leaf adorns the national flag, is not exactly a city slicker. Although sugar maple dominates forests throughout most of southern and central Ontario, it doesn't cope nearly as well with pollution, heat stress, drought, limited soil surface and road salt as other urban trees. Consequently, it's most often relegated to quieter, less-travelled streets, backyards and parks.

There's probably more sugar maple indoors than outdoors in the city, laid down as hardwood floors and used for furniture, veneer, plywood, guitars, cutting boards, bowling pins and many other products that require hard, durable, attractive wood. The tree provides far more hardwood lumber than any other species in Ontario. It also provides first-rate, long-burning firewood and charcoal. In the countryside, maple woodlots maintained on most farms once provided families with their primary source of heat, building materials, sugar and syrup, as well as ashes for soap and a high-potassium fertilizer.

Wherever they do turn up as living trees in the city, sugar maples shine come autumn like no other. Standing out with glowing colours that put the other city maple species to shame, they begin transforming well before most urban trees, which is why fall seems to come much earlier to the countryside. The flaming colours of sugar maples along the slopes of Toronto's Don Valley, however, give hundreds of thousands of commuters a rare opportunity to take in the season's full glory in the heart of the city.

Sugar maples begin to change colour in September, when they've already withdrawn more than half of the nutrients from their leaves back into their branches in

Average mature height:
12–21 m (39–69 ft)

Average mature trunk width:
60–90 cm (2–3 ft)

Ontario giant: 39.6 m (130 ft) tall, 1.2 m (4 ft) wide, in Wellesley Township, Waterloo Region

Average lifespan: 200–300 years

Ontario's oldest known sugar maple: Comfort maple, said to be more than 500 years old, is 25 m (82 ft) tall and 1.9 m (6.5 ft) wide, on the Comfort farmstead, near St. Catharines

Minimum width for sap tapping: 25 cm (10 in), usually when 25–30 years old

Rate at which spring sap rises: 30–120 cm (1–4 ft) per hour

Total spring sap collected per tree: 0.5–4 L (1–8 pt)

preparation for winter and they begin losing their ability to make green chlorophyll. At the same time, their leaves use accumulated sugars to produce red anthocyanin – the same pigments that colour cherries, grapes, beets, radishes and many other vegetables and flowers. The pigment may help protect the leaves from cold so they can salvage as many nutrients as possible before cold nights below 7°C (45°F) cause a waterproof abscission barrier to form at the end of leaf stems. Then the green fades completely to reveal the brilliant red hues.

Sugar maple leaves can also turn yellow and orange. The sunnier the autumn, the brighter the colours, with the best oranges and scarlets appearing on the most exposed or southern side of trees. Eventually, as the anthocyanins in turn break down, red and orange leaves join those in shadier parts of the tree in fading to yellow. Jack Frost is not responsible for painting leaves bright colours. He shrivels and oxidizes them, turning them brown.

Native peoples revered the sugar maple both for its beauty and the gift of its sweet sap. The first run of sap, during the time of greatest privation at the end of winter, was greeted with ceremonies of thanksgiving. In Ojibway legend, a stand of bright autumn maples near a waterfall hid Nokomis, grandmother of the fabled magician Nanabush, from a band of evil windigo spirits chasing her. Through the mist of the waterfall, the windigos were convinced they were staring at a blazing fire in which Nokomis must have died. Nanabush rewarded the sugar maples by giving them sweet, strong-flowing sap.

The Ojibway, Iroquois and other groups collected sugar maple sap by placing a flat stick, hollowed alder stem or reed in a gash in the bark and catching the drips in birch bark containers or hollow logs. A family group commonly spent the better part of a month tapping hundreds of trees and collecting thousands of litres of sap in a hereditary sugar bush within their traditional hunting grounds. The sap was boiled, then strained or dried in the sun on sheets of birchbark. Much of the maple sugar produced was stored for use into the following winter. Until about the 1840s, it was the main source of sugar for pioneers as well.

Average number of litres of sap to make one litre of maple syrup: 35–40

Sugar content of sap: Average 2.5–3%, up to 7%

Average sugar content of sap of most other maples: 1–2%

Alias: Hard maple, rock maple, sweet maple, sugar tree, l'érable à sucre, Acer saccharum

Whereabouts: Backyards, parks, quiet streets and forests with deep, rich, well-drained soil

Leaves: 8–13 cm (3–5 in) long, smooth edges, wide V- or U-shaped spaces between prominently points lobes; growing in opposite pairs on branch

Bark: Smooth and grey when young, becoming darker with age, with long, broad, chunky ridges, often curling outwards

Sex: Clusters of tiny greenish-yellow petal-less flowers, hanging like tassels from branch tips in early to mid-May; first blooms when about 35 years old

Seeds: Green, winged keys, 2–4 cm (0.8–1.6 in) long, joined in pairs with both wings pointing in same direction; only one key in each pair contains a seed; shed in autumn; big crops, up to 12.5 million seeds per ha (2.5 acre), every 3–5 years

Wood: Light yellow-brown, close-grained and often wavy, hard, heavy, strong, durable, 705 kg/m^3 (44 lb/cu ft), very warm burning

Heat equivalent of 1 m^3 (35 cu ft) of sugar maple wood: 196 L (43 gal) of oil

Canuck sluggers: In recent years, dense sugar maple baseball bats made by Ottawa carpenter Sam Holman have become a high-quality alternative in the major leagues to less-durable traditional white ash bats

Roots: Deep, widespread

Companion trees and shrubs in wild: Beech, black cherry, yellow birch, white pine, hemlock, basswood, red maple

Frequent diners: Squirrels, deer mice, chickadees, evening grosbeaks, ruffed grouse and purple finches eat seeds; deer browse leaves, twigs or bark

Common sap sippers: Yellow-bellied sapsuckers, squirrels, chickadees, mourning cloak butterflies, Noctuid moths

Range: Southern Ontario to southern edge of boreal forest; also in Quebec, Maritime provinces; planted in western cities

Early uses of the maple leaf as an emblem: By St-Jean-Baptiste Society in 1834; *Maple Leaf* literary journal, in 1848; first Canadian penny in 1858; coat of arms of both Ontario and Quebec in 1868; Canadian Expeditionary Force in the First World War

One cent botanical blunder: Canadian pennies since 1938 incorrectly depict two maple leaves with stems attached at alternating points along a twig. Maples are among the few native trees, along with ashes and dogwoods, with leaves arranged in opposite pairs

Also see: Norway Maple, Silver Maple, Manitoba Maple, Stars & Constellations

Today, sugar maple sap is collected in some large urban parks for demonstration. Even a few neighbourhoods have organized their own community maple run festivals by tapping the trees on their streets, including some of the lower yielding silver and Norway maples. With many cities and conservation organizations promoting the planting of more native maples, the practice could become more worthwhile in coming years.

March days up to 5 °C (41 °F) and nights below freezing increase pressure within a tree, which stores sugars during winter in spaces within the deadwood portions of the trunk and branches. Sap only flows if there is a tap hole or natural wound in the tree, providing an outlet for the pressurized, melted sugar-water solution. The end comes when sap-swollen buds start producing amino acids, which get into the tree's circulation, giving any resulting syrup a bitter taste. In the country, it's sometimes called the "frog run" because it occurs around the same time that spring peepers start calling from newly thawed forest ponds.

The wider and deeper a maple's crown, the more light it captures and the more abundant and sweeter its sap. Over the past few decades, even in the countryside, the crowns of many sugar maples have withered under the combined assault of acid rain, invading gypsy moths from Europe, low snowfalls and higher temperatures. Because soil nutrients dissolve into acidic water solutions more readily than usual, they are washed away in acid-rain runoff more quickly than they can be replenished by decaying vegetation. At the same time, acid precipitation frees up 10 to 30 times as much aluminium into soil solution as is normal. Aluminium is toxic to trees. To avoid absorbing it, roots diminish their uptake, further starving themselves of nutrients in the process. Once undernourished, trees fall easy prey to root- or heart rot fungi and other natural afflictions.

TREE OF HEAVEN
King of the Concrete Jungle

GROWING BESIDE the foundations of old factory walls, in vacant lots, back alleys and the meanest streets of the concrete jungle, the tree of heaven is a scrappy immigrant that has become so part of southern Ontario's urban landscape, it's largely anonymous. The inner-city dweller's obscurity belies a richly storied past and miraculous powers, not least being its reputation as the fastest-growing species of any tree or shrub in eastern North America.

The tree hails from the Orient, where its ability to shoot rapidly to the sky, growing up to three centimetres (1.2 inches) a day, or three metres (10 feet) in a single year, inspired its lofty name. In the Moluccas of Indonesia, it was called *ailanto*, translated as "tree of heaven" or "tree of the gods," from which derives its other common name, ailanthus. In China, its leaves are the primary food of a moth caterpillar whose cocoons have since ancient times been the source of a coarse-but-durable variety of silk. The bark was, and is, also used to treat many digestive ailments and other problems.

In 1751, the tree of heaven was sent to Europe by a French Jesuit botanist in the employ of the emperor of China. It was a time when early botanists were scouring the world for new and interesting species to record for science and plant in botanical gardens back home. The Asian transplants took well to their new surroundings, where they stood out for their tropical looks, with languidly undulating limbs and palmlike branches. Soon, the instant trees were being planted in city squares and private yards in Britain and about 30 years later made their way across the Atlantic to the United States.

Planting the tree of heaven really came into vogue in the United States in the early 1800s with the spread of

Average mature height:
   10–18 m (33–59 ft)
Average trunk width: 30–75 cm
   (1–2.5 ft)
Maximum height: 25 m (82 ft)
Annual growth in first years:
   1–2 m (3.3–6.6 ft)
Lifespan: Average 30–50 years,
   up to 90 years
Alias: Ailanthus, Chinese sumac,
   stinking ash, ghetto palm, copal
   tree, l'ailante glanduleux,
   Ailanthus altissima
Whereabouts: Vacant lots, back
   alleys, yards, unkept hedges
   and spaces near building foundations, Hydro corridors, railway
   embankments and other
   shrubby open areas
Leaves: Compound, composed of
   11–41 pointy leaflets, each

5–15 cm (2–6 in) long, 1.5–5 cm (0.6–2 in) wide, many with 1–2 teeth near base, dark green on top, lighter below, turning yellow in autumn or falling unchanged with first killing frost; central stalk 25–75 cm (10–30 in) long; smelly if crushed; leafing out in late May

Flowers: Yellow-green, 5 mm (0.2 in) wide, with 5 narrow petals, in upright branched clusters 10–30 cm (4–12 in) long and wide; males and females usually on separate trees; pollinated by bees, flies, beetles and other insects

Seeds: Each in the middle of a flat, spirally twisted wing, 3–5 cm (1.2–2 in) long, 1 cm (0.4 in) wide, yellow to purple-red at first, maturing in Sept. and fading to brown, hanging in large clusters, like ragged pompoms, into winter

Bark: Smooth and greenish with white speckles at first, soon turning more olive, later grey-brown and rough with thin, wavy yellow-tan fissures

Twigs: Thick, blunt-tipped, reddish brown with large, distinctive heart-shaped, tan-coloured leaf stalk scars in winter

Roots: Widespread, shallow, many at surface, few reaching below 45 cm (1.5 ft)

Wood: Streaked, light-yellow heartwood, thick creamy white sapwood, wide-grained, soft, smooth, brittle, weak

Common nibblers and ailments: Tent caterpillars, ailanthus webworm, honey mushroom

the notion that it could somehow absorb poisonous contagions from the air. At the time, infectious diseases were popularly believed to be caused by noxious vapours emanating from swamps and other "unhealthy" places, as suggested by the Italian word *malaria*, literally "bad air." But repeated epidemics, especially devastating visitations of cholera in crowded American cities in the 1830s and 1840s, turned paranoid public opinion against the foreign trees. Perhaps, it was reasoned, they were really trees of hell, giving off all of their stored deadly gases when they bloomed in late June and July. The male flowers, indeed, waft a conspicuously stinky-sock smell that's a characteristic scent of early summer in the city. Denunciations soon led to widespread persecution of the wayward silk trees. Meanwhile, in France, Louis Pasteur and his microscope confirmed for the first time the existence of germs as the cause of contagious disease in 1868 while investigating a plague that was devastating France's domestic silkworms and the high-fashion industry they supported.

As it turns out, the tree of heaven was in North America to stay. The species is virtually impossible to eradicate. If cut down, it sprouts up faster than before from its roots. It flowers when as young as six weeks old and can eventually produce up to 350,000 winged, wind-borne seeds a year. It's been called the most pollution-tolerant tree known, thriving in dusty downtown margins, free of competition from most other plants. The tree grows from cracks where pavement meets fence, wedges into awkward spaces between walls and posts, and rises up through metal grates in back alleyways. Its urban spunk was immortalized as the symbol of perseverance in a tenement slum in the famous Second World War–era novel, and film, *A Tree Grows in Brooklyn*.

The tree of heaven also takes root along recently cutback Hydro corridors, rail embankments and other disturbed sites, where it often forms dense thickets from suckering root sprouts. With rows of pointy leaflets, crooked trunks and sparse, wavy branches, an ailanthus colony can resemble a clump of staghorn sumac, but lacks the velvet fuzz that covers the sumac's similarly thick, blunt twigs. Colonies fight back competing plants and trees by producing a chemical, called ailanthene, that inhibits the seeds and early growth of other species. Because it breaks down in only four days, it's being studied for possible use as a natural herbicide. Both in thickets and alleyways, though, most young trees of heaven never come close to the heights for which they're named, their weak, brittle stems and branches commonly breaking in storms, heavy frosts and snow.

Another Oriental ornamental, the **white mulberry** tree, grows in many southern Ontario yards and often escapes to join the tree of heaven on unkept property lines and vacant lots. It has shiny spade-shaped leaves, some with one or two narrow notches, and bears dark raspberrylike fruits in early summer. Milky-sapped mulberry leaves are the raw material eaten by the common silkworm caterpillar to produce cocoons yielding the finest soft, smooth, glossy silks, once worth more than their weight in gold in the Roman Empire, at the other end of the ancient Silk Road. The attendant caterpillars for both the mulberry and the tree of heaven were imported with the trees in failed bids to set up a silk-making industry in North America in the 1800s.

Ginkgo, the sacred tree of Buddhist and Taoist temple gardens in China, is also planted in Ontario parks, cemeteries and around public buildings as far north as Sudbury and Sault Ste. Marie. Also known as the maidenhair tree, it has unique, delicately ribbed leaves shaped like little fans. It's considered a "living fossil," the sole surviving member of one of the first families of deciduous trees that emerged more than 250 million years ago. There are also no known populations of ginkgo in the wild, even in its homeland. Like the tree of heaven, it comes in either one sex or the other, but in the ginkgo's case, the female tree is the smelly one, bearing rank fruits resembling tiny plumbs.

root rot, leaf spot fungi, black mildew, verticillium wilt fungus
Range: In southern Ontario to about Kitchener, Toronto and Belleville; also in southern Quebec and British Columbia
Also see: Manitoba Maple, Weeping Willow, Moths, Wetlands

TREMBLING ASPEN
Blowing into the City

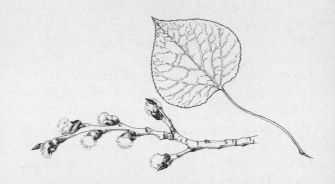

MURMURING AND SHIMMERING in the slightest breeze, the trembling aspen has a name that fits. The trembling is due to long, flat leaf stems that are more easily swayed by the wind than if they were round. According to certain European legends, aspens shake because the wood of Christ's cross was made from one. North American natives called the tree "noisy leaf "or "noisy tree," while in several European languages it is referred to, as least by the men, as "woman's tongue."

Light, tiny aspen seeds, borne on tufts of fluff in June, travel for kilometres in the air to find open natural areas even in cities to germinate and take root. The narrow-crowned trees are also planted in suburban neighbour-hoods and parks, around malls and other commercial buildings, and along parkways and hillsides needing erosion control. Though not the most stately, impressive city trees, they cover much of Ontario, especially in the boreal forest, where their windborne seeds quickly find areas newly opened up by fires, logging or other distur-bances. Once established, they spread rapidly with suck-ering roots that produce vast colonies of clones.

Aspens grow quickly and die young. In nature, the sun-loving trees begin to give way in 60 years or so to shade-tolerant maple, beech, spruce and other species that are nurtured in the nutrient-rich aspen leaf litter. But if a forest is ravaged frequently enough, aspen root networks, protected below the soil, can continually send up new shoots and survive indefinitely. In Utah, a stand of more than 47,000 genetically identical trembling aspens is estimated to be one million years old and to weigh six million kilograms (13.2 million pounds), making it, by some definitions, the world's largest and oldest organism.

Another native poplar species, **eastern cottonwood**, usually produces new sprouts from old stumps, rather than its roots. Named for its fluff-fibred seeds, cottonwood grows along sandy waterfronts and riverbanks in Toronto, Windsor, Kingston and other cities and towns along Lake Erie and Lake Ontario. Its shiny green leaves are generally larger than those of trembling aspen, with sharply pointed tips and wide, straight bases. Though only living up to about 50 years, cottonwood is Canada's fastest-growing native tree, reaching up to 30 metres (98 feet) tall and more than a metre (3.3 feet) thick, developing very deeply furrowed, dark-grey corky ridges.

Lombardy poplar, an introduced European species closely related to cottonwood, is a widely planted ornamental tree, distinctive for its dense, trunk-hugging, upward-pointing branches, forming a very slender, pillarlike crown. It grows in rows as a suburban property-line and driveway tree, or in narrow spaces between downtown office buildings. The tree is often killed, however, by fungal cankers and boring beetles when only 15 to 20 years old and is increasingly being replaced by a similarly slender variety of the hardy European white poplar.

Wider-crowned **white poplar** cultivars are common in cities as well, sometimes growing along streets and highway embankments, sporting variable, widely toothed oval to maplelike leaves strikingly brightened with white, woolly hairs on their undersides. They're usually female trees, but are often pollinated by closely related native aspens and release seeds that sprout as hybrids among the city's wild-growing aspens.

reach about 10 cm (4 in) long; germinate or die within a few days; big crops every 4–5 years

Roots: Mostly shallow, very widespread, producing numerous suckers; thin sinker roots can reach down 3 m (10 ft)

Wood: Greyish white, with a fine, straight grain, soft, brittle, weak, 450 kg/m³ (28 lb/cu ft), much heavier when green

Wood specialties: Extensively cut for pulp, especially for magazine stock; also used for chipboard, plywood, matches, chopsticks, crates and fine shavings for stuffing and packing

Heat equivalent of 1 m³ (35 cu ft) of trembling aspen wood: 117 L (26 gal) of oil

Common nesters: Robins, juncos, warbling vireos and yellow-rumped warblers in branches; woodpeckers, tree swallows, chickadees, nuthatches and wood ducks in cavities

Frequent diners: Beavers, mice and rabbits eat bark; deer browse twigs, leaves and catkins; evening grosbeaks and ruffed grouse eat winter buds

Fungal feeders: False tinder conk commonly infects 40–70% of mature aspens; also other bracket fungi, *Hypoxylon* canker, root rot

Range: All of Ontario to the treeline; also in all other provinces and territories except Nunavut

First appearance of poplars: About 100 million years ago

Number of poplar species native to Ontario: 4

Number of poplar species worldwide: 35–40

Also see: Beaver

WOODS
Remnant Patches of What Was Once Wilderness
Still Hold a Powerful Allure

Portion of Ontario's forest cover south of the Canadian Shield that remains: Less than 20%

Forest cover in extreme southwestern Ontario (around Windsor, Chatham and Sarnia): 4%

Area of original forests left in southern Ontario: 60 km² (23 sq mi)

Average age of forest stands in southern Ontario: Less than 70 years

Carolinian forest zone: Area south of a line running from Toronto to Cambridge, Stratford and Grand Bend

Largest tract of Carolinian forest left in Ontario: Backus Woods, southwest of Simcoe, 4.2 km² (1.6 sq mi)

Tallest deciduous tree in eastern North America: Tulip tree, up to 35 m (115 ft) in Ontario, where it's a rare Carolinian species; more than 65 m (213 ft) in southern United States

Ontario's latest-blooming tree or shrub: Witch hazel, a shrubby Carolinian understory tree, has bright-yellow flowers with long, thin, twisted petals in late Sept. and Oct.

Some other Carolinian forest trees: Shellbark hickory, pignut hickory, blue ash, flowering dogwood, sassafras, black gum, pawpaw, Kentucky coffee-tree, cucumber tree

Number of tree species considered rare in Ontario: 40

PATCHES OF WOODS in large parks, ravines and other refuges persist in varying states of natural order within most cities in Ontario. Many, especially smaller woodlots, are highly disrupted, mixed with many invasive species or harbour little ground cover on heavily travelled, hard-packed forest floors. But the deepest reaches of the best tracts can still abound in a rich diversity of native trees seldom seen on city streets and bloom in almost otherworldly displays of flourishing spring wildflowers. They also ring with choruses of forest-interior nesting birds that are absent elsewhere in the city. Some urban woods as far north as Toronto additionally host smatterings of Carolinian species, inhabitants of the biologically richest, but most threatened, forest zone in Canada.

Beech   18–25 m (59–82 ft) tall

Silvery smooth, curvaceous trunks make beech one of the most attractive trees in the woods, especially on a sunny, leafless winter's day. The trees are favourite signposts for lovers' initials and other graffiti because a permanent layer of cork rises up like a bump along the incisions made in their thin, seamless bark. Such wounds, however, can also allow wood-rotting fungi to get a foothold. In the autumn, bristly husked beech nuts rain down on the forest floor and later produce hardy, shade-tolerant seedlings.

White Ash   10–21 m (33–69 ft) tall

Finely furrowed, light-grey bark, forming patterned, interlacing ridges, instantly sets white ash apart from all other trees. The trunk is straight and elegant, often not branching until near the top. High above in the branches, ash leaves bear five to nine oppositely paired, pointy leaflets, while the tree's narrow, paddle-winged seeds dangle in thick tassels.

Hemlock   20–25 m (66–82 ft) tall

Commonly growing on cool, north-facing ravine slopes and hillsides, hemlocks are big, graceful, short-needled evergreens that throw the densest shade of any trees in the woods. There's usually little beneath a small grove of hemlocks except a thick, soft mat of fallen needles. The chunky-ridged evergreens are often the oldest trees in the forest, sometimes having grown extremely slowly in the dark understory for 200 years before suddenly shooting upwards when a spot opens in the canopy after another tree topples.

Yellow Birch   18–23 m (59–75 ft) tall

The bronze, shaggy trunks of yellow birch often mingle with those of hemlock or white cedar in moist woods. The trees' thick, flexing roots sometimes clutch the ground, stumps or boulders like giant birds' claws, while the trunks may bend and contort around other trees. Unlike the short-lived white birch, they can survive for 200 or 300 years, with the smooth, paper bark of their youth greying and cracking into deep fissures as they become thick-bodied, towering monarchs.

Black Cherry   20–22 m (66–72 ft) tall

Unlike its shrubby relatives, black cherry matures into a tall tree, with distinctive dark, flaky bark, deep in the forest, scattered among other hardwoods. It rises on a strong, narrow trunk and has a relatively small crown that produces dark-red, almost black cherries in August and September.

Black Walnut   20–30 m (66–98 ft) tall

Probably the most common of the Carolinian nut trees, black walnut grows mainly in rich, low-lying river valley forests. Its thick, wide-spreading limbs reach upwards to form a lofty, rounded profile. Walnut leaves are composed of 15 to 23 individual leaflets arranged along a stalk up to 60 centimetres (two feet) long. Large, round green fruit containing the tree's creased nuts plunge to the ground in autumn.

Number of rare Ontario trees that are Carolinian species: 32

Southern Ontario tree species listed as threatened: American chestnut, Kentucky coffee-tree, blue ash, cucumber-tree

Portion of forest wildlife species that use cavities in dead standing trees for nesting, roosting, hibernating or evading predators: About 25%

Common forest plants: Wild ginger, toothwort, Canada mayflower, wild sarsaparilla, doll's eyes, blue cohosh, white snakeroot, foamflower, bellflower, Indian cucumber, wood anemone, Dutchman's breeches, starflower

Urban forest nesters: Red-eyed vireos, white-breasted nuthatches, wood-pewees, great crested flycatchers, great horned owls, downy woodpeckers, pileated woodpeckers, wood thrushes, veeries

Southern Ontario forest nesters listed as at risk: Acadian flycatcher endangered; red-shouldered hawk, red-headed woodpecker, hooded warbler threatened; Louisiana waterthrush, yellow-breasted chat, cerulean warbler vulnerable

Also see: Sugar Maple, White Pine, White Trillium, Solomon's Seal, Skunk Cabbage, Violets, Alien Invaders

Ironwood   8–12 m (26–40 ft) tall

Rising like a sturdy pole, ironwood grows straight up above the shrubs in the understory, but not beyond the shade beneath the forest canopy. With the densest, strongest wood in Canada, the tree is justly compared to an iron bar growing in the forest. The thin trunk is distinguished by its narrow strips of fine, shredding grey bark, almost like cedar in texture. Jagged-edged, spearhead-shaped ironwood leaves, too, are notably soft and supple. In the fall, the tree litters the ground with distinctive bunches of overlapping seed sacs, resembling hop fruits.

Wild Leek   15–60 cm (6–24 in) tall

Emerging patches of bright-green, onionlike leaves of wild leek are often the first sign of life on the drab forest floor in early April. The pairs and triplets of the strong-scented leaves don't last long after fully spreading out, however, usually shrivelling before their small white flowers bloom in June. The flowering stalks remain standing into early autumn, with clusters of tiny black seeds outstretched like little BBs at the ends of thin, delicate stalks.

Trout Lily (Illustrated)
10–25 cm (4–10 in) tall

Long before tree buds burst, fresh green and brownish-purple trout lily leaves spear up through the leaf litter, unfurl and present their nodding yellow, pointed-petalled flowers. By the time of leafout in the trees above, the flowers are finished, with even the tuliplike leaves dying back by June.

Spring Beauty   10–20 cm (4–8 in) tall

Dotted in the carpet of green trout lily leaves in April, tiny bouquets of spring beauties offer pink-and-white greetings in early spring. They too are short-lived, with the plants' basal leaves usually dying by the time the flowers bloom, and the flowers setting seed soon afterwards.

Bloodroot   15–25 cm (6–10 in) tall

Another early bloomer, bloodroot usually has eight delicate white petals spreading from a yellow centre. A single kidney-shaped, lobed leaf initially cups closely around the flowering stem. Lying flat in the morning, the flower petals point straight up by late afternoon and close in the evening. The red juice of the plant's roots was once used by native peoples as a dye.

Hepatica   5–15 cm (2–6 in) tall

Fortified from the chill of April by woolly stems, hepatica bears small white, pink or lavender-blue flowers with six petals. After the flowers finish, the plant produces new three-lobed, low-lying leaves that last through winter.

Mayapple   30–50 cm (12–20 in) tall

Colonies of mayapple unfold their broad, deeply lobed leaves like umbrellas to form a low, even canopy over the ground in late April or early May. Then, in the shade below, each fertile plant blooms with a single waxy-white, nodding flower, which later develops into a green "apple," about five centimetres (two inches) wide.

Jack-in-the-pulpit   30–40 cm (12–16 in) tall

Sporting a green or purplish-brown, often-striped hood surrounding a thick green or purple club, jack-in-the-pulpit is unlike any other flower in the woods. After blooming in May and June, the hoods of female plants persist until late summer to protect their small clusters of bright-green berries, which later turn scarlet.

Wild Columbine (illustrated) 30–60 cm (12–24 in) tall

With elaborate hanging blossoms of red spires joined at a frilly yellow centre, wild columbine sets itself apart where sunbeams reach patches of thin soil on rocky forest outcrops. Blooming from late May to July, the flowers reserve rich caches of nectar at the apex of their long spires for the long, probing beaks of hummingbirds.

WEEPING WILLOW
Source of Beauty, Relief and Magic

A TREE THAT everyone knows and most admire, the weeping willow seems to come alive in the breeze, lifting and sweeping like a woolly mammoth shaking its luxuriant mane. The long, wispy, whiplike branchlets, hanging to the ground, make the willow appear much larger than other trees of equal size. In late autumn, the branchlets turn into golden tresses, their thin, pointy leaves presenting a final show after a growing season appearance that lasts longer than that of just about any other deciduous tree in Ontario.

Weeping willows originate in China, home to the world's greatest diversity of willows, which comprise a very large genus. The tree's sublime form accompanies pagodas and sugarloaf mountains in recurring motifs in traditional Chinese art. Most of Ontario's weeping willows, however, are not really the same trees. Rather, they are "golden weeping willows," hybrids between the original and the European white willow, and are much better suited to cold northern winters than the classic Chinese weeping willow. Named for their yellow twigs, the golden weepers also tend to grow six or seven metres (20 to 23 feet) taller than the Chinese tree.

Confusion reigns among the willows because most can crossbreed easily with others. **White willow** is also planted in Ontario, but is also crossed with **crack willow**, another large European species that was used by British colonial garrisons to provide the charcoal used for fine cannon powder. Often miscalled black willow – which is the name for a smaller native species – wild-growing hybrid crack willows dot many urban ravines and rivers, with their thick-ridged, bent, craggy trunks and branches sometimes leaning out over the water. Yet the trees do not produce seeds. Instead they spread when

Average mature height:
10–15 m (33–49 ft)
Average trunk width:
60–120 cm (2–4 ft)
Maximum height: Up to 25 m (82 ft)
Alias: Golden weeping willow, *le saule pleureur dore, Salix x sepulcralis*
Meaning of *Salix*: From the Celtic words for "near," *sal*, and "water," *lis*
Whereabouts: Watersides, parks, cemeteries, golf courses, yards
Leaves: 4–12 cm (1.6–4.7 in) long, 1–2 cm (0.4–0.8 in) wide, with finely toothed edges and gradually tapered ends, shiny green on top, pale and finely haired on bottom, turning yellow in autumn

their brittle limbs and branchlets snap off during storms. Falling onto the ground or carried away in the current, the severed branches can, like those of most willows, sprout roots and grow into new trees wherever they make contact with moist soil.

Almost all willows share an affinity for water and grow rapidly in moist or mucky spots. Waterside weeping willows can reach up to 14 metres (46 feet) in 20 years. Like other fast-growing trees, their thirsty roots also spread extensively, sometimes invading old clay drains when grown in backyards and siphoning off moisture from gardens. A heavy litter of leaves and whippy branchlets in late fall doesn't make everyone happy either.

But in early spring, before there's much green anywhere, the tree miraculously brightens with the growth of shiny new yellow shoots. Soon afterwards, soft, thin catkins emerge. Though not resembling conventional flowers, the yellow catkins do produce nectar to entice many pollinating insects. Early flowering species, such as the shrubby pussywillows growing in many backyards, provide bumblebees rousing from winter dormancy with their first square meals, allowing them to lay eggs early enough for large numbers of offspring to be around for the floral parade later in the year.

Willows have also been of great importance to people for thousands of years. Willow bark contains sugar-based chemicals – possibly serving to purge impurities – which have been among humankind's most important medicines. Both the ancient Greeks and native healers in Ontario used the bitter bark, often brewed as a tea, to ease pain and break fevers. The Ojibway applied the bark to sores and wounds as well, and smoked it mixed with tobacco. Europeans used it specifically for headaches at least as far back as the 1400s. In the early 19th century, chemists discovered the compound salicin to be the active ingredient. By the end of the century, synthesized salicylic acid was being sold as a new German wonder drug called Aspirin.

Prehistoric cultures around the world used willows for many things. Branchlets and twigs were perfect for basketry, one of the oldest crafts. Pieces of baskets 10,000 years old have been found in caves in Utah, and

Sex: Minute flowers crowded on upright, thin yellow catkins, males 2–5 cm (0.8–2 in) long, females 2–3 cm (0.8–1.2 in) long, appearing on separate trees, May to June; insect- and probably wind-pollinated

Catkin **word origin:** From the Dutch *katteken*, meaning "little cat"

Seeds: Very tiny, attached to tufts of fluff, released in June, germinating within 1–2 days or dying

Bark: Light brown to dark grey, corky, forming wavy, twisting ridges and deep furrows with age

Roots: Widespread

Wood: Light-coloured, straight-grained, light, soft, weak but tough, shock absorbent

Willow wood specialties: Because it does not split, has been used to make clogs, artificial limbs, bats, balls and mallets for cricket and croquet; also wicker, folksy furniture

Polo connection: Polo comes from the Persian word for willow root, *pulu*, from which the sport's balls are made

Range: Southern Ontario north to North Bay, Wawa and Thunder Bay; also in all other provinces

Portion of modern medicines originally derived from wild plants and trees: More than 40%

Willow-pattern ware: Popular blue dinnerware design depicting the story of two recently eloped young Chinese lovers caught on a garden bridge, beside a large willow, by the bride's infuriated father. To save them, the gods change the lovers into birds and they fly away. Said to be an ancient Chinese legend, the story was really a marketing ploy invented by British manufacturers in the 1780s selling cheap knockoffs of imported Chinese porcelain. Chinese potters adopted the design and still sell thousands of tonnes of willow-pattern ware to the West

Charcoal production: Created when wood smoulders slowly under low-oxygen conditions, originally achieved by partly covering piles of wood with earth and setting them on fire

World's most northern shrub: Arctic willow

Number of willow species native to Ontario: About 30

Number of species worldwide: 200–500, depending on classification of species, subspecies and frequent hybrids

Also see: Trembling Aspen, Goldenrod; Bees, Wasps & Hornets; Hummingbird

in the Middle East impressions made by baskets in mud are 6,000 to 7,000 years old. Houses in Europe's first farming communities had wattle walls of willow stems woven between upright posts. Branches were also used to make fishing weirs, bows, grain sieves, snowshoes, kayak ribs, coffins and many other items. The bark of some species, such as Ontario's sandbar willow, was used to make rope, string, clothes, bags and blankets.

Archeological evidence shows that at least in some areas, basketry led to pottery when the clay covering baskets used for cooking became fired and took a hardened, permanent form. Willow may well have figured prominently in the genesis of metal working and smelting as well, which was best accomplished with the intense heat reached by burning charcoal. Though not good firewood, willow is slow burning (as it lacks oils) and is therefore ideal for making charcoal.

Willow was also preferred for making magic. Wands brandished by pagan priests and priestesses were most commonly willow switches. Both "wand" and "willow" come from ancient Germanic and Indo-European words meaning "bend," describing their flexibility. In China, the Taoist goddess of mercy, Kuan Yin, used a willow wand to sprinkle her followers with the divine nectar of life. The Chinese collected furry-budded willow switches on the Ching Ming festival as a rite of spring, as did Christians in Europe on Palm Sunday.

On the other hand, willows were also once linked with Persephone, Hecate and other Greek goddesses of death, perhaps because they usually grew around sacred springs, considered portals to the underworld. Even into modern times, willow boughs are often depicted on tombstones. Along with its connotations of death and sorrow, the tree in Europe came to stand for forsaken love, maybe in part because it is short-lived.

WHITE BIRCH
Water-Resistant, Born to Burn

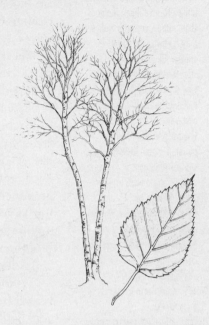

B IRCH FORESTS figure prominently in Canada's wilderness fabric and psyche. But in most cities, especially in southern Ontario, white birch plays a relatively minor role in the urban forest. Still, sometimes planted in yards, especially in the suburbs, it stands out with its famous papery-white bark and the purple haze of its bare winter branches.

Birchbark has a special quality that makes it famous: it resists water and decomposition. A natural wax base makes the bark impermeable, allowing it to last for years on the ground and still burn long after the wood it surrounds turns to mush. Fossilized birch has been found in Siberia with bark still in its original state, while birchbark manuscripts in central Asia are up to 2,000 years old. This characteristic was of inestimable importance to northern woodland peoples, who depended on the bark for their wigwams, canoes, containers and moose-calling cones, as a quick fire-starter even when wet and to wrap their dead for burial.

European white birch, too, was used to make boats and other amenities in the boreal forests of Russia. The tree, which has found its way to many Canadian lawns, resembles the North American white birch, but its bark tends to peal less and its trunk develops scaly black fissures rising from the base and rough patches beneath branches. Its leaves are a little smaller, more sharply tapered toward the tip, and stay on their dangling branches three to four weeks longer than those on the native tree. Some varieties also come with deeply cut, sharply lobed leaves or weeping branches.

Perhaps because of its beauty, birch was considered a magical tree in northern Europe. Brooms were made out of its twigs to sweep away evil, and the Maypole of pagan spring rites was a birch. In Ontario, various Ojibway stories tell of birchbark acquiring its black marks from

Average mature height:
12–21 m (39–69 ft)
Average mature trunk width:
25–40 cm (10–16 in)
Ontario giant: 1.2 m (3.9 ft) wide, 13.6 m (45 ft) tall, in Sundridge
Maximum height: 25 m (82 ft)
Lifespan: Usually 80–140 years, up to 225 years
Time it takes a white birch log to rot: 1–2 years
Time it takes a pine or spruce log to rot: 5–10 years
Alias: Paper birch, canoe birch, silver birch, *le bouleau à papier*, *Betula papyrifera*
Whereabouts: Yards, young woodlands, forest edges
Bark: Shiny dark reddish-brown for about 10 years until peeling back to reveal mature, papery white bark with prominent black

285

hatch marks, called lenticels, which allow air through the bark; stripping bark off trees leaves black scars, weakens and sometimes kills them

Leaves: Light green, about 5–10 cm (2–4 in) long, spade-shaped, serrated, amber or yellow in fall

Sex: 7–10 cm (3–4 in) long, hanging greenish-tan, tassel-like male catkins at twig tips; upright green female flower catkins, 3–5 cm (1.2–2 in) long, farther back on branch; open before leaves in May; first blooms when about 15 years old

Seeds: Winged, 4 mm (0.166 in) long; most released Sept.–Nov. from 4–5-cm-long (1.6–2-in-long), brown, hanging cones; the rest fall through the winter; big crops every 2 years

Wood: Thick, creamy white sapwood, pale-brown heart-wood, with fine, straight grain, smooth, hard, strong, 640 kg/m^3 (40 lb/cu ft), very warm burning

Heat equivalent of 1 m^3 (35 cu ft) of wood: 155 L (34 gal) of oil

Roots: Generally shallow, less than 60 cm (2 ft) deep

Range: From the northern treeline south to about Toronto, London and Sarnia, though planted farther south; also in all other provinces and territories

Number of birch species native to Ontario: 6

Number of birch species world-wide: About 50

Also see: Trembling Aspen, Beaver

the magician-deity Nanabush variously thrashing the tree for allowing some meat it was supposed to be guarding to be stolen by birds, or from a collision with pursuing thunderbirds whom he craftily deked out.

Though its thin, flammable bark makes white birch an unlikely forest-fire survivor, flames are actually its salvation. Having evolved around the cycle of renewal brought by frequent lightning strikes in tinder-dry, resin-soaked boreal woods, birch was born to burn. The tree cannot grow in shade, but by flaming faster than almost any other natural material, birchbark fosters the best conditions for regeneration. Newly burnt-over areas provide sunlight and exposed mineral soil for birch to take root and prosper, often in pure stands. Winged, confetti-sized birch seeds, released from August into winter, can travel great distances to find such sites, especially when blown across the surface of the snow. Birch also resprouts from the base of stumps, producing clumps of two to six trunks, nurtured by surviving root systems that give them a leg up on the seeds of the competition. Like other pioneer species, white birch in general grows more rapidly than the progeny of most other trees, reaching up to three metres (10 feet) in its first five years.

Because birch trees grow quickly, however, their trunks are composed mostly of porous sapwood and contain considerable moisture and sugars, relished by wood-rotting fungi. The wood is also low in the rot-resistant chemicals common in conifers. When little more than 60 years old – and often only 30 years old in the city – white birch tends to become susceptible to heart rot, wood-boring insects and the woodpeckers that seek them, causing the tree to gradually die from the top down. Such trees provide ideal sites for cavity-nesting birds and animals. In the woods, the upper branches are often already in advanced decay before the trunk finally topples.

WHITE CEDAR
The Tree of Life

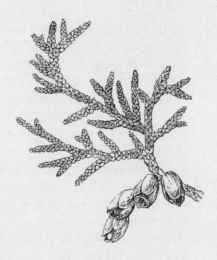

WHITE CEDAR SEEMS to don many guises, depending on where it takes up residence. In the city, especially the suburbs, more than 120 cultivated varieties form orderly hedges and grow as well-behaved, contained ornamental lawn and doorstep trees. They make good hedges because they form new shoots even after heavy trimming and continue growing all summer. They're also pollution-tolerant and are bothered by relatively few pesky insects and diseases, making them healthy, happy, civilized little trees, probably the most popular ornamentals in North America.

Yet feral cedars also frequent dry, gravelly, neglected and forgotten pockets of the city, such as old backroads and warehouse and storage lots. Still others are water hounds, thronging around remnant urban wetlands. The highly adaptable trees take to both situations because of duel abilities of both drought- and rot-resistance.

Cedar wood's durability long made it the material of choice in Canada's early history for fort palisades, log cabins, split-rail fences, shingles, decks and posts. Together with western red cedar, white cedars were once most widely seen in cities as utility poles, before being gradually replaced with stronger, stouter Douglas fir and red, jack and lodgepole pine treated with preservatives for the job. Having the lightest wood of any tree

Average mature height: 10–18 m (30–59 ft); some ornamental varieties 3–6 m (10–20 ft)

Average mature trunk width: 30–45 cm (1–1.5 ft), often divided into 2 or more stems

Ontario giant: 22.6 m (74 ft) tall, 1.1 m (3.6 ft) wide, in Acton

Average annual seedling growth rate: 8 cm (3 in)

Lifespan: Commonly 200–300 years, maximum more than 1,000 years on cliffsides

Alias: Arbor vitae, eastern white cedar, northern white cedar, swamp cedar, eastern thuja, le thuya de l'est, Thuja occidentalis

Whereabouts: Lawns, parks, woods, wetlands, cliffs, dry open areas

Foliage: Light, yellow-green, flat, waxy, scalelike splays, lasting up to 5 years before turning bronze in winter and shedding

Bark: Light grey to reddish-brown, soft, in stringy, shredding vertical strips, spiralling slightly up trunk

Sex: Yellowish male conelets, 1–2 mm (0.083 in) long, on tips of leaves in late Apr. and May; pinkish female conelets, 7–12 mm (0.3–0.5 in) long, usually on separate branches

Cones: 8–13 mm (0.3–0.5 in) long, in dense bunches at tips of branches, especially near treetop, pale green at first, turning brown as they ripen by end of summer, dropping most seeds mid-Sept.–Nov., the rest through winter; big crops every 2–5 years; first cones produced when trees 15–20 years old

Seeds: Light-chestnut brown, encased in 2 wings, landing 45–60 m (150–200 ft) from parent tree

Average annual seedling growth rate: 3 in (8 cm)

Roots: Shallow, thick, extensive on wet and rocky ground; deep taproot formed on thicker, drier soil

Wood: Light yellowish-brown heartwood and thin whitish sapwood, soft, weak, brittle, 304 kg/m^3 (19 lb/cu ft), non-resinous, aromatic, snaps, crackles and pops when burned

Heat equivalent of 1 m^3 (35 cu ft) of white cedar wood: 98 L (21.5 gal) of oil

Companion forest trees: Balsam poplar; red maple, black ash, white spruce, fir and speckled alder in wetter areas and swamps; yellow birch, hemlock, white birch, aspens, white pine and sugar maple on drier sites

in Ontario, much less than half the density of oak, white cedar has also always been popular for canoe and boat frames.

But, in Hamilton, St. Catharines, Owen Sound and other communities along the Niagara Escarpment, white cedars display their most incredible qualities as tenacious, age-old cliff dwellers. The calcium-loving trees fringe the lip of the ancient limestone ridge rising across the breadth of southern Ontario and cling to its sheerest rocky walls. They also grow on cliffs above the Ottawa Valley near the nation's capital. Defying gravity, desertlike conditions and subarctic winter blasts, the unsheltered twisted, gnarly, cliffside cedars wedge their snaking roots into the narrowest crevices and tiniest pockets of soil and hang on for centuries. Eking out the most meagre of livings, they grow at a glacial pace. Many are little more than a metre (3.3 feet) tall and a few centimetres (a couple of inches) thick. Some, with annual growth rings only one cell thick, are considered the slowest-growing trees on Earth.

Protected in their inaccessible locations from wildfire and lumberjacks, communities of the scraggly Escarpment dwarfs probably form the most ancient old-growth forests in eastern North America. Dendro-chronologists – people who study tree rings – have found trees up to a thousand years old and one dead cedar with 1,890 annual growth rings still lying at the base of the cliff from which it had fallen on Flowerpot Island, off the tip of the Bruce Peninsula, around A.D. 856, during Europe's Dark Ages. In 1993, a Canadian Navy mini-sub exploring a flooded canyon in the waters nearby found cedar stumps that were more than 9,000 years old.

White cedar was revered by native peoples. To many, it represented the east, one of the four sacred directional elements (north, west and south were sweetgrass, tobacco and sage respectively). The sweet scent and smoke of its crackling, burning foliage was used to purify a person, place or thing, or to make offerings of thanks to the Creator. A common Québécois name for white cedar is *balai*, meaning "broom," because early settlers fashioned the tree's aromatic green splays into brooms that at once swept and deodorized their homes. Even today, cedar leaf oil is used in perfumes and medicines, and as a deodorizer and insect repellant.

The tree has also been used as medicine for a vast array of ailments. Natives and settlers made an effective poultice from its fibres and placed it on the eyes to cure snow blindness. Tea was also brewed from its foliage for headaches, congestion and scurvy. Like the needles of many other evergreens, cedar contains more vitamin C than oranges. Natives saved Jacques Cartier and his crew from the ravages of scurvy during their first winter in Canada, in 1536, with cedar tea. Cartier brought the seedlings of the wonder tree back to France, where the king promptly named it *arbor vitae*, the "tree of life." Cedar is believed to have been the first North American tree planted in Europe.

In many residential yards, **red cedar** looks much like white cedar from a distance. But its foliage is more sharp and needly, not flat and blunt like white cedar. It also grows naturally in dry, sandy, rocky fields and meadows. The small tree is actually a juniper, in the same genus as several species of native and non-native juniper shrubs also grown around houses, often as hedges. All junipers and white cedar, though, are members of the cyprus family. They were named after true cedars of Lebanon (part of the pine family) because of their similarly aromatic wood. Red cedar was long used to line chests and closets because its aroma was shunned by clothes moths.

Associated plants: Canada mayflowers, false Solomon's seal, mitrewort, oak ferns, lady ferns, northern beech ferns

Common nesters: Robins, blue jays, cardinals, house finches, grackles, song sparrows, yellow warblers, catbirds, cedar waxwings, house wrens

Frequent diners: Rabbits and deer browse foliage; squirrels, mice, goldfinches, cedar waxwings, crossbills and pine siskins eat seeds; winter wrens and yellow-bellied flycatchers also forage on trees

Tiny nibblers: Carpenter ants, cedar leaf miners (moth caterpillars), porcelain grey moth caterpillars, arborvitae aphids, arborvitae weevils

Range: From about Chatham (also planted in Windsor) north almost to James Bay and northwest to Kenora; also in Manitoba, Quebec, the Maritimes and planted in the other western provinces and Newfoundland

Closely related foreigner: Oriental Cedar, with thicker, fleshy foliage, sometimes planted on lawns

World's most widespread shrub: Common juniper

Number of cyprus family species native to Ontario: 4

Number of cyprus family species worldwide: About 60

Also see: White-tailed Deer

WHITE ELM
Angling for a Comeback

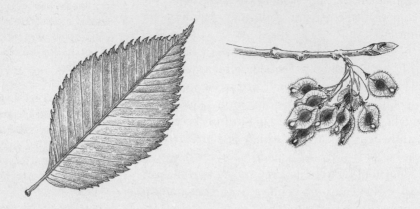

P ROBABLY THE OLDEST and best-known poster tree for the consequences of alien invasion, the fabled white elm still graces city streets with its classic V-shaped form in choice scattered locations. The few great elms that survive, towering a head above surrounding neighbourhood trees, stand as sentinels in the urban forest, bearing witness to a bittersweet past and holding out hope for the future.

Like many native tree species well suited to town and city streets, white elm comes from natural habitats where it often has its feet wet, in and around flood plains, swamps and riverbanks that are inundated in spring. Wherever it gets enough space, the tree's great, upreaching limbs and drooping branch tips form its much-loved symmetrical, expansive, shaggy umbrella canopy. Early pioneers clearing their lands were so taken with the elegant, arching "lady of the forest," they often spared the tree and built their houses beside it. They also enthusiastically planted it along their fencerows.

Freshly shed elm samaras, falling like dime-sized confetti, were easy to collect in late spring and produced hardy seedlings that could be transplanted in autumn. That, and the fact they rose 15 metres (50 feet) in 25 years made them hot items for early nurseries. Soon elm-lined streets forming vaulted corridors of deep shade became *de rigueur* for every pleasant little town and quiet residential neighbourhood across North America. By 1930, there were an estimated 77 million elms in Canadian and American towns and cities, commonly comprising 80 percent of all street trees in many communities.

At the same time, white elm was the third most commonly cut hardwood in Ontario, after sugar maple and yellow birch. Its hard, tough, attractive wood was very popular among 19th-century farm families for kitchen tables and other utilitarian furniture because it always washed very clean and white. The interlocking grain was hard to split, which made it bad for firewood, but ideal for tool handles, hockey sticks, wagonwheel hubs and spokes, and for bending into boat frames. Because it has little scent and held screws better than just about any other wood, it was also widely used to make cheese barrels and crates and baskets for fruits and vegetables.

It was a shipment of such crates, infected with Dutch elm disease, that brought disaster to eastern Canada's shady neighbourhoods, starting in Quebec in 1944. The scourge, which had been ravaging elms south of the border since 1930, is caused by a fungus from Asia that was first identified by a Dutch scientist. It's spread by both foreign and native bark beetles. Stricken elms die of thirst after a few years, with the fungus invading the sapwood's hollow tubular cells and blocking the flow of water. The epidemic reached Ontario in 1946 and was soon denuding cities of their once-magnificent elms. By the early 1970s, the only white elm commonly seen by most Canadians was the one figured prominently in the idyllic rural scene on the back of the two-dollar bill. Soon that one was gone too. Of the 36,000 elms that once greened neighbourhoods around downtown Toronto, about 450 remain. About 2,000 are left in all of Ottawa.

In the countryside, before dying of the disease, most young fencerow and forest elms grow into seed-producing saplings. But by the time they're about 25 years old, with stems 15 to 25 centimetres (six to 10 inches) wide, they're big enough to entice tiny bark beetles to feed in the crown and leave the infamous fungal spores that may spell their ends.

prominent ribs on each side, turning yellow in autumn

Bark: Dark grey-brown with shallow irregular orange-brown fissures when young; deeply furrowed with long, thick ridges on mature trees

Sex: Tiny, reddish-tinged, light-green flowers, 3 mm (0.1 in) wide, with red-tipped stamens; dangle like little tassels in small bunches in Apr., 2–3 weeks before leaves; wind pollinated; trees bloom as young as 15 years old

Seeds: Centred within flat, green, fuzz-fringed, oval wings, 8–12 mm (0.3–0.5 in) long, with sharp, tiny notch at front tips; hanging in small clusters, most falling in late spring within 100 m (328 ft) of parent tree, some more than 400 m (0.25 mi) away; big crops every 2–4 years

Roots: Thick, shallow, widespread, but sometimes reaching down to about 3 m (10 ft) in good, well-drained soil

Wood: Light yellowish- to reddish-brown heartwood, wide whitish sapwood (for which species is named "white elm"), with alluring interlocking grain, 625 kg/m^3 (39 lb/cu ft), rough, hard, tough, water-resistant

Heat equivalent of 1 m^3 (35 cu ft) of white elm wood: 162 L (36 gal) of oil

Companion forest trees: Silver maple, black ash, balsam poplar, Manitoba maple, red maple, slippery elm, black walnut, cottonwood

Common nesters: Flickers, Baltimore orioles, downy

woodpeckers, starlings, yellow warblers, chickadees, brown creepers, white-breasted nuthatches, red-tailed hawks, great horned owls

Frequent diners: Squirrels, opossums, mice, goldfinches, rose-breasted grosbeaks, purple finches, mourning warblers, pine siskins, wood ducks and grouse eat seeds; deer and rabbits browse leaves and twigs

Nibblers and ailments: Elm bark beetles, caterpillars of mourning cloak, question mark and hop merchant butterflies and of cecropia, elm sphinx and elm spanworm moths, Dutch elm disease fungus, honey mushroom, black leaf spot, cankers, artist's conk and other bracket fungi

Number of foreign tree-feeding insect species that have invaded North America: More than 300

Range: Southern half of Ontario to about Timmins, Lake Nipigon and Kenora; also in Maritimes, Quebec, Manitoba, Saskatchewan and planted in Alberta and British Columbia

Commonly planted foreign elms: Wych elm, English elm, Siberian elm

Number of elm species native to Ontario: 3

Number of elm species worldwide: About 18

Also see: Alien Invaders, Green Ash, Silver Maple, Horse Chestnut

Though some large elms have been protected by repeated injections of expensive fungicide, a small remnant core of great-girthed old giants around the province have withstood Dutch elm disease on their own. In many cases, a single large elm may stand in an area that once had hundreds. Over hundreds of years, the offspring of these trees might repopulate Ontario with healthy elms. But the Elm Recovery Project, launched in 1998, aims to do the job within a human lifespan by giving Mother Nature a helping hand. In the mid-1990s, the University of Toronto's forest pathology department cracked the code of genetic tolerance to Dutch elm disease after 20 years of research. Cuttings taken from trees confirmed to be naturally resistant are being used to establish an elite orchard at the University of Guelph's Arboretum, where the disease-tolerant elms can cross-pollinate and create genetically diverse, super-resistant seed crops for commercial nurseries. Derived from a native population adapted to Ontario's climate, such trees should cope far better than the disease-resistant clones or hybrid crosses of white and Siberian elms imported from American nurseries.

Urban riversides, creeks and ravines are also frequented by native **slippery elms** and introduced **Siberian elms**. Named for its slimy, aromatic inner bark, slippery elm is more spindly than white elm and has rougher, larger leaves, 15 to 20 centimetres (six to eight inches) long. Siberian elm, a fencerow tree that has also escaped into vacant urban lots and other neglected spaces, has smooth, little leaves, only two to seven centimetres (0.8 to 2.8 inches) long. Confusing everything, the Siberian and the slippery native often hybridize, producing offspring with leaf sizes falling in between their two ranges. **Wych elm**, a European species planted in parks and yards, bears leaves that often have two additional points, like a pair of horns, on either side of the main terminal tip.

WHITE PINE
Pivotal in Ontario's History

Canada is the scent of pines.
I left my land and returned
to know this and become
   Canadian.
– Milton Acorn, "Poem for
The Astronauts"

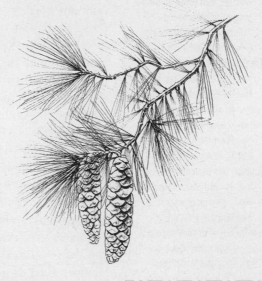

LONG BEFORE Queen Victoria stuck a pin in the map of Canada to choose a capital, white pine was king in Ottawa. The great tree, whose sweeping, wind-sculpted form still rises over many city parks and urban woods, serves as Ontario's official arboreal emblem because of the central role it played in the history of the province, beginning in the once-vast pineries of the Ottawa Valley.

The story starts with Napoleon Bonaparte, who, among his many feats, had a profound and lasting influence on the forests of Ontario. In November 1806, after defeating Prussia and becoming master of northern Europe, he closed the Baltic seaports, cutting off Britain's biggest source of lumber. With supplies dwindling, the huge British Baltic trading fleet sailed to Canada in 1809, sparking a logging boom that quickly spread up the Ottawa Valley and through rich green veins of white pine deep in the interior. Within a year, wood surpassed furs as Canada's biggest export, with tens of thousands of pines cut annually.

White pine was the focus of logging for almost 100 years. Central Ontario's virgin forests were dominated by ancient pines that towered more than 10 storeys, making surrounding hardwoods look like shrubs. Its size and grace, and the many medicines it yielded, made the white pine the Iroquois tree of peace.

Its thick, straight trunk, tapering very gradually and often free of branches for 25 metres (82 feet) or more, made white pine ideal for the masts of Britain's

Average mature height:
   15–30 m (49–98 ft)
Average mature trunk width:
   60–90 cm (2–3 ft)
Ontario giants: More than 56 m (151 ft) tall, in Gillies Grove, Arnprior; 45.1 m (148 ft) tall, 1.7 m (5.6 ft) wide, in Cardiff Township, Haliburton County
Lifespan: Often 200–250 years, maximum more than 450 years
Alias: Eastern white pine, yellow pine, Quebec pine, *le pin blanc*, *Pinus strobus*
Whereabouts: Parks, large yards, cemeteries, golf courses, woods
Ontario's largest remaining old-growth white pine stand: Obabika Lake, Temagami, 2,400 ha (6,000 acres)
Needles: 5–15 cm (2–6 in) long, in bundles of 5, soft, flexible, with finely toothed edges; turn yellow and fall after 1–4 years

Bark: Smooth grey-green on a young tree, with age becoming deeply furrowed, with wide, rough, frosted grey-brown ridges

Sex: Small, light-green male flower conelets appear in bunches near branch tips in May; female flower conelets pink or purplish, at ends of new shoots, mostly near top of tree

Cones: 8–20 cm (3–8 in) long, slender, light green at first, turning woody and tan-brown as they mature over 2 summers, opening in Sept. to release seeds; big crops every 3–5 years

Seeds: With wing about 2 cm (0.8 in) long, averaging 70 per cone

Roots: Widespread, somewhat deep, with 4–10 often visible, thick main roots reaching out from base of trunk

Wood: Pale to reddish-brown heartwood, creamy white to yellow sapwood, soft, strong, clear, with straight, even grain, 415 kg/m^3 (26 lb/cu ft)

Specialty products: Doors, window casings, trim, cabinets, furniture, panels

Heat equivalent of 1 m^3 (35 cu ft) of white pine wood: 103 L (23 gal) of oil

Range: Southern Ontario north to about Timmins and Wawa and west from Lake Superior to Kenora; also in all other eastern provinces, a tiny portion of Manitoba and planted in British Columbia

Number of pine species native to Ontario: 4

Number of pine species worldwide: About 100

Also see: White Spruce, Fungi

world-dominating naval and merchant fleets. Royal Navy warships required main masts 37 metres (120 feet) high and 40 inches (one metre) thick, previously supplied by heavy, pieced-together trunks of smaller Scots pine from the Baltic. In 1811, 23,000 Canadian pine masts were shipped across the Atlantic. Even larger numbers of pines were cut into 12- to 18-metre-long (40- to 60-foot-long) square timbers, tied together and floated down the Ottawa and St. Lawrence Rivers in huge rafts, bound for the saw pits of Britain.

Lumberjacks followed the tributaries of the Ottawa and Trent Rivers far into the headlands of Haliburton and what is now Algonquin Park in the 1830s and 1840s. They spawned legends, such as those of Joe Montferrand – "Joe Mufferaw" of the Stompin' Tom Connors classic – which many believe to be the basis for the American tall tales of Paul Bunyan. Montferrand, though, was a real person, the champion of Québécois *bucherons* against the Irish in the Shiners' War brawls around the swampy little logging settlement of Bytown – later redubbed Ottawa.

Though most of the great stands of white pine were gone by the Second World War, the mechanization of the logging industry has since allowed companies to get many of the remnants. Bulldozers, trucks and logging roads replaced horses and rivers for transporting logs out of previously inaccessible high country. Today, there are only 10 known stands exceeding 500 hectares (1,235 acres) of old-growth white pine left in Ontario.

Even as much of the province's white pine was falling to the axe and saw, Austrian and Scots pine was being planted in towns and cities across Ontario. **Austrian pine**, native to the southern half of Europe, bears dense tufts of stiff, very dark-green needles, up to 16 centimetres (six inches) long, in bundles of two, and large, wide flaky plates of dark-brown to whitish-grey bark. Unlike white pine, it tolerates smog and road salt and is grown along highways and around industrial parks. **Scots pine** has paired twisted needles that are only four to eight centimetres (1.6 to 3.2 inches) long. With the rising interest in restoring native trees to the urban landscape, however, white pine is gaining on both of the foreigners.

WHITE SPRUCE
Bringing Green Cheer to Winter Streets

A CANADIAN tree through and through, white spruce sweeps across most of the country from the northern timberline to just shy of Lake Ontario. Given a helping hand, it's happy to spread its densely needled branches in towns and cities all the way to Windsor, where winters become too short for the northerner, in natural conditions, to maintain an advantage over broadleaf trees. Farther north, spruces and other conifers get the jump on deciduous trees because their evergreen needles can begin to photosynthesize as soon as temperatures rise above 0°C (32°F), allowing them to be productive for the entire short growing season, instead of having to wait for new leaves to unfold.

Individual spruce needles last for five to 10 years before finally falling. New needles, which appear each spring on shoots growing from spruce branch tips, have a brighter, bluish cast than on the older needles that gradually fades with age. The trait is especially pronounced in **Colorado spruce**, native to the U.S. Rockies, from which the landscape industry has developed the extremely popular silvery-blue cultivar known as blue spruce. **Norway spruce**, from northern and central Europe, is also commonly planted in yards, set apart from native white spruce by the distinctive dangling branchlets along the length of its boughs, said to resemble the tooth of a comb or a ragged skirt. Its cones are also much longer than those of white spruce.

Fir trees – both balsam and various non-native species planted in residential neighbourhoods – resemble spruce as well. However, they have flat needles, unlike four-sided spruce needles, which are easily rolled between the thumb and forefinger.

Portion of Ontario's forest that is spruce: 42%

Average mature height: 18–25 m (60–82 ft)

Average trunk width: 30–60 cm (1–2 ft)

Ontario giant: 39 m (128 ft) tall, 79 cm (2.6 ft) wide, in McClure Township, Hastings Co.

Lifespan: Commonly 100–250 years, up to 300 years

Age of 2 m (6.6 ft) high spruce Christmas trees: 7 years

Alias: Cat spruce, Canadian spruce, skunk spruce, l'épinette blanche, Picea glauca

Needles: 1.5–2.2 cm (0.6–0.9 in) long, 4-sided, often with bluish tint; last 7–10 years before dropping

Bark: Light grey and smooth when young, turning darker and scaly or flaky with age

Sex: Male conelet flowers, 1.5–2 cm (0.6–0.8 in) long,

red at first, turning yellow; green to deep-red female conelets, 2–2.5 cm (0.8–1 in) long, high on trees; appear mid-May; wind pollinated

Cones: About 5 cm (2 in) long, with thin, light-brown scales, dropping most of seeds Sept.–Oct., but continue winter and spring; big crops every 2–6 years

Seeds: Attached to rounded, fan-shaped wings, 4–8 mm (0.15–0.3 in) long, 30–140 per cone

Roots: Usually shallow, wide-spread, but putting down deep taproots in well-drained soils

Wood: White or yellowish, soft, smooth, straight grained, durable, 415 kg/m^3 (26 lb/cu ft)

Heat equivalent of 1 m^3 (35 cu ft) of wood: 98 L (21.5 gal) of oil

Special wood qualities: Resonance favoured for pianos, guitars and violins; used for food containers because of lack of taste and odour

Range: From about Kingston, Peterborough and Bruce County north to the treeline, and planted in southern Ontario; also in all other provinces and territories

Number of Christmas trees grown and sold in Ontario annually: About 1 million

Number of spruce species native to Ontario: 3

Number of spruce species world-wide: 35–40

Also see: White Pine

Together with Scots pine, white spruce and balsam fir are the most popular Christmas tree species in Ontario. The Christmas tree tradition traces back to pagan times, when Germans celebrated the winter solstice Yule festival by bringing evergreen boughs, holding the promise of spring and providing shelter for visiting elves, into their homes. Hundreds of years later, they brought the custom with them to North America. It really caught on in Canada in the late 1800s after Queen Victoria, herself of not-distant German lineage, was pictured with her family gathered around a tabletop Christmas tree in the *London Illustrated News*.

Neither trees in the living room or backyard, however, comprise the greatest presence of white spruce in the city. The tree is the biggest source of two-by-fours and other construction lumber, though commonly sold as pine, a general softwood group label. After the big pines were cut from many forests in the 1800s, lumberjacks turned to the next best thing that floats (in log drives). Spruce, with its tall, thick trunk and strong, durable wood, has been a mainstay of the sawmills across North America ever since.

The discovery of efficient techniques for making paper from wood fibre in the 1860s redoubled the economic value of spruce. Paper, invented by the Chinese 2,000 years ago, was previously made from straw or rags. Spruce, even spindly black spruce, was ideal for the new process because its wood is long-fibred, light-coloured and less resinous than other conifers. As supplies of prime lumber trees, a foot (30 centimetres) or more in diameter, dwindled in many areas around the turn of the century, the lumber barons gradually sold their cutting rights to the new pulp and paper companies, which thrived on smaller trees. By the 1930s, they were penetrating deep into the boreal forest, and today an area more than three times the size of Toronto is cut every year in Ontario, the majority for pulp and paper.

THE HEAVENS

Day Sky

WE TALK ABOUT the weather, even with strangers, because it's one thing we all have in common. It is the most all-encompassing aspect of nature. A mostly indoor existence minimizes the place of weather in the lives of many city dwellers, and some seem to dress, drive and act as though they can ignore it. But we all feel the elements, and the effects of what the sky is doing. The sun, or the absence of it, has a huge impact on the way we feel. And there's nothing like a bone-rattling thunder-and-lightning storm to awaken the city to the force of nature. The elements and phenomena of the sky have had a profound impact on the human mind through the ages, taking a central place in myths, legends and concepts in religion.

Cities themselves also influence the local weather. All the sun-absorbing asphalt, roofs and unshaded lawns, together with churning car engines and other machinery, create the noted "heat island effect" in which cities are often several degrees Celsius (Fahrenheit) warmer than the surrounding countryside. Urban smog also adds to the haziness and general misery of hot, humid summer days.

Most weather phenomenon can occur both night and day. But for simplicity, we've grouped all the weather-related topics in this section.

CLOUDS
Nature Above the Cityscape

Name origin: The Old English word *clud* originally meant "rocky mass" or "hill"

Amount of water in a cloud: A cloud the size of a typical two-storey house may contain up to half a sink full of water

Number of cloud particles needed to form 1 raindrop: 30,000–1 million

Dew point: Warm air holds more water vapour than cold air. Air at 10°C (50°F) holds twice as much invisible water vapour as at 0°C (32°F), and 8 times as much at 33°C (91°F) before condensation occurs

Relative humidity of clouds and fog: 100%

Ontario's cloudiest city: Owen Sound, with an annual average of 4,980 hours of overcast skies

Now my mind penetrates the liquid sky
and bodiless through wandering clouds I fly.
– John Milton, "Fifth Elegy: On the Coming of Spring"

LONG BEFORE AND after Milton's day, countless daydreamers, romantics and sages have gazed into the sky and pondered the wonder and meaning of clouds. It's a pastime far too neglected in the city today, where more often than not, many urbanites haven't a clue what is happening in the dome above their heads. While many complain about being separated from nature, they need only to look up to get the big picture. For those with the presence of mind to pull up a piece of park grass or stretch out on a rooftop deck and lift their eyes, the billowing white, shape-shifting forms drifting across the deep-blue sky are a sumptuous salve for the stresses of everyday toil and concern.

The main attraction on days like this are cumulus clouds, the familiar giant cotton balls with flat bases that metamorphose into fanciful shapes of the imagination. *Cumulus*, Latin for "heap," is one of 10 main cloud types described in 1803 by English pharmacist Luke Howard, a part-time naturalist who spent many hours flat on his back looking at the sky. He dreamed up the first system for classifying cloud types, one that remains in use today. The German poet Goethe was so impressed with Howard's system that he wrote four poems to the man of science with his head in the clouds.

Clouds are airborne reservoirs of water. All air carries water, which can remain invisible as vapour at concentrations of as high as 4 percent in the hottest weather. The cooler the temperature, the lower the concentration of water vapour needed to reach the dew point, when it condenses around bits of dust in the air, creating

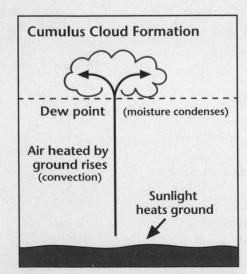

Cumulus Cloud Formation

Dew point (moisture condenses)

Air heated by ground rises (convection)

Sunlight heats ground

minute droplets. Billions upon billions of these droplets form visible clouds. When it's cold enough, the water droplets freeze into small, six-sided ice crystals.

Cumulus clouds are created when air, heated near the ground, rises and then cools at higher altitudes. Moisture-laden air moving over mountains also cools as it rises, and clouds may result. Large cloud banks occur along weather fronts, where a parcel of warm air meets a parcel of cold. Exhaling on a cold day produces a minicloud as warm, moist breath heated by the lungs hits the cold air outside. Condensation trails from high-flying jet aircraft are artificial cirrus clouds. As hot moisture-laden exhaust from jet engines cools, the water vapour condenses into ice crystals. The scores of contrails made over large cities every day actually affect the weather, like natural clouds reflecting heat from the sun away during the day and holding warmth in at night, shaving an average of 2 °C (3.6°F) off the range between daytime highs and nighttime lows.

The presence of certain cloud types in the sky is useful for predicting weather. Wispy cirrus clouds, including the type known as "mares' tails," often precede a storm front by a day or so. Veil-like cirrostratus clouds also usually mean poor weather is on the way. When these clouds obscure the sun or the moon, they may produce faint halos around the heavenly bodies, leading to the old saying "a ring around the sun or moon brings rain or snow upon you soon." Sky-covering altostratus clouds are another sign of rainy weather.

Cumulus clouds are less common in winter because snow reflects sunlight that would otherwise heat the land and cause air to rise. Southern Ontario winters, however, are dominated by unbroken, low-lying nimbostratus clouds associated with low-pressure weather fronts. When they roll in, it usually means at least a day or two of grey, dreary skies. Cloud watching then is an exercise in hope.

HOWARD CLOUD CHART

CLOUD NAME	DESCRIPTION	AVG. HEIGHT
Cirrus	Wispy, feathery, very high	8–12 km
Cirrocumulus	Blotchy cirrus clouds, may be rippled	8–12 km
Cirrostratus	Thin veil, doesn't block out sun, may cause halo	7–9 km
Altostratus	Thicker than cirrostratus, midlevel, partially blocks sun	2–6 km
Altocumulus	Puffy midlevel clouds, small puffs	2–6 km
Cumulonimbus	Giant cumulus clouds, thunderheads, maybe anvil top	450 m–15 km
Stratocumulus	Expansive, puffy clouds	150 m–2 km
Cumulus	Low puffy clouds, detached, flat bases	450 m–2 km
Nimbostratus	Grey layer of solid or almost solid cloud, rain	1–2 km
Stratus	Low-lying dull clouds, may drizzle	0–450 m

MIST, DEW, FOG & SMOG
When Calm Is Not so Clear

MISTY MORNINGS CAN have an unsettling ambiguity in the city. While mist is associated with calm, tranquil moments, urban environs are sometimes subject to a stinky, yellow-brown haze, known as smog, that has its origins in belching car exhaust and smoke-spewing industries. Both phenomena arise during calm conditions, most often in the summer.

The process that causes mist begins at night, when the darkened Earth cools. The air cools faster than water. When water vapour from warm lakes, streams and low, moist places rises into the cool air, it soon condenses into tiny water droplets, forming mist that spreads to surrounding areas. Mist vanishes when the morning sun heats the air and vaporizes the water again. If it's overcast at night, mist usually will not occur, because the air doesn't cool enough. Similarly, wind turbulence disrupts the steady cooling process.

Meteorologists define fog as any bank of mist that reduces visibility to less than one kilometre (0.6 miles). In spring and summer, water vapour in the warm air over land tends to condense when it hits cooler air over large bodies of open water. A fog bank appears. Fog, however, is most common in southern Ontario on early mornings in fall and winter, after light winds cool down the land at night or cool, dry air draws up moisture over lakes.

Smog is generally not as thick as mist or fog in Ontario, unless it's mixed in with them. It also suffuses with the natural haze caused by evaporation on hot summer days. Smog is composed mainly of fine particulate pollution and ground-level ozone, which forms mostly between May and September when nitrogen oxide and hydrocarbon emissions photochemically react with intense sunlight and heat. Hot, stale, humid weather, which has become more common with the apparent march of global warming, traps the pollution in, resulting in more frequent and prolonged smog episodes.

RAIN & RAINBOWS
From Sky to Earth and Back Again

ONTARIO HAS NO regular wet or dry seasons. April showers do bring May flowers, but the first full month of spring actually receives usually a little less total rainfall than most other non-winter months in much of Ontario. April skies, however, are often overcast and send down lots of moderate, steady rain, rather than the intense thunderstorms of summer. For winter-worn city dwellers longing for warmth and sun, it sometimes really can seem like the cruellest month.

Beyond obviously ominous clouds, or recourse to the Weather Channel, some traditional rhymes and sayings about the prospects for rain still ring true, even in the city. The Roman poet Virgil noted that "when swallows fly low there will soon be rain," or Latin words to that effect. This happens to be the case, because certain insects the swallows eat hang low just before a storm. One of the characteristics of a storm front is that the air is more humid higher up. Water vapour tends to condense on the little bugs and make them less airworthy. So they stick closer to the ground.

Many other urban creatures and plants react to atmospheric changes before rainfalls. Backyard ants may be more active just before it rains because the relatively warmer temperature of a low-pressure rain system heats up their blood. Likewise, spiders pick up the pace in

Maximum falling speed of rain: 30 km/h (18 mph); air friction prevents faster velocities

Falling speed of snowflakes on calm days: 6 km/h (3.7 mph)

Raindrop size: 0.5–5 mm (0.03–0.2 in) in diameter; average 2 mm (0.08 in)

Cloud droplet size: About 0.01 mm (0.001 in)

Average annual rainfall in Ontario: 70–100 cm (2.3–3.25 ft)

Annual precipitation that falls as snow: From 12% in Windsor-Chatham area to 33% in Owen Sound, Midland and other communities in snow belts along Georgian Bay and Lake Huron

Average worldwide precipitation that falls as snow: 5%

Most rainfall recorded in one hour in Ontario: 8.7 cm (3.4 in), in Fergus, June 10, 1967

Most rainfall recorded in 24 hours in Ontario: 26.4 cm

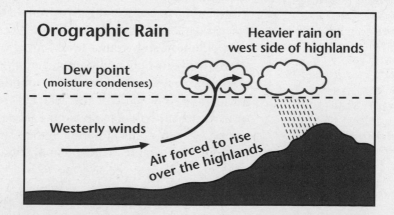

Orographic Rain

Heavier rain on west side of highlands

Dew point (moisture condenses)

Westerly winds

Air forced to rise over the highlands

(10.4 in), in Harrow (south of Windsor), July 19–20, 1989

The walk-or-run debate:
Scientists have proven that a runner stays drier (or, more accurately, less wet) than a walker while getting to shelter during a rainstorm. Although a runner does run into more raindrops than a walker in the same unit of time, the greater time a walker is out in the rain means a worse soaking. The only exception is when rain is falling on a slant in a tailwind. If this is the case, running faster than the wind would mean catching up to raindrops that would otherwise fall in front of the runner. But one mathematician has calculated that if the rain were falling at a 45° slant, this would entail running faster than the 4-minute mile

How radar tracks rainstorms:
Radar waves are sensitive enough to bounce off raindrops; even before raindrops occur, new Doppler radars can also detect concentrations of flying insects that pile up in the updrafts of the leading edges of air masses, where about 85% of storms form

Smell of rain: With the sharp rise in humidity just before a shower, airborne aromatic molecules given off by trees, plants, moulds and soil expand with moisture and stick much more readily to phlegm in the nose, resulting in everything smelling stronger. High humidity also enlarges the pores of plants and trees, allowing them to release

fixing and reinforcing their webs just before poor weather. Cones on ornamental pine trees absorb the moisture of an oncoming rain front, closing up and becoming more supple. The leaves on other trees, such as aspens and cottonwoods, often turn bottom side up just before rain. Moisture-laden air softens their stems, and strong updrafts associated with thunderstorms cause them to rustle. "When the leaves show their undersides, be very certain that rain betides," as one saying goes.

Most rain betides when heated air rises and then cools at higher altitudes. Water vapour in the air condenses into microscopic water droplets around dust, soot and organic particles always present in the sky. As these droplets are tossed about in the cloud, they may collide and grow bigger. Eventually, the raindrops become heavy enough to fall to the ground. Contrary to popular depiction, they are not shaped like tears, but rather like hamburger buns, flat on the bottom and rounded at the top.

Often temperatures inside a cloud are cold enough for the water droplets to freeze into six-sided ice crystals, even in summer. These form the nuclei of snowflakes, which grow as other water droplets condense along their edges. If the air beneath the cloud is warm, the snowflakes will melt and fall as rain. In Canada, they more often fall as snow.

The appearance of a rainbow at the end of a shower commonly signifies, if not literally a pot of gold, improved fortunes in the weather. A rainbow needs two ingredients, sunlight and raindrops. The sun must be located low in the sky and behind the rainbow watcher. The raindrops must be in the air in front of the observer. Late-afternoon rainbows may foretell good weather because it means the sun is unobstructed in the west. Since weather systems generally come from the west, clear skies are probably on the way. And since the rain in the east is moving away, the bad weather has probably passed. For the same reasons, the opposite is true of an early-morning rainbow. The clear skies have already passed to the east, and the rain in the west is bearing down upon the observer, to dampen the day.

Rainbows are created by sunlight penetrating billions of falling raindrops. Most of the light passes straight through the drop; however, a small amount of light is bent as it enters the drop, and refracts into the seven main colours that make up the visible spectrum: red, orange, yellow, green, blue, indigo and violet. The back of the raindrop acts like a mirror to reflect these colours out the front of the drop, toward the observer.

A rainbow watcher sees only one colour from each raindrop. But because the sunlight is refracting and reflecting off countless raindrops, the full spectrum is visible in the beautiful arc of a rainbow. Red is always the outside colour, and violet the inside. Because each observer is positioned at a different angle to the raindrops, each sees his or her own rainbow.

The most beautiful rainbows usually appear after a thunderstorm, because the large raindrops of that type of storm reflect more light. But rainbows can appear through the mist of a waterfall or the spray of a lawn sprinkler. All it takes are water droplets and the sun at the right angle. Sometimes double rainbows are visible, with the secondary rainbow much fainter. This occurs

more terpines and other organic essences into the air

Average number of umbrellas lost annually on Toronto buses, subways and streetcars: 5,600

Why rainbows are semicircular: Rainbows are actually circles, which can sometimes be seen from airplanes. From the ground, only the top portion of the circle is visible because of the angle of view. The bottom portion is below the horizon. A low sun produces taller rainbows, and vice versa

Why rainbows appear in only late afternoon or early morning: Sunlight reflects off each raindrop at angles

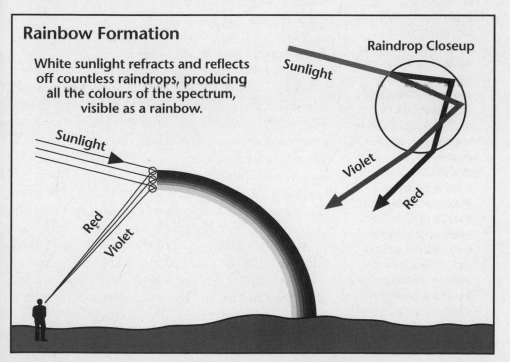

Rainbow Formation

White sunlight refracts and reflects off countless raindrops, producing all the colours of the spectrum, visible as a rainbow.

Raindrop Closeup

Sunlight

Sunlight

Red

Violet

Violet

Red

between 42° (red) and 40° (violet). When the sun is higher than 42° in the sky, the colours from a rainbow pass over an observer's head and are not visible. Generally, rainbows appear in a 3-hour period before sunset or after sunrise

Pot of gold: A rainbow is brightest where it touches the ground, its colours merging there into a golden glow marking the ethereal spot where leprechauns keep their riches

Rainbow duration: Normally only a few minutes, though one appearing off the coast of North Wales on August 14, 1979, stuck around for three hours

Location with world's most frequent rainbows: Honolulu

Moonbows: The light from a full moon can sometimes produce a dim rainbow, if the same conditions that create a normal rainbow are in place

Iris: Name for the coloured circular ring around the pupil of the eye, comes from the Greek word for *rainbow*, also the name of the Greek rainbow goddess, who was an Olympian messenger, usually dispatched when there was bad news

Also see: Clouds, Thunder & Lightning, Wind & Weather Systems, Mist, Dew, Fog & Smog

when sunlight reflects off the interior of raindrops twice. Each reflection dims the intensity of the light. The order of colours in the secondary rainbow is reversed.

In Old World mythologies from Japan to Scandinavia, a rainbow was a bridge between the heavens and Earth. The Babylonians believed it was formed by the necklace of the goddess Ishtar. In the Bible, it is a sign of God's promise to never again send the kind of flood that set Noah to boat building. In a Cree story, rainbows were said to be made of flowers. A young girl who loved rainbows was carried up to one by a thunderbird, and she sent some of the flowers back to Earth to beautify the land.

AVERAGE ANNUAL NUMBER OF WET DAYS, FROM ENVIRONMENT CANADA

LOCATION	RAIN	SNOW	THUNDERSTORMS	FREEZING PRECIPITATION
Windsor	117	45	33	–
Toronto	99	47	26	10
Kingston	109	46	27	12
Ottawa	107	62	24	16
North Bay	105	85	23	19
Sault Ste. Marie	98	79	22	9
Thunder Bay	88	61	26	8
Timmins	94	96	17	14

SUN & SKY

Setting the Balance of Life

THE SOURCE OF all life on Earth begins with a slim surplus of mass deep inside the sun. Under pressure 250 billion times greater than the atmospheric pressure on the Earth's surface, and in 15 million°C heat, four hydrogen atoms fuse into one helium atom. But the helium does not equal the mass of the hydrogen parents; a tiny amount, 0.7 percent, is left over. This missing mass is converted into energy that ultimately becomes the heat and light that bathes our planet and all the other worlds in the solar system.

Science has uncovered many of the secrets of nuclear fusion, as this process is called. But most ancient cultures understood that the sun is the giver of life and had a sun deity or being who played a prominent role in their mythology. Shamash was the sun god of Babylonia; he was responsible for justice. The Egyptian Ra was the great creator and defender of goodness. Helios of ancient Greece rode his sun-chariot across the sky and lived in a palace where darkness never fell. Apollo was also identified as a Greek sun god, although more properly he was the god of light and truth. The sun in Ojibway stories was a symbol of the Great Spirit or Kitche Manitou; sometimes it was referred to as the Great

Sun's period of rotation (the sun's "day"): 25 Earth days at its equator

Diameter: 1,400,000 km (840,000 mi), or 109 times Earth's diameter

Mass: 333,000 times Earth's

Temperature: 15,000,000°C (27,000,000°F) at core; 5,500°C (9,900°F) at surface

Magnitude: -27

Closest distance between the Earth and sun: 147 million km (88 million mi) at perihelion, early January

Farthest distance: 152 million km (91 million mi) at aphelion, early July

Vernal (Spring) equinox: Mar. 20–22 (exact date changes from year to year)

Summer solstice: Jun. 20–22

Autumnal equinox: Sept. 21–23

Winter solstice: Dec. 20–22

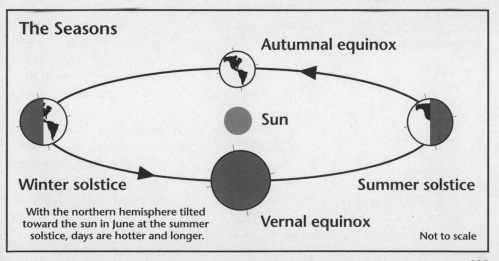

The Seasons

Autumnal equinox

Sun

Winter solstice

Summer solstice

Vernal equinox

With the northern hemisphere tilted toward the sun in June at the summer solstice, days are hotter and longer.

Not to scale

Spirit's wigwam. An Inuit fable describes the sun and the moon as a brother and sister who committed incest while they were humans. In the sky they were to be forever parted. Nearly all cultures identify the sun with the masculine or fatherhood, perhaps because Earth and the moon are so closely associated with the feminine, and sunlight is the agent that fertilizes life.

Great festivals, such as the rowdy Roman Saturnalia, often marked significant solar events. Saturnalia was held around the winter solstice in December. At that time, the North Pole is tilted away from the sun because of the Earth's 23.5° axial tilt to its orbital plane around the sun. At the summer solstice in June, after the Earth has travelled halfway around its orbit, the North Pole is tilted toward the sun. The northern hemisphere thus receives the sun's warming rays at a more direct angle in summer. In December, when shadows are longest because the sun is low, the northern hemisphere receives the rays at an oblique angle. In other words, the same amount of sunlight has to heat a far greater area of land in the winter than it does in the summer. The seasons are reversed in the southern hemisphere.

On summer solstice the sun rises at its most northerly point along the northeastern horizon, and traces its highest arc across the sky. It is the longest day of the year. On the winter solstice, it is the opposite, the sun rising in the southeast and looping low across the southern sky. On the vernal and autumnal equinoxes, the sun rises and sets midway between the points demarcated by the solstices. This happens to be due east and due west. On the equinoxes, the hours of the day are split into roughly equal amounts of light and darkness.

Although the sun is a great benefactor, it does emit ultraviolet radiation. Most is absorbed by ozone, a form of oxygen, in the outer atmosphere. But manmade chemicals have eaten away at the ozone layer in recent decades, allowing more UV radiation to reach the surface. This radiation causes sunburns and in the long term may lead to skin cancer in humans. Increasing carbon dioxide pumped into the atmosphere by cars and industry is also causing increasing amounts of heat to be trapped underneath a thickening layer of the gas – a

Time it takes for sunlight to reach Earth: 8.3 minutes

Speed of light: 299,792 km (186,282 mi) per second

Sun spots: Cooler areas of the sun's roiling surface, or photosphere, caused by fluctuations in the sun's powerful magnetic field, usually accompanied by eruptions of violent flares and enormous gas prominences; fluctuations occur in cycles, so that they are most pronounced once every 11 years

Sun's fuel reserves: Enough for about 5 billion years, at which time the solar orb will swell into a "red giant," engulfing Mercury, Venus and Earth, and then contract into a small, dense star called a white dwarf

Solar radiation reaching Earth that is absorbed into the ground and converted into heat: About 50%; half the radiation reflects off clouds and the Earth, or is absorbed by the atmosphere

Why the sky is blue: Air is transparent, which is why we can see the stars at night. The daytime colour comes from the complex interaction of sunlight striking gas molecules and particles of dust and moisture. White sunlight is actually composed of the seven main colours of the spectrum. During the day, all these colours except blue travel directly to the Earth's surface. The blue light is scattered by gas molecules throughout the sky. The sun, which is white when viewed from outer space, appears yellow from the Earth's

process known as the greenhouse effect – producing a steady rise in global warming.

The sky, like a security blanket, also protects all life from the deadly vacuum of space. But it's a fragile, relatively thin blanket. If the Earth was the size of a beachball, our sustaining layer of air would be about as thick as a paper towel.

There was a time when the atmosphere wouldn't support human life at all; it was composed mostly of carbon dioxide, water vapour and ammonia spewed out of volcanoes. Only in the past 40 percent of the planet's history has the atmosphere been oxygenated, by blue-green algae and other primitive plants, which converted carbon dioxide into oxygen through photosynthesis. They also provided the ozone shield against ultraviolet radiation. Our modern atmosphere, of 79 percent nitrogen, 20 percent oxygen, and other trace gases, remains relatively stable because of the ongoing exchange of oxygen and carbon dioxide via photosynthesis.

Long before the age of TV forecasts, our ancestors watched the sky for clues to tomorrow's weather. Memorable ditties or sayings that pertained to long-range forecasts were more superstition than science, but short-range predictions were often quite accurate, for sound reasons:

"Red sky at night, sailors delight. Red sky in the morning, sailors take warning." If the sun is shining in the west at sunset, this means it is not obscured by clouds. Since weather systems generally move from west to east in Ontario, it's a good bet that the following day will be clear. If the sun is shining in the morning, that means good weather is far to the east. It may not be long before bad weather arrives.

"If there's enough blue in the sky to make a sailor a pair of pants, the weather will improve." Low-pressure systems associated with bad weather have many layers of clouds. If large patches of blue sky are present, it means there are fewer levels of clouds, and the storm system is likely moving on, especially if the blue is in the west.

"If the maple sap runs faster, it is going to rain." Low pressure enables the sap to run more freely. Low pressure means bad weather.

surface – all the colours of the spectrum minus blue

Composition of atmosphere: 79% nitrogen, 20% oxygen, 1% other gases including carbon dioxide, ozone, hydrogen, methane and helium

Origin of "sun": From ancient Indo-European *sau* or *su*. Some groups of sun-related words adopted an "l" suffix, including *soleil* in French, *solar* in English and *hellios* in Greek. Others adopted the "n" suffix, including *sun*, *sonne* in German and *zon* in Dutch

Historic expedition: In 1768, the British dispatched astronomer Charles Green and Captain James Cook – the latter of whom had distinguished himself in the Gulf of St. Lawrence during the English conquest of Canada – to Tahiti to record the transit of Venus across the face of the sun. The measurements were to be used to determine the distance of the sun from Earth. On his way back from Tahiti, in 1770, Cook became the first European to encounter eastern Australia. His ship sailed into Botany Bay and changed the history of that continent forever

Also see: Moon; Stars & Constellations; Planets & Comets; Rain & Rainbows

THUNDER & LIGHTNING
Flashes Hotter Than the Sun

A SUDDEN SUMMER thunderstorm, full of sound and fury, is one of the most awesome and regular reminders in any city of the full force of nature. It takes little effort to imagine the profound effect the howling winds, crashing thunder and alien lightning bolts must have had on the minds of the ancients. Perhaps that's why the thunder gods of many past civilizations were supreme beings, even more than the sun deities. Zeus of Olympus and Thor of Asgard hurled thunderbolts with impunity. Marduk, the supernatural hero of ancient Babylon, was also a thunder god. One of the manifestations of the Semitic god Baal was a storm god with an arsenal of thunderbolts. Maybe they're all the same god – one story passed down and altered through the millennia.

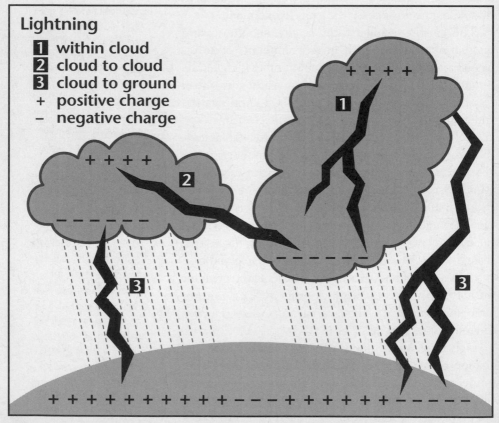

Lightning
1 within cloud
2 cloud to cloud
3 cloud to ground
+ positive charge
− negative charge

Native peoples of Canada also respect thunderstorms. To the Ojibway and many other nations, mythic thunderbirds, or *pinesi* – important beings who played roles in many old stories – brought thunderstorms. When storms were raging, the thunderbirds were said to be hunting. Thunder came from the flap of their wings, lightning from the flash of their eyes. Though *pinesi* had no definite shape, they are generally associated with hawks, which are most numerous around the same time of year that thunderstorms mainly occur, from April to October.

Another Ojibway conception of thunderstorms linked them to grandfathers. Because grandmothers were traditionally closer to their children and grandchildren than granddads, they were given a more regular, symbolic presence in Grandmother Moon. Grandfathers, angry at this lack of attention, returned as thunder, or Grandfather Thunder. Families offered tobacco in thunderstorms to appease the grouchy old man.

The classic thunderstorm occurs on hot, humid summer afternoons, when massive amounts of moist, heated air rise to form huge cumulonimbus clouds. The turbulence of powerful updrafts of warm air within thunderheads, together with the rapid condensation and crystallization of water vapour, jostle electrons – the juice of electricity – out of place from water and air molecules. A huge excess of electrons accumulates at the base of the cloud, while a deficit emerges at the top, creating a massively charged, bad-news bank of mist. The ground immediately below a thunderhead becomes positively charged too. Nature seeks to correct the electrical imbalance by transferring electrons from the positive ground or positive cloud top to the negative cloud base as soon as their forces of attraction become too great for the air to resist. Most lightning occurs within a cloud or between clouds. Only about 20 to 30 percent is cloud-to-ground lightning.

Lightning forms along a route called a tunnel or channel. In cloud-to-ground lightning, one end of the tunnel starts at the cloud base and moves downwards, while the other starts on the ground – generally from a tall point such as a tower or tree – and moves upwards.

Temperature of lightning bolt: 10,000–40,000°C (18,000–72,000°F)

Temperature of sun's surface: About 5,500°C (9,900°F)

Lightning bolt voltage: About 1 billion volts

High-transmission Hydro-line voltage: 500,000 volts

Typical speed of a lightning bolt: 150,000 km/sec (90,000 mi/sec)

Speed of light: 299,792 km/sec (186,282 mi/sec)

Speed of sound: 332 m/sec (362 yd/sec)

Typical width of a lightning bolt: 2 cm (0.75 in) at point of strongest current

Thunderstorm travelling speed: Up to 100 km/h (62 mph)

Typical size of a frontal thunderstorm: 10–15 km (6–9 mi) wide, 200–300 km (124–186 mi) long

Time it takes a fluffy, white cumulus cloud to turn into a thundercloud: 20–30 min

Maximum height of a thundercloud: 20 km (12 mi)

Height of Mt. Everest: 8.8 km (5.3 mi) above sea level

How far away is the lightning: Count the number of seconds between a lightning flash and its resulting thunder. Each second is about 300 m (1,000 ft)

Length of a lightning bolt: From 50 m to 35 km (55 yd to 22 mi), which is why a "bolt from the blue" can sometimes strike ahead of or behind storm clouds. Safety gurus recommend staying indoors if thunder can be heard within 30 seconds or less of seeing distant lightning, and for 30 minutes after a storm ends

Maximum distance thunder travels: About 40 km (24 mi)

Winter thunderstorms: Rare because there is not as much heating of air (convection) in winter as in summer

Lightning and trees: Most healthy trees can withstand a direct lightning strike without serious damage, its moisture conducting the charge down to the ground, leaving perhaps a 1-cm-wide entry hole in the bark. Trees that come down are usually dead or dying, with rotting wood, or very dry

Forest fires caused by lightning in Canada: About 55–60%

Average annual lightning casualties in Canada: 6–10 people killed, about 120 injured

Chances of ever being hit by lightning: 1 in 350,000–600,000

Chances of winning the jackpot in Lotto 6/49, per $1 play: 1 in 13,983,816

Fear of thunder and lightning: Brontophobia, from the Greek *bronte*, meaning "thunder"

Tennyson's description of lightning: "Flying flame"

Speed of falling hail: 160 km/h (96 mph)

Largest recorded Canadian hailstone: 11.4 cm (4.5 in) wide, weighing 290 g (10.2 oz), in Cedoux, Saskatchewan, Aug. 27, 1973

Average number of full-fledged tornadoes reported in Ontario annually: 15–25; 90% do minimal damage

The two meet, usually at within 100 metres (328 feet) of the ground, and the circuit is completed. The visible lightning bolt emanates from this point, moving up and down the tunnel in about 1/10,000 of a second. The explosive bolt heats the air instantly, up to seven times the temperature of the surface of the sun, and the resulting air expansion vibrates as thunder. The sound of the electric bolt itself, audible only close to the strike, is akin to the ripping of cloth.

Sheet lightning is not another form of lightning, but simply the glow of lightning bolts that occur within a cloud. Contrary to popular belief, lightning often hits the same place twice, especially tall towers.

Houses, buildings and hard-top cars are the safest places to wait out thunderstorms. High-rises and power lines absorb most of the strikes in cities. When houses are hit, the charge is usually conducted into the ground through eavestroughs, plumbing and wiring. For that reason, appliances should be unplugged during a storm and it's a good idea to keep off the phone and away from sinks and bathtubs.

Outside, it's dangerous to stand under isolated tall trees, light poles or shelters in the middle of open areas or atop hills in a thunderstorm. Swimmers, windsurfers and boaters should get out of the water as soon as they hear thunder. Woods are relatively safe, as long as you're not beneath the tallest tree. If you're caught in the open, the "golfer's crouch" can prevent serious injury or death: squat down in the position of a baseball backcatcher, balancing on the heels of the foot. If a lightning bolt strikes nearby, the charge should pass under you without striking vital organs. Don't lie flat. Lightning strikes are lethal about 20 percent of the time, when the charge passes through the heart or spinal cord.

Another hazard associated with thunderstorms is hail. These ice balls can kill animals, damage cars and wipe out fields of crops in seconds. Usually they are the size of peas, but grapefruit-sized monsters have been recorded in Canada. Hail occurs when ice crystals in a thunderhead are carried up and down by violent air currents. The crystals grow along the way as more moisture condenses and freezes on their surface. When they are too heavy to be supported by air currents, they fall explosively out of the bottom of the cloud.

Tornadoes may also accompany the biggest thunderstorms, and are usually preceded by heavy hail. They're set off when high-altitude winds put a spin on a powerful updraft within a storm cloud. Tornado winds can reach 500 km/h (300 mph), about twice as fast as the worst hurricanes. The area between Windsor and Barrie usually gets the lion's share of Ontario's twisters, along with the most thunderstorms and hail in the province. It lies at the end of the central region of the United States known as Tornado Alley, where tropical air from the Gulf of Mexico commonly collides with cold fronts, producing the severe weather.

Average duration of a tornado: 10–15 minutes

Average tornado travelling speed: 40–60 km/h (25–37 mph)

Most common time of day for tornadoes: 3–7 p.m.

Also see: Clouds; Rain & Rainbows; Wind & Weather Systems; Red Oak, Flicker

WIND & WEATHER SYSTEMS
A Blow-by-Blow Account

WIND IS ESSENTIAL for life on Earth. Many trees and plants owe their existence to winds that carry pollen and distribute seeds. Wind transports moisture around the world, bringing life-sustaining rains. Tailwinds and vertical air currents called thermals enable birds to migrate thousands of kilometres (miles). Worldwide wind patterns distribute heat more evenly across the planet. Even in antiquity, wind was considered one of the four essential elements, along with fire, water and earth.

The science of wind is complex. Many questions about its behaviour still stump researchers, not to mention novice sailboarders. But the basics are well understood. Put simply, wind occurs when air rushes from a high-pressure zone to a low-pressure zone, answering nature's call for equilibrium. A vacuum cleaner uses the same principle. In the machine, a powerful fan creates an artificial low-pressure zone. Air outside the vacuum cleaner, now suddenly under higher pressure, swooshes up the nozzle toward the low-pressure area, carrying dust, dirt and lost bus tickets along with it. The greater the difference in pressure, the faster the wind. Hurricanes and tornadoes are like enormous vacuum cleaners: both are extreme low-pressure systems, sucking deadly winds toward their centres and picking up everything in their paths.

Typical low-pressure systems aren't as violent, but they generally bring bad weather. In a low, the inward-rushing air is warm and moves upward as it converges toward the centre. As the warm, moisture-laden air ascends, it cools. Water vapour condenses into cloud banks, and it often rains.

High-pressure zones are characterized by heavy, cooler air that sinks as it moves outwards. Cool air contains less moisture; therefore, the air is sometimes cloudless. A high-pressure system in the

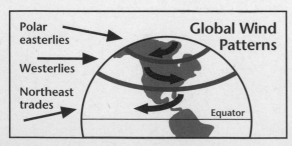

Global Wind Patterns

Polar easterlies

Westerlies

Northeast trades

Equator

winter brings cold, clear air. In summer, the air in a high-pressure system doesn't seem so cool because it heats up during the day as intense sunlight warms the ground. Both high-pressure and low-pressure systems generally move westward across the continent because of the prevailing westerly winds.

Though cities are generally less windy then the surrounding countryside, winds often get channelled into urban canyons of downtown office buildings and clusters of condo and apartment high-rises. When these canyons are at right angles to the air flow, they redirect the wind downwards, redoubling its strength as it's deflected into powerful street-level gusts, especially at intersections. In Ontario, Toronto's shopper-tossed Yonge and Bloor junction is one of the most notorious of these urban wind tunnels.

In the summer, winds usually die down at night because their creator – the sun – disappears. During the day, the sun heats the ground, which then warms the air. As the warm air rises, other air rushes in to take its place, creating wind. Once the sun is gone the process stops.

ground. The larger the lake, the stronger this effect

Why wind feels cool or cold against skin: Wind evaporates moisture in the skin, a process that removes heat energy

Gust fronts: Cold, moist air rushing ahead of storms, caused by falling raindrops inside storm clouds creating strong downdrafts that spread out as they reach the ground

Downbursts: Gust fronts of up to 250 km/h (155 mph), caused by the high-altitude jet-stream feeding into storm downdrafts

Jet stream: A shifting, 50–150 km-wide (31–93-mi-wide) band of wind encircling the northern hemisphere 8–14 km (5–8.7 mi) above the ground, usually blowing at 100–200 km/h (62–124 mph); normally positioned over southern Canada in summer and the southern United States in winter

Frequency of tropical hurricane remnants reaching Ontario: About once every 2 years, in late summer or early fall

Ontario's windiest city: Sudbury, average annual wind speed 18 km/h (11.2 mph)

Also see: Clouds, Red-tailed Hawk; Mist, Dew, Fog & Smog; Mosquitoes, Rain & Rainbows, Thunder & Lightning

BEAUFORT WIND SCALE
Named after Francis Beaufort, a British admiral, who invented the scale in 1805

NUMBER	WINDSPEED KM/H	DESIGNATION	CHARACTERISTIC
0	up to 1	Calm	Smoke rises vertically
1	1–5	Light air	Smoke drifts, leaves rustle
2	6–11	Light breeze	Wind on face, small wavelets
3	12–19	Gentle breeze	Flags flutter
4	20–29	Moderate breeze	Dust blows, branches move
5	30–38	Fresh breeze	Flags stretched, trees sway
6	39–50	Strong breeze	Wires hum, wind whistles
7	51–61	Moderate gale	Walking impeded
8	62–74	Fresh gale	Twigs break off, high waves
9	75–86	Strong gale	Branches break, tiles blown
10	87–101	Whole gale	Trees uprooted, damage
11	102–120	Storm	Widespread damage
12	over 120	Hurricane	Major destruction

Night Sky

T HE BRIGHT LIGHTS of the big city, while perhaps dazzling, are antithetical to good night-sky viewing. Only a small fraction of the constellations visible from an unlit countryside location, together with Venus, Mars, Jupiter and Saturn, shine enough to cut through the urban glare. But since the brightest, best-known constellations make it through, the city is a good place to learn the basics of the roadmap to the night sky, without the appearance of the galaxy of background stars to overawe and confuse. Once the main configurations are known, they can act as guideposts in learning the other constellations in the dark skies beyond the city.

MOON
The Original Timepiece

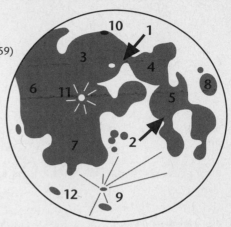

FRENETIC URBANITES TEND not to pay much attention to celestial sights, but a brilliant full moon rising low over the cityscape rarely fails to elicit a "wow." The proximity of the yellowish orb against buildings creates the illusion of a gargantuan moon, appearing much bigger than when it is higher in the sky. But it is, indeed, an illusion, easily checked by comparing the size of a round Aspirin tablet held at arm's-length against the size of the moon's disk at any point in its nightly journey. The moon doesn't shrink.

The moon is perhaps the best target for city stargazers armed with a pair of binoculars. While light from faint stars or nebulas gets washed out by city lights, sunlight reflecting off the moon's surface easily penetrates the urban glow, providing great views of craters and the flat plains called seas or mares (from the Latin). A crescent moon provides spectacular views of the "terminator," the line dividing light and dark on the moon's surface. The angle of the sunlight creates shadows on mountains and crater rims that gives the surface a tangible three-dimensional quality.

Naked-eye views of the full moon reveal – depending on the culture or myth – a man on the moon, a rabbit,

Number of one-way trips between Windsor and Ottawa it would take to travel the mean distance between Earth and the moon: 505

Distance from Earth: 356,500 km (213,900 mi) at closest (perigee); 406,500 km (243,900 mi) at farthest (apogee)

Diameter: 3,476 km (2,085 mi)

Width of Canada at longest point: 5,514 km (3,308 mi) from Cape Spear, Newfoundland, to the Yukon Territory–Alaska boundary

Moon gravity: About one-sixth Earth's gravity

Age: 4.6 billion years

First lunar probe to land on the surface: The Soviet's *Luna 2*, crashed Sept. 13, 1959

First man on the moon: Neil Armstrong, *Apollo 11*, July 20, 1969

Last man on the moon: Eugene Cernan, *Apollo 17*, Dec. 11, 1972

Magnitude: -12.7 at full moon

Why do we see only one side of the moon? Just as the moon causes tides on Earth, the Earth's gravity causes "tides" on the moon. There is no sea, of course, but the landmass does shift. Over time, friction caused by the shifting land has slowed down the moon, so that the period of rotation on its axis — its "day" — exactly matches the 27.3 days it takes to orbit Earth. In other words, Earth's gravity has locked onto the moon so that only one side ever presents itself to us. Tides on Earth are also slowing down our planet. The day is getting longer by one second every 60,000 years. When Earth was first formed, the day used to be 22 hours

Tides on lakes: Even a cup of tea is affected by the moon's gravity. But lake tides are imperceptible to all but the most sophisticated equipment

Moonrise: The moon rises in the east about 53 minutes later each day. At full moon, the moon rises in the east at dusk, just as the sun sets in the west. At new moon, the moon rises in the east at dawn, at the same time as the sun

Eclipses: When the moon passes exactly in front of the sun at new moon, a solar eclipse occurs. But because the moon's orbit is tilted 5° to the plane of Earth's orbit around the sun

an elephant jumping off a cliff, a girl carrying a basket on her back, or dozens of other images projected by the imagination. The myth of the moon made from green cheese dates from at least 400 years ago, when a writer noted, perhaps mischievously, that our satellite was made of unaged (green) cheese, judging by a visual comparison. The theory stuck. Scientists, always good for a laugh, disproved the green-cheese hypothesis some years ago by comparing the density of moon rock, determined by seismographic experiments from the Apollo missions, to the density of various types of cheeses.

While city dwellers may not pay much attention to the moon, the moon played a central role in the rise of civilization and thus cities. The first calendars were based on the phases of the moon. There is evidence that cave dwellers in France recorded the lunar cycle with notches in animal bones and antlers, 25,000 years before the first writing in Mesopotamia. Life's been on a schedule ever since.

In Europe the year was based on a lunar calendar until 45 B.C. – an imperfect system because 12 lunar months do not add up to a solar year of 365 days. Julius Caesar, with the help of an Egyptian astronomer, resolved the problem when he abandoned the idea of lunar months and divided the year into 12 independent calendar months, with a leap year every four years. The month of July is named after him. Later, in 1532, Pope Gregory XIII refined the Julian calendar because it was coming up short one day every 128 years. Gregory artificially shortened October that year – Oct. 5 to 14, 1532, do not exist in history – and made other changes, so that the calendar is now accurate to within one day every 3,200 years.

Although the Julian/Gregorian calendar has been adopted almost worldwide, some cultures retain the lunar calendar for religious, festive and day-to-day use. Muslim countries use a lunar calendar that began the day Mohammed was chased out of Mecca by unruly citizens enraged by his preachings (on July 16, 622, by the Gregorian calendar). The Muslim year of 12 lunar months makes no provision for the solar year. Every year the seasons begin earlier, until, in 32 1/2 years, the cycle starts repeating. The Jewish calendar is also based on the lunar month, beginning with the biblical moment of creation (3761 B.C. Gregorian time). It is adjusted for the solar year, however, with the addition of a 13th month every three to four years. Another lunar calendar, the Chinese, has been abandoned for civil use, but important Buddhist and Taoist festivals are still held around new and full moons. In Christian societies, Easter is still timed to the lunar and solar calendars: the Sunday after the first full moon after the spring equinox.

The lunar cycle was of great importance to Native peoples in Ontario, who also used it as a calendar. Full moons were often named after natural events occurring around the same time, and were sometimes associated with human activities such as hunting, fishing or food-gathering. The Ojibway call the full moon in May the Sucker Moon. That is the month suckers spawn up north woods' streams. June is the Blooming Moon, July the Berry Moon, August the Grain Moon and September the Leaves Turning Moon.

The rhythms of the moon are also deeply linked to fertility. The 29½-day period between full moons closely matches the average female menstrual cycle. The word *menstruation* comes from the Latin word for "monthly." Charles Darwin suggested that since humans ultimately evolved from the sea, it followed that menstrual periods were a distant echo of the tides. Whether the female and lunar cycles have a rational connection is a matter of debate. The menstrual cycles of other mammals, for example, do not match the average 28-day human one. But the fact that lunar and human periods do coincide has led some scholars to suggest the earliest timekeeping evolved through the need of women to know the season of birth of their children, which would have required a knowledge of the link between menstrual and moon phases, and the nine-month or nine-moon gestation period. This could have led to the first calendars, perhaps those same cave calendars of France.

Symbolically, the fact the moon is "reborn" each month has led to its deep association with women since ancient times. Many mythologies and religions have moon goddesses; the most famous is probably Artemis,

(called the ecliptic), most times there is no eclipse at new moon; the moon's shadow shoots out into space instead of falling on our planet. Similarly, a lunar eclipse occurs only at full moon, when Earth's shadow falls on the moon as our planet passes directly in front of the sun. But usually that 5° tilt causes Earth's shadow to miss the moon's disc

Once in a blue moon: The full moon sometimes appears blue due to atmospheric conditions created by high dust content after volcanic eruptions or large forest fires. In recent years, the second full moon in a month with two full moons (it happens twice every five years or so) is said to be a blue moon, though this is not the original meaning

Harvest moon: The full moon closest to the autumnal equinox, occurring either in September or October. Owing to the alignment of Earth, moon and sun at this time of year, the bright moon before, after and during the harvest moon stays in the night sky longer than other times of the year — ideal for farmers harvesting their crops at night

Moon goddesses: Artemis, the Greek goddess of hunting; Selene, a Greek Titan sometimes associated with Artemis (selenology is the study of the moon); Hecate, the Greek goddess of the new moon (and thus darkness); Diana, the Roman goddess of hunting; Mama Qilla, the Inca moon goddess; Isis, the mother of Egypt; Galata, the Celtic moon goddess; Hina, of Polynesia

How to tell if the moon is waxing or waning: If the right side of the moon is illuminated, the moon is waxing – heading toward full moon. If the left side is illuminated, it is waning – past full moon and heading into new moon

Also see: Planets & Comets, Sun & Sky

the Greek goddess of hunting, whose Roman equivalent is Diana. The Ojibway think of the moon as Grandmother Moon, the first mother in the creation myth who still keeps watch over her offspring.

The moon is related to another aspect of the human condition: madness. Lunacy, from the Latin *luna*, or "moon," has been attributed to a mysterious connection between the full moon and our mental state. It is traditionally thought that lunar gravity – the same force that causes the tides and probably earthquakes and volcanic eruptions – somehow pulls our psyche out of kilter, perhaps in the same way it starts the menstrual flow. There is little proof for this, although there is no doubting the fact that 200 years ago, inmates in English lunatic asylums were flogged just before the full moon to deter violent behaviour. Who was actually mad in this case is another question.

One moon mystery remains unsolved even after visits to the silvery orb by several well-educated, middle-aged American men: How was it that Earth came to have a companion in the first place? Scientists have a few theories. The moon may have formed close to Earth at the same time Earth condensed out of the cloud of dust and gas that became our solar system. Alternatively, the moon may have formed elsewhere in the solar system, but was somehow captured by Earth's gravitational field. The most popular theory proposes that a huge asteroid, possibly as large as Mars, smashed into Earth early in the planet's evolution, and threw up debris that eventually coalesced into the moon. No one knows for sure.

PLANETS & COMETS
Wanderers of the Night Sky

FOUR PLANETS MAKE regular naked-eye appearances in the urban night sky: Venus, Mars, Saturn and Jupiter. Tiny Mercury is also visible to the naked eye, but because it is the closest planet to the sun, it never rises high in the horizon and is often obscured by buildings or the sun's glare. Uranus, Neptune and Pluto are too distant to be seen without the aid of a good telescope and advanced stargazing abilities.

But Venus and Mars – rocky terrestrial planets like Earth – and Jupiter and Saturn – the famous gas giants – offer plenty of fine viewing from backyards, porches, and balconies. Each has its own orbit that dictates when the planet is visible from Ontario night skies. The orbits are predictable, but the timing of appearances changes from year to year; to check where the planets are now, consult magazines like *SkyNews*, Web sites such as <www.space.com>, almanacs and sometimes newspapers. The peripatetic nature of planets is the root of the word: *planetes* is Greek for "wanderer." All the planets rotate around the sun in the same direction and on a rough plane called the ecliptic.

From Earth, Venus is the brightest planet, the brilliant "evening star" often seen perched in the deep blue-black western sky shortly after sunset. It can be confused for a jetliner with its landing lights on, until it becomes apparent that it's not moving. The closest planet to Earth, its greenhouse-gas atmosphere acts as a giant mirror, reflecting three-quarters of the sunlight hitting it. Due to the geometry of its orbit compared to ours, Venus actually has "phases" like the moon, including crescent phases that can be seen through a good pair of binoculars. The naked eye, however, usually can't discern the shape because of the distance.

Mars, the second-closest planet to Earth but much smaller than Venus, appears red even to the naked eye. The surface is covered in red, iron-oxide dust that is sometimes blown into huge dust storms. Mars's blood-like colour explains how the planet got its name: Mars was revered as the Roman god of war. The Greeks called

MERCURY ☿
Distance from sun: 58 million km (35 million mi)
Diameter: 4,880 km (2,928 mi)
Day: 59 Earth days
Year: 88 days
Surface temperature: 430°C (806°F) dayside, -180°C (-292°F) nightside
Moons: 0
Magnitude: +1 to +2
Successful probes: *Mariner 10*, 1974
Day of the week: Wednesday, from *woden*, Norse for "mercury"; *mercredi* in French; *miércoles* in Spanish
Notable: Craters on Mercury are named after men and women of the arts, including Rubens, Dickens and Beethoven. Mercury has a highly elliptical orbit

VENUS ♀
Distance from sun: 108 million km (65 million mi)
Diameter: 12,100 km (7,260 mi)
Day: 243 Earth days
Year: 225 days
Surface temperature: 480°C (896°F)
Moons: 0
Magnitude: -4.0 to -4.1
Successful probes: *Mariner 2*, 1962; *Venera 7* (landed), 1970; *Venera 9* (landed), 1975; *Magellan*, 1990–92
Day of the week: Friday, from Old English *frigg* or Norse *freya*, translation of Latin *Venus*; *vendredi* in French; *viernes* in Spanish

Notable: The Venuvian day is longer than its year. The planet spins in the opposite direction from Earth and most other planets. Venereal diseases are "diseases of Venus." Surface features are named after famous women.

EARTH ⊕

Distance from sun: 150 million km (90 million mi)

Diameter: 12,756 km (7,654 mi)

Day: 23.9 hours

Year: 365.2 days

Spinning speed: 38,400 km/h (23,040 mph)

Orbital speed: 105,600 km/h (63,360 mph)

Surface temperature: Avg. 15°C (59°F)

Moons: 1

Atmosphere: 77% nitrogen, 21% oxygen, traces of carbon dioxide, methane, neon and other gases

Notable: Earth was the centre of the universe until 1543, when Nicholas Copernicus pointed out that we circle the sun, not vice versa. (Some early Greeks also thought this, but like Copernicus, they had a hard time convincing people.) Earth is considered a double planet, like Pluto, because of its relatively large single satellite. Its name comes from the Old English *oerthe*, meaning "dry land."

MARS ♂

Distance from sun: 228 million km (137 million mi)

Diameter: 6,787 km (4,072 mi)

him Ares. The red star Antares in the summer constellation Scorpius looks a lot like Mars. *Antares* is Arabic for "rival of Mars."

Of all the planets, Mars captures our imagination the most. Until recently, hopeful (or fearful) humans thought there was intelligent life on Mars. Evidence was supposedly found in 1877, when Italian astronomer Giovanni Schiaparelli reported seeing natural channels on the planet's surface, and others such as famous astronomer Percival Lowell mistook this as to mean artificial canals were present. Reputable scientists dreamed up various schemes for communicating with Martians, including a giant mirror to engrave words on the Martian desert with the focused rays of the sun. On Halloween 1938, Orson Welles caused widespread panic in North America when his Mercury Theatre of the Air broadcast a radio adaption of H.G. Wells's *War of the Worlds*, a story about an invasion of Earth by Martians. In 1976, two *Viking* landers failed to meet any welcoming committees, but the idea of some kind of life on Mars has been gaining ground in recent years. In 1996, headlines around the world proclaimed the possibility of life on Mars after scientists examined a chunk of rock blown off Mars that subsequently landed on Earth as a meteorite. Many scientists came to the conclusion that unusual microscopic patterns on the meteorite were fossilized evidence of bacterialike organisms. Recent close-up photos of Mars by space probes reveal topographic features that strongly suggest water once sloshed on the surface, and water is believed to exist in the polar caps and perhaps even underground. Such promise has led to the recent flurry of orbiters and robotic landers to Mars, as humanity prepares to make its first leap to another planet.

The next planet out from Mars, Jupiter, represents an entirely different world: not a rocky ball but a giant sphere of swirling gas. The largest planet, Jupiter contains 70 percent of the mass of the entire solar system, excluding the sun. Though not as brilliant from Earth as Venus (because of its great distance), through binoculars Jupiter appears as a distinct white disc against the starry dots in the blackness. Some of those dots are Jupiter's

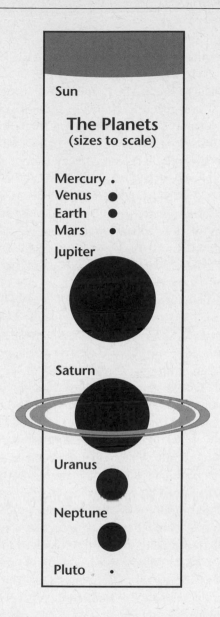

The Planets
(sizes to scale)

Sun

Mercury .
Venus ●
Earth ●
Mars •
Jupiter

Saturn

Uranus

Neptune

Pluto .

Day: 24.6 hours
Year: 687 days
Surface temperature: Avg. -50°C
   (-58°F)
Moons: 2, Phobos ("Fear") and
   Deimos ("Panic"), Mars's dogs
   in Roman mythology
Magnitude: +1.1 to +1.4
Successful probes: *Mariner 4,*
   1965; *Mariners 6 & 7,* 1969;
   Vikings 1 & 2 (landed), 1976;
   Mars Observer, 1993,
   Pathfinder (first roving vehicle
   on another planet), 1997; *Mars
   Global Surveyor,* 1999;
   Odyssey, 2001; *Mars Express
   Orbiter,* 2003 (lander failed);
   Spirit and *Opportunity* rovers
   (landed 2004)
Day of the week: Tuesday, from
   Old English *tiw,* equated with
   the Latin *mars; mardi* in French;
   martes in Spanish
Notable: Mars has polar caps like
   Earth, but they are composed of
   frozen carbon dioxide and
   water. They advance and recede
   with the planet's long seasons

JUPITER ♃

Distance from sun: 778 million
   km (467 million mi)
Diameter: 142,800 km
   (85,680 mi)
Day: 9.9 hours
Year: 11.9 Earth years
Temperature at cloud tops:
   -130°C (-202°F)
Moons: 17, largest Ganymede
Magnitude: -2.1 to -2.3
Successful probes: *Pioneer 10,*
   1973; *Pioneer 11,* 1974;
   Voyagers 1 & 2, 1979; *Galileo*
   (with atmospheric probe),
   1995; *Cassini,* 2001

moons. Four of its 17 satellites – Io, Europa, Ganymede and Callisto – are easily visible through a small telescope or binoculars mounted on a tripod, even in the city. The sight of Jupiter and its moons is one of the most thrilling nighttime views for a novice stargazer. Each night the moons are in a different position. A small telescope will also reveal the bands of gas on Jupiter's surface, while more powerful telescopes can detect Jupiter's famous

Day of the week: Thursday, from the Norse god *Thor*, equated with the Latin *Jupiter*, *jeudi* in French; *jueves* in Spanish

Notable: The surface area of the Great Red Spot is larger than Earth's. The Chinese studied Jupiter at least as far back as 1000 B.C., when the 12-year orbit was observed

SATURN ♄

Distance from sun: 1,427 million km (856 million mi)

Diameter: 120,600 km (72,360 mi)

Day: 10.7 hours

Year: 29.5 Earth years

Temperature at cloud tops: -185°C (-300°F)

Moons: 18 (at least), largest Titan

Magnitude: +0.7 to +0.6

Successful probes: *Pioneer 11*, 1979; *Voyager 1*, 1980; *Voyager 2*, 1981; *Cassini-Huygens*, 2005 (scheduled descent into Titan's atmosphere)

Day of the week: Saturday

Notable: Saturn's moon Titan is bigger than Mercury and Pluto and has a dense nitrogen atmosphere. It can be seen with a backyard telescope

URANUS ♅

Distance from sun: 2,870 million km (1,722 million mi)

Diameter: 51,300 km (30,780 mi)

Day: 17.2 hours

Year: 84 Earth years

Temperature at cloud tops: -200°C (-328°F)

Moons: 21, largest Titania

Magnitude: +5.7

Great Red Spot, a 300-year-old storm in the planet's swirling hydrogen-rich atmosphere.

As befitting its size, Jupiter is named after Rome's supreme god, who was fashioned after Zeus, the chief Olympian in ancient Greece.

But no planet has launched more astronomy careers than Saturn, the next gas giant. While astronomers have detected faint rings around Jupiter, Uranus and Neptune, they are nothing like the great rings of Saturn. The first sight of Saturn's rings through a backyard telescope is unforgettable. Suddenly, the solar system seems tangible.

The rings themselves are composed of billions upon billions of icy particles, ranging in size from dust flakes to garages. There are thousands of separate rings, but only two main bands separated by a gap (called the Cassini division) are visible from typical backyard telescopes. The whole system, estimated to be only about 200 metres (218 yards) thick, revolves precisely around Saturn's equator. Depending on where Saturn is located on its orbit relative to Earth, the rings can be distinctive at an oblique angle, or they can virtually disappear as they tip "edge on" from our point of view. No one knows why Saturn alone has rings so pronounced.

Not only is Saturn beautiful, for the ancients it had certain pleasant associations. Saturn was the Roman god of agriculture, and every December a great festival called the Saturnalia was held to mark the winter solstice. Businesses and public institutions were closed, citizens exchanged presents, wars were interrupted and slaves were freed. In other words, the people partied.

Among the rarest of celestial sights observable from the city, or anywhere else on Earth for that matter, are comets. Comet Hale-Bopp, readily seen from even the downtowns of our largest cities, put on a great show in March and April 1997, with a thick blue-white tail clearly visible. Several comets each decade are visible through telescopes, but naked-eye beauties like Hale-Bopp are typically a once-in-a-lifetime event.

Astronomers describe two kinds of comets. Long-period comets are believed to originate from the distant Oort Cloud, a massive zone that forms a spherical casing around the solar system, with an outer edge perhaps two light-years, or about 18.8 trillion kilometres, away from the sun. Comets born from this nursery are seen once and never again. Short-period comets, or those with orbits of less than 200 years, appear to come from the closer Kuiper Belt, a zone just beyond the orbit of Pluto.

Comets are icy, rocky chunks of space debris left over from the birth of the solar system. The average comet is composed of a rocky nucleus about a kilometre or two (3,300 to 6,600 feet) in diameter. An icy layer around the nucleus is warmed as the comet approaches the sun. The ice vaporizes into a cloud called the coma. Solar radiation blows some of the material away from the cloud, creating a tail that can be hundreds of thousands of miles long (the word *comet* comes from the Greek *kometes*, "long haired"). In both the Kuiper Belt and Oort Cloud, theory holds that every once in a while a gravitational bump will knock one of the space snowballs off its regular route. The newly born comet then begins its long trek toward the sun.

Successful probes: *Voyager 2,* 1986

Notable: Uranus spins "horizontally" on a 98° tilt. Scientists speculate that a gigantic passing object may have knocked it on its side

NEPTUNE ♆

Distance from sun: 4,497 million km (2,698 million mi)

Diameter: 49,100 km (29,460 mi)

Day: 16.1 hours

Year: 165 Earth years

Temperature at cloud tops: -200°C (-328°F)

Moons: 8, largest Triton

Magnitude: +7.9

Successful probes: *Voyager 2,* 1989

Notable: Neptune's moon Triton has nitrogen geysers and revolves around the planet in the "wrong" direction. *Voyager 2* passed only 4,900 km (3,000 mi) above Neptune's north pole, a cosmic pool shot of unbelievable accuracy

PLUTO ♇

Distance from sun: 5,900 million km (3,540 million mi)

Diameter: 2,300 km (1,380 mi)

Day: 6.4 Earth days

Year: 248 Earth years

Surface temperature: -230°C (-382°F)

Moons: 1, Charon

Successful probes: none sent

Notable: Pluto has an exaggerated elliptical orbit. From 1979 to 1999, it was actually closer to the sun than Neptune was

STARS & CONSTELLATIONS
A Seasonal Tour of the Night Sky

TORONTO'S OLD MCLAUGHLIN Planetarium, shut down in 1995, had a star show that began with the lights dimming in the theatre and a few dozen stars appearing on the dome overhead. On the horizon line – the rim around the bottom of the dome – a cityscape appeared. The narrator would announce that this was the sky Torontonians might see on a typical night. Then the show would "move" out to the country. As the sky (and theatre) darkened, thousands of more stars and the Milky Way popped out of the void, to the oohs and ahhs of the audience. No doubt about it, a dark sky seen from the countryside or wilderness is an awesome sight.

But to an attentive urbanite, there is still much to enjoy by stargazing from city streets and yards. (Suburbanites enjoy even better views, being one step removed from light-polluted downtowns that wash out the dimmer stars.) Urban stargazing is an excellent way to learn the major constellations, which serve as guideposts to dimmer stars and deep-sky objects such as nebulas, star clusters and galaxies visible from darker environs. For some, a simple knowledge of the major constellations brings pleasure through a heightened sense of the changing seasons, and also a connection to our ancestors who gazed upon the same points of light.

Some stars are visible all year, as they never set below the horizon. These "circumpolar" stars are closest to the North Star (from our point of view). The North Star, Polaris, remains fixed in one location in the northern sky about halfway between the horizon and the zenith. Stars farther out from Polaris will set below and rise above the horizon in different seasons and at different times of the night. Because of the rotation of the Earth, all the northern constellations and stars appear to revolve counter-clockwise around Polaris. Meanwhile, the motion of our planet along its orbit makes some constellations seasonal.

The Big Dipper is a circumpolar constellation, appearing in different positions as it makes a complete

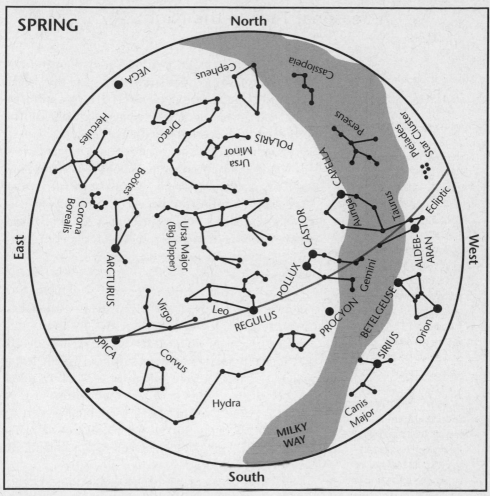

SPRING

North

West

East

South

VEGA
Cepheus
Cassiopeia
Hercules
Draco
Perseus
Pleiades Star Cluster
Corona Borealis
Ursa Minor
POLARIS
CAPELLA
Boötes
Auriga
Taurus
Ecliptic
ARCTURUS
Ursa Major (Big Dipper)
CASTOR
Gemini
ALDEB-ARAN
POLLUX
Virgo
Leo
PROCYON
BETELGEUSE
Orion
REGULUS
SPICA
Corvus
SIRIUS
Hydra
Canis Major
MILKY WAY

(See "How To Use the Star Charts," page 334)

circle around the North Star, as the following urban stargazing tour through the seasons will show.

Spring

On a clear spring night, around 9:30 p.m., the distinctive Big Dipper is in the northeastern sky, positioned upsidedown as if dumping its contents onto the Earth, the handle pointing to the right (east). It is perched high above Polaris, with the two stars at the front of the "ladle" of the Dipper pointing down to the North Star. (Over the course of the evening, the Big Dipper will move westward.) The North Star is dim compared to

system, the brightest stars were ranked 1 and the dimmest ranked 6. The modern magnitude system rests on this foundation; some very bright stars, such as Sirius, now have negative values, while stars invisible to the naked eye but apparent in telescopes have values greater than 6

Magnitude of Polaris: 1.97. Stars with a magnitude of about 3 or less (dimmer) are difficult to make out from light-polluted urban areas

Regulus: Magnitude 1.3, distance 69 light-years

Name meaning: "Little king," from Latin

How Arcturus lit up Chicago: At the 1933 World's Fair in Chicago, organizers used the star's light to turn on the fair's floodlights. The starbeam was focused through a telescope onto a photoelectric cell, which generated the voltage to flip the switch. The starlight hitting the cell would have begun its journey to Earth in 1896, since Arcturus is 37 light-years away

Magnitude of Arcturus: -0.05

Closest star in Big Dipper to Earth: Mizar, 78 light-years away

Farthest star in Big Dipper: Dubhe, 124 light-years away

Brightest stars: Alioth and Dubhe, both magnitude 1.8

Double-star names: Mizar (larger star) and Alcor. This pair is called an optical double, because they are close to each other only by virtue of our line of sight from Earth. They are not gravitationally linked to each other like a true double-star system. Telescopic observations show that many stars are actually double-stars, also called binaries. Mizar appears as a double-star in telescopes

Latin and Greek names: *Ursus* is the Latin word for *bear*, evident in such modern words as *ursine*, meaning "bearlike." The Greek word for *bear*, *arkitos*, is the

the stars in the Big Dipper, but they are all visible on a dark night from a reasonably dark spot in the city.

Remember the North Star's location: it is conveniently positioned in the sky almost directly above the North Pole on the Earth's axis, and thus does not move around the sky like the other stars. The fixed nature of Polaris makes it perhaps the most important star in the heavens, as it was essential for navigation.

The North Star appears in all mythologies. Its apparent immobility in the whirling procession of the stars must have been observed by the earliest cave dwellers. The Moguls called it the Golden Peg that fastened the universe together. In Scandinavia's violent mythology, it was the World Spike, the Veralder Nagli. (The Norse gods constructed their sky out of the chopped-up bits of adversaries; the nail in the centre of the universe finished off the job.) In an Arab myth, the Big Dipper was a coffin that held the body of a great warrior killed by the evil North Star. The stars that revolve around the North Star, including the Big Dipper, formed a funeral procession. Chinese stories about the North Star relate it to T'ai Chi, the great Absolute or Unity; it was the perfect union of the yin and yang principles. The North Star was also a symbol for the Emperor, representing permanence in a transient world. The Pawnee people of the Great Plains called it The Star That Does Not Walk Around.

The pole star has actually changed over the millennia because the Earth wobbles slightly on its axis, a phenomenon known as precession. Four thousand years ago the pole star was Thuban, in the constellation Draco. Archeologists have discovered that Egyptian pyramids were built to align with Thuban. Polaris will be nearest the spot that is the true celestial north in the year 2100. Astronomers predict the bright star Vega will become the pole star 12,000 years from now.

In modern astronomy, Polaris is placed at the end of the constellation Ursa Minor, the lesser bear, commonly called the Little Dipper. Ursa Minor is a dim constellation, generally not observable from urban sites.

In the southern sky, the bright star Regulus is a spring favourite. Regulus has a slight yellow-red cast, and is known as representing the heart of the constellation Leo, the lion. The other stars in Leo, easily forming the shape of a lion and described as such since at least 3500 B.C., may be seen on a good night. Regulus lies almost exactly on the ecliptic, the imaginary line in space defined by Earth's orbital plane, along which all planets travel and the zodiacal constellations lie.

Rising in the eastern sky in spring is a star that northern civilizations have awaited eagerly or anxiously each year for millennia: Arcturus. It is the harbinger of spring, a signal to start thinking about planting crops or opening up the cottage. Arcturus climbs over the horizon into the early evening sky around the time of the spring equinox in late March.

Arcturus means "guardian of the bear" in Greek. The star was thought to herd Ursa Major, the Great Bear or Big Dipper, around the North Star. To find Arcturus, follow the curve of the handle of the Big Dipper to the bright star – the famous "arc to Arcturus." As spring turns into summer, Arcturus moves higher across the night sky. It is almost directly overhead as darkness descends in late June and early July.

Arcturus, also with a distinct yellow colour, is the brightest star of the spring and summer sky. This giant nuclear furnace is about 120 times more luminous than our own sun and 25 times wider. It's also relatively close to Earth, a little more than half the distance of the Big Dipper's nearest star to Earth. The only star to outshine Arcturus in the northern hemisphere is brilliant Sirius, the "dog star" of winter that burns low in the southern sky.

Summer

By now the Big Dipper has moved into the northwestern sky in early evening. It is a good jumping-off point for a night of summer stargazing, and has been for thousands of years. Through the millennia, people in the northern hemisphere have gazed into the night sky and connected the same starry dots to form what we now call the Big Dipper. In fact, long before the Golden Arches came to exist, the Big Dipper was one thing many civilizations had in common. A surprising number

root for Arcas, son of Callisto, the bright star Arcturus and even King Arthur, who was sometimes called Arturus. Because the stars associated with the bear stories lie in the northern sky, things relating to the north often contain the *arkitos* root, e.g., "arctic"

Scan zone: The Summer Triangle is one of the best areas of the sky to scan with binoculars. The Milky Way runs thick through this part of the skydome, and hundreds of stars invisible to the naked eye materialize

Vega: Magnitude 0.0, distance 25 light-years

Altair: Magnitude 0.8, distance 17 light-years

Deneb: Magnitude 1.3, distance 1,467 light-years

Lucida: The brightest star in a constellation, from which we get the word *lucid*

Closest star in Cassiopeia to Earth: Eta Cassiopeiae, 19 light-years away

Farthest star in Cassiopeia: Gamma Cassiopeiae, 613 light-years away from Earth

Brightest star in Cassiopeia: Schedar, magnitude 2.2

The Sea Monster: Cetus, sent by Poseidon to terrorize Cassiopeia's subjects, took its name from the Greek word for whale, *ketos*. The modern word *cetacean* refers to the order of animals than includes whales, dolphins and porpoises; cetology is the study of whales

Orion's origins: Some say he was the son of the sea god Poseidon, but others say he

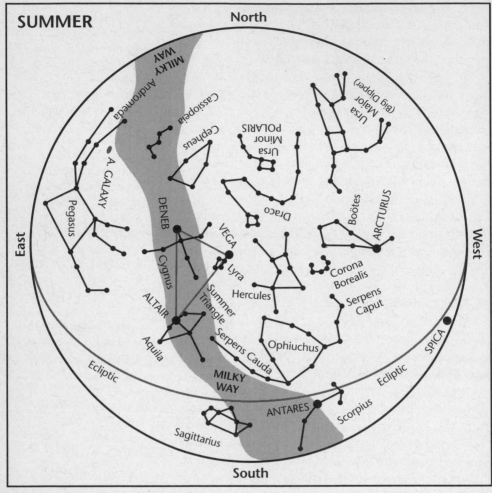

SUMMER

North

West

East

South

MILKY WAY

Andromeda

Cassiopeia

Cepheus

Ursa Minor POLARIS

Draco

Ursa Major (Big Dipper)

Boötes

ARCTURUS

A. GALAXY

Pegasus

DENEB

VEGA

Lyra

Cygnus

Hercules

Corona Borealis

Serpens Caput

ALTAIR

Summer Triangle

Aquila

Serpens Cauda

Ophiuchus

SPICA

Ecliptic

MILKY WAY

Ecliptic

ANTARES

Scorpius

Sagittarius

(See "How To Use the Star Charts," page 334)

emerged from the hide of an ox upon which Poseidon, Hermes and Zeus had peed (leading to his original name, Urion, meaning "urine")

Brightest star in Orion: Rigel, magnitude 0.1, distance 1,400 light-years

Betelgeuse: Pronounced bet-el-jooz, is a red supergiant that may be in the final stages of

of myths from Europe, Asia and North America refer to the Big Dipper as a bear. It's thought the bear story comes from prehistoric Asia, and travelled both eastward and westward with various human migrations.

The Mi'kmaq first nation has just such a story, in which the four stars making up the cup of the Big Dipper represent a bear. The three stars of the handle, plus other nearby stars, represent birds. From high in the sky, the birds chased the bear closer to earth. In autumn, the lead bird, Robin, shot an arrow at the bear. Blood splashed Robin, giving the bird its red breast. Blood also dripped onto the leaves below, giving them autumn colour. The hunt's cycle is repeated every year, with the position of the constellation serving as a calendar to record the seasons. The motion of the bear through the sky during the night also serves as a clock.

The Greeks, as always, saw in the Dipper constellations a star opera of love and jealousy. In one version of the legend, Zeus seduces the nymph Callisto. Zeus's betrayed wife, Hera, retaliates by turning Callisto into a bear. Out of compassion, Zeus turns Callisto's son Arcas into a bear too, to keep her company, placing both of them in the heavens to protect them from hunters.

There, they are known by their Latin names Ursa Major, the greater bear, and Ursa Minor, the lesser bear. Zeus's manner of delivering both bears to the heavens – a cosmic heave – explains their stretched tails.

The constellation is not always known as a bear, however. The Saxons called it a wagon, as did the Babylonians. In Britain it is still sometimes called The Plough. Ancient Egyptians looked up in the sky and saw a bull's thigh. Back in the United States, slaves called it a "drinking gourd" because it resembled the shape of gourds they hollowed out for drinking cups. The celestial drinking gourd became a navigational beacon pointing northwards as slaves fled under the cover of night along the Underground Railroad in the mid-1800s. Popular folksongs contained coded lyrics with instructions for getting north to Canada and other safe areas. The chorus for the most famous song went:

Follow the drinking gourd,
follow the drinking gourd
For the old man is a-waitin'
to carry you to freedom
Follow the drinking gourd.

While the Dipper is the main attraction in the northwestern sky, a new set of three stars takes prominence in the southeast: the Summer Triangle. Comprising the bright stars Vega, Deneb and Altair, the Summer Triangle dominates the heavens from June to September. Over the course of a summer night, the Triangle flies high across the sky like an enormous

life; magnitude 0.5 (varies); distance 1,400 light-years

Sirius: Magnitude -1.4

Procyon: Magnitude 0.4, distance 11 light-years

Dog days of summer: During summer, Sirius and Procyon are located in the day sky, but like all the other stars are not visible because of the sun's glare. Ancient Egyptians knew this fact, and believed that the heat from the "dog star" Sirius was added to that of the sun, thus producing the dog days of summer. *Sirius* comes from the Greek, seirios, meaning "hot" or "scorching"

Aldebaran: Magnitude 0.9, distance 60 light-years

Distance of Pleiades: About 410 light-years

celestial kite, passing almost directly overhead. The formation is called an asterism because it is not an official constellation. But its distinctiveness makes it one of the first groupings of stars introduced to novice stargazers.

Each of the three stars in the Summer Triangle is a member of its own constellation. Vega, the brightest of the three, is the lucida of the constellation Lyra. It is named after the lyre the Greek musician Orpheus used to enchant listeners during his various adventures. The most famous story concerns his attempt to rescue his wife, Eurydice, from the underworld of Hades. Orpheus took his lyre and entered the gates of hell to bring her back to life. His beautiful music so charmed Hades that the god granted Orpheus's wish, but with one condition: he must not look back as his wife followed him to the land of the living. Orpheus obeyed until, just as he stepped out into the sun, he could resist no longer and glanced back. It was too soon, and Eurydice disappeared. Orpheus was later reunited in death with his wife, and Zeus placed the lyre in the heavens to commemorate the musician's sweet melodies.

Vega is an Arabic word meaning "the stooping one," or "vulture" – the ancient conception of the constellation before the Greeks. The other two constellations of the Summer Triangle, Cygnus and Aquila, represent birds to this day. Cygnus looks much like its namesake, the swan. It is easy to imagine the outline of the great white swan as it flies along the shimmering path of the Milky Way. Deneb marks the tail of Cygnus; the word is Arabic for "tail of the hen." Early Christians also gave their own name, the Northern Cross, to Cygnus.

One of the Greek myths for Cygnus is said to explain the origin of the expression "swan song." Phaeton, the young man who created the Milky Way during a wild ride in his dad's sun chariot, had a close friend named Cycnus. When Zeus struck Phaeton dead with a thunderbolt, the mortal fell into a river. Cycnus tried several times to retrieve the body of his friend for burial, but his dives were unsuccessful. As he sang songs of grief along the riverbank, the gods took pity on him and placed him in the heavens as a swan. Thus was born, supposedly, the superstition that swans sing sad songs before they die.

Aquila, the constellation that includes Altair, was another bird of Greek mythology – the eagle that transported Zeus's thunderbolts. Aquila is Latin for "eagle," and the modern word *aquiline* means of or like an eagle. Altair is Arabic for "the flying one." In Hindu mythology, Altair and the two bright stars nearby were thought of as the footprints of Vishnu, the preserver spirit.

A comparison of Deneb and Vega gives a good idea of how difficult it is to judge the size of stars and their distance from Earth. To the naked eye, Vega is slightly brighter than Deneb. Yet Deneb is, by astronomical reckoning, almost 60,000 times more luminous than Vega. The explanation, of course, is distance. Vega is only about 25 light-years from Earth while Deneb, a colossal star 60 times wider than our sun, is about 1,500 light-years away.

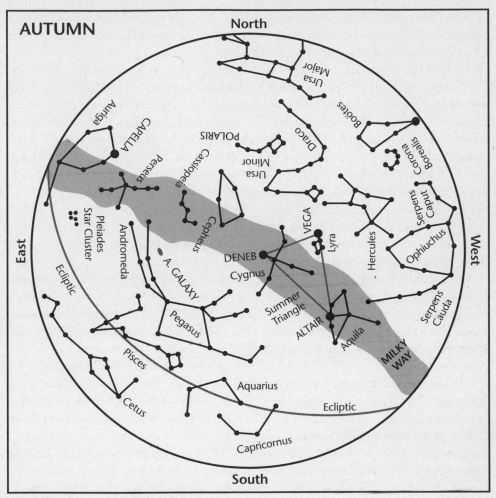

AUTUMN

North

Ursa Major

Boötes

Auriga

CAPELLA

Perseus

POLARIS

Cassiopeia

Draco

Corona Borealis

Ursa Minor

Serpens Caput

Pleiades Star Cluster

Cepheus

VEGA

Lyra

Hercules

Ophiuchus

East

Andromeda

A. GALAXY

DENEB

Cygnus

West

Ecliptic

Pegasus

Summer Triangle

ALTAIR

Aquila

Serpens Cauda

Pisces

MILKY WAY

Cetus

Aquarius

Ecliptic

Capricornus

South

(See "How To Use the Star Charts," page 334)

Autumn

By fall the Big Dipper has moved low in the northwestern sky in the early evening, so that it's just skimming the horizon and may be hidden by buildings. From spring's upside-down position, the Dipper is now right-side up.

Another circumpolar constellation, meanwhile, primps for attention in the north-eastern sky. Cassiopeia is about the same distance from Polaris as the Big Dipper, but almost directly opposite the Dipper from the North Star. The W-shaped constellation is named after the Queen of Ethiopia in Greek mythology. Married to King Cepheus, Cassiopeia was by reputation an unpleasant woman. She bragged that she was more beautiful than the sea nymphs – not a smart move, since the nymphs were the off-spring of the mighty sea god Poseidon. The enraged god dispatched the monster Cetus to attack Ethiopia's coast. An oracle advised Cepheus that the only way to save his

331

citizens was to sacrifice his daughter Andromeda to the briny beast. This he reluctantly did, although Andromeda was rescued by Perseus before Cetus could get his flippers on her. Cassiopeia was strapped to a chair and placed in the heavens as punishment for her boastfulness. The other characters in this myth, including Cepheus, Andromeda, Cetus and Perseus, have nearby constellations named after them, but they are dimmer and harder to make out from urban locations.

Other northern cultures gave various meanings to Cassiopeia's distinctive shape. When it is low in the sky it looks like a giant W. As it moves higher it turns upside down to become an M. To the Inuit people of the Arctic this outline reflected the pattern of stairs cut in snow, an astral stairway connecting Earth to the sky country. The ancient Egyptians called it the Leg; to the Chinese it was the charioteer Wang Liang.

Winter

Though not the most comfortable season for stargazing, winter offers perhaps the most dazzling night sky. Contrary to popular opinion, it's not because the clear, crisp air provides a better view of the cosmos. The sky sparkles with bright stars because there just happens to be more of them in winter, from our point of view at this particular spot on Earth's orbit.

The Big Dipper is still there, now low in the northeastern sky in the early evening, heading toward the spring location where this tour started.

But the main action is in the southern sky, with the unmistakable constellation Orion filling a good chunk of the view. He is accompanied by Sirius, the brightest star in the northern hemisphere; the Pleiades star cluster, apparent even from the city; the orange-red star Aldebaran in the constellation Taurus; and several other bright stars including Capella and Procyon.

Orion is named for the great hunter of Greek myth, and it's easy to discern his form in the stars. The three distinct "belt stars" define his waist. Below them, another string of dimmer stars make up his sword or scabbard. To the upper left of the belt stars shines the bright star Betelgeuse, a red giant whose name is usually translated from the original Arabic as "armpit of the great one." Many ancient sky maps indeed show the star as marking Orion's armpit or shoulder. His other shoulder is marked by Bellatrix, somewhat dimmer but still easily visible to the naked eye from light-polluted cities. Kitty-corner from Betelgeuse, on the other side of the belt stars, is Rigel – from the Arabic for "foot" – one of the earliest-named stars. Orion's right foot is pinpointed by the star Saiph, though in some old maps Saiph and Rigel mark the hunter's knees.

There are many versions of the Orion story, but the most intriguing involve another constellation, Scorpius. Orion was a hunter who boasted that no animal could get the better of him. As usual with the Greeks, this hubris proved fatal. The spiteful goddess Hera sent a tiny scorpion to deliver a mortal, mocking sting. Orion was placed in the heavens as a lasting warning to all, and opposite Scorpius so that the two constellations would never appear together in the night sky. Scorpius is a dim summer constellation that scuttles close to the horizon, never rising very high into the night sky.

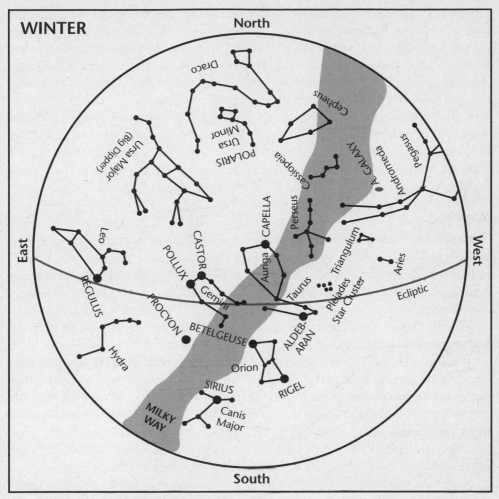

(See "How To Use the Star Charts," page 334)

The story goes that when the Greek gods placed Orion into the heavens after his encounter with the scorpion, they also thoughtfully included his hunting dogs as companions. These are the "dog stars" Sirius and Procyon. Blue-white Sirius is the brightest star in the night sky, a brilliant white point piercing the black velvet of a winter's evening. It's bright because it's big and close; the closest star to our own sun visible from the northern hemisphere, and the fifth closest overall. Astronomers reckon it's about twice the diameter of the sun, and 23 times as luminous. It is 8.7 light-years away; a hop and a skip in cosmic terms, but still distant enough that it would take our fastest spacecraft about 300,000 years to get there. Procyon, the other dog star, ranks eighth in the astronomical Top 20.

Following a line formed by Orion's belt stars, the gaze of the urban astronomer is directed westward to Aldebaran, the brightest star in the constellation Taurus the bull.

It is said to represent the bull's eye. Continuing along the same line brings the viewer to the Pleiades star cluster, a slight smudge in the sky visible from the city on a dark night. The Pleiades are a fine binocular target, with the lenses revealing the individual stars that make up the cluster. The Pleiades are also called the Seven Sisters, after the seven daughters of Atlas and Pleione in Greek mythology. They are sometimes mistaken for the Little Dipper, for the shape (especially through low-power binoculars) is similar. Officially known to astronomers as M45, the Pleiades are young stars borne of an interstellar nebula of gas and dust. The youngest stars are estimated to be about 20 million years old. By comparison, the rocks in Ontario's Canadian Shield regions are one billion years old or older.

How To Use the Star Charts

The rotation of Earth makes it appear as if all the stars are circling Polaris, the North Star, in a counterclockwise direction. Because of this motion, the star charts reproduced here are not exact for every time of night, every night of the year, or every location in the northern hemisphere. But they are good guides to the heavens shortly after nightfall in the middle of each season in south-central Ontario.

To use a chart, hold this book upsidedown, place it over your head and face north. The side of the chart marked "north" should point toward the north. The side marked "east" should face the east, and so on. The position of the constellations in the night sky will roughly match those in the chart. Find the most prominent features first – the Big Dipper, Summer Triangle or Orion in winter – and use them as guideposts to the other constellations. Star names are printed in UPPER CASE, while constellations are printed in upper- and lowercase. If you're in a light-polluted urban area, you'll see fewer stars than are indicated here. If you're under clear, dark skies in a wilderness area, you'll see many more.

To find planets, look for what appear to be bright stars along the ecliptic. Planets travel along this imaginary line in space. The ecliptic roughly defines the plane of the solar system – technically, it's the plane defined by Earth's orbit around the sun.

To help your eyes adjust to the dark, use a flashlight with red cloth or red paper wrapped around the light.

Recommended Reading

There is an increasing number of excellent field guides and books on many of the subjects included in *Wild City*. We recommend the following:

Legacy (McClelland & Stewart), edited by John Theberge, is a thick, comprehensive compendium of the natural history of Ontario, written by the province's leading naturalists and featuring some of the best colour nature photography.

The ROM Field Guide to Birds of Ontario (McClelland & Stewart), by Janice Hughes, includes colour photographs, range maps, descriptions, species status and brief behaviour and habitat notes on more than 300 species. It's part of a new series of handy field guides from the Royal Ontario Museum.

Peterson's Field Guide to the Birds of Eastern and Central North America (Houghton Mifflin), by Roger Tory Peterson, has long been one of the best guides for birds in the region, complete with detailed colour illustrations, brief descriptions and range maps.

Bugs of Ontario (Lone Pine Publishing), by John Acorn, is a field guide to some of the most common insects and spiders in the province, many of them frequently seen in the city. It features good colour illustrations and amusing natural history notes.

The National Audubon Society Field Guide to Insects & Spiders (Alfred A. Knopf), by Lorus and Margery Milne, covers more than 600 species, with colour photos, descriptions and notes on the food, habitat, range and life cycles for each.

The Encyclopedia of Canadian Fishes (Key Porter Books), by Brad Coad, is a thick tome with black-and-white illustrations and detailed accounts on all of the country's fish.

Mammals of Ontario (Lone Pine Publishing), by Tamara Eder, is a field guide with colour illustrations, range maps and short accounts for 76 mammal species.

Familiar Amphibians and Reptiles of Ontario (Natural History/Natural Heritage), by Bob Johnson, provides good accounts of all of the province's frogs, salamanders, turtles and snakes, along with illustrations and range maps.

The ROM Field Guide to Wildflowers of Ontario (McClelland & Stewart), by Timothy Dickinson, Deborah Metsger, Jenny Bull and Richard Dickinson, has multiple colour photos, range maps, detailed descriptions and short notes on each of 550 species covered in the book.

Newcomb's Wildflower Guide (Little, Brown and Company), by Lawrence Newcomb, is one of the most widely used field guides in North America, covering 1,375 species. It features clear black-and-white illustrations, succinct descriptions and a renowned key for systematically each flower.

Trees in Canada (Fitzhenry & Whiteside), by John Farrar, is the definitive hard-cover reference from the Canadian Forestry Service. It has colour photos of leaves, seeds, flowers, buds and bark for each species.

Trees of Ontario (Lone Pine Publishing), by Linda Kershaw, is a smaller, soft-cover field guide that is also very useful, with colour photos, range maps and interesting notes on the traditional uses of each tree and the wildlife attracted to them.

Nightwatch: An Equinox Guide to Viewing the Universe (Camden House Publishing), by Terrence Dickinson, is an excellent guide to observing the night sky, with everything from superb star maps to advice on how to take pictures of the heavens.

On Nature (the magazine of the Federation of Ontario Naturalists), **Nature Canada**, **Canadian Geographic**, **Cottage Life** and **Wildflower** magazines are all excellent sources of ongoing information on nature in Ontario.

Resources

Canadian Museum of Nature, 240 McLeod St., P.O. Box 3443, Station D, Ottawa, Ont., KIP 6P4, 1-800-263-4433, www.nature.ca

Canadian Nature Federation, Suite 606, 1 Nicholas St., Ottawa, Ont., KIN 7B7 1-800-267-4088, www.cnf.ca

Carolinian Canada, Grosvenor House, 1017 Western Rd., London, Ont., N6G 1G5, (519) 433-7077, www.carolinian.org

Conservation Ontario, P.O. Box 11, 120 Bayview Parkway, Newmarket, Ont., L3Y 4W3, 905-895-0716, www.conservation-ontario.on.ca (can provide contact information for local conservation authorities throughout southern and central Ontario)

Evergreen Foundation, 355 Adelaide St. West, 5th Floor, Toronto, Ontario, M5V 1S2, 1-888-426-3138, www.evergreen.ca

Federation of Ontario Naturalists, 355 Lesmill Rd., Don Mills, Ont., M3B 2W8, (416) 444-8419, www.ontarionature.org (the FON can provide information to contact local field naturalist groups throughout the province)

Field Botanists of Ontario, www.trentu.ca/fbo

Ministry of Natural Resources, Natural Heritage Information Centre, P.O. Box 7000, 1st Floor, 300 Water St., Peterborough, Ont., K9J 8M5, 1-800-667-1940, www.mnr.gov.on.ca

Ministry of Tourism and Recreation, 900 Bay St., 9th Floor, Hearst Block, Toronto, Ont., M7A 2E1, (416) 326-9326, www.tourism.gov.on.ca

Ontario Field Ornithologists, P.O. Box 455, Station R, Toronto, Ont., M4G 4E1, www.ofo.ca

Pollution Probe, 625 Church St., Suite 402, Toronto, Ont., M4Y 2G1, (416) 926-1907, www.pollutionprobe.org

Royal Astronomical Society of Canada, 136 Dupont St., Toronto, Ont., M5R 1V2, (416) 924-7973, www.rasc.ca

Royal Ontario Museum, 100 Queen's Park, Toronto, Ont., M5S 2C6, (416) 586-5549, www.rom.on.ca

Society for Ecological Restoration, Ontario Chapter, www.serontario.org

World Wildlife Fund (Canada), 90 Eglington Ave. East, Suite 504, Toronto, Ont., M4P 2Z7, (416) 489-8800, www.wwf.ca

Index

Page numbers in **bold** indicate illustrations.